Advance praise for *A Turquoise Life*

"[Kathy Bird has] done an incredible job of telling Diann's story but also of describing some very significant mental health issues. [This] book can help others who are struggling to…overcome their abusive pasts and find peace. This book is fast paced, sad, gut wrenching, charming and, ultimately, uplifting."

—Joan Gabrielson, MBA Executive Director of Excelsior Youth Center (formerly The Good Shepherd Home).

"*A Turquoise Life* is an important story for survivors of sexual abuse to know healing is possible. Just when you think this child can't endure another trauma, Diann does. Her life bravely illustrates the strength of the human spirit. It is difficult…real… with a happy ending."

—Feather Berkower, M.S.W.,
Co-author of *Off Limits: A Parent's Guide to Keeping Kids Safe from Sexual Abuse.*

"Diann's story will give you an empathic workout – lots of pain and lots of gain. She rewards readers with honest proof that a thriving life is possible after a heartbreaking childhood. Not easy, but possible."

—Julie Golden,
author of *Vagilantes—Pedophiles, Be Afraid. Very Afraid.*

"*A Turquoise Life* is a powerful account of one woman's experience of a childhood full of unspeakable sexual abuse and trauma, and her difficult, but ultimately successful journey as an adult. Her resilience and her drive to keep moving forward are compelling and inspirational! As a professional working in this field for more than forty years, I believe her *Turquoise Life* is a beacon of hope for survivors and a profound insight for professionals who offer support and treatment to victims of sexual abuse."

—Bob Cooper, MSW,
former CEO and currently Chief Development Officer
of Tennyson Center for Children

"This is an important work on trauma from the victim's perspective. . . a must read for all, but especially lawyers, judges, mental health workers and law enforcement people who encounter trauma daily."

—Randall C. Mustain-Wood, JD, MA,
former family law litigator and currently family law mediator with JAMS, Denver

"*A Turquoise Life* is a visceral account of the level of emotion and physical pain a child can experience, yet Diann found a way to not only heal but thrive. This book's powerful message is about resilience, courage, strength and is truly heroic as she helps others now from her story. [Kathy Bird's] writing is amazing."

—Melissa (Missy) Bradley-Ball, MS, NCC, BCETS, FAAETS, psychotherapist
and nationally recognized clinical educator, corporate consultant, and author

A
Turquoise
Life

One Woman's
Triumphant Journey

Diann M. Kissell
with
Kathy Bird

Diann's family photos provided by Diann Kissell
Kathy Bird's photo courtesy of Gabe Rovick
Diann's photo courtesy of Bettinger Photography
Photo of Diann and Kathy courtesy of Jeff Fuller

To protect their privacy, Diann's siblings have requested their first names and the family's last name be omitted from the book. All the characters portrayed in this memoir are real although some names have been a changed in order to maintain anonymity. The locations, circumstances, and events recounted are derived from Diann's memory and are depicted as accurately as possible, but accuracy and completeness cannot be guaranteed. The dialogue, of course, is according to Diann's best recollection and not a precise retelling. The veracity of some of the information described is a matter of public record which lends to credibility. Some statements are a matter of opinion.

Although the authors have made efforts to ensure that the information in this book is correct, the authors and publisher disclaim any liability, loss or damage caused by the contents of this book.

First published by Dog Ear Publishing
4010 W. 86th Street, Ste H
Indianapolis, IN 46268
www.dogearpublishing.net

ISBN: 978-1-4575-2902-3

This book is printed on acid-free paper.

Printed in the United States of America

This book is dedicated to all my loving siblings, my children
and to my ever wonderful
Prince Charming, Fred.

Turquoise – most efficient healer, solace for the spirit
well being for the soul

"I made it through the rain."
—Barry Manilow

A Turquoise Life

December 2012

I'd been living my happily-ever-after life for so long it was hard to remember how it felt before. In my "other" life, the holiday season filled me with trepidation. But the horrors of my past are gone. The trauma and pain caused by incest, murder, suicide, and abusive relationships all seem insignificant compared to the love and peace I feel today.

Grateful for my life's lessons, I'm happy I chose to do the hard work of remembering, talking about, and dealing with the past, in order to live this healthy present. As incredible as it may seem, the pain was worth it because I'm now experiencing life at its fullest. As a whole person, I'm able to be the best wife, mother, nana, and friend to those in my life.

At age six, I no longer felt the magic of Christmas nor believed in its miracles. Those gifts had been stolen from me. As a young adult, I tried valiantly to recapture the joys of the season, but had only a modicum of success. Then, twenty years ago, I was able to bring back the magic in full when I, together with my husband Fred, transformed the dreaded Decembers of my past into special times of celebration. At one of our annual Christmas gatherings, a professional Santa Claus appeared on our doorstep. He came bearing gifts and insider information on each of our grandchildren's wonderful traits and accomplishments, and when warranted, comments about naughty behavior. That the old fellow has found his way to our home every year at the exact date and time of our family party is amazing.

It was December 22, 2012 and our family Christmas party was well under way. Our home was packed with our children and their families. Gauging from history, Santa would be arriving soon. As I surveyed the happy scene, heart bursting with love, I knew my life was filled to the brim with blessings.

I let my senses settle into my surroundings. I saw my adult children's happy expressions as they watched our adolescent grandchildren's antics and the innocent, animated faces of the younger ones. Above the peals of laughter and family chatter I could hear the now comforting sounds of my favorite Christmas carols. The bright colors, appetizing smells, and wall-to-wall chaos filled me with peace. Hugs and love abounded. I felt so blessed.

My husband brought me out of my reverie with a tap on my shoulder. He smiled and nodded his head toward the front door. I spied a jolly old man in a red suit with a long white beard surrounded by a swarm of very excited young children. Fred said, "Santa Claus has arrived."

"Indeed he has," I said. "Indeed he has." And I meant it.

*   *   *

Turquoise is my color of well being. My story is one of hope. Through my healing journey I chose to replace the dark days of survival with the color and light of living a turquoise life.

Dad and 5-year-old Diana (Diann), 1955

PART I

SURVIVING

CHAPTER 1

The Sinner

Spring 1957

So far it had been a grey day, but as usual, the second I went outside, the sun's rays shone through my cloudy thoughts. Under an umbrella of blue sky, we, Mrs. Anthony's second-grade class, marched in a straight line from our school to St. Dominic's Catholic Church. Our journey was short but serious; we were leaving behind our carefree childhoods and entering the world of grown-up responsibilities, which involved admitting our big and little sins to Father Ronney. Father, who was God's ambassador on earth, had the power to forgive in God's name. God, through Father Ronney, was going to decide if we should be forgiven, and if God forgave us, Father Ronney would tell us what we had to do to make things right. On this sunny Thursday afternoon in May, we were marching to the church to have our first confession heard. If we passed the test, we could take our First Communion on Sunday.

As we marched to the church, we passed by our empty playground. It beckoned to me, wanting me to play. I couldn't play because I was on a mission from God. But despite my best intentions to focus solely on the Church and the solemn task at hand, I stole a glance at the playground. I felt guilty for not wanting to be a strong, seven-year-old soldier. A big part of me didn't want to shoulder the responsibility of confessing my sins. The truth was that I was *bad*, and I didn't want to admit it. I really just wanted to stay outside and play.

My family's life had revolved around St. Dominic's ever since I was a baby. I knew the minute I entered the church on this day that it felt different. Its dimness blinded me, making me see stars; its cold stillness sent chills through my body; and the huge, cavernous space made me feel small, insignificant, and alone. On Sundays, my church was packed full of families, friends, happy voices, warm bright colors, and familiar songs and words. This Thursday, the church was an empty, colorless space filled with a loud silence.

En route to the pew, where I was to kneel and wait for my turn in the confessional, I could hear the footsteps of my black-and-white saddle shoes echoing on the cracked cement floor. Kneeling, I knew I should focus on Jesus nailed to the cross, but I found myself looking around. For the first time, I noticed that the large stone walls felt cold and unforgiving to me. This feeling made me think of Father Ronney's face. Father's pale skin and bald head, his hard eyes, and his rigidly held mouth reminded me of the church walls. No way, after what I had to say, would I be forgiven. No way would I get to make my First Communion. My stomach suddenly became queasy again as my mind wandered back to my classroom earlier that day.

That morning, my class had been buzzing with anticipation. My classmates seemed unconcerned about confessing their sins, probably because they had only tiny sins to think about. Everyone was focusing on making their First Communion. The girls in my class were mostly excited about their new dresses. Everybody was happy except me.

My mood that morning had been heavy. I knew I was the only mortal sinner in my class, and my concern was that if I confessed my mortal sin, Father Ronney might think me too horrible to forgive. If that happened, I would be barred from taking part in the First Communion ceremony. Dad would be mad and my family disappointed. I wouldn't get to wear my new white dress.

For months, Mrs. Anthony had prepared our class for our First Communion. In the Catholic Church, the rule is that before you can take communion, you have to confess your sins. We learned about the difference between venial (little) sins and mortal (big) sins. We memorized the Ten Commandments. These ten rules—by which we were to live—were set in stone. Any one of these commandments, if broken, would send you straight to hell when you died. The way to avoid that fiery place, swarming with red-horned devils carrying pitchforks, was to confess your mortal sins. Confessing was the way to erase one's sins and start the new week with a clean slate.

Thinking about my first confession, I easily came up with three little sins. They were the run-of-the-mill, typical sins of a normal kid. I wasn't concerned about the venial sins; they were too tiny to get me thrown into hell.

No, the thoughts that penetrated my nights, invaded my days, and upset my stomach were about my mortal sin. I didn't have words to explain my mortal sin but I knew I had to confess something Father Ronney would accept. I don't remember consciously searching through the Ten Commandments looking for the commandment that most closely fit my activity with Dad, but I know I did. I probably started with the fourth commandment stating it was a mortal sin not to honor and obey your father. The problem was that what Dad and I were doing together in secret seemed like a big sin too. As far as honoring God and going to church was concerned, I was doing fine. This took care of the first three commandments. The fifth and seventh didn't apply to me because I definitely hadn't killed anyone or stolen anything big. Commandments eight, nine, and ten had to do with neighbors. For the most part, I liked both the Garcia and the Engel families. I got mad at George Garcia sometimes, but I certainly didn't bear false witness against him. Coveting Mrs. Garcia or Mrs. Engel or their goods wasn't a problem. Besides, my neighbors didn't have anything to do with Dad and me.

The only commandment that could possibly apply was number six: Thou shalt not commit adultery. Even though I didn't understand what the word meant, I just knew it applied to me. It was clear that I was a very bad girl. If I stopped letting Dad touch me, I would be dishonoring my father, which would be committing a mortal sin. If I allowed him to touch me, I was committing a mortal sin also. In my seven-year-old mind, it was clear that no matter which commandment I obeyed, I would be a mortal sinner. I knew I couldn't win. Confession seemed to be my only solution. Even a seven-year-old knows you don't want a bunch of sins, especially the mortal kind, hanging over your head.

A hard tap on my shoulder from Linda, a girl in my class, made me jump. Mrs. Anthony was furiously motioning to me. I got up off my knees and rushed to the confessional booth. I took in a large gulp of air and entered the dark, small space. I knelt down, gathered up my courage, and recited the memorized words. "Bless me, Father, for I have sinned. This is my first confession. I ate a cookie before dinner. I fought with my brothers three times. I lied twice. And I…"

"Go on," Father Ronney's clipped voice demanded. Looking up, I glimpsed the shadowy image of Father's face behind the screen. He was waiting for me to finish my sentence. I couldn't speak or breathe. The words were stuck in my closed-up throat. I wanted desperately to stop kneeling and run out of St. Dominic's Catholic Church and never come back. Luckily, my body stayed frozen long enough for my mind to remember the last and biggest sin. I had practiced my confession probably a hundred times in the past week. So finally, out of habit, my small, seven-year-old voice was able to squeak out, "And I committed adultery."

After what seemed like forever, Father Ronney said, "Yes, well, you try to be a good girl this coming week, won't you? For your penance, say two Our Fathers, ten Hail Marys, and one Glory Be."

I had done it! My first confession was over. I was free and absolved of all my sins, even the big one. I was going to be allowed to take my First Communion on Sunday in my beautiful new white dress and veil. My daddy would be so proud.

CHAPTER 2

My Big Family

M y life at the beginning was healthy, happy, and quite normal. I was born to Luis and Leonarda on January 13, 1950. I arrived into an already big, Catholic, Latino family. I was child number five. Although I have no memory of my baby years, I am sure I was a contented bundle of baby. There were many arms to hold and hug me, many lips to kiss my cheeks, and many smiling eyes to watch me grow. Laughter filled my ears and covered me with the warmth of belonging. We were a family in all respects. We even looked the part by all displaying distinctive features in various parental combinations. We had all inherited Dad's dark hair. Half the family sported Mom's green eyes, and the other half had Dad's dark brown.

My first real memories are from when I was almost three and a half years old. It was a nice, sunny day. The bushes with the sweet-smelling purple flowers, which I found out later were lilacs, were everywhere. It was a great day to move. Our family of eight was moving from a cramped duplex to a new house across the alley. Actually, it was an old house, long and made of painted white wood, but it was new to us. The house was located on a quiet, Grandma-laden block in a North Denver neighborhood. Since we all played in the front yard, we were about to add youth, noise, and excitement to the boring street.

Of course, everybody in the family wanted to help move. In our family there were no slackers. Michael, the oldest, was directing traffic and keeping my brothers on task. Al and Paul turned every chore into a fierce but fun competition. Sometimes they got so carried away with the fun competition part that they forgot about the job. At these times, my oldest brother was in charge of reining them in. As a ball whizzed across the room, almost hitting Michael in the head, he yelled, "Guys, quit goofing off and get busy. You don't want Dad to get mad." This comment seemed to do the trick, for not even my fun-loving brothers wanted to raise Dad's ire. Dad's anger often translated into a belt whipping. I think Dad thought use of the belt was the best tool for keeping us in line. I think it just made my brothers sneakier.

Mom must have told my sister Jean to be in charge of me on moving day. Gesturing to a huge, heavy, unwieldy object I thought was a mattress, Jean said, "Diana, you take this." Proudly puffing myself up, I grabbed the large mass with both hands. In my three-year-old mind, I was an industrious worker ant walking a long distance, all the while grappling with a huge load. I was young and short, my burden big and bulky. It smashed against my face and was so gigantic I couldn't see around the sides or over the top. I didn't have a clue as to what lay ahead. I felt my way easily through the old duplex and out the old back door. But there I wobbled, almost toppling off the big step onto the dirt alley below. I caught my balance just in time and held tight to my huge responsibility. I made my way cautiously, sliding my feet low along the ground, feeling around for more surprises. Finally, I arrived at our new house, where I immediately dropped my bundle.

My sister was watching, so I dramatically brushed my hands back and forth for effect and said in a slightly out-of-breath voice, "Whew, heavy mattress!"

Jean just laughed, shaking her head. "You silly, that's not a mattress; that's just a pillow."

The new house had two bedrooms and a large attic. Mom, Dad, and baby Patrick took one room. The other boys packed into one part of the attic, while Dad laid claim to the second part for his projects. Since Jean and I were the only girls, we got our very own room. We both squealed with delight at seeing our room. We twirled around, our fingers brushing against the smooth wallpaper full of flowers and the cold radiator full of bumps. We jumped up and down on the bare double bed that we would share and then on the hardwood floor. We peered out our window past our backyard to the field beyond.

In the spirit and excitement of exploring every nook and cranny of our new room, we accidentally got locked in our closet. There we were in a dark, small, unfamiliar space. Jean, three years older than I, calmly tried the knob, pushed on the door, and then did what any normal six-year-old would do: She started screaming. "Help us! We're trapped in here. We might die! Get us out of here!" Each sentence was punctuated with rapidly pounding fists.

I tried to follow her lead but with less command of the English language. I pounded the door after every word: "Help! Trapped! Die! Out!" Just when we feared all was lost, and we would be trapped forever and definitely die, our brother Alfred heard us and came to our aid. Jean and I said to him in unison, "Our hero." Indeed, Al stayed our hero for at least the rest of the day. He had saved us, but I knew our loud mouths and fists did their part in saving us too.

That night at dinner, Michael had barely finished saying the blessing when everybody started talking at once about their moving experiences. Jean was yelling, "Listen to me. I have a story."

Dad put his fingers to his mouth to quiet us, "Listen to Jean." One comment from Dad and the table was quiet, and Jean had the floor. Jean stood up and began to act out our adventure.

Dad loved mealtime with his big family. He seemed to enjoy the constant chatter. He even laughed at the mess the baby in the high chair made. Dad wasn't one of those guys who got mad when you accidentally spilled your milk. He did have some mealtime rules, though, and even I knew that standing up at the dinner table wasn't usually permitted. On this night, I quickly checked to see what kind of face Dad was wearing. I let out a big breath when I saw that he had smiling eyes, a smooth forehead, and wrinkle-free eyebrows.

Jean was good at acting; she pretended to turn the stuck knob, put on a scared face, and started yelling while making pounding motions with her fists. By this time, I was out of my chair, jumping up and down screaming, "Me too, me too!" When it came to the rescue part, Al stood and dipped his body gracefully to the ground in a proud bow. The whole family clapped and cheered. I looked at Dad. His whole face was laughing from his mouth to his eyes.

Dad was Puerto Rican born and looked it, with a handsome Latin face and deep, dark brown eyes. He did a lot of talking and listening with his eyes. His eyes would sparkle with his own stories and would laugh at ours too. Sometimes when he didn't think we were looking, his eyes spoke of sad and faraway times. When he was angry, even though his eyes were wide open, they couldn't see. It was as if he slammed a door shut. When he was mad, no matter what was said, he couldn't see or hear us.

His face was framed with thick, wavy black hair. He was short, standing only five feet seven inches, but his height didn't seem to fit with anyone's perception of him. He was big and powerful in our lives. I think he brought out feelings of both love and fear. I thought there were two parts to my dad—the fun-loving part and the scary, mean part.

Mom was often too busy to play with us, but not Dad. It was true he worked hard to provide for us. In my early years, he drove a bread truck, and when I was about nine, he became an insurance salesman. On weekends, to bring in extra cash, he picked up newspapers that needed to be recycled. Yet despite some long hours, when he came home from work, he was almost always ready to play with us. His two-toned blue station wagon turning into our driveway caused a ripple of excitement in us. We could hardly contain ourselves. We swarmed like buzzing bees around the car door. As Dad emerged from the car, he was tugged and pulled in different directions by many little hands and voices. He would smile, hugging and speaking to each of us. Sometimes, if he was feeling energetic, he would pick us up and toss us into the air.

When things calmed down, the older kids would ask if he wanted to participate in the activity of the hour. Dad usually gave a big smile and an emphatic yes. If the weather was even remotely passable, we played outdoors. In the evenings and on the weekends, Dad played outside games with us. He especially loved playing volleyball and baseball. We played a game called "bases," which he learned growing up in New York. Since New York City's narrow streets and alleys couldn't accommodate a regular baseball diamond, bases consisted of one base and home plate. In our Denver neighborhood of big open spaces, our large family still played bases New York-style in honor of our dad.

When we were stuck indoors, Dad could be just as fun. He made sure there was a jigsaw puzzle in progress at all times. As we went about our busy lives, we often passed by the puzzle table and paused for a moment to glance at the scattered puzzle pieces. Occasionally, one of us found a fit for one or two pieces. Dad was definitely the king of the jigsaw, for he would find the perfect place for five or six pieces at a time. Life was never boring with Dad around.

Even though Dad had only an eighth-grade education, we thought of him as very smart and creative. He used some of his creativity to build toys and games for us. He made us a "murder board," which was a combination of Parcheesi and Chinese Checkers. We played it often as a family. It was named, in jest, to represent the overzealous and fierce competitive nature of our family. Sometimes Mom even took time from her active schedule to play games with us. She was also a fierce competitor, but she didn't care about the outcome. According to her, good effort, attitude, and having fun were far more important than winning. I felt the same way, which was lucky, because the fifth child rarely won.

In a big family, if you were mad at one sibling, you simply switched to another available playmate. Patrick was my most constant companion.

I was older, but only by a year and a half, so we had much in common. We lived across the street from Ashland Elementary School, which boasted state-of-the-art playground equipment. The playground's proximity to the house was handy for Mom because she could keep an eye on us. Mom had a system whereby the older kids watched over the younger kids. I watched over Patrick. Luckily, he loved the playground just as much as I did and was always ready and willing to accompany me. He could be a bit of a trickster and sometimes annoying, but he was definitely my best playground buddy.

Playground time occupied almost every day, all day, in the summer. Through the nights, I would dip in and out of the deepest sleep and the richest of dreams, but when the night's black backdrop faded into grey, my thoughts seemed to line up in order of daytime importance. When the daylight coaxed my eyelids open and the blue of the sky filled my vision, the leader of all thoughts and the first word through the door of my mind was "playground." The playground was sweeter than candy and more fun than any other activity in my world. The playground was my safe place. The playground let me be free to be my happiest kid-self.

On the playground, I felt like a boy, or at least a tomboy. I thought swings, slides, and teeter-totters were fine for babies and girls. I liked the stilts and pogo sticks we brought with us. Tetherball, foursquare, and any game my brothers wanted to play were fun, but I especially loved the ringers. This great piece of playground equipment consisted of a tall pole with eight bars fanning out from its top to make a large circle, like spokes in a bicycle wheel. Each bar held a hanging chain with a ring at its tip. It looked to me like a circle of exclamation marks. The look matched the exhilarating feeling of swinging high like a monkey, hand over hand and ring after ring. For hours, I went round and round and never touched the ground. I became better at the ringers than my sister or any of my brothers. The summer I was seven, my siblings and friends called me queen of the ringers. This crowning achievement came after weeks of agony during which my raw and red palms, piled high with blisters, screamed, *No more rings. We're through! We hurt! We can't take it anymore.* I didn't listen to this chatter because I wasn't a wimp or a quitter. In no time, my hands were so numb and calloused that they didn't feel the pain. Some of my family and friends thought I was crazy to go through so much pain and practice just to be queen, but sometimes the pain is worth it. I loved being the best, and I loved the title "queen of the ringers." If I had to be a girl, I at least wanted to be queen.

It was good to know that I could count on Mom being home to welcome me after a grueling day on the ringers. She was a stay-at-home mom who never learned to drive. One Sunday, Dad was driving the family home from church. All seven of us were squished in the back of our station wagon, anxious to get home. I was five and ready to be on the playground. Meanwhile, Mom was talking to Dad about wishing she could learn how to drive. Dad got our attention by abruptly veering to the side of the road and stopping the car. "Leonarda, if you want to learn how to drive, I'll teach you."

"Now?" my mom said in a squeaky voice.

"Now," Dad stated. He looked in the back seat with a warning stare. "No talking or squirming. Your mother needs to concentrate." We all looked at each other. We thought teaching Mom to drive was a terrible idea. Mom tended to be pretty excitable, and we were all afraid learning how to drive would put her over the edge.

It turned out we were right. In the driver's seat, Mom looked stiff and scared. She touched the gas pedal, the car lurched, and then she screamed, closed her eyes, and mumbled a prayer. The car, and all of us, ended up in a ditch. Mom was mortified, but Dad was gentle. "It's okay, Leonarda; we'll try again another time." With that comment, Dad drove us out of the small ditch and home. The experience didn't cause a scratch on metal or skin, but it did wreck Mom's self-confidence. She refused to try driving again. This left Dad in the driver's seat in all aspects of our lives except the day-to-day routine at home which was Mom's realm.

Mom's given name was Leonarda. Because Dad hated nicknames, he called her Leonarda, but all her friends called her Nora. She was of Spanish descent and fit the image of her Barcelona heritage. I thought she was beautiful with her sparkling green eyes and auburn hair. I felt proud that my eyes, smile, and cheekbones mirrored Mom's. If I'd had red hair, I could have looked just like her. Mom and I were both born fifth in our respective large families. I wanted to feel an extra-special bond because we looked so much alike and had the same birth order, but I didn't. I know Mom loved us all, but I think she felt most attached to Jean because Jean was the oldest girl and her number-one helper.

Mom was usually so busy that there was not time for much one-on-one attention. There were a lot of us and only one of Mom. I do, however, remember one special time when I was five. The situation evolved because Mom, in a distracted state, gave me permission to play with a metal Band-Aid box. I had no idea that she had stashed fifty dollars in the container for safekeeping. I did what any five-year-old worth her salt would have done: I played with the box for a few minutes, lost interest, and put the box in an interesting hidden location. I then pushed the place out of my mind.

I was sitting on the floor, immersed in a Dr. Seuss book, when Mom entered the living room. "Diana, come snuggle with me on the couch." My ears thought they had heard incorrectly, so my eyes looked up to see if she was really there. She was standing by the couch, smiling and motioning me to sit down with her. I jumped up and ran into her arms, causing us to topple over onto the couch laughing. She pulled me close and with a soft voice said, "Remember the Band-Aid box I let you play with yesterday?"

"Yes," I said.

"Do you know where it is?"

"Nope, I don't."

"Maybe I can help you remember." Mom kept asking me questions in a soothing voice, and I kept answering. I was paying more attention to my body filling up with joy because Mom was paying attention to me than I was trying to remember where I had put the box. Mom's usual roving eyes were still and soft as they landed right on my face and connected with my eyes. Her normally fast-moving hands slowed down enough to brush some hair out of my face. Her warm arms wrapped around my shoulders. I melted down and rested my head on her tummy. It seemed like she had all the time in the world just for me. I didn't want the moment to end. She finally moved, but the snuggling memory remained.

I never found out whether the Band-Aid box with the money was ever recovered. I do know I liked the feeling of snuggling with Mom. I liked it so much that I wished for another snuggle time. I bargained in my head, giving up ice cream and candy for one little snuggle. None of my bargaining worked because although she was affectionate with all of us, I never received that one-on-one snuggle time again. I often wondered if it was possible for a person to receive too much snuggling. There was no such thing as too much snuggling, I finally decided. I resolved that when I was a mommy, I would snuggle with my kids every day. Mom was a very good mother, but she was just too busy.

I think Mom treated us all the same in the snuggle department. She just didn't have time to snuggle. I hardly ever saw her snuggling the boys. Maybe boy-snuggling wasn't a good idea if one wanted to develop toughness. Mom didn't snuggle Jean a lot either, but her eyes would brighten and she would laugh more when she was around Jean. She may not have held Jean in her arms, but Mommy sure snuggled her with her attitude.

My parents' native language was Spanish but it wasn't spoken in our house unless they wanted to hide their words from us. I don't think they were ashamed of their ethnicity; rather, speaking English was more an attempt to give us a language that might protect us from the prejudice my

Puerto Rican father experienced growing up in New York City and the "wetback" label Mother had endured throughout her childhood. Dad was strongly against all prejudice. "You never judge people by the color of their skin," he would say, "only by their actions." I understood, but I wished I knew Spanish so I could speak to my grandparents in their language.

Mom's parents, Grandpa Amado and Grandma Predicanda, lived just around the corner from us. My siblings and I would often visit their house with the red chili peppers hanging on the outside door. Our grandparents always welcomed us by wrapping us in hugs, kisses, and the sweetness of Brach's chocolate star candy. I remember Grandpa with his white hair, dancing green eyes, high cheekbones, whiskery tickles, and big grin. Mom said her whole family worked in the fields of Colorado picking corn and beans. Years of backbreaking work under a hot sun sounded horrible to me, but my happy grandpa disagreed. His English words poking through his Spanish accent said his life had been full and satisfying. He wasn't old fashioned either—he even liked the "pop" music that I liked.

I also remember Grandma. She had a tiny body topped with a cloud of white hair. She would cook up a storm, bombarding our noses with the enticing smells of tortillas and beans. With her needle and thread, she sewed the love of practice and passion into my life. I would often sink into Grandma's soft Spanish words as she snuggled with me on the couch.

When I was seven, I asked for a doll for Christmas. Even though Grandma didn't speak English and I didn't speak Spanish, she was the only one who spoke my language on the subject of dolls. She knew exactly what I wanted and bought me a cuddly doll that reminded me of my love for her. She died when I was ten, and I was devastated. As was the custom in the Catholic Church, Grandma lay in an open casket. Mom instructed me to kiss her cold cheek, but I fainted and collapsed instead. I don't do well with dead bodies, open caskets, or funerals.

It felt like our religion had strong opinions on just about all life-and-death matters. Some of the opinions were more like hard-and-fast, right-and-wrong, black-and-white rules. When I was little, the difference between right and wrong was obvious and comforting. It was nice to know the rules. In second grade the clear choices of the past became increasingly fuzzy. Most of the time around Father Ronney, it didn't seem to matter what I did, I felt like a bad person. This feeling gave me a little hope because I knew I wasn't a quitter. *If I'm bad, I'll just try harder to be good. If I can't totally be good on the inside, I'll pretend to be good until I figure out how to be truly good.* Dad wanted all his kids to be good, pious people. He thought performing Catholic rituals would help in this department. I think I was a tough case because kneeling just hurt my knees and often didn't make me feel any closer to God. Dad tried his best to help me be a good Catholic, but despite his efforts, I knew I was a bad girl.

Dad seemed to embrace all the church's traditions and rituals. In our community, he was considered to be a model Catholic. He attended church twice each Sunday: once as an usher and then to sing in the choir. He was viewed as an ideal family man because he, unlike some of the other dads, always provided for us, didn't drink, and came home each night. Although he was stern, he loved his big family very much. I think he thought loving and supporting each other was just about as important as loving God.

Dad was a strict Catholic who demanded that we respect God, him, and each other. He thought we should be devout Catholics every minute of every day and especially on Sundays. We were required to show our reverence to God daily, which included a blessing before dinner and the rosary each night.

All my relatives were Catholic, but Mom's family was raised with a more lenient brand of Catholicism. My parents often invited Mom's relatives over to our house to socialize. A fun time was had by all until about sunset. I noticed as the light began to fade so did my cousins' spirits. They began to look longingly toward the front door. Sure enough, without fail, Dad stopped us mid-activity and made everyone kneel and say the rosary. My cousins hated the ritual. I'm not sure how my aunts and uncles felt because no one ever said anything. People rarely crossed Dad, especially about being a good Catholic.

For the most part, though, these frequent get-togethers with our relatives meant we were a part of one big, happy, extended family. Mom's best friend was her sister Ruby. She and her husband, Frank, lived close to us in North Denver. Mom's brother Tom and his wife, Lily, also lived close by. I liked Mom best when my aunts and cousins came to visit. At these times, she smoothed the worry wrinkles from her forehead, her green eyes smiled, and she became "laugh-out-loud" fun. She loved spending time relaxing, laughing, and playing jacks on the kitchen table with her sisters.

I had mixed feelings about Mom's laugh. Her laugh was like a huge wave crashing overhead, drowning out all other sounds. Mom's laugh was so loud, a part of me wanted to hide in embarrassment, but most of me laughed along with her. The truth was, her laugh was contagious; it tickled my insides. The most disconcerting aspect of Mom's laugh was that it was identical to mine.

When I was little, I remember thinking my mommy smelled fresh like the laundry hanging outside on the line. She felt soft like a snuggly blanket. To supplement the family income, Mom took in ironing for friends and relatives. As she went about her daily chores, she enjoyed listening to and singing along with the radio. Her clear, sweet voice floated through the house. The sound always wrapped around my body and hugged my heart, giving me a warm, safe, cozy feeling. She especially liked the tune of the song "Tom Dooley" by the Kingston Trio. She would belt out the "Tom Dooley" chorus with gusto:

Hang down your head, Tom Dooley.
Hang down your head and cry.
Hang down your head, Tom Dooley.
Poor boy, you're bound to die.

I picked up the words to songs quickly and thought it fun to sing along with her. One day the song came on the radio, and I immediately chimed in. My voice began to fade when I noticed the music was playing but Mom wasn't singing. In fact, her mouth was pencil-thin and clamped shut. Her eyebrows wrinkled into an angry "V" over a pair of flashing green eyes. This was a signal for me to stop any Dooley singing immediately. "Mommy, why aren't you singing the Tom Dooley song? It's one of your favorites."

"Not anymore, it isn't," she declared. "I don't like that song. Tom Dooley wasn't a nice man. In fact, he was a very violent man. I don't support violence, and neither should you."

Evidently she had recently listened to the verse and chorus and found out Tom Dooley had actually murdered a woman and was to be hanged for his crime. After discovering Dooley's villainy, she denounced him and would never again sing along.

I thought Dad's use of the belt on our bare bottoms fairly violent, but I think she considered it a normal way to teach us right from wrong. In my mind, I questioned how violence could teach us what was right if, in fact, violence was wrong. I didn't ask the question. I figured my parents knew the right answers, and that I would understand when I was older.

When Dad told us to do something, no one ever questioned him. If we disobeyed him, and we were younger than five, he would merely hit us with his open hand on our bare butts. After turning five, if we didn't live up to his expectations, it was *the belt*. I began to think that he used the belt more often for punishing us than for holding up his pants. Dad's snarl would suddenly bite into the peaceful air, "On your knees, pants down." One second the belt was around his waist, and the next, the leather was cutting the skin of our bare bottoms.

Many behaviors caused the belt response. Swearing almost always ended with a whipping or at the very least getting your mouth washed out with soap. We were not to say the word "damn." We couldn't even say the word "dang," because it was a four-letter word starting with "d" that meant "damn." The words "shut up" were not allowed. In order to avoid the belt, we could say "shush up" if we were very careful to enunciate the "sh" sound at the end. Dad never swore himself. When he did get riled up, the worst we ever heard him say was "Oh, gefilte fish" or "fudgesicle."

Sometimes the belt would miss our butts and land on our thighs. I remember not wanting to wear shorts for a couple of days because of the welts that would show. After Dad had left the room, the rest of us would gather around to comfort the one who received the belt. Murmurs of, "Are you okay?' and whispers of, "You'll feel better tomorrow" filled the air. I would be truly grateful I was spared and feel bad for the one who was punished

I was often afraid of Dad, but seldom afraid of Mom. She rarely got really angry. On occasion, though, all the kids and the chaos would frazzle her so much that she would shake us. I remember when she shook me. I can't recall why I was in trouble, but I do recall her eyes flashed a deep emerald green, and her hands squeezed tightly around my shoulders.

"I'm sorry, Mommy," I said in a loud voice. She didn't seem to hear my apology. Her quiet voice was scary. Seemingly out of control, she began shaking me, which caused my head to bob so hard I was afraid my neck would snap. Shaking, although rare, was terrifying because Mom wasn't being Mom; I think I actually preferred Dad's belt as punishment.

Mom never complained about her situation, but she often seemed overwhelmed. I believe being pregnant and trapped in our small house all day; every day really weighed her down. Mom was a major baby maker. In 1945, a year after my parents were married, my oldest brother took his first breath. From the age of twenty-seven, she had a baby almost every year unless she miscarried: 1946, 1947, 1948, 1950 (me), 1951, 1955, 1957, 1959, and 1960. She would have had another child in 1963 had she lived. When I picture Mom in my head, I always see her pregnant. I still remember staring in shocked disbelief at a photo of her with a flat stomach; it looked very strange to me. I wonder if she ever longed to have her body and some time all to herself. She didn't share her personal aspirations with us, so I'll never know.

What I did suspect was that Mom was always ready for our bedtime. At nine o'clock p.m., it was lights out. Dad was strict about bedtime, and we knew not to argue. What Dad didn't know was that Jean and I were seldom sleepy. At the end of our active playing, eating, praying day came our active playing, singing, foot-fighting fun bedtime.

From the time I stopped sleeping in a crib, I shared a double bed with my sister. The side of our bed pushed against the wall was Jean's side. I slept on the outside because Jean didn't want me disturbing her sleep by crawling over her in the middle of the night to go to the bathroom. At least she hoped I would go to the bathroom. Many times I disappointed her by wetting the bed. My sister wasn't particularly fond of the fact that I was a bed wetter. Sometimes during the night Jean would nudge me awake. She would yell in a grossed-out, disgusted voice, "Diana, you wet the bed again!" I could clearly feel the sheets were wet. This was most upsetting because I would swear that I had gotten up to go to the bathroom. I actually felt the cold tiles on my feet as I trudged to the bathroom, sat on the chilly toilet seat, and began to pee. All that was really happening was that I was having a very vivid, recurring dream, and when I let my bladder go, it would be in my bed.

My parents never punished me for wetting the bed because they felt I didn't have control over my bladder. More importantly, I had a physical problem; my urethra was too small. From the ages of three to five, I had to go to the doctor to get my urethra stretched. This procedure was extremely painful, but I liked the lollipop I received afterwards. No matter the reason, bedwetting was a great embarrassment to me and a never-ending irritation to my sister. By the age of ten, the situation improved because I was finally able to stop wetting the bed and still keep my vivid dreams.

CHAPTER 3

Big Girl

I officially became a "big girl" when Mom thought I was old enough to help with the babies and housework. Our brother Lee was born when I was five, and I got to hold him and change his diapers. Mom counted on Jean and me to work around the house, although Jean was a better helper than I was. For one thing, Jean was three years older than I and much more experienced at being a good helper. For another thing, I was a tomboy and not interested in any women's work except taking care of the babies.

The boys worked on chores outside the house while Jean and I handled the inside duties. The boys had paper routes by the age of ten. Shoveling snow, mowing the lawn, and taking out the trash were all boy tasks. The girls helped Mom with housecleaning, laundry, cooking, and caring for the younger kids. Jean played second mom to Lee and Alan. Later on I became second mom to Vincent and Teresa.

We were a stay-at-home working family until the summer I was five and a half. That summer, Dad decided the family would take a vacation to New York City. Dad loved his big family and wanted to show us off. He also wanted us to see his childhood haunts. All seven kids piled into the old Ford station wagon. Dad, as always, was in the driver's seat, while Mom sat beside him in front. The rest of the crew sprawled out in the back with the seats folded down.

After thousands of miles, chatter about every subject that came to mind, endless car games, fights, and many "are we there yet?" inquiries, we began to ask Dad about his early life. With gentle encouragement from Mom, he finally told us a little about his history.

He rarely talked about his childhood, I think because remembering was painful for him. "My father, your grandfather," he started in his best storytelling voice, "was old when I was born."

18

"How old?" my older brothers asked in unison. My ears, which were half asleep, suddenly woke up for Dad's reply.

His normal voice was gone and was replaced with a faraway little boy's voice that said, "Sixty-nine." I wondered if Dad had grabbed his long-ago self from Puerto Rico because the man's deep, roughened English words were softened by the boy's high-pitched Spanish accent. "I think I was a surprise baby 'cause my brothers and sister were a lot older. I grew up by myself. When I was eight, Dad died. Two months after Dad, Mom passed. I was all alone in Puerto Rico until my brother, Fernando, brought me here to the U.S. I wanted to live with Fernando, but he was only fifteen, and the people in charge wouldn't let him take care of me. I went into foster care and lived in the Bronx. The end."

"No, Dad, tell us more," Jean pleaded.

"Yeah, we want to hear about the Bronx," Michael piped in.

Dad's regular hard, loud, gruff voice suddenly returned, "I said *the end*, and I mean the end." He began to cough a violent, wheezy cough.

Often in the summer and especially when he was stressed, he would have an asthma attack. The car became very quiet waiting for him to catch his breath and hoping he would catch his temper, too. I was only five, but even I knew this was a time to keep my mouth shut. I wouldn't hear another word about what happened when Dad was in foster care until I was much older.

Even though Dad wouldn't talk about his foster care experiences, he tried to soothe the painful memories of his troubled childhood in other ways. Around the holidays, our family would take in orphans for weeks at a time. His being a foster child with asthma created a big soft spot in his heart for any abandoned or sick kid. An asthmatic orphan was beyond special. I believe caring for other lonely, sick children and creating a big family of his own were two ways that Dad attempted to fill the void of his empty childhood.

On this New York vacation, a particular thought floated to the surface of my mind. It caused my five-year-old face to wrinkle up like I had just tasted a lemon; it was the fact that all Dad's siblings looked like him, including his sister, Amparo.

"Mommy, Auntie Amparo is a woman. Why does she look exactly like Dad's brothers? She looks ugly. She has a man's face."

Before she could help it, Mom nodded her head in agreement, and her mouth started to curve up in a smile. I started to smile too, proud of my astute observation.

The shared moment vanished so quickly, I thought I had made it up. In an instant she had straightened her mouth out, frowned, and pointed a wagging finger at me. To Mom, being polite and considerate of others was of the upmost importance. I was considered to be an abject failure in this department because of my many inconsiderate "why" questions. I frequently asked questions that were rude, like "Why do you have so many wrinkles?" or "Why do you snore so loud?'" or "Why do you walk funny?" Mom often admonished me for my insensitive remarks, declaring me too bold.

My observation about Auntie Amparo elicited a version of Mom's normal scolding. "Diana, that isn't a nice thing to say. Wipe that smile off your face. You're being extremely rude." I wanted to please Mom, but sometimes I couldn't quite figure out how to tell the truth and be nice at the same time.

That summer in New York we visited the Bronx Zoo. My young mind could not shake the frightening image of the gorilla I saw there. The animal devoured my dreams for about five years. Month after month, the nightmares were the same: The deranged beast crashed through our front door, destroying everything in its path. My family was pleading for mercy, but the hairy monster proceeded to kill everybody in my family except for me, because I would always hide. I would awaken shaking, sweating, and sure I was totally alone. It was a relief to hear Jean's voice yelling at me to be quiet.

The most disappointing memory I have was recalling that I didn't get to see much of New York City. Because of a kidney infection, I was forced to stay with Aunt Millie and Uncle Peter while everyone else went sightseeing. I had a rotten time at my aunt and uncle's house because, besides being sick, I fell out of the bunk bed and hurt my butt, and an aspirin got stuck in my throat, which ruined pill-taking for me for a long time. To make matters worse, upon arriving home, I had to have daily shots to cure my infection. Since Mom was too nervous to learn how to give the shots, a neighbor lady came over to do the deed.

With the summer, shots, and infection over, I looked forward to school. My excitement turned to shocked disbelief when, on the first day of kindergarten, I was scolded for already knowing how to read. This seemed a very strange attitude for a teacher to have. I thought teachers liked good readers. Maybe because she was a nun-teacher she wanted to teach me to read her way and only her way. I had learned to read and write from my older siblings, and evidently this was not acceptable in Catholic school.

I loved to read. I knew I was supposed to honor and respect the teachers at my school, but as much as I tried, I just couldn't feel bad about being able to read. Trouble seemed to follow me even though I tried to be good in kindergarten. I remember one day at naptime, my friend asked me a question. I was answering her when the nun-teacher snuck up behind me. In a loud voice that made me jump almost to the ceiling, she yelled, "Diana, no talking. You're a naughty girl." She grabbed my hand, squeezing it white, and yanked me into the cloakroom. I had to lie on the floor alone. It was very hard to breathe because the walls pushed close together like a monster squeezing all the air out of the very small space. The single light bulb above scared me, and I promised myself I would never get caught talking during naptime again.

To add to the school trouble, I started having trouble at home. One night, Dad quietly tiptoed into our room as we slept. He let Jean continue to sleep while he gently lifted me out of bed. He carried me in his arms down the hall to the bathroom by the kitchen. When he picked me up to hold me close, I felt two things: I felt special to be snuggled by Dad, but also strange and confused. Why would he take me out of bed when I was sleeping and had kindergarten the next day?

After locking the door, he sat on the toilet with me on his lap facing away from him, pulled down my panties, put his hand under my flannel nightgown, and rubbed me between my legs. My body thought the rubbing felt good, but my mind disagreed, saying, *Stop it; this is weird. I can't breathe. Stop! This feels yucky.* It felt like when someone started tickling me and wouldn't stop. Of course, I didn't say these things to Dad, because he was the boss. I knew I would get in big trouble for asking him questions. I didn't know exactly what was happening, but to my five-year-old mind, his erection felt to me like he was trying to put something in my butt.

After Dad woke me up four or five more times, each time doing exactly the same strange butt thing, I decided it was safe to ask Mom a "why" question. Something just didn't feel right. I remember, as clear as a Colorado sky, Mom and me standing and talking right outside their bedroom when I asked my important question, "Why does Daddy take me out of bed at night?"

"What do you mean?" inquired my mom.

"He tries to stick something in my butt," I explained. Mom didn't get mad at my "why" question or say I was too bold. She merely gave me a strange, faraway, sad look and told me not to worry. I know she talked to my dad because he stopped taking me out of my bed and didn't rub me again until I was almost seven.

I quickly pushed the dad incident out of my mind. My first- and second-grade years were focused on one of my great passions: reading. I was a good reader and was often picked to read aloud in class. I loved to be chosen even though the kids teased me because I read with such expression. The dramatics earned me the name "expression hotel." I especially loved Dr. Seuss books. At home, where our huge Seuss supply was in high demand with my younger siblings, I used my best acting abilities. Since I felt it important to act my age, I pretended to be disinterested in the good doctor. After much begging by my younger siblings, I would eventually agree to read. I would read book after book, day after day, acting as if I were merely being a good sport when secretly I loved every minute of Seuss time.

My favorite Dr. Seuss character was an extremely likable elephant named Horton. Horton protected the little people. One of his refrains was "a person's a person no matter how small." Sometimes being the fifth kid, and the youngest girl so far, made me feel like a little person who needed protection. Mostly, though, because of my large family, I felt like Horton, big and tough. I liked myself best when I was like my favorite elephant: kind, determined, and sticking up for the underdog. He was my spirit, the wise and honest part of me. My affection and love for Horton soon spread to all elephants. I'm crazy for elephants.

CHAPTER 4

The Day the Music Died

D ad loved music, and that love spilled over onto us. He taught us all
to sing and my sister and me to dance. In the early years, the waltz
and foxtrot were our specialties. He loved to listen to music, especially to
the great tenor Mario Lanza. People strolling past our home would often
pause in mid-stride to hear a record playing Mario's powerful voice.

Dad possessed a big, beautiful, booming tenor voice as well.
Around the house he would break into song frequently and spontaneously. The whole family was bitten by the singing bug. He sang in the
church choir, and all of us practiced often to perform as a family at the
church talent shows. We all had good voices, but Patrick's voice was
exceptional. His voice gave me goose bumps and was so beautiful it
caused my heart to soar to heaven. People said he had the voice of an
angel. Dad thought our family's talent so great he nurtured the idea that,
given enough dedication and practice, we could be the next Trapp Family Singers.

Christmas caroling was a family production. After weeks of practice,
Dad would deem us ready to sing in public. We, along with our cousins,
would carol our hearts out going from house to house. I'd like to say we
did this simply for the satisfaction of singing to honor the birth of Jesus,
but being a normal kid, I have to admit I also welcomed the money and
candy given to us by appreciative audiences.

The holiday season of 1956, just like every holiday season in my
memory, meant nightly practices for our big Christmas caroling event. I
loved the magical music of Christmas. It filled me up until I swelled with
contentment. The Christmas season when I was almost seven was proving to be the most magical time ever. This was because the whole season

rested on top of a good start in second grade, complete with loads of friends and books.

One evening in December, our family was practicing hard in the living room. My voice was loud and full of expression as I belted out "O Come, All Ye Faithful." Dad's eyes smiled at me with approval, so I sang even louder. When the practice was over, Dad looked at me and said, "Diana, come with me." He motioned with his arms to follow him up the stairs to the attic.

"Okay, Daddy." I felt proud that he'd singled me out.

He turned to the rest of the family and said sternly, "No one bother us. I want to talk to Diana in private."

Dad walked fast, and I ran to catch up. I arrived at the boys' room huffing and puffing. He was already through the boys' room and waiting for me in his projects room. He was looking at me with a big, friendly grin.

"Come here, Diana," he said, opening his arms. I ran and jumped in my dad's arms, and he lifted me high into the air, my green dress billowing around me like a parachute. He gently placed me on top of his table.

"Diana, look at you. You're getting so big." I giggled. Yes, I was big. Standing on top of the table, I was even bigger than my dad. Suddenly he reached under my dress and pulled down my panties. Below the folds of my green dress I saw the white material of my panties pooled around my ankles. I could barely see my black-and-white saddle shoes peeking out from my underwear. How embarrassing. I wanted to run, but I couldn't move my legs. Maybe I could use my voice. *Mommy, help me. Somebody, anybody, help me.* But my feet and my voice got stuck.

Then I remembered Dad was the big boss. Nobody, including Mom, would or could tell him what to do. Besides, if I ran, or talked back to him, he would really be mad. He would take off his belt and whoop me. I felt trapped in every way. As Dad started rubbing my private parts, he said, almost breathlessly, "You're so pretty."

No, Daddy. Look at me. I'm a tomboy. I don't care about being pretty. If pretty is the reason you're rubbing me, I don't want to be pretty. When he touched my private parts, it felt sort of good and sort of bad. But mainly his touch made me feel ugly and dirty. I was thinking it'd be much better if I were a boy. I was pretty sure my dad wasn't rubbing my brothers' private parts. What about Jean? Jean was much prettier than me. Jean was also older and stronger. I'd seen her stand up to Dad. If I couldn't be a boy, I wished I could be a girl like my sister. Why me? Maybe Dad chose me simply because I was a bad girl.

It seemed like I was stuck to the table and that the rubbing went on for hours, but maybe it was just minutes. My mind couldn't stand hanging around, however much time elapsed, so it went to the library. In the library, I could hide in stories.

When he was finished, he said softly, but dismissively, "Pull your panties up."

"Yes, Daddy," I said, my mind coming back to the attic. As I pulled my panties up, I caught a glimpse of my black-and-white saddle shoes. They were sitting on the table. I couldn't feel my feet or legs, but I'm sure they were still in my shoes. As Dad lifted me off the table and set me on the ground, I suddenly felt very small. I could barely make out Horton's voice saying, "A person's a person, no matter how small." I was six and didn't know much about the world, but I sure hoped Horton was right.

After the attic, every time I heard Christmas carols, my eyes would tear up. I wanted so much to recapture the magical Christmas feeling through the singing of carols. Whenever I sang Christmas songs, the sound took me back to the hopeless feeling of Dad touching my private parts in the attic. My heavy, yet empty, heart would grieve for the loss of the music that I loved. Just as the words had ruined the tune of "Tom Dooley" for Mom, the attic abuse ruined Christmas carols for me.

The attic incident seemed to spur Dad into a frenzy of activity. He would trap me inside, outside, day and night, in the attic, in the car while doing errands, at night when tucking me into bed. The weekends were the worst. It seemed to me that he used all his creative energy to corner me. Before my seventh birthday, Dad had pulled down my panties to rub or finger my private parts dozens of times.

Dad took me on errands with him whenever he could. A usual weekend errand would be picking up newspapers to recycle for extra cash. Since he picked up the newspapers in alleyways, he had ample opportunity to stop the car and indulge in his newfound favorite activity: groping me.

One time, when there was a lull in the activity, I dared to ask him a question. I knew I wasn't supposed to question him, but my curiosity got the better of me. "Daddy, why are you doing this to me?"

To my amazement, he didn't get mad. His brown eyes looked at me with an expression I hadn't seen before. He appeared a little sad and maybe a little scared. But no, I was making that up. Dad was never scared. After he glanced at me, he quickly looked down. He pretended he was searching the floorboard for something, but I think he was looking for the right words to say to me. Finally, when he looked at me again, it was with one of his normal expressions. His stare said, *Listen to me carefully. Your only choice is to do what I say.*

Out loud he said, "What we're doing is our little secret. You're not to tell anybody, including your mother." I must have had an alarmed or distrustful look on my face because he quickly added, while patting me on the shoulder, "Don't worry; all daddies do this."

I didn't want to believe Dad was lying to me, but there was something about "our little secret" that didn't seem right. If what we were doing was truly okay, then why was it a secret? I thought about his answer for several days and finally asked my cousins and friends, "Does your daddy ever touch your private parts?"

The answers ranged from "What are you talking about?" to "Of course not!" to "Gross," but the answer always meant no. The answers told me Dad was lying about his idea that "all daddies do this." Not one of my friends' or relatives' daddies touched or fingered their private parts.

After I realized I was alone in this, my brain filled with smashed-together, competing thoughts. The fight in my head that gave me a major headache was the battle between Church rules and Dad's rules.

As a seven-year-old attending a Catholic school, we were taught the Ten Commandments. Teachers drilled into us every day that disobeying any one of the big ten was a mortal sin. This was a very bad dilemma because I didn't understand how I could honor God and my father at the same time. Why did I feel like "our little secret" was a big, mortal sin? What did it mean about me that sometimes when Dad fingered me it felt good? I knew exactly what it meant. I was a horrible girl, because a mortal sin should never feel good. If I stopped Dad, I was bad. If I let him touch me down there, I was bad.

Another fight in my head was about Dad's rules and having a life. It seemed that from second grade on, I constantly had to do a balancing act in my mind. I continually had to decide whether it was worth it to fight off his sexual advances. Most of the time I complied, but sometimes I would be so sick of the fondling I would say, "No, Daddy, don't touch me. Not now, Daddy. I don't want to go with you, Daddy, not today."

Some of these times, although he didn't like what he heard, he didn't force me. He usually stomped out of the room and slammed the door. I had an instant of feeling big and powerful until a minute later a voice would come blasting through the walls. It pierced my head and invaded my brain. This shattered my big and powerful feeling into little pieces.

"Diana, weren't you supposed to dust? Look at this dirt," he would say, holding up a finger with a speck of dust on it. "Take down your pants now." And his belt would hit my skin. *Swat! Swat! Swat! Sting! Sting! Sting!*

"You never learn, do you? Until you learn, no phone, no playground. You're grounded. Now dust."

Dad's rule stated, *I am the undisputed ruler of this house. You will obey me. I'll win in the end.* I learned fast with Dad. When I let him have his way with me, he didn't hit me with the belt. When I let him touch my private parts, I could visit with friends and, most importantly, have playground time. When I let him molest me, he rewarded me with special treats, like candy and soda, which my sister and brothers didn't receive. I chose not to fight him because it wasn't worth it. Between having no life and having a life, I mostly chose to have a life.

My biggest inner battle was my mind fighting my body. Every night I slept with my ears partially awake. Many nights, I heard his footsteps. I heard his saliva making a slurping noise through his teeth. My heart would beat faster. I would see the shadows of movements through the slits in my eyes. I would wrinkle my nose closed, guarding against the coming pungent sex smell. I would tighten my eyelids down into my eye sockets, guarding against the sight of Dad's body, and move my head slightly, shaking it back and forth and saying *no* in my mind, over and over again. At these times I braced, waited, and braced again until I felt his hands on me, pulling down my panties. My mind told my body to stay asleep, or at least to be numb, to lay still and not respond. This didn't seem to ever matter because as loud as my mind yelled *no*, my body betrayed me and was loyal to his touch. I responded to him fingering me. My body would start to tingle and then get wet, and in direct opposition to my mind's wishes and without my mind's consent, my body would begin to move in rhythm. My mind hated me and my body, because if my body liked the feeling of doing this wrong thing, the only logical conclusion was that I, Diana Christine, was rotten. Sometimes the feeling grew too big, too out of control, and too intense. It was like being tickled to death.

When this happened, my brain would burst open and my mind would take a vacation. I would go to safe places. One time when Dad visited my bed, my mind went to the library. In the library I was reading a book from the *Beany Malone* series. These stories were about Beany, a girl my age who had fun times and didn't have to deal with a dad who molested her. I transformed into Beany. As Beany, I had a "Leave It to Beaver" life. Or, and I chuckle at this, a "Leave It to Beany" life. I lived in Denver, and I was a part of a secure, attentive family. I got into many scrapes and adventures, but my life remained safe. My mind was free and able to breathe again.

Then, suddenly, I was traveling at hyper speed, hurtling through space. I found myself back in my house, back in my bedroom, and back in my bed. I was no longer Beany. I was me. I opened my eyes a crack to see if Jean was still sleeping. She was. Out of the corner of one eye I saw Dad walking away and gently closing the door. In the following years, I often wondered why Jean never seemed to hear him when he came into our room until I realized that she didn't have the sexual abuse antenna that I had. She hadn't heard him because she didn't have to participate in his sex games.

To handle the horror, I gradually split myself in two: the normal Diana and the Diana whose job was to cope with being alone with Dad. My normal side was, well, normal. I loved my school, St. Dominic's. Most of the nuns were nice teachers the majority of the time. They were, as a rule, only hard on the students who acted out. Therefore, I tended to listen attentively, to be polite, to be diligent with homework, and to keep a rein on laughing and talking until I hit the playground.

On the playground, I was known as a tomboy and a daredevil. I had a reputation for always championing the underdog. If I noticed a kid being shunned for any reason, I would always come to the rescue and immediately invite that person into our crowd. I was popular enough with my peers to get away with this. No one ever accused me of being shy. Whether at school or playing with friends, the normal Diana was always present. I was the extroverted sort who loved people and spent a lot of time cultivating and maintaining friendships.

To me, though, family was even more important than friends. I loved my big family. Dad stressed family togetherness, and many of our activities, including church activities, centered on the family. Even after being abused on a consistent basis, I still loved to play games with Dad and my siblings. His presence in a group setting didn't bother me a bit. During family time, I don't recall the other Diana ever appearing.

When we were doing activities as a family, Dad treated me like the rest of the kids in that he frequently tried to rid us of our nasty habits. Swearing was the biggie for the family, but my nasty habit was sucking my thumb. I loved to suck my thumb. It was a way I could comfort myself—any time, anywhere. Dad thought it babyish and told me so. When the name-calling didn't work, he began coating my thumb with Tabasco sauce. The result of this tactic was that I learned to love the burning, hot pepper-flavored mixture, but continued to suck my thumb.

Dad, as powerful as he was, didn't have the power to stop me. Even as a child, I knew there was a more powerful force than Dad. When I was seven, I decided I would stop sucking my thumb on the day of my First

Communion. I remember thinking, *Jesus made a big sacrifice for all of us; I'll make a big sacrifice and give up sucking my thumb for him.*

At that time, when I was seven, the babies in my life were Lee and Alan. Lee was five years younger than I. Although he was technically Jean's charge, I helped with him as well. Saturday dinner was always spaghetti night, also fondly known by our entire family as "pig night." This name was due to the mess the youngest child made with the spaghetti in his high chair. I link pig night most closely with Lee. He was like spaghetti: thin, flexible, wiggly, and delightful. Mommy had a mangle, a large press used mainly for ironing sheets. It sat next to the high chair, and on spaghetti night, Lee took it upon himself to completely decorate the mangle with red sauce and noodles. I can still picture him covered from head to toe with a big grin of satisfaction on his face. Everybody loved pig night.

Alan was born when I was seven and a half. For some reason he didn't get the oxygen he needed at birth and was labeled "mentally retarded." Now I say he was born "slow" or "mentally challenged." If we had ever taken a family vote, he would have unanimously received the "all-time favorite child" award. He was a special-needs child who loved everything: food, toys, people, dogs, naps, boxes, TV, and music. He was a bundle of energy, wriggling in excitement with each adventure, every moment fresh and new in his mind.

Alan had a round shape. He was stubby; his chubby legs held up a ball-shaped torso topped with a spherical head. His eyes were two big circles of green. He could fall asleep any time, anywhere. When he was a toddler, it seemed we were always searching for him. We'd locate him in the most unusual places. He could be found in the closet curled up in a laundry basket or behind a couch, always fast asleep.

We, as most children do, invented games mirroring the adult world around us. I remember one time when my "alone-with-Dad" world and my "regular" world collided. When I was seven and Patrick five, we played a version of house that we called "Mommy and Daddy." I'd play-act washing the dishes and cooking. "I'll stay home and take care of the babies," I announced.

"I'm going to work," my brother stated. "I'll be back for dinner."

One day I talked Patrick into playing a different game, one that I called "Mother and Father." We were both naked, simulating the sex act, when Mom found us. "What are you two doing?"

"We're playing Mother and Father," I replied.

"Stop it this instant," she said, flustered. "Get your clothes on right now. Diana, you are very naughty."

My face felt hot, my throat got tight, and the tears pushed on my eyes. "I'm sorry, Mommy. I didn't mean to be bad."

"Where did you come up with this idea, anyway?" she queried.

"I don't know." I said, shaking my head. But I did know. I was just afraid to tell her.

Dad had showed me pictures of naked grown-ups on top of each other. I learned that those pictures were just another secret of Dad's I had to keep. Dad continued to play his secret sex games with me, but Patrick and I only played Mommy and Daddy, never playing Mother and Father again. A short time after this incident, I stopped thinking of my dad as a daddy and myself as a little girl. In my mind, daddies were supposed to protect their little girls' innocence, keeping them safe from danger. Dad was the exact opposite of my idea of a daddy; he was scary. I was the opposite of my mommy's idea of an innocent, good little girl; I was bad. What was I supposed to learn when Dad thought what we were doing was right and Mom thought it was wrong? It seemed no matter what I did, I was hardly ever good.

I felt like I was Mom's least favorite child. She believed I was bad. My boldness and getting into trouble caused her lots of headaches and worry. She tended to be anxious and emotional anyway, and I got the feeling my behavior caused her condition to be much worse. It seemed like she thought I could never do anything as well as my older brothers and sister.

Dad liked me when I let him touch my private parts but seemed to hate me when I didn't. He said it was my fault he wanted to touch me. He said because of me, he couldn't help himself. His favorite child was Alan because he was so innocent and happy.

The only time I remember being filled to the brim with love was when I was hanging out with the babies. My younger siblings thought I was great. They truly loved me and I loved them. I decided early on that the feeling of being loved and needed was what I wanted as a grownup. So when others would ask, "What do you want to be when you grow up?" I didn't answer a doctor, a dancer, or a fashion designer. I said without hesitation, "That's easy. I want to be a mommy."

Deep down, I knew my parents loved all of us, including me. What hurt was my belief that they loved the other kids a little bit more. The feeling of being my parents' least favorite lay like tiny, jagged black stones in my heart and stomach. The stones were always there, but I wasn't consciously aware of them. I was too busy living to focus on negative feelings.

My life was filled with ordinary kid stuff: chores, play, and school. Our busy household continued to have that normal "at-home" feeling like wearing an old, favorite, comfortable pair of blue jeans. Through elementary school, I was comfortable in my skin because I knew I was an average kid. I was a daredevil. I was a tomboy. I was outspoken. I loved babies. I fought with my siblings. I was a protector of the underdog. I was queen of the ringers. I was an extrovert. I loved reading, laughing, and making friends. I knew I was normal.

"Diana, you come with me." Dad's words shattered my normalcy. It felt in an instant that I—the real me—left, and Diana #2, the girl who dealt with being alone with Dad, appeared in the shape of a phantom shadow. This Diana had little resemblance to my normal self. This Diana exuded the flat, grey color of resignation. An expressionless, powerless, hopeless, docile, compliant ghost of a girl did his bidding without complaint.

Thankfully, she was the Diana who was present throughout the abuse. She hated it when Dad would say nasty sex words to her. Out of his mouth came many four- and five-letter words for vagina, penis, and breasts. The words sounded like swear words to her. His rules about swearing evidently didn't apply when he was alone with her. He would also show her pictures, such as Kama Sutra cards, which were cartoon people depicting sex positions. I know these pictures gave me the idea of the Mother and Father game.

I was always aware of the other Diana and knew she was just another side of me. I talk about this side of me in the third person, however, because I felt so detached and separate from my shadow side. I think the reason I was able to handle the abuse and enjoy a normal life was because I could separate the two sides of me and leave my body during the abuse. I was almost sure, as crazy as it sounds, that splitting myself into two parts helped me to survive and not go crazy.

CHAPTER 5

New Developments

I n the life of a child, there comes a time when passing thoughts suddenly become strong opinions and insignificant urges spring into action. My time for strong opinions and action began in the summer of 1958, before third grade. I started classifying my perception of things into three basic categories: Like, Dislike, and Horrible. My opinions, for the first time, significantly differed from the establishment; i.e., parents and teachers.

My thick, wavy brown hair, which hung down to my waist, had just reached the Horrible designation. For years, Mom and her brush valiantly fought the daily battle of my untamed, tangled mass and my equally out-of-control, complaining mouth. "Ow, that hurts. I hate this. I don't want my hair brushed," I would whine.

"Hold still. I'm almost finished," Mom's slightly frustrated voice would reply.

As an eight-year-old, I received my very own torture device: a brush. I was now in charge of taming my own obstinate strands. I didn't have time for this task. I had higher priorities, and frankly, my hair was weighing me down. I begged Mom to let me cut my hair. I had all sorts of valid arguments, such as long hair is old-fashioned, and my friends' mothers let them get their hair cut. It was my hair. My heavy hair got in the way on the playground. When the reasoning tactic failed, I went back to my younger, more emotional approach; I simply stated with a sad expression and quivering lips, "I hate long hair!" I don't have a clue what caused her to acquiesce. My devotion to my goal may have made her see the light, or maybe she wanted me off her back. Whatever the reason, I received my first real haircut.

The scissors clipped away as I watched my hair fall to the ground, circling the high barber chair. You might think that the sight of endless waves of my hair on the floor should have caused a pang of regret or loss; on the contrary, I felt light and free. I swung my short, stylish, ducktail hairdo vigorously and let out a whoop of joy. My spirits soared and weren't dampened in the slightest when Dad's angry voice threw his heavy punch: "You look terrible. You look like a boy. Girls should have long hair!" The only tiny moment of doubt came when I glimpsed a girl at summer camp with hair down to her ankles. After an instant, my thoughts and I skipped lightly away from the poor girl. I felt sorry she was carrying such a heavy burden.

The family dynamic was placed in the Dislike category the summer of my first haircut. In addition to Dad's belt-happy behavior, I felt like I was often being blamed for my siblings' offenses. Patrick, the little sneak, was the worst offender. One day Patrick disappeared. Everyone was calling his name. Mom was frantic. "Diana, you were in charge of Patrick. Now he's missing. I thought I could trust you to watch your brother. Jean's responsible; why can't you be more like Jean?"

Thank goodness we finally found him on the playground. When asked why he was there, he calmly answered with a smirk, "Diana said I could."

"Dang it, Patrick, I didn't. You're a big, stinking liar," I protested. I knew I was in big trouble before I even looked at Dad's red face and squinted, dagger eyes. When he started to take off his big, stinking belt to whip me, I winced and averted my gaze. I braced for the words, but when Dad didn't tell me to pull my pants down, I looked up.

To my astonishment, he was uncoiling his belt and threading it back through his pant loops. I couldn't believe my luck! I had committed an unforgivable sin in Dad's eyes; I'd uttered a swear word. But for some reason Dad decided not to whip me. I was almost thinking this constituted a miracle.

Then I remembered there was no miracle. I wasn't being punished for the simple fact that I had been letting him touch me. He never punished me when I was letting him have his way with me. Still, I was fed up and angry. I'd narrowly escaped a whipping for a situation Patrick had caused.

Patrick had deflected the blame away from himself and onto me one too many times. I decided to take action by running away. Instead of honoring my usual playground schedule, I walked directly to the Piggly Wiggly. As I walked to the store, I'm fairly certain it was another great Colorado day: The sky was probably really blue; my favorite flowers, daisies, were in bloom; and the birds were chattering away. But I didn't notice. The scenery merely provided a neutral backdrop for my runaway thoughts: "I'll show them. They'll be sorry."

I sat down on the stoop in front of the store and pictured perfectly everybody's reaction to my homecoming. In my mind's eye, I saw all my siblings running out to greet me, saying, "Diana, we were so scared. We thought we lost you." Patrick clung to me, sniffling; he apologized to me for getting me into trouble and promised never to let me take the blame for his mistakes again. Mom dropped her ironing and raced to my side. She gave me a quick body scan to see if I was okay. She snuggled me, smothering me with kisses. She then pushed back to focus on my face, and said, "I'm sorry I yelled at you. I trust you and know you're responsible. I love you so much. I'm glad you're home. You're safe here with me." This entire visualization, detailed as it was, took a very short time.

I was then left to sit. I sat, and I waited. I sat and sat and waited and waited. I watched the sun slowly lift itself to the top of the sky. The sun's hot fingers drilled directly into the top of my head. I was hot and bored, but I still waited. I waited for the right moment to return home and show my face.

My stomach began to growl, and luckily that coincided with the perfect time to be welcomed home. I speed-walked, all the while anticipating my homecoming and lunch. As I entered the walkway to the house, I slowed my pace slightly and looked around. Where was everyone?

Everyone was doing what everyone always did in the summer at this time of day; eating lunch. I paused at the kitchen's entrance for effect. No one even looked up as the family chatter continued. No one had noticed I was gone. No one had even missed me! While eating my lunch in silence, I pondered the flaws in my thinking.

Running away hadn't solved the problem; it had only made matters worse by cutting into playground time. I couldn't imagine ever running away again, but if I did, it'd be for a *dang* good reason!

The Dislike category extended to school as well. It's not that I was a perfect child; in fact, far from it. I'd once stolen and smoked a part of a cigarette from Mom's stash, and I'd sneaked half a glass of my aunt's leftover wine. But if caught, I was willing to tell the truth and take responsibility for my actions. What I deeply disliked was being blamed unfairly. In late third or early fourth grade, Mom showed us an interesting *Life* magazine. On the cover, in living color, there was a fetus curled up, resting comfortably in a uterus. There was an accompanying article that explained the birth process in detail. Since Mom was always pregnant, I thought this subject, article, and picture fascinating and brought it to school to share with my friends.

Out of respect for my teacher, I waited until playground time to show my fellow students. I found myself in the middle of a good-sized crowd of awed classmates. I'd started to point out developing baby parts when the air stilled and the crowd suddenly dispersed. I stood alone, body braced, my magazine hiding my face, sensing the impending danger. Slowly I brought the magazine down just far enough to get a glimpse of a nun's habit, two furrowed brows, and glaring eyes.

"What's this?" Sister Angelina exclaimed as she ripped the magazine from my grasp. This must have been a rhetorical question because before I could answer, she went into a tirade. My face was hot, and my hearing dimmed. I only caught bits of sentences: "You nasty girl," "trouble," "tell your parents." Why did the Sister think showing a picture of a baby growing in a uterus made me a nasty girl? A picture of a baby wasn't bad, because babies were never bad.

Dad and Mom were indeed called in. I don't know what was discussed. All I know is that I did not receive any punishment from the school or my dad. Maybe my parents had talked some sense into the nuns about babies. I guess I should have forgiven Sister Angelina because she probably didn't know anything about babies, but I couldn't because I was still mad.

My heart filled with love imagining Mom and Dad standing up for me and successfully pleading my case to the nun. I giggled when I envisioned my devout Catholic parents going up against the self-righteous nun. In the end, I didn't ask about the meeting because I liked my imagined version, and deep down I really didn't care just as long as I wasn't in trouble.

At the age of ten, my intentions for the most part were to be both a dutiful fourth-grader and a helpful sister. I tried to be a nice sister most of the time, and one day my big brother Michael called to me, "Hey, Di, you going to the library today?"

"Of course," I said.

"Take this book back for me."

Since I practically lived in the library, I was only too happy to oblige. Because my brother was so much older, I wasn't usually interested in his reading materials. I remember thinking the book was awkward and heavy, but I wasn't the least bit curious about its subject matter. Walking down the hall, holding the big book in both hands, daydreaming as usual, I nearly bumped into Sister Maria. She was in my path, standing quite still with a stern look on her face.

"Sorry," I mumbled. "I didn't see you. I should watch where I'm going." As I attempted to go around her, her actions mirrored mine. She blocked my way. I stopped.

"Let me see your book."

"What book?" Then, following her gaze, I looked down and with much relief remembered the errand for my brother. "Oh, no," I said, handing the book to the nun, "this isn't my book. This is a library book I'm returning for my big brother."

It turned out that the biology book in question was being used as research material for one of my brother's ninth-grade class projects. The shameful subject contained within, according to Sister Maria, was the section on reproduction. I was blamed, the book confiscated, and my parents called in. I don't remember anything more happening to me, but I do remember feeling that being unfairly labeled and falsely accused were enough to get this incident placed in the extreme Dislike category. The controversial book must have been held for thorough examination by the powers that be, because my parents had to pay a hefty fine when it was finally returned to the library.

Since I'm a glass-half-full kind of girl, I seldom wallow in the negative. I left the Horrible and Dislike classifications on the shelf as I explored my own taste in music. I found myself no longer quite as interested in Dad's Trapp Family Singers goal for us. I wasn't interested in his music, either. When Dad wasn't home, Mario Lanza's operatic voice was quickly replaced by the doo-wop sounds of rock and roll. My sister and I fancied ourselves background singers, always singing the popular songs. Silverware turned into microphones and dishtowels into props as we doo-wopped the nightly dishes clean and dry. We even added a few well-choreographed dance steps to convey the dishes gracefully to their places in the cupboard.

From the time I started school, I liked boys. Boys were fun because they were feisty, tough, and competitive, which corresponded with my daredevil tomboy traits. I also liked boys who made me feel special, and loved. I was, in fact, boy crazy.

Michael, my kindergarten boyfriend, kissed me daily. George Gonzales, my boyfriend in third grade, carved my initials in his arm with a razor blade, which I thought was totally crazy, bloody, and messy. Billy Dietz was the next in a long line of boys I liked and who liked me. I especially enjoyed kissing him on the fire escape steps, despite the pigeon droppings. I instinctively knew one had to be discreet when "making out," so I was careful. I guess I was a little more mature in the boy department, because my girlfriends weren't interested or experienced in making out.

The boys were a different story. They seemed extremely interested in kissing. Some of the boys tried to pry open my lips with their tongues for a French kiss. I liked the good old American kiss, so I kept my mouth clamped shut. I didn't even want to try the French way. Too gross!

*　　*　　*

I'm not sure how many errands a typical father runs on a weekly basis, but it seemed to me Dad carried errand-running to the extreme. He, I believe, had developed a severe errand obsession. This fit into the Horrible category because he demanded I accompany him on every errand. One such errand stands out in my mind. It started out normally enough; Dad's left hand did the driving while his right hand groped my body. Usually his hands were disconnected from his talk. The other Diana, on duty in these circumstances, was usually bored with Dad's repetitive groping and inane conversation.

On this day, though, the other Diana noticed a different tone. He was ecstatic over the changes in my ten-year-old body: my pubic hair, my budding breasts, and the change from my little-girl stick figure to curves. "Look at you," he said excitedly. "You're not a little girl any more. You've grown up. Pretty soon you'll have tits like the women in my magazines." Then he went on and on about his sexual fantasies.

All the time he was talking, we—Diana #2 and I—were thinking if he liked us "grown up," we would definitely be in favor of "growing back down." We wanted to return to being a stick-figure tomboy. We tuned into what Dad was saying when his light, clipped cadence slowed to a heavy sigh. "Because of the way you look now, I really won't be able to help myself." His statement may have revealed shame and guilt for his actions, but I began to believe my changing body was responsible for Dad not being able to change his behavior. It was my fault he couldn't stop.

As the months passed, he seemed to rid himself of any misgivings he'd had about abusing me. He was convinced my newly developed body meant Diana #2 would be interested in porn magazines and fantasies about other women. Since she was exhibiting womanly features, he also felt he had license to broaden his sexual activity. She was not remotely interested in either the fantasy talk or the additional sexual activity; both made her sick.

We moved to a big new house in another section of North Denver, off 23rd Avenue and Irving Street, when I was ten. My brother Paul bragged that he was the first to see this house, yelling to any sibling in earshot, "Na na na na na, I saw the house before you did! I got to use the toilet in the new house."

Long before our family purchased this home, Paul had been the previous owner's newspaper delivery boy. One day Paul asked if he could use their bathroom. The request was graciously granted, giving him a preview of our future home.

The house, a veritable palace compared to our previous home, sported five bedrooms and two bathrooms, easily accommodating our growing family of nine children. Jean and I continued to share a room. Our room featured an alcove—the perfect place for three-year-old Alan to sleep in his crib. One-year-old Vincent claimed the crib in my parents' room.

I liked everything about the new space except for two things: There wasn't a playground across the street, so we were relegated to playing in our yard with pogo sticks, stilts, and jacks. The fragrant smell emanating from the lilac bushes dotting the perimeter of the house and the big, soft patch of grass made our playing area pleasant, but it didn't compare to the playground of old.

The second problem was the basement. The basement was Dad's newest lair. I'm not fond of unfinished basements; the musty smell, the cold floor, the creepy insects, and the shadows all make basements scary. Danger lurks in unfinished basements.

Two developments that coincided with our move to the new house were my bodily changes and Dad's growing a mustache. My changing ten-year-old body, in addition to our new basement space, seemed to embolden him to do more and more to me sexually. Somehow I linked hating my changing body and the increased sexual activity to Dad's changed appearance. His mustache became a sinister symbol. It reminded me of the villains in the Saturday morning cartoons.

I was glad when school started for the change of pace. This year was exciting because Lee was starting kindergarten. I'm not sure to this day why, but Lee was the first to attend a public, rather than a Catholic, school. We thought this weird because Dad liked everything Catholic, especially the discipline of the nuns.

It was a Saturday morning after Lee's first week of kindergarten. All of us, including Dad, were outside playing bases. Lee ran to catch a ball, and as he dropped it, he said, "Oh, fuck." The game stopped. We all froze in our positions. We must have looked like statues.

"Where did you hear that word?" Dad hollered.

"At school," Lee said, his lips quivering.

"That's what we get for sending you to public school," Dad growled. He started to undo his belt buckle, then looked at five-year-old Lee and seemed to change his mind. Yanking on Lee's arm, he wrenched him upward and dragged him into the house. We all followed as he took him to the master bathroom. Lee continued to cry as Dad washed his mouth out with soap. Our friendly game of bases ended abruptly with all of us being reminded of how quickly things could change.

By that evening, the tension had died down, and I was in high spirits after a particularly great dishwashing doo-wop session with Jean. I sank down into our blue-green brocade couch. I loved this couch because it was well worn and comfortable. I basked in the warmth and familiarity of my big family. My homework finished, my tummy full, the dishes done, the rosary said—all was well. I started to feel the drowsy drift as my body relaxed in comfort and contentment.

I was almost there, sinking into the soft pillows of safety, when a voice pierced the air, invading my space. The second the sound of Dad's voice penetrated my ears, my brain gave my body the signal to brace. "Diana," the voice simply said. The sound of my name caused my heart to pound hard against the walls of my chest. *One of these days*, I thought, *I'm sure it's going to crash through and make a break for it.*

I agreed with my heart. I desperately wanted to run as fast as my legs would carry me. Where should I go? I checked with my legs; they were jelly, stuck to the floor. My mind was totally focused. I didn't look at Dad, but I knew his exact location. My senses were super acute; they detected even the tiniest shift in atmospheric pressure. I heard the sound of saliva slithering through his teeth. I smelled the scent of Dad's clothes, a newspaper smell mixed with Mom's cooking smells. I felt his hungry eyes looking me up and down. I saw his shadow shifting slightly as he contemplated his next move. All my nerve endings stood at attention. I was frozen alert. *Move, Diana, move*, my internal voice hissed. I jumped off the couch and took one step, two steps, three steps. *Don't run.* I was walking...walking. "Diana! Did you hear me?"

I stopped. I mean I stopped everything: my step, my hands moving, my eyes blinking, my breathing.

"Come with me. You have clothes to fold." Then, as he opened the basement door and ushered me through, all feeling vanished and the other Diana appeared. Numb, she turned like a zombie and said in a monotone, "Yes, Dad."

Dad used code; he had one message for me and another command for the rest of the family. My message was to join him in the basement. To everybody else, he would bellow from the black hole, "I'm working; nobody come down here." No one ever came to my rescue, for no one dared defy his orders.

This evening, I heard laughter up above as the door creaked open. This had never happened before. I held my breath as Patrick's young voice called down, "Hey, Daddy. Do you want some ice cream?"

Dad bellowed back, "No. Close the door, I'm busy. I told you not to bother me."

A moment passed. "Now, where were we? We're going to try something different tonight." As he unzipped his pants and removed his penis, he said, "I would like you to kiss my dick."

Diana #2 refused. Good for her; she had more spunk than I thought. He, not to be deterred, began using his mouth on her while saying, "I love your sweet cunt."

Diana #2 couldn't stand the feeling. She hated the sucking sound of sex. She hated the feel of his scratchy mustache on her body. She hated the musty, moist, concrete smell of the basement mingled with the pungent, putrid sex smell. She let her mind leave. She went to the mountains and lay in a field of wildflowers.

I hovered above, watching and listening to this scene. I was getting more furious by the second. True, this was normal basement talk, but I couldn't believe the filthy language tonight after punishing Lee so harshly today. *How could you, Dad? Get mad at him*, I mouthed to the other Diana. *Tell him "gross, nasty!" Tell him you'll wash his mouth out with soap.* Alas, Diana #2 couldn't respond to me because she had gone to the mountains. She was enjoying a slight warm breeze. She looked up into a deep blue sky and noticed a few oddly shaped clouds. She smiled as she spied a cloud girl on a pogo stick.

Then, suddenly, I noticed Diana #2 had returned to the basement. She was cringing. Dad's mustache hairs felt like spiders, spiders that were crawling all over her private parts. We, both Dianas, detest spiders. "No!" we said in unison, and pushed Dad away.

"No, Dad, I don't want to do this anymore." I ran upstairs and locked myself in the bathroom. I took a bath. I scrubbed and scrubbed, trying in vain to rub out the dirty feeling. I repeated over and over, "I hate it, I hate it. I'm never doing that again!"

I held my ground for a week that time. Whenever I said no to Dad, I would become very nervous. I would try to do everything perfectly so he wouldn't have an excuse to punish me.

The first night after I told him no, Jean and I were doing the dishes. It was a quiet and serious affair. I couldn't risk having fun because Dad was sitting at the table watching Jean and me. I could tell by Jean's uncharacteristic sulky demeanor that she didn't care for Dad's scrutiny either. There would be no doo-wop singing tonight, I thought. I had to concentrate very hard on doing my job perfectly. My job was to dry the dishes. My hands were shaking so hard, I was afraid I might drop the plate I was holding.

I managed to dry it and was starting to put it away when Dad jumped up from the table and rushed up to me saying, "Let me see that plate, Diana." He grabbed the plate out of my hand. "Just as I thought— this dish isn't completely dry; there are still drops of water on it. Bend over and pull down your pants." In one fluid motion, his belt was off his pants and on my butt and thighs. A searing pain tore through my body. I bit my lip as the belt bit into my tender skin. I was determined not to cry.

The next day the infraction was not dusting correctly. Whipping on already welted skin is extra painful, and I couldn't help but cry out in agony. Welt upon welt on my buttocks was a far worse pain than blister upon blister on my hands when I was queen of the ringers. Besides, being queen was rewarding; being whipped was not. I remember my bottom hurting so badly I had trouble sitting at my desk at school.

Whipping was not his only method of punishment. For the next couple of days, he would jump out of nowhere as I was doing my chores and knuckle me on the head, saying, "You're too slow," and, "Knuckle down to business." Despite my determination, the knuckle would bring the sting of tears to my eyes.

But out of all the punishments, losing my privileges was worst of all. The beatings were temporary. Losing privileges meant I was stuck in the nightmare with no escape. Without my friends and activities, I felt hopeless. I didn't have a choice; I had to give in to him. He was in total control of me. He always won in the end. And so by the time Saturday came, I'd acquiesced. I was no longer being punished and had my life back. A few days later, I'd forgotten to put away the clothes I had folded. I was in a panic Dad would lash out. He didn't. Again, I was reminded Dad never punished me, in any way, when I allowed him to molest me.

I also became aware that when I denied Dad sexually, he was impatient with the entire family. He lashed out and was quick with the belt with all of us. At the time, I thought my siblings didn't have a clue about Dad's abuse, and I wasn't going to tell them. I certainly didn't receive or expect any kudos from the family for sacrificing my body sexually so they wouldn't get hit, either. But I felt good that I was helping them whether they knew it or not.

When I resisted, Dad's face would become cloudy, dark, and surly, sitting atop a tense, heavy body. It was like the tension buildup of an alcoholic needing a drink or a drug addict needing a fix. I guess I was his drink, or his fix. I was his addiction. When I let him have his way with me, the storm would pass and we could have a life. As was often the case, however, after a time of forced abstinence, he was even more demanding.

*   *   *

My life was turning into a series of splits. I guess Superman and I had some similarities: We both changed costumes and personalities, and we were both good at leading two distinct, separate lives that sometimes intersected. We definitely also had our differences: Whereas he changed costumes externally, my costume was an internal one. He was a super-hero and a normal guy; I was a normal girl and a sad, sick, shadow-person. He changed quickly in a phone booth, while I shifted more gradually step-by-step up the stairs from the basement or scrub-by-scrub in the bathtub. Sometimes my shift occurred spontaneously. It happened when I left the grey, isolated, underground existence with Dad and ascended into the colorful world of people. Family, friends, and school constituted a different world.

I was a tough kid in many respects, but I was also developing a reputation as a "scaredy-cat." The name, I had to admit, resembled me more and more. This scared feeling crept up on me. It probably started when I was three with the closet scare. In kindergarten, the fear jumped out at me in the cloakroom. From five until seven, a gorilla stalked my dreams. By the time I reached the age of eleven, I was often spooked by my own shadow. My list of fears was long and kept getting longer. Basements, old buildings, the dark, spiders, closets, sudden loud sounds, being alone, and scary television shows like *Alfred Hitchcock Presents* and *Twilight Zone* made my top-ten list.

When I walked into Sister Kent's classroom every morning of my fifth-grade year, however, I left my fears and all thoughts of Dad and Diana #2 in the basement.

"*Bonjour, ma chère Sœur,*" our fifth-grade class greeted our teacher.

"*Bonjour, ma classe,*" she replied.

"*Comment allez-vous aujourd'hui?*" we inquired.

"*Très bien, merci, et vous?*" she responded.

"*Très bien,*" we replied.

Yes, indeed, I was doing very well. Thank you, Sister Kentagern (or Sister Kent, as she preferred the class to call her) for taking me and my fifth-grade classmates out of our small, closed, cloistered St. Dominic's and inviting us to travel the world. Every day, the French greeting connected us to another thrilling, exotic adventure.

Sister Kent had taught children of diplomats in Chicago before coming to St. Dominic's and thus had connections all over the world. She encouraged curiosity, creativity, learning, and growing. My life seemed an easy flow when Sister Kent was around. I could be myself. She seemed not only to accept me but to celebrate me: the bold, outspoken, and imaginative me. How different from my kindergarten teacher and the typical rigid, rule-bound nuns. Sister Kent and her worldly connections opened the international door to pen pals.

My pen pal was a girl from India. I wrote telling her about my life in Denver and sent her a current picture of me. She immediately answered with stories of life in India, enclosing a picture of her riding her pet elephant. Fueled by my fierce love of elephants, I immediately considered moving to India primarily for the chance to own an elephant.

I quickly quashed the idea, knowing I would miss my family and friends too much. I decided the solution was to bring the elephant here to Denver. Mom loved pets, so I asked. I knew it was a negative when her voice and eyes went soft to lessen the blow. She patiently explained that our backyard simply wasn't big enough to hold that large an animal. I didn't argue.

Sister Kent wasn't my only exciting fifth-grade experience. After going to school since kindergarten with the same old St. Dominic's kids, we received an infusion of new blood in the form of a bunch of boys from St. Vincent's orphanage. Alfred, Sammy, and Paul, three cute, mischievous musketeers, soon became my close friends. By applying some sort of cosmic Catholic guilt factor, the school thought that due to an orphan's tough life, they should now be coddled and exempt from the normal punishments meted out to the general St. Dominic's population.

The musketeers, being a clever lot, were forever conspiring to cause me trouble. They counted the garter snake down my blouse as their most daring and successful trick. They had surrounded me one day, and I knew something was up because their overly sweet voices didn't match their impish eyes and sly smiles. When the musketeers were at their best, they worked like a piece of well-oiled machinery; one held me, one pulled open the neck of my blouse, and one grabbed the twisting snake and put it down my back. Then, as if on cue, they all took three steps back in order to get a good view.

It was apparent that the terrified snake and I were on the same wavelength. The snake was desperately writhing and thrashing, trying to break free of its blouse bondage. I was in step with the reptile's contortionist dance movements. I screamed and wiggled wildly. I frantically pulled and yanked at my tucked-in top to allow the snake to escape. The three poor, hard-luck-case orphans were laughing hysterically, enjoying every minute of the show.

Their expressions changed quickly from hilarity to shocked, embarrassed disbelief the instant they spied Sister Mercedes approaching. I finally became snake-free just as she arrived. Unseen by Sister, the reptile slithered quietly away. She quickly took in the scene and immediately chastised me for the indecent exposure of evidently pulling out my shirt from my skirt in front of three innocent boys.

I had a crush on all three of the boys, but Paul was the cutest. With his compact, athletic body, his handsome, dark Latino face, and his expressive brown eyes, he eventually clinched the number-one boyfriend spot. Another important factor was that he had a crush on me too. To express his feelings in his eleven-year-old style, he penned a poetic love letter to me. Receiving my first romantic letter caused a severe case of puppy love. I was lightheaded and had trouble concentrating. I clutched the letter close to my heart. I kept the letter with me wherever I went.

Somehow the note caught my dad's attention. He ripped it from my grasp, read it, and then proceeded to interrogate me. "What's this? Who's this Paul, and how do you know him? This will not happen again. Do you understand me? I don't want you hanging out with this kid."

I didn't fully understand his intense reaction. He didn't even know Paul. Didn't he want me to feel special? He was judging Paul unfairly. If I were to explain that Paul was an orphan just like he was, he might soften. To my dismay, he became more incensed. I thought at the time that he was just being an overly protective father, concerned for my safety.

Years later, after Dad was gone, Paul contacted me. "Did I tell you that your dad came to see me when I was eleven and living in the orphanage? It was so strange. He told me to stay away from you. He sounded almost as if you were his sweetheart, and I was a threatening rival." This news made me physically ill. I wanted to vomit. His actions weren't the actions of a concerned father. His actions were the actions of a jealous lover, and I, his daughter, was his girlfriend.

In the 1950s, black-and-white television shows such as *Father Knows Best*, *Leave It to Beaver*, and *The Donna Reed Show* featured the whiteness of Caucasian-American family values. The darkness of sexual and physical abuse didn't exist on these TV shows. In the 50s, as depicted on television, the father was the head of the household and was in charge of discipline. He would dole out consequences in a safe, nonviolent, wise, and compassionate manner. The wife's primary role was to serve her husband. Her secondary role was to take care of the home and to be a mother to the children. She would, of course, submit to the husband's wishes in all areas of life. All the sitcoms of this era show the parents sleeping, pajama-clad, in twin beds. It was assumed they had intercourse at least the minimum number of times needed to match the number of their offspring. In the 50s and early 60s, the subject of childhood abuse was rarely, if ever, discussed.

Our family was hit with a triple whammy because we not only had to cope with the prevailing attitudes of the 50s and early 60s but also with our ethnic background and religious affiliation. I believe the Hispanic hierarchy, as do many ethnic cultures, placed the father as the undisputed head of the household.

It's now apparent to me that for years much of the Church hierarchy blindfolded itself so as not to see the sexual predator problem that existed within its own body. I believe that this fact largely contributed to the denial of the abuse that went on among some of the parishioners. It seems to me that the Church's stance on pedophilia among the clergy spilled over into Catholic families. I was one of those ignored victims drowning in a sea of secrecy. I believe Father Ronney adhered blindly to the dictates of the Church.

Since my first confession, I had been confessing adultery to stern Father Ronney. His judging eyes certainly didn't ever appear forgiving, and so I had held my breath week after week, year after year, waiting for his negative answer. I was afraid he might find me to be so bad that I would be beyond forgiveness. He forgave me my mortal sin every time. But by not asking me questions and by giving me my penance, he made me feel the molestation was indeed my fault. I knew I was a horrible person to keep committing a mortal sin, but luckily the good Father kept on forgiving me. In the seminary, he must have memorized just one penance with slight variations. Throughout the weeks, I noticed that if my penance was not exactly the same, it was certainly similar.

One part of confession that confused me was that if confession wiped my slate clean, why did I feel so dirty? I had only two answers to this question. Either I wasn't confessing the right way, or Father Ronney wasn't doing his job correctly.

I, Diana Christine, was the girl in my family who didn't fit the pure, innocent image of the dutiful daughter, like on *Father Knows Best*. Dad didn't mirror the father on *Father Knows Best* either, but that didn't matter because he wasn't a white father; he was Hispanic. He not only knew best, but what he knew was never to be questioned.

Discipline-wise, there was almost no resemblance in our household to that of Ward Cleaver's *Leave It to Beaver* family. Ward Cleaver discussed his son Beaver's errant behavior with him. More often than not, after the

Beav calmly acknowledged his error, the consequences would be quietly discussed and a joint decision would be made. Dad's discipline consisted of immediate corporal punishment; the belt, not discussion, was his favorite approach.

Ironically, Dad was split into two parts, just like I was. He was a devout Catholic who expected us to lead stellar Christian lives, and he was an upstanding community member. Yet he continued to molest me daily. I had to tolerate the distinctive smell of sex on both of us each and every day. He frequently made inappropriate sexual comments directed toward various family members. He had girlie magazines down in the basement that my brothers, one by one, secretly viewed. No one, including Dad, acknowledged the magazine stash. When he was alone with me, however, I was forced to view them with him.

I realize now that Mom was a product of the times and adhered to her upbringing and religious training. She remained mute, never challenging Dad in front of us or in public. We were all victims. We all knew subconsciously what was going on, but to keep the family intact, we couldn't know.

I had to trust Mom talked to Dad about the abuse when I was five and she believed Dad had stopped molesting me. I had to believe my brothers weren't aware of my abuse even though they saw Dad's behavior toward me every day and listened to his inappropriate comments about women. I had to believe that Jean, with whom I shared a bed, didn't know Dad fingered me in our bed while she slept. Jean had to believe Dad wouldn't abuse me even though he tried to sexually abuse her at the age of seven. In her case, she gave Dad a firm no, jumped up, and immediately told Mom. Dad, in order to keep up his respected community image, had to count on our silence. He thought his iron rule, corporal punishment, and undisputed head-of-the-house status ensured our cooperation. Every family member was to stay in denial so we could continue to be one big, happy family.

As kids, we all thought our parents were always right. If anything was amiss in the family system, it had to be the child's fault. I believed the situation was totally my fault. I was bad because sometimes my body liked the sexual stimulation. I was bad because I let him have his way with me so I wouldn't be hit or grounded. He wasn't doing this to Jean. I was bad and weak because I wasn't like Jean. If I were stronger, I could make him stop. I was bad—a huge, mortal sinner—because I was somehow causing Dad to sexually abuse me. In truth, we were all living with a heavy, grey, gigantic secret.

Our family's big secret was the proverbial elephant in the living room. It had been there for years. As much as I like elephants, they are simply too destructive, too out of control, too smelly, too messy, and too hard to keep clean to hang out in our living room.

CHAPTER 6

The Worst of Times

"My Diana, my beauty," purred Dad. "Why are you torturing me like this? I can't resist you anymore." And so it was, on a Monday night in April, when I was eleven, that Dad had intercourse with me. At the moment he entered me, I thought, *Why does being beautiful have to feel so bad and ugly?*

I had a feeling Dad had been building up to this event for a long time. He'd used his fingers in my vagina so often that actual intercourse didn't hurt physically or feel much different than all my other sexual experiences with him. But when he pushed his penis inside me, it was more horrible than anything I had experienced in my entire life. The feeling was so awful that for the first time in my life, I didn't know if I was going to make it. Diana #2 was doing the best she could, but the ordeal was even too much for her to handle. All the time Dad was having sex with her, she was shaking and ready to cry, but luckily she didn't throw up. Dad would've been really disgusted with her if she'd vomited. She was worried that he wouldn't like her shaking, but he didn't seem to notice her at all. He didn't look real happy about what happened, either. It was as if she had caused him to do something he didn't want to do, but he couldn't help himself.

After he finished, he told me, in a soft voice, without looking at me, that I could go play. As I put my clothes on, I wondered if I'd ever be able to enjoy playing again. Both my insides and outsides felt dirty. I wanted to scrub myself clean, but I was concerned that if I started scrubbing, there might be nothing left of me. I left the basement and ascended the stairs out of what I now thought of as the "hellhole." I knew I shouldn't have been using swear words even in my mind, but I couldn't help it. I'd have to confess everything on Sunday. In addition to my usual confession

48

of adultery, I'd have to confess to having sex. I realized at that moment in time, in a very concrete fashion, beyond a shadow of a doubt, that all daddies, dads, and fathers definitely didn't do this and shouldn't ever do this. No one should ever do this.

I went straight to the bathroom to scrub myself in the bath. In the process of taking off my clothes, I noticed blood in my panties. I freaked! I knew enough about making babies to be totally terrified. At school the next day, at the first opportunity, I told a friend, saying, "I think I might be pregnant."

My friend raised her eyebrows and opened and shut her mouth two or three times. She asked who did this. I replied, "My dad." Her eyes did that wild back-and-forth thing, and then we went to class. As with most big pieces of information too big for fifth graders to handle, my friend told a nun, who in turn told Father Ronney, who then brought my parents in for a consultation. I learned later Dad admitted to sexually abusing me.

On Tuesday, the day I talked, my body felt so tense I was afraid it would crack. A guarded relaxation overcame me when I arrived home to our normal, happy, chaotic family scene. The anger I had been dreading from Dad never came. When he didn't touch me for the next two nights, I felt more relieved than I had in ages. I was still slightly worried about being pregnant, but for the first time, I was hopeful the abuse would finally stop. I had done the right thing by talking.

Thursday, I felt so good I was tempted to skip home from school. Since popular fifth graders wouldn't be caught dead skipping, I merely walked but with a lightness in my step. I was humming softly as I entered the house. Two-year-old Vincent was beside himself with excitement at my appearance. His skinny little body wriggled, his soulful, big, brown eyes pleaded, while his voice yelled, "Nana, Nana up!" He called me Nana because he had trouble saying Diana.

I picked him up, smelling his sweet baby smell, and kissed his soft baby cheek. Then I swung him around and around. We laughed until we were out of breath. Alan heard the laughter and came running. He "wiked to swing too" and showed me with big sweeping arm movements as he made *whishing* sounds. Every time I stopped, both of the little ones yelled, "More, more." When my arms were tapped out and I didn't have another swing in me, I used my favorite distracting technique; I picked up a Seuss book, sat on the couch, and began reading silently. Both boys jumped on the couch, one on each side, and snuggled down to quietly listen to a book they had heard a hundred times before.

By dinnertime, all of the family had arrived home except for Dad. Our dinner was unusually quiet that night. We were all probably worrying about him.

"Maybe he just was delayed," Michael stated.

"Maybe he had a meeting we didn't know about," Al piped up.

Jean, on the verge of tears, stated, "This isn't like Dad. Maybe something terrible has happened!"

I didn't say anything because I knew why he'd left. He wasn't delayed and he wasn't hurt. He had intentionally disappeared because I had talked. I couldn't eat because my stomach was full of dread. Thursday and Friday were sleepless nights. By Saturday, the police had posted a statewide alert.

Great! I'd done it now. I'd caused Dad to run away because I'd opened my big, fat mouth. And now Mom had to deal with the nine of us by herself. The only money we had was the little that my brothers brought in from their paper routes and the money Mom made from ironing. Not only had I made Dad go away, and caused my family to suffer, but now it seemed all of Denver knew he was gone! To my chagrin, the story was splashed across the local newspapers.

Dark clouds swallowed my days. Mom cried often. I knew who had caused those tears—me. The tears had been mostly tears of sadness, but I also sensed some fear and frustration. She was anxious about how to make ends meet. She expressed worry about my dad's health, happiness, and whereabouts. Both Mom and I knew why he had left. Mom wasn't mad at me, and she didn't blame me, but she was just being nice. It was my fault; I blamed myself.

If you were to compare our family structure to a house, what you would see would be a heap of rubble. Dad walked out, taking with him our foundation—the money we needed to survive, money for food, electricity, and transportation. He took a sledgehammer to our family structure by vacating his role as the benevolent dictator. We were lost without the rules, ritual, and order of our chief enforcer. It became clear we were all very dependent on Dad. Without him, Mom crumpled. Michael and Jean, being the oldest kids, picked up the leadership role to the best of their abilities, but they were, after all, just children. The others all pitched in to maintain some sense of normalcy. I did what I could, but all the while I knew beyond a shadow of doubt that I was the real destroyer. I was the home wrecker.

My sky-high stress level combined with my current sense of self-hatred led to me stealing and smoking Mom's cigarettes. Smoking helped to deaden my nerves and snuff out any lingering good feelings I had about myself.

In the *Rocky Mountain News* dated April 9, 1961, a nice headshot of my father sat atop an article entitled "Statewide Hunt On For Denver Father of Nine." The article went on to say that Dad, "who had the reputation of being an ideal family man," had disappeared Thursday night, April 6, 1961. The police thought maybe there was foul play involved because he, an insurance salesman, may have had some cash on his person. They'd found his abandoned car in Five Points, a dangerous part of town on his route. Even though Mom knew exactly why he'd disappeared, she told the police he'd been in "good spirits and good health." I remember thinking she wasn't telling them the truth because she was protecting me by not exposing my shameful behavior to all of Denver.

In another newspaper article written later in the month, all ten of us were pictured, a family pleading for the return of our dad. We all missed him. You may think I felt a sense of relief at having him gone. On the contrary, my intense shame and guilt plunged me into the darkest and heaviest of times. I'd blabbed to my friend. How silly of me to think just because I had blood in my panties I was pregnant. I'd talked and caused my whole family fear and pain.

Dad was gone for two long months. The church, neighbors, and relatives came to our aid. The community provided food and necessities. A friend even made shirts for our uniforms out of old sheets. We all pulled together as a family, doing what we could to bring in money. I felt distant from my siblings for the first time because I believed if they knew what I had done they would want nothing to do with me.

To make matters worse, in May I started bleeding in earnest. When Mom gave me a pad and told me about menstruation, I felt even more down and dumb. Down, because I wasn't so sure I wanted to grow up, and dumb because I'd thought I was pregnant before having my first period. How stupid I'd been! I'd panicked and caused these devastating events to happen for no reason. I made some solemn promises during the first month of Dad's absence. I vowed that if he returned, I wouldn't be such an alarmist. I would handle my own problems and would never go public again.

The last month of Dad's absence was shrouded in a grey fog. The blackout days would come and go. Deep, dark memory holes smothered my light. I had no thoughts, no feelings. An abundance of pervasive nothingness entered my life. Perhaps this time was too much for me, and the other Diana took over to handle the stress.

Dad came back sometime in June. I don't remember his homecoming. Then one day, the sun's fingered rays gently pushed the fog away. It seemed to coincide with Mom talking with me while sitting on my parents' bed. She took my hands in hers. Her green eyes focused on me with sincerity as she spoke in her most reassuring voice: "You don't have to worry about your dad bothering you anymore. He promised me he wouldn't." I was hopeful that Mom was right and that, in these two months, the bad dad had been exorcised out of his body and left to die. I hoped only the good dad had returned. I had missed the fun, creative, game-playing family man, and I was glad he was home.

When I was finally able to really see him, he no longer resembled his normal, well-groomed self. He looked terrible. He had big boils on his face and neck. His mustache hadn't been trimmed, and there was stubble on his chin. He seemed gaunt and looked like he hadn't had a good meal in months. Mom began immediately to fatten him up.

His story came in pieces that never quite fit together. All of us had lots of questions we couldn't ask because Dad didn't want to discuss hard subjects. "I had amnesia. I don't remember very much," he said, making it clear by his gruff tone that the little he did remember he didn't wish to discuss. Dad's blanks were later filled in by the newspapers. He was arrested for hitchhiking in Baton Rouge, Louisiana, a week after he disappeared. He served a twelve-day sentence for vagrancy under the name of Luis J. Martin. Of that period, Dad told reporters everything had gone hazy, and he didn't realize who he was or where he belonged until later. When he finally came out of the haze, he called his brother Pedro for a loan in order to return home.

Sometime in July, despite his promise to Mom, Dad started molesting me again. He had intercourse with me at every opportunity. I guess he was worried about pregnancy, too, because he put on a condom before penetrating me. When intercourse wasn't possible, he'd revert to mere fondling. His gentle "all daddies do this" became a harsh "if you tell anyone, I'll kill you."

Dad determined the Sunday schedule. He sandwiched having intercourse with me in between two Masses. He and I attended the early Mass, where he was an usher. Mom and the rest of the older kids attended the middle Mass, and Dad went back to church to sing in the choir for the later Mass. The middle Mass was when Dad had me stay home under the pretense of babysitting the little ones. Year round, he would send Alan and Vincent into another room or, if the weather permitted, outside. He would then molest me in the master bedroom at the foot of their bed. On days other than Sundays, when the family was present, he took me to the basement. I would open the door to the basement slowly, and as I descended the stairs, I shifted with each step into my shadow-self. By the time my feet touched the basement floor, I was the other Diana, the docile one who was in charge of dealing with Dad and sex.

Dad welcomed her with a soft, sultry voice, a voice dripping in sweetness, a voice a man might use to entice a lover. "Come here, my sweet, and sit with me on the couch so we can talk. Would you like a soda? I bought your favorite. Come let me look at you." Then his hands would do the looking by reaching up her shirt and groping her breasts and pulling down her panties. Even though her body responded, she always hated these encounters and felt shame at her body for betraying her.

"Today we're going to do something I know you'll love. Mrs. X, on my route, went wild when I did this with her." Then he would show her.

Never once did this kind of talk stimulate her in the least. In fact, both of us hated every minute of it—it wasn't motivating, but simply nauseating. He would then show her his 1960s porn in hopes of eliciting an excited response. The most he got from her was disgust. She unwillingly witnessed Dad's many perversions. After he had his way with her, she would slowly climb out of the black basement hole. As she ascended, she would gradually shed the heavy, thick slime that enveloped her. By the time she reached the light of the main floor, I was back, transformed into a normal kid.

Life went on. Dad was like a sex-starved dog seeking out his bitch in heat. I was as far from heat as Siberia is from Arizona. I was polar ice—frozen, numb, and indifferent. He began monopolizing all my free time. I would beg to stay overnight with friends and cousins. Sometimes Mom would intercede and I'd be allowed to go, always with a proviso from Dad that I wouldn't share the "secret." There would frequently be a comment subtly reminding me of certain death should I talk. "You may go just this once, but remember what we talked about. You'll be here tomorrow morning early for your chores; there's the laundry, and we've errands to run. I'll hear about it if you misbehave or talk too much."

My memory of the next couple of years is of a solid wall of obstacles. I was constantly pushing against Dad, wanting and needing to have a life. Dad wanted the opposite, needing me to be the object of his voracious sexual appetite.

School for the most part was a welcome reprieve from the constant violation at home. There were a couple of instances, however, where school situations were similar to the home violations. In sixth grade, my friend Linda and I were stopped in the hall by the principal, Sister Anastasia.

"Come with me," she growled as she grabbed both our arms in a death grip and ushered us into her office. I had no inkling as to why we were there. I couldn't recollect any misdeeds in the last week. I'm sure Linda couldn't either. Sister Anastasia shut the door, looked at us fiercely, and without preamble, stuck her hands down our blouses. Her hands found four developed breasts. She simply removed her hands and said, in her guiltless-nun way, "Oh, I thought you might be wearing falsies." I felt totally violated and angry, but I'd learned that talking to Sister Anastasia did absolutely no good and would often cause more problems. I remained quiet as she sent us on our way without an apology.

The babies kept me sane and lit up my darkest days. Alan's antics were a constant joy. He was a walking, talking, dancing TV commercial. "Mr. Clean, Mr. Clean," he would sing while puffing up his arms and showing his sparkling white smile. Mr. C was one of his favorites, and he would belt out the jingle with great expression any time, any place. Our laughter would encourage him to go through his whole commercial repertoire again and again.

My smart-as-a-whip, wriggly little Vincent was also a delight. He became my charge when I turned eleven. I was in charge of getting him ready for the day and putting him to bed at night. For half an hour each night, we would explore the world of imaginary words. One of us would come up with an unusual-sounding word. "Flobber," Vincent would say. We would laugh hysterically, and I'd write down the word. Then it would be my turn. "Snaggle," I'd reply with a serious face. Gales of laughter would take away our breath and bring tears to our eyes.

Teresa was born in July of 1962, which caused a chain reaction of musical beds. Teresa took Vincent's crib. Vincent kicked Alan out of the alcove in our room, and Alan moved into the bedroom with Patrick and Lee. On school days, I would awaken early, get dressed in school garb, and wake up Vincent, who would be sleeping soundly in a crib in the alcove. With a gentle nudge, I'd awaken my little bundle of energy. Vincent's big brown eyes would immediately pop open. His eyes opening would then spark an instantaneous smile, which lit up his little face. That triggered a flurry of activity in his skinny, wiry body.

At almost three, Vincent thought he could do everything by himself. Now twelve, I remembered myself as a three-year-old. I understood his stubborn, tough, opinionated, independent spirit. I was patient as he struggled to put on his clothes by himself. My discreet help came only when we were pressed for time. When he was finally dressed, we would walk down the stairs together to breakfast. I was in charge of getting his morning meal and wiping a good deal of the food off the high chair, the floor, his face, hands, feet, and all other parts of his body because he insisted on eating without help.

Around Christmas, Mom allowed me to take charge of five-and-a-half-month-old Teresa. After getting Vincent ready for the day, I would head to the master bedroom where she slept in her crib. My little cherub would often be awake, calmly entertaining herself with her feet, trying to put anything and everything in her mouth. As I approached the crib, there would be a second of silence as she registered my presence. Then I could hear a flurry of flapping of her chubby arms and legs slapping hard against the mattress. Cooing sounds emitted from the crib. My face slowly coming into view over the crib rails would send her into ecstasy—excited, wild, staccato body movements complete with giggles and coos.

Every morning at that moment, all my twelve-year-old problems would dissolve, and I would be bathed in the warmth of complete adoration and unconditional love. I would pick up my sweet girl, look into her sparking brown eyes, tousle her dark brown, curly hair, twirl her around, kiss her soft cheeks, breathe in her sweet scent, and change her stinky diaper. I was in heaven. I not only loved playing mommy to Vincent and Teresa, I knew I was an excellent mom.

December of 1962 produced the usual family merriment. The holiday spirit floated throughout the house, spurring all manner of hustle, bustle, decorating, and holiday baking. Five-year-old special-needs child Alan was enthralled with the idea of Santa. Alan focused on Santa like our Doberman Hilda focused on a bone. Alan was obsessed; he talked of nothing else but being Santa. He asked us all to help with his fantasy.

One day he came to me with an urgent request. "Nana come," he said, pulling my hand. "I Santa Claus." Over his shoulder he carried a bulging old pillowcase.

"Santa," I inquired, "what's in your sack?"

With his twinkling green eyes and a big grin, he lowered the sack and opened it wide. I looked in amazement, for my sweet little brother had packed the pillowcase full of his toys.

Before I could speak, he pulled my arm. "Come on, Nana, we go." Hoisting the pillowcase over his shoulder, he took my hand and headed out of the house into our neighborhood. He happily marched up to a neighbor's door, rang the doorbell, and waited for the door to open with gleeful anticipation.

"Yes?" said Mrs. Martinez, our curious neighbor.

"Ho, ho, ho," replied Alan, introducing himself as Santa by using the deepest Santa voice he could muster. He swung the sack off his back, reached in with a chubby arm, and pulled out one of his special toys, which he eagerly handed to the lucky recipient. "Ho, ho, ho," he concluded, and off he went to the next house.

After witnessing Alan's generous actions, I pondered giving up my selfish wish list but ultimately decided to delay my decision until the next year. I do believe, however, that Alan was the only kid in our family who understood the real meaning of Santa Claus and the true spirit of giving.

Shortly after Christmas, my thirteenth birthday ushered in the beginning of my teen years. To my astonishment, I was allowed to hold my first real birthday party at our house, complete with six of my very favorite girlfriends. My previous birthdays were strictly family affairs. This time I received some very "cool" gifts, but my hands-down favorite was an album by Johnny Crawford, who played the son of the Rifleman on TV. He was so cute. I had a major thirteen-year-old crush on him. I would sit gazing dreamily at the album cover as I listened to Johnny's crooning for hours at a time. His voice transported me directly to teenage, puppy-love heaven. My brothers teased me about being the first person to actually wear out a record. My favorite song on the album was "How High the Moon," a song that symbolized for me my ascent to adolescence.

My teenage bliss was suddenly shattered one day by Alan. He came to me crying, holding up pieces of my broken record.

"I sorry, Nana. I didn't mean it. I sat down on it, and it cracked. I so sorry."

Alan had broken the most prized possession of my entire life. I put my hands on my hips and sighed disapprovingly. My response caused Alan to heave a series of great, jagged sobs. Even in my deepest teenage anguish, I couldn't be angry at Alan. "It's all right, buddy; don't cry. It's just a record," I said softly while putting my arms around him.

I relished leaving behind childhood and advancing gracefully into the freedom and responsibility of being a teen. I felt confident and excited about being thirteen, having watched three older brothers and one sister ascend to the high rank of teenager. I knew how to be an adolescent.

Devastatingly, I found myself locked in juvenile jail. No, worse: a pubescent prison. While Dad had gradually loosened the parental reins on my siblings, he consistently tightened mine. He constantly watched me, monitoring my every move. He tightly controlled and limited my activities and incessantly demanded sex. My freedom died, swallowed alive by a sex fiend. A monster gripped my throat, choking the color from my life, leaving only shadow and stagnation.

Dad dragged me down, darkening the bright colors and dampening the fragrant smells of my spring days. The babies seemed to provide the only light in my life. They lifted my spirits by showering me with rays of sunshine love. Alan, Vincent, and Teresa were a constant source of delight. Alan with his antics kept my belly aching with laughter. My Vincent, with his thousands of curious questions and boundless energy, provided a perfect distraction from the heavy side of my life. Baby Teresa filled my heart with such tenderness that it felt like it might burst, spilling joy everywhere.

She started walking at nine months, and now at eleven months she was running. She would hear me coming up the walk. I would see her run excitedly to the window. When she spied me, she would jump up and down and squeal, "Mommy!" I would open the door, and my little bundle of baby would take a flying leap into my arms. "Mommy," she would say again, her baby limbs hugging me tightly around my neck. I know I didn't give birth to her, but in all other respects I was her mommy.

School ended, and summer's colorful carpet covered the ground. Usually I loved this season because it meant hours of happy, unencumbered playground time. My thirteenth summer produced in me a different sensation. Instead of my usual buoyant, free feeling, I felt like I was drowning. I was being sucked into the tar pit of Dad's domination. I was a puppet, and Dad controlled the strings. Lately, even the babies' love couldn't shine through the dark days. It was the end of June, the week my playmate Patrick was away at church camp, when I decided to take action.

I couldn't sleep. My heart was pounding hard on the walls of my chest as I lay in the dark thinking about my life. *I can't stand it anymore! I'm trapped. If I don't get out of here I'm going to die.* Contemplating my future, I pictured myself through the years as Dad's sex slave girlfriend. *Nothing will ever change. What future? I have no future.* My brain screamed, *You don't own me, I'm not your girlfriend!* This thought led me to remember Dad's death threat. *I'm going to talk, Dad. If you're going to kill me, kill me. I'm already dying.*

At precisely ten p.m. on Sunday night, June 24, 1963, I chose to run for help. The other Diana and I had just endured another horrible Sunday. My decision might have been a response to the particularly disgusting perversion my father made us witness or the despicable activity in which we were forced to participate. Running away might have been spurred on because of the sleepover with my cousin that Dad wouldn't allow me to attend so he could have sex with me. My choice to tell might have been because, on that morning, Lee, Alan, Vincent, and Teresa were left outside by themselves again without my supervision while Dad committed incest with me at the foot of their bed. Whatever it was, my thirteen-year-old brain just couldn't stand it anymore.

I dressed silently. My heart beat so loudly, it plugged up my ears with its pulsing. I think it was trying to beg me to reconsider this impulsive decision; but my brain was focused, a mastermind in control and on a mission.

Just past little Vincent's crib, the alcove window in our bedroom squeaked as I opened it. Stopping, I strained to hear whether Vincent or Jean stirred, but my heart was still causing a racket in my ears I crawled slowly out the alcove window and onto the roof. I inched myself to the roof's edge.

Not seeing a waiting ladder, I realized I hadn't planned very thoroughly; I thought about returning to the safety of my bed. *Safety of my bed? Safety? That's a laugh. Ha, ha, funny*, shouted my head. And then, without my mind consenting, I jumped. I hit the uneven ground hard and crumpled, twisting and bending an ankle in the process. In queen-of-the-ringers fashion, I successfully stifled a scream, pushed myself to my feet, and hobbled down the street.

With every step, I winced with the physical pain of putting weight on my badly sprained ankle. The emotional pain, however, seemed to lessen as I limped farther away from my house. My destination, although it seemed like miles, was only nine blocks away. I headed toward St. Claire's Orphanage, where my mother's cousin Judith was a nun. This place, I was sure, would provide me with some sort of a solution.

As Sister Judith listened intently and sympathetically to my story, I started to calm down, but anxiety returned with the suggestion that she call my parents. We compromised by calling my Uncle Tom, my mother's brother, and his wife, Aunt Lily. Soon their daughter, my cousin Sharon, and her boyfriend, Richard came to St. Claire's to pick me up. We chatted about nothing in particular, never touching the subject of my abuse. As we drove, the black night enveloped the sleeping suburb. We turned into their neighborhood; a single lit house beckoned to us. We reached the front door, and I suddenly realized I didn't know what to say.

Aunt Lily was my glamorous aunt. She worked outside of the home and was always impeccably dressed, her makeup perfectly applied. She was the sophisticated sort, not prone to hugs, kisses, and mushy words. So when my aunt's authoritative words boomed from the bedroom, "Come snuggle with me, Diana," I was surprised at the suggestion of affection.

When I entered her bedroom, however, it was like the board game Mousetrap. Aunt Lily's open arms started the process. I collapsed on the bed, which triggered a gigantic breath, which then opened the "mouth gate," allowing all my words to tumble out, one on top of the other, until my mind emptied. My aunt listened sympathetically, but as I talked about Dad, her eyebrows furrowed, her eyes became slits, and her mouth tightened into a straight line. She said through clenched teeth, "We need to talk to your Uncle Tom." It turned out she meant they were going to talk to me. In the discussion that followed, Uncle Tom and Aunt Lily said emphatically that they were going to have my parents come, and they were going to have a frank talk with them.

"No, you can't. Dad will be really, really mad. Please, please don't call," I cried. The word "mad" had to do because I didn't have the courage to tell them about his threat to kill me. Besides if I told them about the threat it might make it real. *Dad won't kill me. I'm his daughter and he loves me.*

Despite my objections, they called my parents over. From the other room, I heard only snatches of my Uncle Tom's voice: "Luis," "sex," "that's sick," "better not happen again." This definitely hadn't been in my plan. I was glad about the anger being shown toward Dad, but I was sick about the prospect of going back home.

The drive home with Mom and Dad was in silence. Like dry ice, I felt both steamy and cold due to my ice-cold fear and red-hot anger. I went straight to bed without a clue as to what my future held.

I was wary, and my ankle still throbbed, but as the days passed, I thought my extreme measures had accomplished their intended goal. Miracle of miracles, Dad finally stopped bothering me; he didn't touch me for five days, almost a week. I began to have hope, but my faith died when Friday night arrived; the door slowly opened, and the shadow-side of Dad crept toward the bed. I braced as his hands slithered under the covers.

Just then, as the resigned Diana was about to appear, Jean's voice penetrated the darkness, which caused Dad's hands to jump and yank away, like hands caught in the cookie jar. For the first time ever, Jean had awakened to catch Dad in the act.

"What're you doing, Dad?"

"I'm tucking Diana in," he replied in an out-of-character, unconvincing voice.

"No, you're not. Leave her alone, or I'm going to tell Mom." *Way to go, Jean, my savior*, I thought, as Dad skulked out of the room.

CHAPTER 7

Is There Life After Death?

That night after Jean confronted Dad and hope was temporarily restored, I fell into an unusually deep sleep. I slept soundly until three a.m., when the air pressure in the room shifted and the night watchman of my mind sensed movement. I opened my eyes to find a large man in a uniform standing at the foot of our bed. To keep my panic at bay, the dream maker, who was still in charge, tried to convince me the man was a figment of my vivid imagination. When the man introduced himself, the panic, in one fluid movement, twisted my stomach into knots and grabbed my throat. The policeman must have had the same effect on Jean because we asked in tandem, "Why are you here?"

"Your dad hurt your mom," he replied.

Oh, my God, no, no, no. Jean and I both jumped out of bed and raced out of the room, away from the messenger. We ran toward some semblance of familiarity and safety: We ran toward our brothers.

We didn't have to run far, because fast approaching were Michael, Paul, and Al. We all congregated in the hallway in front of our three younger brothers' bedroom. All of us peered in to glimpse the three beds; two were empty. A sharp intake of breath, then relief washed over me as I remembered Patrick was away at camp. Thank God he wasn't here. *Look, Lee is sleeping soundly. Alan, where is Alan?* All of us seemed to focus on the empty bed at the same time. Many voices spoke as one: "Where is Alan?" We turned to a policeman, who was coming up the stairs.

We wanted answers, and yet at the same time we didn't want to know. When he finally spoke, it was as if it were in slow motion. He said in a maddeningly calm voice, "Your dad hurt Alan, and your other little brother, and your baby sister."

Mommy, where are you? Mommy? No, not Alan. Vincent, Teresa. My babies; don't hurt my babies. Hurt? My ears homed in on the hope accompanying the word *hurt. Maybe they're just hurt. Maybe they'll be all right.* "What do you mean, 'hurt'?" asked one of my brothers.

We could tell the detective didn't want to say any more. He had trouble meeting our eyes. We waited for what seemed like a long time while he swallowed hard a couple of times, trying to keep down his emotions. Finally, after one giant gulp of air and a swipe of his hands across the tears forming in his eyes, he choked out, "They aren't hurt. I'm so sorry. They're all dead."

Dead? No, my babies can't be dead. Time stood still. I couldn't hear the crying and howls of my siblings. I couldn't feel the hugs. A scream started in the depths of me and grew like a flash flood pushing, surging, pressuring my body, opening my mouth. My mouth gaped open, stretched like a rubber band ready to snap. No sound came out. Terrible competing thoughts pummeled my brain, fighting for recognition. *Dad did this because of me,* and *I killed her; I killed Mom* alternated with *No, not the babies. Please, God, not my babies.* My mouth remained open and silent.

After what felt like an interminable length of time, my brain registered colored, revolving lights reflecting against the hallway. They reminded me of the strobe lights that we had at one of our school functions. *Where are those lights coming from?* My sluggish brain slowly followed the lights to the window. Of course, I thought, as I looked out the window to the street below; the lights are coming from the top of a patrol car.

I saw movement. Someone was out there. *No.* I squinted harder. Three people were out there. An ear-splitting scream ripped through the night sky and reverberated into the heavens as I realized I was seeing two policemen escorting Dad in handcuffs to the waiting vehicle. The sound of the wail was so deafening, the pain so loud, it was almost unbearable. I was vaguely aware that the sound—the soul-splitting howl of a wounded wild animal—was coming from deep within me. "Noooooooo!" I screamed. I kept screaming. I was hysterical. I was drowning in screams and tears, pounding and clawing, all the while being sucked down into a whirlpool of black nothingness.

An ambulance opened its wide doors and swallowed me whole. Inside the machine's body, it was ghostly quiet. Everyone was moving in slow motion. I saw the surreal, shadowy figures of Jean and Lee. I noticed their mouths were open wide, and their faces were unusually red. Rivers of tears streamed over their puffy cheeks, but I couldn't hear anything.

Why couldn't I hear? I touched my face, but I couldn't feel my skin. Why couldn't I feel? In my mind, I said two words over and over: *my babies, my babies.* Someone must have heard my brain because a paramedic appeared. He mouthed some words I couldn't decipher, but he had a gentle, friendly look of concern on his face, so I let him give me some drugs that made me sleepy.

The ambulance dropped Jean, Lee, and me off at the hospital early Saturday morning. We stayed in the same room all day, where we spent the time together crying. Jean and Lee were handling things better than I, so they were released that evening. I, on the other hand, was a mess; my insides were all shaky. I tried very hard to look normal on the outside, and on the whole, I thought I was doing a pretty good job controlling the trembling except for my hands. I couldn't seem to control my hands. They were shaking so badly that I had to hold a glass of water with both hands like I had taught my baby to do so she wouldn't spill. Teresa at eleven months old had done a better job than I was doing now. Even holding the glass in both hands, I spilled water down the front of my shirt. I was afraid I would chip my teeth. What was wrong with me?

I knew exactly what was wrong with me. I knew why I wasn't handling things as well as my brothers and sister. I knew why I was the one left in this hospital alone with my thoughts. It was because I was guilty of murder. I was bad through and through. Even though I didn't have the details—I hadn't yet talked to the police or my family, and I hadn't seen a single newspaper—I knew the truth. Dad had murdered Mom and my babies because of me. I had run away. I had told. Dad had warned me not to tell or something bad would happen. Why hadn't I listened? Why didn't he just kill himself? Why the babies? Why Mom? If I could have been stronger, I could've stopped the abuse and none of this would have happened. I should've just let him have his way with me. It was my fault. I killed Mom. I killed my babies. I was all alone. I was alone while crowds of thoughts shouted in my head, *You're horrible, I hate you, you should die, murderer.*

I was alone because I deserved to be alone. Clearly there was something wrong with me. I didn't know another kid that had been sexually abused by their dad. I saw the facts of my life standing huddled together in frozen, terrified, shamed silence. If I wanted the little family that was left to love me, if I wanted to have any friends at all, I could tell no one what I had done. No one must know the real me; I had to keep the horrible, bad part of me hidden.

A surreal quality blanketed existence. Time and space distorted themselves into another world. I knew cognitively that Mom, Alan, Vincent, and

Teresa were dead. What was unimaginable was that life was still happening. I noticed people around me were eating, talking, walking their dogs, taking out the trash, and driving. More astonishing was the fact that some people were actually laughing. How could anyone laugh when the world had crashed?

Stranger yet was the fact that my life hadn't stopped. I had just been released from the hospital into the custody of my mom's sister Ruby and her husband, Frank. They brought me to their two-bedroom duplex where my siblings and I were going to live. This arrangement indicated that life would go on. Nature certainly hadn't stopped: The Colorado sun was still shining, the birds were singing, and the flowers were blooming.

Some time the following day, Jean and Michael had gone to pick up Patrick from camp. Al and Paul were off somewhere. Aunt Ruby was watching Lee. My friends from the neighborhood, twins named Mary and Alicia, came by the duplex and asked me to go for a walk. I gladly accepted.

We found ourselves at my favorite radio station, KIMN. We made our way inside the station. Although it isn't clear now how I ended up talking to my favorite disk jockey, I heard my voice, as if through a tunnel, asking him if he had heard about the murders. I think I needed some kind of verification that what my family was experiencing was real.

Of course he knew. "I'm the murderer's daughter," I said for shock value. He was shocked, but it didn't help me feel better.

The remaining family—Michael, Jean, Al, Paul, Patrick, Lee, and I— were packed into Aunt Ruby's duplex. Everything was shrouded in grey fog. I remember very little of those next few days. I picture lots of crying, hugging, and wall-to-wall cots. Our family was in the center of a storm, a hailstorm of information that pummeled us at every turn.

I could stand the barrage of questions from the police and the media frenzy surrounding us for only so long. When the feelings became too big to handle and the monstrous guilt, pain, hysteria, and shame began to strangle me, I numbly retreated to the safety of a tranquilized state. The doctors had given Aunt Ruby a supply of tranquilizers that she was instructed to give me if she thought I needed them. Luckily, the pills were small. Most of life had a surreal, nightmarish quality, yet some events seemed absurdly normal. My brothers, for example, because they had jobs and Dad would have expected nothing less, delivered their paper routes in the days following the murders. What seemed ridiculous was that they were spreading the news to their customers about the murders their father committed.

As the days passed by, the blow-by-blow descriptions of what happened that night came out, little by little, from different sources. From my siblings, the police, television, radio, and the newspapers, I was able to piece together the sequence of events.

The verbal picture of my murdered family came from my brothers. The night of the murders, after being briefed by the police, my skeptical teenaged brothers Al and Paul decided to verify the unbelievable story. After climbing out an upper window, they were able to peek into my parents' bedroom window. They described to us the horrifying, vivid picture imprinted on their brains. They saw a line of unmoving faces sticking out from the bed covers: First Mom with a ghostly white face and protruding belly; beside Mom lay the inert, pasty-white baby face of Teresa; next lay little Vincent, his thin features looking translucent blue; and last, sweet Alan's motionless, opaque round face.

I tried to avoid the extensive media coverage, but I couldn't. Like a moth is drawn to light, I was inexplicably drawn to the pictures and commentary on the television. The sound of our family name on the radio caught the attention of my ears and wouldn't let go. For the first time in my life, I didn't want to read. Every single one of my brothers over the age of ten had a job delivering newspapers. These same brothers had lately taken to leaving the news scattered around our tight living quarters for me to read. I didn't want to read a word, yet I devoured every sentence.

The motive, said the various articles, was that "Luis J. M. was attempting to have sexual relations with one of his children when he was discovered by another family member."

Another article stated that Luis J. M. told the police he was terrified the second child would tell his wife, who had warned him if it happened again, she would tell the authorities.

My heart jumped for joy. *You stood up to Dad the night I ran away. You were going to help me.* Just as soon as I thought that good thought, the bad thoughts rushed down into my stomach, making me sick. *Mommy, why'd you tell Dad that? You shouldn't have. If you hadn't said anything, everybody would still be alive. You should've thought about the other kids too. It's not your fault; it's my fault. If I'd been stronger, I could've stopped him—then you wouldn't have had to say anything. I'm so sorry, Mom, that I let you down.*
*   *   *

The newspapers quoted Dad as saying, "I started thinking more and more, and I thought the best thing was to kill them and myself too. I knew they'd be embarrassed by what I'd done." The papers went on to say that Dad planned to kill all of us to save us from "public disgrace." *You were crazy, Dad. You were going to kill us all, but you forgot Patrick was at camp. How could you forget Patrick?* With a rare feeling of anger, I thought, *I wish you would've just killed yourself.* The minute I had the thought, I tried to take it back, but it was too late. I was drowning in a sea of guilt. I was the reason Dad did what he did.

Today, after years of reading countless articles and replaying the incident in my mind, I believe this is what happened: Dad sat in the living room stewing for a couple of hours after Jean's reprimand. He was, after all, a pillar of his community, a devout Catholic, and thought of as an outstanding family man. With public exposure, his reputation would be trashed and his family disgraced. Jean would tell Mom. Mom would call the authorities, and the dishonor he would bring to himself and his family would be excruciatingly painful. Dad was in agony. He couldn't stop abusing me, but at least he could save us from humiliation. Death would be preferable. Death would be the solution. He thought, through murder, he could save himself and his family from never-ending shame.

At one a.m., the decision made, he walked deliberately yet zombie-like to the master bedroom where my mom, seven months pregnant, lay sleeping. In his hand he held his weapon, a thirteen-and-a-half-inch steel poker. *This is for the good of the family*, he thought, as he covered Mom's mouth with a towel so her screams wouldn't wake us up. He then brutally struck her on the head three or four times until she died. He cleaned Mom up and left her in their bed.

Teresa was sleeping soundly in the same room in her crib. Now on autopilot, Dad picked up my sweet, eleven-month-old baby girl, covered her mouth, and stabbed her in the chest with a souvenir stiletto he had brought back from Mexico. In a detached manner, he cleaned her body in the bathroom and placed her next to Mom.

Like a corpse himself, he came up to our room to get Vincent from his crib. Jean and I were sleeping soundly. He took my four-year-old precious Vincent down to the basement where he squeezed his little throat and choked off his breath. He carried Vincent back upstairs and placed his limp body in bed beside Mom and Teresa. So far his plan was working. So far, in his warped reality, he had saved three of his family members.

Next in line was Alan, the family favorite, *his* favorite. He picked up his sleeping little retarded child who was so good and carried him downstairs. When he reached the basement, the child that made him laugh, his source of joy, woke up. Dad told him to go back to sleep. When Alan's eyes closed and his head drooped, Dad hit him over the head with the same steel bar he had used to kill Mom. Alan woke up and wailed, "Daddy, Daddy!" Alan's voice awakened Dad's heart and brain. So Alan wouldn't suffer, Dad continued to hit him until he was dead. Dad was crying as he gently cleaned up his son with a towel, carried him to their bedroom, and placed him on the bed beside Vincent.

Dad told the police that Alan's dying pleas shocked him out of his killing rampage, and he couldn't continue with his plan to kill the rest of us.

I've done it now, thought Dad. *I'll kill myself, at least.* Dad went to the garage, got in the car, and started the engine. He tried to asphyxiate himself with carbon monoxide but decided against the plan. He knew as his mind began to clear that he needed to take responsibility for his actions.

He went back inside to call his brothers. In hysterical sobs, Dad told Uncle Pedro and Uncle Fernando what he had done. He then called the police at two-thirty a.m. Saturday morning, admitting to the murders. When the police arrived, they found Dad sitting in the living room shouting hysterically, "They're in the bedroom." I have no idea why none of us heard him.

While the family was in chaos, the patrolman was asking Dad if he would like to talk to a priest. Dad, being a devout Catholic, said, "Yes. Please contact Father Ronney."

This was the same Father Ronney who had heard my confessions for years in which I admitted adultery. The same Father Ronney who confronted my parents before Dad disappeared for two months, and the very Father Ronney who heard my dad's confessions regularly. While Jean, Lee, and I were being taken to the hospital, Dad was being hauled off to jail where he was met by Father Ronney. They talked for about half an hour.

On Sunday, when I was spending time alone in the hospital, Uncle Pedro and Uncle Fernando flew in from New York to visit Dad in jail. Dad, who was so distraught he couldn't stop crying, calmed down when he talked to his brothers.

On Monday as I was taking a walk with friends, formal charges were filed against Dad. On Tuesday, Dad pled guilty to murdering Mom and the babies. He stated, "The crime I committed I know I am guilty of. That is all there is to it."

He told the judge he didn't need an attorney because he knew he was guilty. The judge retorted, "The court is going to protect your constitutional rights in every way possible." This statement meant Dad would receive a court-appointed attorney. Then Dad talked about us. "I would appreciate it if it would not cost my children any more grief."

I was thankful to Dad for thinking of us. Looking back, it is hard to fathom his thinking; that he actually believed that by killing us he was acting in our best interests. Then he started talking about God, which was his way. "I want to get this matter over as soon as possible. I know I'm guilty. Nothing whatever under God is going to change it. Let God's will be done." The judge told Dad to come back the next week for a new arraignment.

While Dad was pleading guilty to the murders, my siblings and I attended a private family viewing of the bodies. The people lying in the coffins looked like strangers. I squished my face tight with revulsion as I peered through squinted eyes at Mom. Mom didn't look at all like Mom. The bouffant hairdo was totally wrong. She, I believe, would have never swept her curly auburn hair across her forehead like that, even to cover a wound. Her face was grey and covered with makeup. *Don't you mortuary guys know Mom is so beautiful she doesn't need makeup?* She wore an expression I had never seen before.

"Oh, God! No," I said, as I saw Mom's lifeless arms holding my baby, Teresa. Uncontrollable sobs racked my body as my eyes rested on her little face. She was still, grey, and lifeless. *Wake up, little girl, wake up. Please, God, let her live. Take me. I deserve to die, not my baby.*

I was now sick to my stomach and dizzy, but I made myself look at Vincent. His face had a strange blue pallor because he had been strangled. Why hadn't I heard Dad? Maybe I could have saved my baby Vincent. Maybe I could have saved them all.

Alan's innocent face was bashed in just like Mom's. *Alan, you stopped him; you saved us.* Out of all of us, Alan was the most innocent, the most loving, and, it turned out, the most powerful. *Why you? My good little Santa, why'd you have to die? Why didn't he kill me?*

The voice in my head told me to scream, run, shake, vomit, or pull my hair out—anything to stop the pain. I couldn't stand it; I couldn't stand looking at the hollow, grey-faced strangers who now represented my once full-of-life family. My body felt like running screaming out of the building, but my family was walking quietly. So I followed their lead, stepping silently into the fresh air.

That night they visited me. Each time I closed my eyes, I saw the grotesque faces of my dead family. I would awaken sweating and nauseated. I was living the worst nightmare imaginable. The feeling was beyond horrible, the pain beyond excruciating. I couldn't go on this way. This had to be hell. Things couldn't feel any worse.

I was wrong. Perhaps if not worse, the Rosary and funeral were just as bad. The Rosary was held on Wednesday night, July 3. The church was packed. I sat with my family in the front pew. I don't know what my siblings were feeling because in our family we weren't accustomed to sharing emotions, but I had the surreal sensation of being a sideshow freak.

An endless line of kind, sympathetic people filed past. They squeezed my hands, hugged my body, and said things like "I'm so sorry... I loved your mother... You look just like her... It's so sad."

The tears streamed in rivers down my cheeks, converging with my runny nose and pooling on my collar. I responded to the kind words by nodding and sobbing. My open mouth blew wet, silent bubbles. There was absolutely nothing to say. I would periodically calm myself down only to fall apart again. A caring look would melt my insides. A great chest heave would cause the dam to break and my eyes to flood anew. A soft touch would often trigger a fearful, out-of-control vulnerability. *Go away. Leave me alone. I don't deserve to be loved. I'm a murderer.* I couldn't breathe. I was being smothered by a stifling stream of sympathy, a continuous, constant circus parade of compassion. I guess I should have cherished the fact that so many people came to pay their respects, but I didn't. I hated every minute of the Rosary.

The next day, the funeral was held at St. Dominic's Church. The large, hundred-year-old church was filled to capacity. People sat shoulder to shoulder in the dark wooden pews. Just as at the Rosary, we sat in the front pew. I can't be sure, but I think Father Ronney said the Mass. I was unable to concentrate on the words because behind the priest sat one large coffin and two small coffins.

My imagination began to run wild, and my heartache eased for a moment as I thought about the contents of those three boxes. I could picture the family searching everywhere for little Alan, when all the time he had crawled into a comfortable box just his size and was fast asleep. Sneaky little Vincent was playing a funny prank on me. When I opened the lid to the second coffin, he surprised me by suddenly popping up, cleverly employing the old Jack-in-the-box trick. He was laughing hysterically at his own joke. In the large box, I saw Mom holding baby Teresa, both taking a peaceful afternoon nap.

I was pushed out of my reverie—and the pew—by Jean. Evidently, Mass was over and the family was ushered up the aisle after the coffins and into the hearse.

We led the procession to Mt. Olivet cemetery. I looked out the window to see who was following our lead. A huge train of cars caravanned behind us as far as the eye could see, looking like a giant, twisting, turning tail. We emerged from the hearse and watched as the coffins were placed in a mausoleum for safekeeping. Since it was Independence Day, a national holiday, Mom, Alan, Vincent, and Teresa had to wait another day to secure their final resting place in the ground.

Everything in its place, the family waited for the rest of the mourners to arrive at the grave site so we could proceed with the service. We waited and waited. The vehicles and my tears kept coming. It felt like hours had passed. I was sure my sobbing and the cars would never end.

Finally the last auto arrived. The service began, and my waterworks continued. The service concluded, and my weeping, which had begun to subside, intensified as people commenced hugging me, clasping my hands, and repeating the sympathetic statements expressed at the previous night's Rosary. What was I supposed to say or do? I wanted to crawl out of my existing body and run as fast as I could away from everything and everybody. The funeral was on July Fourth, Independence Day, but I felt trapped. I was held hostage by my guilt and shame.

That evening, as a family, we went to watch a fireworks display. It seemed that relatives, professionals, friends, priests, nuns, and well-meaning acquaintances all agreed that the family viewing of fireworks was an "excellent idea in order to achieve some sense of normalcy." I was thinking everyone was crazy because feeling normal simply wasn't going to happen. I was just happy I had some tranquilizers to help me feel numb. I thought it strange to be celebrating anything, much less a day representing freedom.

The following day my family went back to our house to retrieve our belongings. From the car window I anxiously studied the structure that was formerly our home, the home that housed the crime scene. I wanted to rescue my possessions, but I was afraid of the ghosts.

My plan was a focused run upstairs to my bedroom, where I would hurriedly grab my most treasured items and then sprint down the stairs and out the door in record time. I have heard it is very difficult to outrun ghosts, but I was going to give it my best effort.

I slowly started up the walkway, the gangplank leading to flashbacks, and entered our former house. My siblings went ahead of me through the front door and immediately upstairs to their bedrooms. Something was wrong. Michael was yelling from his upstairs bedroom that someone had stolen his coin collection. Then everybody started yelling at once about the various items they were missing. "Where's my baseball bat?" "Somebody took my silver dollar collection." "Where's my mitt!" "They took my pogo stick."

I entered my room and stood in the doorway. It had also been ransacked. Our belongings were strewn across the room. Most of our clothes and shoes were missing. How could this happen? How sick! The thieves must have been the only people in North Denver who didn't attend the funeral.

I flopped face down on my messed-up bed and contemplated my messed-up life. It was true that I was an inexperienced thirteen-year-old, but if my money hadn't been stolen, I would have been willing to wager a small sum that I had been slammed into the hard surface of the bottom of life. I was being shoved toward the cliff of the grey, anchorless void that stands between life and death. It seemed I was hanging onto sanity by a thread.

I was slipping into a crazy place, not quite knowing the difference between real and unreal. I knew enough to realize I did not wish to be dead like Mom and the babies, but I didn't want to feel like this, either.

A gentle touch on my shoulder brought me back to my room. I turned over to see Jean looking at me with soft eyes. She said simply, "Things will get better. It'll be all right."

She was my big sister and never lied, so I sat up, wiped my eyes, and nodded my head in agreement. We grabbed our meager possessions and walked out of our room.

Jean ran down the stairs to see what was causing a commotion in the kitchen. I paused for a second longer in the doorway to look back into my past. I noticed the alcove where Vincent slept, our bed, and some scattered belongings with memories attached that I chose to leave behind. As I hoisted over my shoulder my pillowcase full of keepsakes and articles that might come in handy in my future life, I thought of Alan. I also brought with me a bundle of thoughts and feelings that I promptly buried deep in my soul. I softly shut the door.

It turned out that the commotion in the kitchen was about the fact that the thieves had even stolen our garbage disposal. I don't know if Dad would consider this swearing, but I called them a "piece of trash" and, even better, "garbage."

Sometime in the week following the break-in, much to Aunt Ruby's disapproval, Michael drove us to see Dad. All I can remember of that place is a windowless, grey room with eight chairs—a seat for each of us. When we entered the room, a slumped-shouldered, disheveled man sitting in a chair slowly raised his head. He was ghostly pale, with blotches of red dotting his puffy skin. It looked like the man had been crying for weeks.

There was a moment of eerie silence as he stared at us with haunted eyes, and then he let out an ear-piercing wail. Reminiscent of the strangers in the coffins, this unrecognizable man was alien to me. The powerful, commanding, confident, meticulous dad I remembered had disappeared, and in his place sat a rumpled, bent, sobbing, broken man. He kept saying over and over, "I'm sorry. I'm so sorry."

We were all sobbing as well, answering him through our tears, saying over and over, "We love you, Dad." This went on for about fifteen minutes until the guard informed us our time was up. Nothing else was said because there was nothing else to say.

On July 12, shortly after our visit, Dad went back to court. He didn't want us anywhere near the proceedings, so we found out from the media that his lawyer had convinced him to enter an insanity plea. Dad reluctantly agreed but told the court, "I do not want my children to go through any more suffering. I do not want a trial. If the doctors find I was not insane, I will put in my plea as guilty." He was sent to a mental institution in Pueblo, Colorado, for a month to be evaluated.

CHAPTER 8

Sandra and the Teenager

Life eventually returned to a semi-normal state. Nobody talked about Dad and the murders. I don't have a clue why my siblings remained mum. I know why I didn't speak. It was simple: I was no good. I deserved what had happened, and I should bear the shame and guilt in silence.

Ten of us were stuffed in a two-bedroom duplex, and both bedrooms were already occupied. Aunt Ruby and Uncle Frank had one room and my cousin, Bob, the other. Our cots were crammed into all the other spaces. Because our beds filled the living and dining rooms, we had to fold them up in the daytime and put them down at night. My aunt and uncle were in charge, but Michael and Jean were second in command. We all had chores and responsibilities. Because they were a part of my old family, I semi-cooperated with Michael and Jean when they asked me to cook and clean. I missed taking care of Vincent and Teresa, my babies. The youngest member of our family now was eight-year-old Lee. I loved him a lot, but he was Jean's charge, not mine.

I may have been acting like your average teen, railing against authority, or I may have simply resented anyone trying to take Mom's place. Whatever the reason, I found myself incredibly angry. I took out my adolescent rage on Aunt Ruby. My defiance started within a week after the funeral.

One day, Aunt Ruby, noticing my nicked shins, asked, "Diana, what happened to your legs?"

In a typical teen, isn't-it-obvious tone, I replied, "I shaved them."

She sternly responded, "You're not old enough to shave your legs."

I am too. I'm thirteen, and that makes me a teenager. Besides, you're not the boss of me.

72

I said, verging on hysteria, "My mom let me shave my legs because my legs are hairy like Dad's."

I don't want to be like Dad. Mom didn't want me to be like Dad. Stop making me be like him.

"I don't care. In this house you don't get to shave your legs."

I screamed, "You're not my mom. You can't tell me what to do." I stomped out of the duplex, slamming the door as hard as I could. I marched, steaming, to the library to get some peace. I gradually calmed down by immersing myself in the imaginary world of books.

Upon exiting the library, the bad girl inside me began her chatter. This part of me was an extension of the other Diana. The other Diana showed herself only when she was alone with Dad. Since Dad was locked up, Diana #2 needed a new job description. Her job now was to remind me I was bad, a mortal sinner, and an accomplice to Dad's crimes. Dad wasn't around, but the bad part of me who had been sexual with Dad seemed to want to carry on the tradition of evil deeds and wrongdoing. She was determined to continue to act out our feelings about ourselves. *We're no good. We're nothing. We're worthless.* I could feel the sinner take control.

We were standing outside the library at the corner, waiting to cross the street, when a shiny red sedan slowed to a stop right in front of us. Behind the wheel, a man who looked like he was in his thirties rolled down the window.

He said to me in a silky smooth voice, "Hey, can I give you a lift?"

I innocently pointed to myself, shaking my head slightly, my body language saying, *Who, me?* Then I said, "Thanks anyway; I think I'll walk." But the bad girl smiled, nodding her consent to his "thoughtful" invitation. She knew exactly what kind of a lift he had in mind. This particular kind of lift was exactly what was needed to reinforce her badness. She said yes, without hesitation. And before I, Diana, was able to get a word in edgewise, she had jumped in and settled her butt down in the car's bench seat. Seated, she glanced to her left and saw a brown-eyed man with slicked-back, dark, greasy, Brylcreemed hair. He asked our name. Stating our real name would have exposed us, and so to protect our anonymity, out popped the name "Sandra." Diana #2 had handled sex with Dad; it appeared Sandra would be the one handling sex with strangers.

His slippery voice said, "Why don't you scoot over here beside me, Sandra?" He smiled a big, toothy smile and patted the portion of the seat very close to his body. I was scared and ready to leap out of the car at the first opportunity. Sandra, however, slid over smoothly.

He drove around through the streets of North Denver and stopped at an empty parking lot. Sandra had sex with the stranger, and then he drove us back to the library. I was horrified at Sandra's dangerous, irresponsible behavior. *We could've gotten killed. What were you thinking? What if he hadn't brought us back?* Sandra just smiled, knowing this was exactly what bad girls did.

The summer was replete with reminders of what had happened to my family. With the reminders came the horrible feeling everything was my fault. My world had been turned upside down, and I believed I had done the turning. An out-of-control monster of feelings would arise inside, threatening to devour me. It felt like the beast sucked out all the blood, leaving my body empty. This caused my stomach and chest to hurt. At the same time, tears pushed hard against my eyes, but my brain fought back, making my head throb. I wanted to scream and yell and hit. I needed to do something, anything, to get rid of these feelings; it felt like I couldn't survive them. When I couldn't stand it any longer, Sandra would take action. At that point, I didn't care about the possibility of being mugged or murdered. I was willing to take the risk in order to get rid of the feelings. If they didn't stop, I was sure I'd die anyway. When Sandra took control to try to handle the monster, I felt much calmer. Most of the time, having sex with strangers did a much better job of getting rid of the emotions than the drugs Aunt Ruby was giving me. The problem was that the Sandra solution was temporary; the monster would inevitably start to take control of my body again.

And so Sandra, the bad girl, dominated that summer. Negative feelings would overwhelm me, and Sandra would come to my rescue. She had sex with strangers three or four more times—in a back alley, an abandoned restroom, and a vacant apartment. It wasn't Sandra's purpose to feel any pleasure from these trysts with strangers. She didn't have to worry her body would betray her by liking the sex. In fact, her body's response to intercourse ranged from numbness to disgust. The sexual acting out was done simply to handle the feelings. A second objective was to reinforce the belief we were bad, keeping us in our proper place among the mortal sinners.

Meanwhile, back at the duplex, the police met with me two or three times to question me about my relationship with my father. The policemen and I sat alone at the kitchen table while they questioned me. Dad had taught us to respect authority. I knew the police were just doing their job, and I was respectful, but I hated talking to them. Dad had told them what he'd done with me. They wanted to know what I remembered. I didn't want to remember. When they asked me very personal, embarrassing questions, and the pictures of the abuse came back to my mind, my face got really hot. When they wanted me to describe in detail Dad's sexual perversions, my voice whispered the answers. My eyes tried to look into their eyes, but they ended up looking down at the table, and my hands were shaking so badly I had to sit on them. Luckily, many of the questions had yes or no answers. I always felt particularly dirty after those interviews, even though the detectives tried to be as gentle as they could. These conversations just fortified my feelings about myself and bolstered Sandra's activities.

Because those who knew me would have known from the newspapers I was the child being molested, Aunt Ruby, with input from Michael, decided I should start the school year at a new school. I reluctantly agreed to attend St. Joseph Elementary only because Michael thought it would be best for me. I didn't like the idea one bit, because I was attached to my old friends and my old school. Being separated from my friends and family was yet another loss. Michael, Jean, and Al went to St. Joseph's High School. Paul, who didn't want to go to St. Joe's, chose to go to North High School. Patrick and Lee continued at my old school, St. Dominic's. For the first time ever, I went to a school on my own.

I struggled to fit into my new school. The boys liked me; the girls didn't. The cliques were tight. These kids had gone to school together for many years and were reluctant to accept a newcomer. One of the most popular girls in the eighth grade screamed at me one day, "Your dad is a murderer!" I stopped, frozen in shame and embarrassment. Squeezing my lids tight, I attempted to hold back the flood of tears gathering behind my eyes. *Be strong. Don't let her affect you. Don't cry, you big baby.* At this thought a big-baby wail came from my throat as tears spilled over onto my face. I ran away, sobbing.

*   *   *

In the fall, Dad returned from Pueblo. After the month-long evaluation, the doctors decided he was sane when he committed the murders. Dad, true to his word, pled guilty. The trial to determine sentencing was scheduled for November. The jury had only two choices: life in prison or execution. Dad didn't want us to attend any of his court proceedings, least of all his sentencing. Michael, who at eighteen considered himself to be an adult, chose to speak on Dad's behalf even without his permission. Michael was pretty tight-lipped when he arrived home, so I gleaned my information from the media. *The Rocky Mountain News* reported on November 18, 1963, that Luis J. M., after pleading guilty to murdering his pregnant wife and three of his ten children, had read the confession he had written.

There was nothing new in the confession. He didn't use any of our names. He again talked about Jean seeing him taking indecent liberties with me. He stated he became terrified Jean would tell Mom, who had warned him if it happened again she would tell authorities. It was then he decided to kill the whole family and himself. He described the murders in detail. Dad broke down when he got to the part in his confession where he described killing Alan, his favorite. He told the jury that in the middle of the attack, Alan woke up crying, "Daddy! Daddy!" Dad, right there in court, "threw back his head screaming." Six or seven of his blood-curdling screams rang out before the judge called a recess.

Dad told the court about the time he left for two months. He admitted he left because "he was fooling around with the same child," me, and "he was afraid something drastic would happen." Despite this admission and much evidence to the contrary, I thought my siblings believed I was abused just once. Believing this made me feel better, because if no one knew, they couldn't be responsible for not helping me. At the same time, I felt worse because if they weren't responsible for what happened, it was my fault. If I had tried harder, I could have stopped not only the abuse but the murders as well. I thought if I let my siblings in on my secret, they would not only condemn me but also disown me. When I thought about losing more of my family in any way, I felt as if I would die.

Just before the jury was to retire to decide his fate, Dad called out, "You want to kill me? Kill me."

After much deliberation, the jury decided Dad should be executed in the gas chamber. This information knocked me off my feet and punched me in my gut; it was simply too much to handle. I didn't ever want to be alone with Dad again, but I certainly didn't want him to die. After hearing the terrible news, our remaining family cried and cried. The next day, November 19, 1963, I decided to turn off my tears. I was tired of crying. Three days later, President John F. Kennedy was assassinated. I was glued to the television, and all the sad feelings were there, but the pipes that carried my tears to my eyes were frozen. My whole body was numb. I was tired of feeling sad. Maybe in the future I would be able to cry for others, but I decided I would never cry for myself again.

Just before Christmas, we, the surviving kids, were able to move into the other half of the duplex. Aunt Ruby and Uncle Frank still ruled the roost, but we chickens had more room and privacy. Jean and Michael were second-in-command and ran the day-to-day operations. Jean and I shared a room, as usual. All the boys—Michael, Paul, Al, Patrick, and Lee—were crammed in the other room. I loved having a bedroom and a real bed again. It was just us; our family, in our own space.

Christmas that year was pathetic. Michael and Jean scraped together money to make sure we all had presents under the tree. I think we had a tree. My memory of that Christmas is vague because my mind must have closed the door on the pain. I would almost guarantee the day felt heavy and quiet. There must have been very little conversation, because there was nothing to say. There was almost certainly no caroling with our cousins; no one felt like singing. The whole day was haunted by memories of our family ghosts and Christmases past. I missed Mom's laugh and caring spirit, Alan's twinkling eyes and Santa imitations, Vincent's quirky questions, and baby Teresa's unbridled excitement and affection. I missed the new baby who would have been born in September, the three-month-old who would have soon been my charge. I was certain I would miss them forever. I have to acknowledge I even missed the fun, creative Dad of old. Come to think of it, I missed the old Michael, Jean, Paul, Al, and Lee. I even missed the old me. I desperately wanted my old life back. I couldn't imagine ever looking forward to Christmas or any other holiday again. There was a big hole in my heart. All the happiness had drained out and left me hollow. I needed to patch the hole somehow, but I couldn't fathom how. In my mind there could never be a "happily ever after" ending to my story.

I turned fourteen in January of the following year and began dating an eleventh grader. I remember being a typical teenager, but Aunt Ruby believed I was fast turning into an out-of-control, defiant, atypical sort. A constant comment coming from Aunt Ruby was, "Diana, why can't you be more like Jean? She doesn't cause trouble. She follows the rules."

Jean was perfect. She never seemed to do anything wrong. And if she did, she didn't get caught. Pretty, popular, and smart, Jean was Aunt Ruby's number-one helper. Aunt Ruby thought I was a screw-up, and maybe I was.

For the most part I followed the rules, but feeling the influence of my new, older, and more worldly boyfriend, Juan, I periodically began to skip school and drink liquor. Having started sneaking cigarettes at eleven, I was both a veteran sneaker and smoker by age fourteen. One of my friends and I even tried shoplifting for the first time. I stole a bottle of Jergen's lotion. Luckily, we were stopped before we left the store by an understanding shop owner who didn't report us. After the close call, I decided a life of crime wasn't for me, and never shoplifted again.

Summer came, and I started sneaking out of the window at night to meet my boyfriend. We started having sex because it was what he wanted to do. The sex was just sex; just another part of my rebellion like sneaking out of the duplex, drinking alcohol, and smoking. My body had no value and was available for anyone to use. At the time, like with Sandra, it was a way to cope with overwhelming feelings. I was an angry, lost, empty shell of a girl trying to survive the best way I knew how. I suppose I hoped the sex might lead to filling up my barren life with a baby because I remember saying to him, "Get me pregnant." I guess subconsciously I wanted a different life, and I definitely missed "my babies."

At this point in my acting out, Aunt Ruby told me, "You need more help than we can give you." My aunt and uncle made this declaration without any knowledge of Sandra. I can't imagine what they would have done if they had known about her. They would have locked me up in a mental institution. As it was, they called Social Services. My social worker and Aunt Ruby decided to put me in the Good Shepherd Home for Girls. For my own good, I was being locked up against my will.

Aunt Ruby loved Jean and acted like she hated me. I thought she was punishing me. It felt like one more abandonment; she was getting rid of me to make her life easier. At the age of fourteen, Aunt Ruby was my sworn enemy.

I went to the home kicking and screaming. I yelled at Aunt Ruby, "I hate you. I won't go! You can't take me away from my family. You can't make me! I'll run away." My mean aunt was taking me away from my school, my friends, my boyfriend, and my family. I made up my mind before I entered the home that I despised not only my aunt but also my uncle for marrying her and especially for not sticking up for me. I hated the Good Shepherd Home and everyone in it as well as the courts, Denver, and the world in general.

I loathed myself, the girl called Diana. I was having a major identity crisis, which is developmentally a normal experience for an average teen. My crisis seemed more extreme; I wanted my old life back, but at the same time I wanted to distance myself from the horrible memories and my old self.

I also wanted to defy Dad, and I started with his anti-nickname stance. My teenage solution was to change my name. I decided I would no longer be Diana. When I entered the home, I thought a name change could help me attain one of those elusive clean slates touted by the Catholic Church. My new name from the instant I stepped into the home was Diann. Just in case the name change didn't erase me and my sinful history, I still went to confession. Actually I didn't have a choice; confession was required at Good Shepherd Home.

Father Abercrombie was the resident priest who was in charge of saying Mass and hearing confessions. Mother Nicholas, the Mother Superior, was the boss. She presided over the Home's three dorms in addition to being overseer of the school. I grudgingly admit Father and Mother Superior were nice, decent people. Mother Angela was a different story.

When I entered the home, Mother Angela was in charge of my dorm. Aunt Ruby received the brunt of my anger outside of the home, while Mother Angela received my anger inside. Mother Angela wasn't a happy person and seemed to think making the residents of the Good Shepherd Home miserable her earthly duty. She had all these ridiculous rules. For example, you had to sleep in your panties and bra, and you couldn't have a stuffed animal on your bed unless you were a junior or senior. I was critical of Mother Angela's behavior, and she was critical of mine. She even criticized the way I danced. We girls would crank up the radio or watch the dance shows on television. The doo-wop music of my past was quickly replaced with the new dances shown on shows such as *Hullabaloo*. The black girls could really dance. I discovered my body could move in the same way.

One evening when we were dancing the cha-cha to a Motown song, Mother Angela marched in the room and turned off the TV, abruptly ending our dancing. She singled me out by calling me over. "The way your shoulders move is too sexy," she said with a smug smile.

"I'm just dancing," I replied.

She thought me impertinent. Glaring, with hands on her hips, she said, "From now on, you are forbidden to use your shoulders when you dance."

Since I considered dancing without moving my shoulders a stupid and unreasonable request, I continued to dance, shoulders and all, when Mother Angela wasn't around.

Upon entering the home, all of us felt trapped; we were held hostage, imprisoned against our will. The first four months were horrible because I was completely cut off from my family. The only form of communication allowed with the outside world was through letters, which were read by the nuns before we received them. We were entirely cut off from family and friends. I responded, like most new residents, with anger. I resented being taken away from my family, school, friends, and boyfriend. I even missed family chores: cooking, cleaning, and babysitting. Michael and my family had begun to drive 115 miles south from Denver to the prison at Cañon City every Sunday to see Dad. I'm not sure how I felt about visiting Dad, but I knew I wanted to be a part of my family. I wasn't allowed to go. I blamed all this on Aunt Ruby.

And yet in the first week, much to my surprise, I connected with some of the other girls. Initially, I related to the angry ones. Very soon, a group of new residents and I plotted our escape from the oppressive system of rules enforced by the good Sisters. The plan involved running away while on an outing. Unfortunately, the plan was foiled, landing me in solitary confinement for a week. I ended up on the fourth floor of a very old, creaky building. Like jail, there were bars on the windows. Strange, scary, creepy sounds seeped through the walls, and shadows lurked, ready to pounce on me at any moment. I was so scared! By the end of the first sleepless, terrifying night, I decided I, Diann Christine, would choose my destiny. If I was forced to be in this place, I might as well make the best of my predicament.

On the seventh day, I emerged as a cooperative, communicative, loving person. My positive demeanor further improved when, shortly after I was released from captivity, Mother Angela was transferred out of the home. I prayed she would enter a cloistered nunnery and take a vow of silence. Some people just shouldn't have contact with kids, especially troubled kids. I knew I shouldn't pray in anger, but sometimes these types of prayers are good for letting off steam.

Mother Lawrence took Mother Angela's place. If Mother A. was night, Mother L. was day. We clicked. We liked each other. I bloomed under Mother Lawrence's guidance. In a short time, I gained the trust of the nuns and became a leader among the residents.

I began to talk about the feelings buried under my anger. To my relief, some of the other girls began to share their histories. Several of them had been victims of incest as I had. I was no longer alone. For the first time since I was very young, I felt nurtured and safe. I was able to be one person—Diann. Diana and Diana #2 were my past selves, and Sandra lay dormant, sleeping her life away due to lack of opportunity. I became one of the favorites among the nuns.

I soon became "head girl" in the kitchen, which came with certain privileges. I was allowed to go in the kitchen after hours and take out a certain number of snacks for me and my friends. I never took advantage of the situation until the night I spied a large bag of pistachio nuts. I love pistachios. I stole the bag, went to an unused room, and gorged myself on nuts. I ate the whole bag in one sitting. The nuts and my guilt sat in my stomach, making me sick. Later in the day, I was informed Mother Euphrasia was looking for me. I dreaded the confrontation. When it came, I was sitting on the bed worrying.

Mother Euphrasia came in, saying, "There you are. I wanted to ask you about—"

I couldn't stand the suspense, so I did exactly what I wasn't supposed to do: I jumped up and interrupted her midsentence. "I did it! I'm guilty! I stole the bag," I squeaked with my head in my hands, unable to make eye contact.

Mother Euphrasia looked perplexed. "I was going to ask about your schedule, but this piece of information sounds more interesting." I didn't receive punishment because Mother believed the huge amount of guilt I felt was punishment enough, even for a Catholic.

My eyes and my world widened even more than from my fifth-grade experience with Sister Kent. Sister Kent's international stories were fascinating, but actually living with girls of all different races, nationalities, and circumstances was life changing. We had American Indians, Eskimos, Caucasians, Latinos, and African-American girls at the home. We had three things in common: We were all female, Catholic, and troubled.

One of my best friends was a black girl named Maggie. Hanging out with her helped me to not only straighten out my thinking, but I was able to witness how she straightened her hair. I was extremely glad, for her sake, when the styles changed from straight to curly.

Most of us—despite, or maybe because of, our pasts—loved to laugh. We would kid around with each other. Joking inevitably led to nicknames. "Hey, Di, why do you always wear green?" Pat, my trickster friend, asked, laughing and pointing. Pat reminded me of my younger brother, Patrick, always joking.

"I don't!" I said, glancing down at my green shirt and my green pants. "My socks are white."

"Yeah," Maggie said, joining in the fun. "We should call her the Jolly Green Giant except she's small, so from now on she'll be known as the Jolly Green Shrimp."

"I used to be tall; I just stopped growing," I stated lamely. So the name stuck. That it stuck had no effect on my color preference, for green, hands down, was my favorite color. I didn't have any control over my height, so I let that go. The truth was I liked the light-hearted banter, and I liked my new family of sisters.

Sometimes we talked seriously about our lives. It was such a relief to hear and share stories, as sad as they were, about our abuse and incest. I was able to forge deep friendships in this sanctuary of safety. I also learned how to cook and bake, how to make a bed army-style, and how to cut hair.

As far as becoming a better Catholic, we attended Mass daily, which the nuns hoped would make us more devout. I thought I had reached the pinnacle of pure devotion after seeing the inspiring movie *The Greatest Story Ever Told*. I knew God wanted me to become a nun, and immediately shared this exciting news with Mother Nicholas. I told her in my strongest and most resolute voice, "I'm sure I'm supposed to be a nun."

I caught a brief glimpse of a wide smile and thought I heard the start of a chuckle before Mother Nicholas turned her face away. After a few little choking sounds and clearing of her throat, she turned to face me. She said with a slight smile and kind eyes, "Diann, I don't think becoming a nun is your calling." When she saw my deflated and bewildered look, she quickly added, "I may be wrong. You have time to discover your true passion. Take your time." After a week, the movie and my conviction I was perfect nun material faded. After two weeks, I remembered with startling clarity that I'd always wanted to marry and have a family. My calling had always been and still was to be a mom. I had momentarily lost my head because of a movie that moved me.

After the initial four months, I was allowed weekend visits with my family. I spent my Saturdays cooking, cleaning, and participating in every family activity. Although friends called, and I talked to them on the phone, I had no desire to leave my family.

Every Sunday we made the two-hour drive to Cañon City to see Dad in prison. I hated the grey prison and being frisked by the guards. Every week Jean and I would be taken to a separate area where the female guards would roughly pat our breasts and search between our legs. At least we were being frisked by women. My brothers were probably getting worse treatment from the male guards. Did the prison system really believe children would bring in weapons or drugs?

We were allowed to see Dad for only an hour at a time. On Father's Day we got to see him twice, with an hour break in between. We always visited him in a bare, grey room, complete with institutional grey chairs, and table. We never saw his cell.

On my first visit, it relieved me to see the haggard, alien man I first glimpsed after the murders almost gone. Dad seemed more like Dad. Sometimes I found it hard to remember the contrite, remorseful man because he had readopted his "undisputed head-of-the-household" attitude. He asked about homework, chores, and church. We always told him the truth, and he gave us guidance we weren't to question. Still the boss, he demanded our respect and love as always.

But in some respects Dad wasn't the same. There were two huge differences between the dad before and the dad after incarceration. With the ever-present guard at the door, he used a *Leave It to Beaver* style of discipline with us because he wasn't allowed to yell or use the belt. The best difference for me, though, was he couldn't sexually abuse me. For the first time in my memory, I felt totally safe in Dad's presence. I was assured of a weekly visit with the best side of Dad.

We knew he was probably bored sitting in a cell all day, so we brought him jigsaw puzzles. Dad's face lit up when he saw us, but he was especially animated when we brought him a new puzzle. Dad was upbeat and positive at our weekly visits. He talked about his friends in prison and the creative things they made. He never said anything negative about his stay. After our initial visit in jail, he never mentioned the murders, and following his lead, neither did we. I liked visiting Dad, but I was always relieved to leave the prison and looked forward to our regular weekly stops at McDonald's on the way home. My brother could feed all seven of us, complete with milkshakes, for less than four dollars.

Life at the home was safe and good. The only things that hurt these days were my knees. My dorm room was located on the third floor, which meant about one hundred steps from the bottom floor to mine. Like most girls my age, I was in pretty good shape. But my knees would scream out in excruciating pain, and I would have to stop on the second-floor landing to let the pain subside before I continued.

On the whole, I was doing well emotionally. One of my old behaviors persisted, however. The whole population of the Good Shepherd Home, one hundred-plus girls and nuns, soon became aware I was easily spooked. Invariably, after a scary movie night, my friends would devise new ways of scaring the daylights out of me.

Once we saw a movie called *The Hand*. In the film, a pianist's hand was unjustly severed. Throughout the movie, the hand sought retribution by murdering people. The movie scared me so much I was terrified to lie down that night. I put off preparing for bed as long as I possibly could.

By the time I finally climbed under the blankets, my friend Pat Jones had been patiently hiding under my bed for some time. My eyelids were beginning to droop when I heard movement. My lids flew open, and I spied a hand coming down toward my body, attempting to grab my neck and strangle me. I sat up, my arms flailing, swatting the murderous hand away and screaming bloody murder!

Mother Lawrence came running out of her bedroom with her headpiece askew. "What is it? What's wrong?" she asked, trying desperately to cover her head. Meanwhile, Pat and all the girls in the sleeping room were laughing so hard, tears were streaming down their faces. Mother Lawrence attempted to stifle a laugh as she grappled with her headpiece. After faking an admonishment to Pat for scaring me, she tried to settle us down, but I was so scared the only way to calm me down was to keep all the lights blazing for the rest of the night.

On Halloween, we decided to have a haunted house. I wanted to be a character from *Psycho*: the mother in the creaky rocking chair. I was supposed to scare people when they came into the room, spookily rocking in my chair and reciting the words, "I won't hurt you; I wouldn't even hurt a fly." But instead of frightening others, every time someone entered the room, I jumped out of my skin and screamed. All they did was laugh. I was too frightened to hurt a fly.

The sisters eventually deemed me healthy, stable, and ready to rejoin my family full time in August of 1965. I was released just in time for Jean's wedding. A week before the wedding, I helped with decorations and last-minute details. I met Barry, Jean's fiancé, at the wedding. I liked him immediately, and was impressed and envious that they had attended a Beatles concert. Jean, the "perfect one," had done it again. She had picked a successful husband who would give her a different name and whisk her to another state where she would live a magical, upper-income life away from the family drama.

She was married at St. Dominic's in a traditional Catholic wedding full of people and flowers. I felt pretty as her maid of honor, wearing a turquoise dress with a brocaded top and satin bottom. If I was pretty, Jean was radiantly beautiful. Even though I was a bit jealous, I was happy for her. Lee, however, wasn't happy; he was mad. Lee, who had lost Mom at the age of eight, was about to lose his second mom at ten. He used his best hardball arm to pelt Jean with rice.

During the reception, several members of the wedding party wanted to leave and decorate the newlyweds' car. I felt grown up and special at being included in the outing. The happy, laughing, drinking group thought it harmless to share the fun and bourbon with me, a fifteen-year-old. We arrived at the duplex, and when I got out of the car, I felt the full effect of the bourbon. I stood up and immediately fell over.

The best man, who I could see through my drunken haze, was tall and handsome. He laughed. He then reached down and picked me up, his hands under my armpits, and set me on my feet. Swaying slightly, I again began to topple over. He grabbed me, attempting to steady me, but could see I was too wobbly to stand alone.

"Why don't you lean on me?"

Giggling with embarrassment, I slurred, "Thanks a lot."

I don't remember exactly how I ended up in my brother's room, but my alter ego Sandra and the best man were having sex when Al came into the room.

"What the hell are you doing to my sister? Get off her, you rapist! Call the cops," he yelled to someone in the next room.

I protested, saying in my drunken state, "He didn't rape me; I wanted to."

But the police were called, and the twenty-two-year-old best man was hauled off to jail. I was taken to our family doctor for examination. I heard they charged him with statutory rape. I don't know what happened to him after that; I was afraid to ask. I felt bad because I knew I was the reason he was arrested. I couldn't remember exactly what happened because I was drunk, but I was almost certain I had wanted him to have sex with me.

What was wrong with everybody? Why blame the best man for rape when they knew it was my fault? What was wrong with the authorities? Why arrest an innocent man? What was the meaning of statutory rape, anyway? I had no clue. The statutory part, I guessed, had to do with our ages. I was fifteen and felt pretty grown up. The best man was much closer to my age than other men Sandra had sex with; sex with men in their thirties was her norm. Dad was in his forties. The best man was twenty-two, only a seven-year difference. As far as the rape part was concerned, what rape? There was no rape. He had been very nice; he had been a perfect gentleman.

Yes, I thought he was a nice, caring, gentle man. I just kept destroying my family again and again. I was a bad seed with a rotten core, spoiling everything I touched. The layers upon layers of heavy sins I had heaped upon myself were stacked so high I could hardly recall them all.

On top of the stinking trash pile lay my latest unforgiveable sin; ruining Jean's wedding by having sex with the best man and getting him thrown in jail. Next was Sandra, the whore, having sex with strangers, and there was always being the terrible teen who had been thrown into the Good Shepherd Home. The home was supposed to cure my wickedness, but evidently that hadn't worked. Within a week and a half of being released, I was back to my despicable behavior.

If it wasn't something I did, it was something I said causing disaster to befall the people I loved. Because I ran away and then opened my big mouth, Dad murdered Mom and the babies. My big mouth at eleven resulted in Dad running away for two months, leaving us destitute. I kept on committing adultery, all the while knowing it was a mortal sin. I believed my dad when he told me I'd tempted him even when I knew he couldn't resist me. I wasn't strong enough to stop him, and he couldn't stop himself. Mom was going to call the authorities if he didn't stop, and he would have been arrested for having sex with me just like the best man had been. He was a proud man, and he must have felt he and our family would die of shame if our sexual behavior became public. I loved Dad. He was the only parent I had left. All of it had to be my fault because if it wasn't mine, whose fault was it?

Suddenly a gigantic wave of feelings crashed over me. I couldn't breathe. *No, I can't go there. Too much. My heart hurts. My stomach hurts. I hurt. I hurt my family. I'm empty. I'm a whore. I'm no good. I'm worthless. I need to be locked up. Take me off the streets. I'm not a fit person to be around.*

My sister and her husband left the next day for Kansas without talking to me about the incident. I had ruined Jean's very special day, and I presumed she hated me. I asked to return to the Good Shepherd Home. Thankfully the good Sisters agreed to let me come back.

I didn't deserve my family. In fact, I didn't deserve to be alive. I didn't eat for close to a week. My weight dropped from 115 to 100 pounds. I was inconsolable. Mother Nicholas sat with me, trying to get me to talk about what happened. I said very little except I was evil and didn't deserve to live.

Mother Nicholas adamantly disagreed. "No, Diann, you're not evil. Please, Diann, you need to eat to stay strong. Don't blame yourself; it's not your fault." I knew she was wrong, but even so, her soothing voice and words felt good. I finally began to eat again, but this didn't allay their concerns.

The nuns were afraid I wasn't dealing with my traumatic past or my feelings, so they sent me to a therapist. This therapist and I wanted two very different things. I wanted to avoid any memories and feelings associated with my past. I was afraid of being flooded with feelings that would drown me. Above all, I wanted to avoid crying. On the other hand, my therapist seemed to to want the opposite from me—she was determined I cry. I won every session. I just laughed.

I spent every weekend of the next year taking Jean's place at the duplex. I cooked meals for the week and cleaned the duplex from top to bottom. When friends wanted to visit, I would decline. I wanted to be there for my brothers. At the home, I did my chores diligently. I got good grades and became even more of a leader. I tried to appear squeaky clean on the surface so others wouldn't see the dirt underneath. The only smudge on my nearly spotless image was that, after two years of forced abstinence, I began secretly smoking again.

Even considering the small vice, I convinced myself at the age of sixteen I was healthy enough and ready to venture out again. Besides, many of my friends had left to go into foster homes. They would come back to the home with wonderful stories about their foster families. Their stories convinced me to take a risk.

When Michael turned twenty-one, he assumed guardianship of Paul, Patrick, and Lee. They still lived in the duplex next to Aunt Ruby. I think Dad encouraged guardianship in order to keep the family strong and together. Michael didn't assume guardianship of eighteen-year-old Al because he had moved to New York to try his luck at acting. I considered moving in with Michael, but feared Aunt Ruby's influence. Still extremely angry with her, I chose to go into foster care. I said good-bye to the close family of nuns and girls who had been my life for the past two years.

In late June, 1966, at the age of sixteen, I moved into my new foster family's home in an affluent suburb of Denver. The spacious house with its rich furnishings and manicured lawn took my breath away. I had never set foot in a house so grand. It was hard to believe this was where I was going to live.

My foster father, Rod, was a big, burly, redheaded man with freckles, twinkling blue eyes, and an easy manner. He laughed a lot and immediately began to tease me. I think he thought the teasing would make me feel at home, and he was right. He liked people and they liked him. He had been a football star in college and now was a successful businessman.

My foster mother, Joan, had a coifed hairdo, dyed blonde hair, and was always impeccably dressed in designer clothes. She was an only child with an air of entitlement; she smelled of money. On our initial meeting, she seemed to look me over with a gentle eye. I looked her over also and decided she appeared perfect. Her one flaw was she was a chain smoker. I had high hopes if she ever caught me smoking a cigarette, she might be lenient in her discipline.

They were awfully nice to take me in. It seemed like Rod sincerely liked me and was interested in my welfare. Although Joan seemed to pity my poor and violent background, I felt both became foster parents with good intentions and wanted to help a kid in need. Joan also liked the fact I was good with their kids and could clean house.

When I arrived, there were two children: Holly, aged six, and John, aged four. Joan was eight months pregnant with number three. I loved being around young children again. I was in heaven when in July the third child, Jeff, was born. I was again in charge of a baby. I didn't mind the cleaning, either.

What I had trouble with was Joan's attitude. Although I attended many of the family's high-society functions and learned many social graces that would come in handy later in life, I never really felt part of the family. They told me I was family, but the reality was my wants and needs were always secondary. They were a very active couple, and if they had an engagement, I was expected to stay home and babysit. My plans didn't count, and neither did I. That year they offered to adopt me. I was very clear I wanted to retain my last name and didn't want to be adopted. I didn't need adopting because I was already a part of a family who loved me.

I was living in a *Leave It to Beaver* house where everything matched. The tan carpet color matched the furniture, which matched the pillows and blended with the wall color. The dishes matched each other, and so did the silverware. Although I thought the furniture and accessories were elegant, I wanted more color in my life. I liked the order and space of my color-coordinated house, but I missed the casual and chaotic comfort of my family. The neatly trimmed yard with its pink and red rose bushes was beautiful, but it didn't compare to the fragrant purple lilac bushes of North Denver. I appreciated opportunities afforded by a rich, white neighborhood, like elegant meals and cultural events and plays, but I missed the fun, intimacy, and diversity of the Good Shepherd Home.

Since I knew absolutely no one in the area, Joan set up a tennis date for me to meet a girl who attended my future high school. Louise was a beauty. She had a perfect figure. Her good looks could have made her stuck-up, but she wasn't. She was popular and nice to everyone.

Luckily, Louise and I hit it off right away and quickly became best friends. I could talk to her about almost everything—everything except for Sandra, my shadow-side. Louise was the most wholesome person I'd ever met, and I didn't want to do anything to jeopardize our friendship by introducing her to any of my nasty traits. It was important to keep my bad side hidden.

She'd attended the local schools since kindergarten. She was a god-send, helping me fit in by introducing me to her friends and showing me the ropes at my new school. I went from attending small Catholic schools with large Latino populations, to the Good Shepherd Home filled with a hundred girls from diverse backgrounds, to Thomas Jefferson High School. Even Louise couldn't cushion the blow of trying to fit into an affluent, lily-white school population of four thousand students. I was one of two minority students.

To handle this number of students, the school had split sessions. I went to school from seven a.m. to noon daily. One of my hours was spent in the school office as a student assistant. The office personnel and the school counselors saw how lost I was and took me under their wings.

In addition to Louise and her friends, I befriended other newcomers to the school. The cliques were tight and exclusive; the newcomers were unattached, like me. Whenever I thought I was coming in contact with a potential friend, I'd tell them a brief version of my story.

"Just so you know, I live in foster care because my dad murdered my pregnant mom and three of my siblings." I would say this and wait for a response. If the response was along the lines of "I'm so sorry, let's go to lunch," I knew I had a potential friend. If the response was a wide-eyed stare and a gasp with a statement like, "I'll see you around," then I knew I couldn't trust them and didn't want them for a friend. I devised this tactic to prevent myself from getting hurt.

As far as dating was concerned, I stayed in my comfort zone. I dated a Catholic Latino boy named John from St. Joe's through the eleventh grade. I attended the St. Joe's homecomings and proms, where I fit in just fine. After the fiasco at Jean's wedding, I decided the *good* side of me would definitely abstain from sex with boys I dated, at least until I was engaged to be married. If I cared for a guy, I certainly didn't want to cheapen the relationship by having sex. I cared for John, and so even though I engaged in some light petting with him, we never had sex. I didn't want to have to keep any secrets—other than Sandra—from Louise, either.

CHAPTER 9

The Last Supper

The members of my family still living in Colorado continued to visit Dad every Sunday. Michael, driving a packed car, would pick me up from foster care. Michael, Paul, Patrick, Lee, and I would make the two-hour-long trek to Cañon City. Jean and Al were the two family members missing. Jean was living in Liberal, Kansas, with her husband, and Al was in New York City struggling to become an actor.

It was now 1966. For the previous three years we had been visiting Dad, his lawyers had been working to get a stay of execution. All of us were hopeful life in prison might be the outcome. In the 1960s in the United States, there was growing controversy about the death penalty, which led to a decline in executions. The situation in Colorado also held some hope. A ballot initiative to abolish capital punishment was to be put before the voters of Colorado in November.

The history of capital punishment in Colorado was a colorful one. In 1890, the legislature passed a law requiring executions be carried out at the state penitentiary in Cañon City, the very facility we visited every Sunday. Seven years later, the legislature abolished the death penalty, only to reinstate it in 1901 following three lynchings. Colorado is the only state known to have restored capital punishment in order to prevent lynchings. The thinking was that vigilante justice was unacceptable in every case. It didn't matter how heinous the crime or how strong the evidence, every citizen of the United States was entitled to a legal defense and trial.

In 1966, the battle was heating up on both sides of the issue. Dad evidently was interviewed by a journalist. In the interview, Dad made an off-the-cuff comment about capital punishment that was later taken out of context by the media. The newspapers ran with it, displaying outrageous headlines like "Luis J. M. Wants to Be Hanged on the Capitol Steps."

The media had again put Dad in the spotlight. The scrutiny radiated out to us, upsetting our lives. We all wanted to talk to Dad about his interview but were afraid to bring up the subject. In the three years of our weekly visits, Dad hadn't mentioned his legal issues, the murders, or his view of capital punishment. We all had the impression the subjects were forbidden.

We entered the prison after the media blitz with apprehension. Dad immediately sensed the tension and alleviated our fears. He dispensed with the small talk and said in his softest conversational tone, "I suppose you read the newspapers." We all nodded. "Well, I guess I should set the record straight, because the media said it all wrong." We all nodded vigorously, saying with our body language, yes, we hope so, and please explain. "What I said was if I thought I could prevent anyone else from doing what I did, I would consent to being hanged on the capitol steps." Then Dad teared up and held his head in his hands. "I would do anything to prevent others from doing what I did." His face softened as he looked at each one of us. "So don't worry. I won't be hanged." He chuckled and looked at the boys. "Just deliver the papers; don't read them." We left the prison feeling slightly better, glad Dad had clarified things.

In November, our hopes were dashed because Colorado residents voted two to one to retain the death penalty. The final date was set for my father's execution. Dad was to die in the gas chamber on June, 2, 1967.

The rest of my junior year flew by. I tried not to think of Dad and his predicament. I focused on getting good grades in school; my boyfriend, John, who attended St. Joe's; and taking care of my foster parents' growing family. My foster mother was using me more and more as a resident maid and nanny. Occasionally I would rebel by having my boyfriend over while babysitting. We never did anything remotely inappropriate, but both my foster parents had a fit if they saw him at the house.

*   *   *

In Colorado, skies were often blue, and the sun made an almost daily visit throughout the year. Even so, I felt winter always had a cold and unfriendly, dirty grey feel to it. Every year, in early May, both the spring season and I gladly shrugged off our heavy winter coats. I loved nature's spring colors and the fresh smell of new growth. The lilac bush was my favorite, dripping in flowers of rich purple and scenting the air with a heavenly fragrance. Lilacs sent me back in time to the good parts of my childhood: playing outside with my brothers and sisters in North Denver, remembering Mom and my grandparents, and being surrounded by laughter and love.

I loved the mountain views, too, no matter what season, but for some reason, in the spring they were especially magnificent. Always peeking over the foothills were the fourteen-thousand-foot-high peaks. Their ancient, grey, stony faces were visible from any location.

Pikes Peak stood alone, apart from the others. She was stunning in her beauty. She was the mother of all peaks. She wore a magnificent white cloak so pure it sparkled in the light I had peered out the car window looking for her every Sunday for the past four years. She was present, showing herself from different angles, from Colorado Springs to Cañon City. She never disappointed me. Even when stormy days obscured her form, I could picture her leaning against the heavenly dome watching me. When I sensed her presence, she always filled me with peace and love.

I woke up on Sunday, May 28, 1967, with my stomach a raging, swirling, black mass of dread. On this Sunday, my family would eat a final meal with Dad. It would be the last time I would see him alive. Next Friday, in only six days, he would die in the gas chamber. I'm sure on this particular Sunday, like most spring days, the western part of the state was dressed in its ordinary colorful splendor. I'm also sure the mother of mountains was with me. This day I couldn't see her. I saw only grey. I couldn't feel her; I felt heavy and numb. The grey enveloped me, permeating everything. The fog was so thick it was tough to think, hard to breathe, difficult to move.

Through the thick haze, I tried to grasp the enormity of the situation. Faint, dark shadows of all my losses pushed to the edges of my consciousness. Mom and the babies dead. No, I couldn't go there; I wouldn't go there. Too overwhelming. Our family had suffered so many endings. Today, another ending, another loss, another death. *I don't want you to ever get out of prison, Dad, but I don't want you to die.*

For the last time, Michael piloted his 1966 Chevy Impala to the prison. My Uncle Fernando and my brother Al, who had arrived from New York, sat in the front seat with Michael. As usual, my unhappy, claustrophobic, seventeen-year-old self was squashed in the middle of the back seat with Paul, Patrick, and Lee. The only family member missing was Jean. She was pregnant and too sick to travel.

The car seemed to crawl; the familiar landscape floated by in slow motion. I wanted to yell at Michael, *Hurry up; go faster*, and at the same time scream, *Stop the car; I want out!* After we finally arrived and had piled out of the car, and I could breathe again, I glanced at my watch. My hands were shaking so violently I had trouble reading the time. When I finally read my watch face, to my astonishment and in exoneration of my brother's driving, I realized the drive to the prison had taken the same amount of time this day as on all the other visitation days. I was almost sure the surreal, slow-motion feel was my mind's attempt to stop time.

Our normally talkative family was subdued that day as we slowly walked up to the cold, forbidding prison entrance. I braced as we entered the facility, anticipating the physical violation of being frisked. I hoped this day, the day of our last visit with Dad, might warrant a frisking reprieve. We were frisked as usual; I guess it was an ordinary day for prison personnel.

The walls seemed to close in, and again I found it hard to breathe as we were ushered down the familiar, long, grey corridor. Walking to see Dad was like driving to see Dad; I wanted to slow my pace and accelerate at the same time. I felt an equal measure of burning up, freezing, numbness, and wanting to vomit as I entered a holding cell and saw him. He had been granted special privileges for his "last supper," and we, along with his brother, were allowed to join him for this meal.

All of us, including Dad, did our best to act as if this were just another of our many visitations. In all the years we had been coming as a family, the subject of the murders had rarely been mentioned. Abuse had never been broached. Dad was still the undisputed head of our family, and he didn't want to talk about those subjects. He alone determined what was to be discussed, and so even today, just five days before his death, we all chatted, as usual, about the inconsequential aspects of our lives during dinner. "School is almost out; how are your grades?" Dad asked.

"Fine," the school-goers answered in unison.

"Are you all going to confession every Saturday and church every Sunday?" We all nodded.

After dinner, just before it was time for us to leave, Dad called out, "Diana, come here. I want to talk to you alone."

Upon hearing this command, my brain instantaneously sent my body a neon sign flashing DANGER. My body, upon reading the sign, instinctively braced. Would he, could he, abuse me one last time? For a long second I froze in panic. Then my logic brought me back to the room; I saw the prison guard in the glass door watching us. My siblings and my uncle were a short distance away. I knew I was safe.

I'd just begun to catch my breath when Dad uttered a sentence that hit so hard the words knocked me down: "Try not to let what I did to you affect the rest of your life."

Dad's last words to me just stood there, still, powerful, and absurd: words hanging in the air, waiting. Waiting for what? Words waiting the seemingly interminable length of time it took them to arrive at the entrance of my ears, to travel a circuitous route to my brain, to let my mind have the moments needed to register their meaning, to feel the shock that freezes thought, and finally to thaw enough to pluck out of the air a myriad of responses and questions.

My seventeen-year-old mind screamed, *Are you kidding me? Are you crazy? What a stupid statement!* Stored memories suddenly sprang to life; a crowd of thoughts, or fragments of thoughts, pushed and shoved their way through the double doors of my consciousness. They were all fighting to be heard, vying for attention, jockeying for position. *Try to what? Too late! I'm trash. I'm a slut. You're clueless. You don't know me. I'm a bad girl. I have sex with strangers. I'm a monster. What you did? You made me a monster. Affect? Every minute. Every day. Life? What life?* Then one loud, booming sentence silenced the chatter as it hit my thought waves: *Don't you know your actions have affected every moment of my life?*

The crowd of thoughts stilled as I looked up. Dad was staring at me with a strange, questioning expression on his face. I suddenly realized I hadn't spoken a word. He was waiting for a reply. My head started to spin. Over and over, like a hamster treading his wheel, my mind repeated, *What should I say?* Then, just when I thought I couldn't stand the panic for one more instant, a grey numbness enveloped me, and I stated in a soft, monotone voice, "Okay, Dad."

*   *   *

After school, on the day of the execution, Rod and Joan dropped me off at the family duplex. Inside, the air was heavy and thick with tension as Al valiantly attempted to distract us with stories of his New York experiences while Michael, Paul, Patrick, Lee, and I valiantly attempted to listen. After I made some dinner, we all ate and chatted distractedly, glancing every minute at the clock. At 6:45 we turned on the radio, and all conversation ceased. We just sat in the living room and stared at the black box, willing a last-minute stay of execution.

What came out of the commentator's mouth was bizarre. He was making Dad's execution sound like a sporting event complete with a play-by-play description. I wanted to cover my ears and yell *No! No! No!*

I sat like a stone, my body and mind frozen. "Luis M. asks the guard if the gas will affect his asthma." What kind of question was that? "Luis M. has entered the chamber. He appears to be praying. He has been strapped to the chair. The gas has been released. They expect it to take about twenty minutes. His face is now slack. His body is drooping."

Comment after comment, detail after detail, until he was finally pronounced dead.

Al, who had visited Dad every day for the last week, was howling with grief. The boys were sobbing quietly, but the tears leaning up against my eye sockets refused to come out. Dad died never having to feel our anger; Dad died feeling only our love.

He was gone. Dad was dead. My heart was empty. I spent a sleepless Friday night with my family. The following morning, we all sat around not knowing what to say; the silence was deafening. I was relieved to leave. My foster parents thought it a good idea for me to get out of town. They talked to Father Abercrombie from the Good Shepherd Home, and he agreed to take me with him for the weekend.

Father Abercrombie and I took a road trip to three mountain towns: Granby, Grand Lake, and Kremmling. Sometimes I looked out the car window; sometimes we talked about school, my foster home, my family, the weather, and food. Sometimes we talked about Dad. Father Abercrombie was kind, patient, and always a perfect gentleman.

Years later, after Father Abercrombie's death, I read he was accused of pedophilia. The Catholic Church gave hundreds of thousands of dollars to his alleged victims. Luckily for me, it turned out he liked boys. I felt sorry for the boys he molested but grateful he didn't like sex with girls. I don't think I could have handled being molested that weekend.

Father Abercrombie brought me home to my foster parents Sunday evening, June fourth. There were only two days left of the school year. It took every ounce of energy to get up, get dressed, and go to school. We had our yearbooks, and everyone was making the rounds asking friends and teachers to sign.

The yearbook provided a slight diversion. I actually had brief instances of time when I didn't think about the execution. I walked into my physiology class and asked the teacher if he would mind signing. He said, "Sure, I'd be glad to." As he was signing, he looked up and said in a conversational tone, "Say, did you hear a man with your last name was executed last Friday night?"

I just stared at him. After what felt like eons of time, I said, "Yes. That was my dad."

He didn't know what to say. He swallowed hard a couple of times and had trouble keeping eye contact. "I'm so sorry. I didn't know." After that encounter, the day dragged. The last day of school seemed to last forever. But finally we were let out for the summer.

A day after school was out, a letter came in the mail. The handwriting was eerily familiar. The words just lay there, the black marks of a man's life written on ghostly white paper. My reaction to the letter was the numbness of grey. I don't know what I did with my letter. I may have thrown it away, or I may have put it in my footlocker where I keep important papers. I found out each of my siblings received their letters from Dad the same week.

CHAPTER 10

Graduation to Marriage

Sandra, my shadow-side, got word of the execution and decided that, after being banned since Jean's wedding, it was safe for her to come back into my life. Sandra was indelibly linked to Dad. Whenever I came face-to-face with Dad, Sandra came face-to-face with me, reminding me I was complicit in Dad's debauchery and therefore worthless. If I ever started feeling good about myself, she showed up to "burst my balloon" with the intent of putting me smack-dab in the middle of the mortal sinners once again. Dad might have been physically dead, but he was still actively controlling my psyche. I continued to lead my bad vs. good double life.

The summer before my senior year, I was hired as a temporary employee of Rockmont Paper Company to work the kiosk at the Teen Fair. My job was to man the booth and pass out items to promote and enhance their paper business. Sandra accompanied me and was clear about her job description. She specialized in promoting sex with strangers. She was constantly making herself available to any Tom, Dick, José, or Harry who crossed her path.

Meanwhile, I was still dating John. If Sandra acted like a slut, I, Diann, acted in a wholesome manner. I wasn't a total prude. I was open to *appropriate* heavy kissing and light petting.

The facts of my existence were that Dad was dead but still on my brain, and risk-taking Sandra was back in my life. I certainly couldn't change death and didn't yet know how to get rid of Sandra. I believed my only choice was to figure out a way to skip confession. I simply was sick of admitting, week after week, I was a mortal-sinning adulterer, which had been my standard confession since the age of seven. I knew when Sandra was present, I was forced into the big sin arena. But now Dad was

97

gone and I was out of the Good Shepherd Home, the confession pressure was off.

Even though Dad still seemed to control my errant behavior, his death in many ways set my mind free. For the first time in my life, I began to think outside the proverbial Catholic box. I decided it might be possible for me to talk directly to God. He was all knowing and all seeing; God was the only one who knew about Sandra—besides me, anyway. What possible good could come of going over the same mortal sin every confession? I didn't feel either of us needed reminding week after week.

Once I stopped going to confession on Saturdays, I had to figure out a way to miss taking communion on Sundays. Even thinking outside the Catholic box, I couldn't, in good conscience, take communion without confession. My solution was to sit far away from my foster family in the huge Catholic Church we attended. I'd line up to go to communion, and when the family wasn't looking, I'd sneak back to my seat.

My senior year began. I was still haunted by Dad's death. One of the counselors helped me write a letter to Governor Love asking why he didn't commute Dad's sentence when he'd commuted five other sentences that year. The governor wrote back stating that when he offered to commute his sentence, Dad refused the offer. He said Dad wanted to die. This information was strangely calming to me.

After receiving the governor's letter, I began to feel an even bigger sense of freedom. I finally felt relief instead of guilt at not having to make the prison visit every Sunday. My boyfriend, John, was in a band and into the 60s drug scene, a scene in which I wasn't comfortable. I wasn't interested in adding another addiction to Sandra's repertoire, and I suddenly had the courage to say so. Because I felt free to make my own decisions, I broke up with John.

I still worked in the high school office that year. The office staff took it upon themselves to mentor me. They convinced me I had a bright academic future and encouraged me to apply for a scholarship to Colorado State University. With help, I filled out the necessary forms and sent them in. A few months later, I received an acceptance letter congratulating me and offering me a generous scholarship. I started to feel pretty good about myself. My senior year flew by, and I was able to maintain some semblance of normal teenage life.

Sandra, however, was waiting in the wings, ready to ruin my bright future college plans at the first opportunity. Sandra determined that a despicable whore, slut, and bad girl like me certainly didn't deserve anything, especially a higher education. Sandra's chance to undermine my aspirations came in the form of a phone call.

"Hi. I'm Jeremy from Lowry Air Force Base. I won your picture and phone number in a poker game. Would you like to go out with me?"

"You won what?" Before he could say anything, I said, "Who gave you my name and number? How did the guy get a picture of me?"

"Whoa, take it easy. I think he said his name was Ted. He met you and one of your girlfriends at a roller rink. You gave him one of your senior pictures."

For a short time, Louise and I had dated a couple of nerdy guys we met at the rink. We were just acting silly, and yes, I did vaguely remember giving this Ted person a wallet-sized senior picture of me. Jeremy was telling the truth.

Even if his information was correct, I still needed to get to know him. Sandra, however, needed him to remain a stranger. She was looking for a one-night stand to prove I was bad. After I talked with Jeremy for about a half hour, Sandra had lost all interest. Jeremy was close to my age and seemed like he might be potential boyfriend material. I was interested because I wasn't dating anyone, and he seemed nice. So at the end of the conversation when he suggested we meet sometime in the future, I agreed. He ended with, "I know a bunch of guys from the base who would love to get to know some girls. Do you have any friends?"

"Indeed I do," I said, thinking specifically of Louise, Janice, and Cindy.

I talked to Jeremy on the phone for the next several weeks, but the first opportunity to meet him and his friends came at the graduation keg party Joan and Rod threw for me. I invited a bunch of my friends, and Jeremy agreed to bring several of his friends. Rod and Joan probably would have objected to me inviting a group of twenty-one-year-old males to the party, but they didn't know I had because I didn't tell them.

In 1968, in the state of Colorado, it was legal for an eighteen-year-old to drink 3.2% beer. Rod and Joan were partiers, and most of my friends and I were all eighteen. This kind of graduation party was fairly common. It was a right-of-passage party, and I was delighted Rod and Joan were honoring me. I was, in fact, an eighteen-year-old, grown-up graduate ready to leave foster care. I was no longer a girl but a woman capable of being on my own. I wanted to be an adult making good, responsible choices. I wished for everybody to be proud of me. I wanted everybody to stop worrying about me, especially Jean and Michael.

I was also still an eighteen-year-old teenager out to have a good time at my graduation party, so as soon as the keg was tapped, I started in on the beer. By the time Jeremy and his Air Force base buddies joined the party, I was well on my way to being toasted. I think I liked finally meeting Jeremy, a burly, freckle-faced Georgia boy, but I was too drunk to remember my first impression of him.

In the middle of June, a couple of weeks after the party, I decided to clean my foster parents' house from top to bottom. This cleaning, although not officially my duty, was done as a thank you for taking me in and giving me a wonderful graduation celebration. That afternoon, Joan came home, brushed past me without a greeting, and climbed the stairs to her bedroom. A few minutes later, she called to me. Relieved, I ascended the stairs, thinking I would receive my belated greeting plus acknowledgment and appreciation for a cleaning job well done. Instead, Joan's tone was accusatory as she ushered me into the master bathroom. "Did you clean this mirror?"

"Yes, I did." I replied.

"Well, you didn't do a very good job. Just look at these streaks." Even though this behavior wasn't out of character for Joan, I think I had reached my limit of patience with being in a foster home. That was the moment I decided it was time to move out. I left partially because of Joan's lack of gratitude, but mostly because I was an eighteen-year-old wanting to be emancipated.

Within the week, I was back living with my brothers Michael, Paul, Patrick, and Lee, which, come to think of it, was only semi-emancipation because Michael was in charge. He had purchased a typical North Denver brick home with three bedrooms and a basement. It sat on the northeast corner of 32nd and Raleigh, about four blocks south of our old duplex. Even with my oldest brother looking over my shoulder, I had more freedom to date and be with friends. I didn't miss foster care a bit.

Jeremy's friends, all over the age of 21, provided me and my friends a summer of fun. All of us would get together and hang out. Louise and I started to double-date with Jeremy and his friend Bill. We figured double-dating would be a fun and safe activity that would keep us out of trouble.

On July 4, 1968, Louise and Bill and Jeremy and I drove up to a place near Denver known as Lookout Mountain. There, we were having dinner at a nice restaurant with a spectacular view overlooking the city of Denver. It was a special night. We were celebrating Louise's eighteenth birthday. Jeremy was very affectionate throughout the meal. He frequently squeezed my hand and put his arms around my shoulders. His eyes were soft with desire.

After dinner and birthday cake, Jeremy pulled me out of my chair and away from the table, saying, "Diann and I want to give you two some time alone. We've decided to go for a little drive. We'll be back to pick you up. Is that all right?"

"Sure," said Louise, looking dreamily into her date's eyes. "See you soon."

My part of *we* had no idea about Jeremy's plan. I suspected his motive had nothing to do with Louise and everything to do with making out with me. Louise seemed fine, so I went along with my boyfriend, saying, "Happy Birthday, Louise. We'll be right back."

In an instant, we were out of the restaurant and in his car. Jeremy found a secluded spot off-road, and we proceeded to frantically make out. So, as it happened, Jeremy and I had sex for the first time on Louise's eighteenth birthday. A half hour later, we picked up Louise and Bill and continued our double date. I didn't tell Louise about having sex with Jeremy until months later when the evidence of my unwholesome behavior became obvious.

I didn't intend to have sexual intercourse with Jeremy that night. In fact, I had fairly strict rules about boyfriends and sexual behavior. Heavy kissing and light petting were allowed, but no fondling of my private parts and definitely no intercourse. But Jeremy was a persistent guy who had been gradually wearing me down. I liked him a lot, and I think I was a little afraid he would break up with me if I didn't give in.

Before I knew it, light petting became heavy, and no touching turned into light touching and more. I finally surrendered. It was July 4, Independence Day. I didn't feel independent because I don't remember actually consenting to sex.

Even if I didn't actually choose to have intercourse, this much is true: It was the only time I had ever enjoyed it. I liked Jeremy and for the first time in my life, I wanted to have sex. I never ever wanted to have sex with Dad. I always hated it, even though many times my body liked it. Sandra never enjoyed sex with strangers. The sole purpose of those sleazy encounters was to handle overwhelming feelings and to make me feel horrible about myself. She had effectively achieved her goal. Sex with Juan at age fourteen was simply a combination of having no boundaries and my own teenage rebellion. I was too drunk to know if I had liked sex with the best man, but having sex with Jeremy was different from all the sex I had experienced.

With Jeremy, I felt physically and emotionally close to him. After Lookout Mountain, I abruptly stopped double-dating because my relationship with Jeremy had ascended, or descended (depending on one's point of view), to a new level. We spent the whole summer in each other's arms. My friends, especially Louise, told me they felt ignored and neglected, but I couldn't hear them from la-la land.

La-la land was located in the state of denial, free of nagging thoughts of birth control and natural consequences. Deep down, I knew my family and friends wouldn't approve of my behavior, but I convinced myself having sex with Jeremy was okay because he was the guy I would eventually marry. I broke my rule about being abstinent until I was engaged, but I just knew I was close to getting a ring, I was sure of it.

By the end of the summer, I saw us as a very serious couple on the brink of marriage. So one evening when Jeremy stated in an off-handed manner, "My mother would die if she knew I was dating a spic," I was totally shocked. It was as if he had taken a red hot piece of molten racism and branded me with it. I felt sick; blistered, and burned. Heat traveled up my body and settled in my face. My mouth was ready to spew hurtful words back at him, while my eyes stung with held-back tears of hurt. Blood rushed to my extremities, down my arms, balling up my fists, ready to fight, just as my legs were preparing to run. I just stood there saying and doing nothing. I liked Jeremy a lot and couldn't believe he could say such a thing to me. Maybe I should give him the benefit of the doubt; maybe he was kidding.

In the following days I tried to determine whether I wanted to continue the relationship. I had just come to the conclusion I would try to make it work when I found out I was pregnant.

We didn't have home pregnancy tests in those days, but I suspected something was up. Besides missing my period, I was vomiting everything I ate, I had a pimple on my nose, and my gums were bleeding. Despite these minor irritations, however, I loved being pregnant. I loved the changes to my body and the idea of having a baby. I loved knowing there was a life growing inside me. How I missed little Teresa; to hold a newborn again would be heaven.

When the moment came for me to tell Jeremy about our impending parenthood, my "serious boyfriend" said, "The baby isn't mine, and I never want to see you again!"

Yes, you know the baby is yours, you jerk. I haven't been with anyone but you since Lookout Mountain. How could you leave me? I don't want to be with you anyway, you racist creep. I cared for you; how could you do this to me? My roller coaster emotions rode me day and night. After about three weeks of crying, screaming, and nonstop whining, I decided I was wasting my time brooding about something I had no power to change. Resigned, I joined with my friends Louise, Janet, and Cindy, all no longer dating Jeremy's friends, and became a member of the broken heart club.

What was almost harder than dealing with the ex-boyfriend was coping with Louise's reaction to my pregnancy. "Pregnant? You've got to be kidding me." A flush of shame colored my face. I couldn't look at my friend as I nodded my head slowly. Louise had questions, and she demanded answers. "When did you start having sex with Jeremy?"

"On your birthday."

Her mouth hung open and her eyes widened, trying to absorb this hard-to-fathom turn of events. Her incredulity quickly shifted to hurt and anger. "You're kidding me, right?" she said again. "How could you do what you did any time, but *on my birthday*?" The next question was at the center of her hurt. She said, her voice cracking with emotion, "When were you going to tell me? We're best friends."

"I didn't think you'd understand," I said, listening to my best friend not only criticize my behavior but also chastise me for not telling her about it.

Louise's wounded feelings resulted in my receiving a severe tongue-lashing from her. I almost would have preferred the belt. Almost. Louise's reactions reinforced to me, once again, that my actions often hurt the people I love.

Even though there was a baby filling me up, a pervasive emptiness invaded my happy space because my family, foster parents, and friends weren't the least supportive of me or my predicament. According to my brothers, if I had previously been considered a screw-up with potential to be rehabilitated, the pregnancy now placed me in the no-hope category. Upon hearing the news the baby was due near his birthday, Michael declared if the baby was born on his birthday, it would be Rosemary's baby, a reference to the popular book and horror film. He was talking about a baby possessed by the devil. Jean declared I was a disgrace to the family. She was dismayed I was enjoying the pregnancy and that I was planning on having a natural birth.

Aunt Ruby was disgusted with me. "How could you let this happen?"

I responded, "It just happened."

My foster parents were appalled. I was bombarded with questions of the where, when, and who variety. They were concerned first with their own family. "Did you ever have sex in the house?"

"No."

"Did you have sex around our kids?"

"No."

"We're very disappointed in your behavior."

"I understand."

My friends didn't know what to say, and I didn't know what to say back. Their faces showed a mixture of anger, fear, sadness, and maybe a touch of embarrassment for me. Due to my actions, I had alienated my friends and family. I was again alone with only my badness and morning sickness to keep me company.

Despite my brother Michael's anger, he let me stay at the house until I left for Colorado State University to live in the dorms. When I left for college, I promised myself that under no circumstances was I going to date or get involved with the male species for a long time, maybe for my whole college career.

It was late August when I arrived at the CSU campus, pregnant, scared, and determined to register. I sat in the office filling out form after form. To give my eyes a rest from the tedious paperwork, I looked up. Across the room I glimpsed a dark-haired, dark-eyed, handsome Latino man. He wasn't tall, maybe five feet eight inches, and was very slight of build. I later found out he had just returned from Vietnam, and he was scary-skinny.

After some time with him, I teased him about his skinniness, saying that from the side, if he had his tongue sticking out, he could double as a zipper. He looked familiar and inviting. He reminded me of home. He looked exactly like a St. Joe's boy. Actually, I found out later he not only looked like a St. Joe's boy, he *was* a St. Joe's boy. He had been three years ahead of me in school. He'd been in my brother Al's class, and Al didn't like him.

When our eyes connected, I was interested. When he smiled, I was hooked. He had the cutest little smirk. He wasted no time crossing the room and introducing himself. "I'm Joe. What's your name?" Suddenly I wasn't alone anymore. I light-heartedly abandoned all my resolve my first day on campus.

We had our first date that evening. As we talked, I discerned quickly that he was interested in having sex because he pushed for "making love" on our first date. Sandra wanted me to remember that I was worthless and to go ahead, but I saw a potential for a more meaningful relationship, so we decided to give him a choice.

In the past, strangers would approach me, ask for sex, and I would acquiesce. I left the decisions to the stranger; my job was to perform sex on demand. Even though I didn't know Joe, he wasn't exactly a total stranger. Joe was a former St. Joe's boy, which made him a semi-friend.

Stranger or friend, I guess it didn't matter because I hadn't set rules around sex with my boyfriend Jeremy either, and I had ended up pregnant. I was determined to handle this situation differently. I was proud of myself for saying to Joe, "You can have sex with me now, and I won't ever see you again. Or we could wait, and you could get to know me."

As I figured, Joe wanted more than a night of sex, so he opted for getting to know me. About five days into our relationship, we spent five hours talking on the phone. He appeared to be intelligent and was knowledgeable on a variety of subjects. He challenged some of my ideas and made me think. I like people who make me think. Then the conversation turned personal. He told me he had been a gunner in the Vietnam War and was hoping for a degree in business on the GI bill.

I told him much more than he told me; I told him everything. I told him the detailed story of my life, ending with "I'm pregnant." I waited for him to reject me right then and there, to tell me "see you later." Yet this information didn't faze him a bit. I loved him for that. I was hooked by his acceptance and nonjudgmental attitude. I felt ostracized by everyone else in my world. He seemed to be the only one in the universe willing to listen to me. He appeared to understand me as well. It didn't hurt that he was cute, either.

I believe he told me what I wanted to hear because he liked my looks and, later on that week, the sex. Maybe I should have been a little suspicious of his true intentions when he asked for sex on the first date, but at the time, I didn't notice his behavior because I was focused on mine. Choosing to set relationship parameters of any kind was a major step forward for me. It was true I had broken my vow not to get involved with a man, but at least I was slowing down and thinking things through this time. I had made him wait a whole week for sex! There was even an upside to continued sex with Joe; Sandra would most certainly continue to curtail her dangerous activities, and I wouldn't have to worry about getting pregnant.

And so I attended CSU for a semester, seeing Joe every day and having sex with him every night. Because we both lived in a dorm, Joe's older green Karmann Ghia became our tight-spaced "love lounge." Joe was happy with this arrangement, but Joe's roommate thought he was playing with fire, a flame that would trap and burn him. The first time he met me, he warned Joe, "Be careful of that girl. She's the marrying kind." Joe told me this story, laughing heartily at the absurdity of his roommate's statement. I didn't laugh; I bided my time.

I did have "the talk" with Joe just as I did with every other guy with whom I thought I might be serious. The talk goes like this: "If we were to be married and have kids, and if any of the kids happen to be girls, if you ever touch those girls sexually, I'll kill you."

Three months into the relationship, Joe popped the "would you marry me" question after we watched the movie *Romeo and Juliet*. My ecstatic answer was yes. A few days later, he popped me in the gut with another question: "A couple of days ago, did I ask you if you would marry me?" he asked.

Again my answer was yes.

He said, "I thought so. Would it be possible to rescind the proposal for now?"

My answer was a disappointed okay. He rescinded a total of three more proposals before we finally set a date. I learned fairly quickly that Joe had a fear of commitment and a great desire to party as a single person.

When I was five months pregnant, I left CSU at Christmas break and again lived with Michael. Because of my pregnancy, Michael was not excited to have me home. Although I loved living with my family again, I was not thrilled to have to listen to my disapproving oldest brother, either.

Joe, on the other hand, wasn't judgmental of my pregnancy at all. One time when the marriage plans were on, Joe even offered to raise the baby with me. Joe's suggestion made me feel accepted and loved, but I wasn't quite ready to make a decision about the baby. Despite Joe's generous offer, I was leaning toward adoption. I just needed a nonjudgmental place to live until my baby was born.

Catholic Charities had a program designed to provide employment for unwed mothers, and I quickly secured a job through them. I was hired as a live-in nanny for a large Catholic family until the birth. I made the move from a critical environment to a positive, accepting atmosphere just after my nineteenth birthday.

I moved into a turn-of-the-century home in the Denver Country Club area of town with Tina and Tim and their eight children: seven girls and one boy. If Rod and Joan, my former foster parents, were upper-crust champagne, Tina and Tim were down-to-earth beer. Tina, long and lanky with dark brown hair, had a generous mouth that housed an expandable laugh that could fill a room. Tim was a slim six-footer with sandy hair who claimed many redheaded relatives. This fact explained their plethora of redheaded children. The house with its tall ceilings, four bedrooms, claw-footed bathtubs, banisters, and armoires for closets was inviting, but what made me feel at home were the love, affection, and noise of this large, boisterous family.

I loved the everyday chore of brushing the little girls' red hair and figuring out fun hair styles with barrettes. The children ranged in age from fourteen years to four months. There were two aspects of life in this household that I had trouble with, however: the chaotic mess and my room in the unfinished basement. I was accustomed to order from my years at the Good Shepherd Home and my time at the perfectly organized and matching foster care home. This entire house was in a constant state of disarray. The entryway catchall shelf was the worst, cluttered with coats, hats, books, papers, and unnamable stuff. Many times when Tina and Tim were off to one of their socially and politically active commitments, I would mobilize the troops to do a bit of shelf and house organizing. This effort was futile. Order seemed to last only a matter of hours before the mess began to stealthily encroach again.

I lived in the basement with the laundry, spiders, dangerous bugs, and the dark. One night a hairy, eight-legged monster rappelled down from the shelf above my bed. Dangling from its web above my face, it let out more and more rope. The spider bounced up and down, as if on a bungee cord, extending its extremities to touch my nose. I jumped off the bed and began to scream. I screamed and screamed and screamed.

Tina, fearing I was in the clutches of a murderous rapist, came thundering down the stairs, making spearing jabs with a ski pole. She stopped short when she noticed me panting and pointing to the harmless, tiny arachnid. She gave me a disgusted look, and because the crisis occurred in the middle of the night, she lowered the ski pole, shook her head, turned, and left. I could hear the clunk of the ski pole on each step as she ascended the stairs.

Unlike foster care at Rod and Joan's house, the nanny duties that came with the move to Tina and Tim's were well defined. Strangely, the concise job description made me feel more a part of this family than I ever felt with my foster family. They seemed to be cognizant of my feelings and my need for time off. Joe would come down from Fort Collins on the weekends to see me. Tina and Tim, unlike my former foster family, welcomed him even if they were out of town. We had a great time playing with the kids. I loved the playful, fun side of Joe.

On May 10, 1969, my baby was born at one p.m. at St. Joseph's Hospital in Denver. She was a six-pound bundle of soft, pure love. She had dark brown hair and big eyes. I named her Michelle Therese in honor of my little sister. I took care of her in the hospital for three wonderful days. For nine months I had thought about the decision I would have to make when the time came. I was poor and unmarried. I wanted my little girl to have a stable, two-parent home with a stay-at-home mom who would snuggle her daily. I decided her best chance in life was to be adopted. I knew I was making a healthy decision. I was thinking about my baby, not about me.

That was easy to think before she was born, but holding her, kissing her cheeks, feeding and changing her, loving her and bonding with her and then letting her go was the hardest thing I had ever done in my life. I wanted her to know deep in her soul that her birth mother loved her.

Jean drove from her home in Kansas to Denver soon after the baby was born. Jean's idea was to take me back to Kansas for a sisterly visit. The trip was designed to give me a change of scenery in order to distract me from the ordeal of giving up the baby. Or at least that was what I thought the trip's purpose was. I had just settled myself in the passenger's seat and readied myself for a long, fulfilling, sisterly chat when Jean began pelting me with critical remarks. "You're so irresponsible. This pregnancy has shamed our family. How could you let this happen? It better not happen again." I felt the blood gather in my face.

The words were lined up at my mouth's entrance ready to engage in battle. *You can let me out of the car right now if you think I'm that terrible*, I was ready to say. The real problem was I deserved her remarks; I was irresponsible and bad. I stayed in the car, the words stayed in my mouth, and Jean stopped her lecture. As it turned out, the trip was a nice change and did distract me from thinking about my baby girl.

After returning from my Kansas trip, I left Tina and Tim's home as planned. Deciding not to return to CSU, I moved into a two-bedroom Denver apartment with two other girls, Kristen and Sarah. All of us had been unwed mothers. Kristen and Sarah shared a room, and I had a room to myself, although I invited Joe to share it quite often. My shadow-side, Sandra, had disappeared again. I worked at a printing company during the day and continued to date Joe in the evenings.

Soon, despite Joe's roommate's concern, we became a couple on the road to a serious relationship. Joe's parents, John and Cora, welcomed me with open arms. John looked like an older Joe except for his balding head. He constantly smoked cigarettes, drank coffee, and teased anyone and everyone.

Cora stood 5 feet 1 inch short but seemed tall. She was an attractive woman with a commanding presence. She ran a tight ship, and her house was always spotless. Both welcomed me immediately and decided on our first meeting that I was family. I began spending most evenings at their home.

Joe didn't think it fair that my roommates expected me to cook every night at the apartment. To solve this problem, Joe began to invite me over to his parents' house for dinner on a regular basis. Evidently, he didn't see a problem expecting his mother to cook. The smells coming from Cora's kitchen traveled through my nose and into my heart speaking of Mom and Grandma. I think in a way I married Joe's family before I married Joe.

One time I arrived early to Joe's house. I walked in on Joe screaming at his mom. "I told you my shirts have to be facing the same way in the closet. How stupid are you? How many times do I have to tell you if one of my socks doesn't have a mate, toss it? I can't stand living like this. You can't even do my laundry right."

While we were growing up, it never occurred to any of us to yell at our mother, and if we had, Dad wouldn't have hesitated to hit us with his belt. Dad never yelled at Mom, either. Joe's disrespectful outburst concerned me, so while I was helping Cora with the dishes, I broached the subject. "Does Joe always get mad like that?"

"No," Cora responded. "Vietnam changed him. He never used to fly off the handle." She glanced up from the dishes to see my worried expression and said quickly, "He's been really nervous since he came home from Vietnam, but I'm sure he'll be back to his old self in no time."

I knew even then that Cora had a soft and blind spot in her heart for all her sons. I don't know what she believed about the war and Joe, but I think she saw me as a potential wife for her son and didn't want me to break up with him. Whatever the case, she needn't have been concerned. I had already whitewashed Joe's behavior in my mind with the belief my love would fix it. *My love is so strong it'll erase all his pain and anger. I'll soothe his war wounds and make him happy. My love is the remedy for all his ills.*

Just as a precaution, though, if we were married, I'd be diligent with how I placed his shirts in the closet. And I decided I was going to throw away every sock without a mate so Joe would have absolutely no reason to yell at me. I was so intent at not being yelled at that I went home that very day and rearranged my own closet to his exact specifications.

Sitting on my bed in the apartment staring at my newly ordered closet, I decided I basically liked order, or maybe I preferred it to disorder and chaos. I shuddered as my thoughts instantly walked into Tina and Tim's cluttered environment. I let out a big sigh of relief when my memory moved from that chaotic space to the Good Shepherd Home, a welcome, ordered, safe haven in my out-of-control, messed-up life.

Aunt Ruby had known what I needed. I wasn't any better than Joe; I, too, yelled at my auntie when she was just trying to help me. She took us in, gave us a home, and provided us with a stable parental figure. In return, I gave her a whole lot of grief, disrespect, and anger. As I gazed at my closet, I thought the organization of my outside life didn't mean very much if my priorities were out of order on the inside. I got off my behind, called my aunt, and paid her a long-overdue visit.

Aunt Ruby, as was her nature, welcomed me into heart and home. "Diana, it was wonderful to get your call. It's great to see you. Is everything okay?" That was my auntie, always concerned about other people's welfare.

A rush of love filled me up and overflowed; my eyes teared, and my throat closed up. The words came out husky and halting, filled with emotions. Aunt Ruby, before hearing a word, was crying, hugging me, and saying, "My poor, poor Diana."

I gently pushed her away from my body. I kept my hands on her shoulders. I needed to face her. I needed to look her in the eye. "I'm...so, so sorry! I was so mad. I was mad at the world, and I took it out on you. I'm so sorry I yelled at you. I was mean to you. You were just trying to help me. You sent me to the Good Shepherd Home not because you hated me. You didn't want to get rid of me. You loved me. You loved me."

Aunt Ruby was crying and nodding and wanted to say something, but I didn't let her. I put one finger to my lips because I needed to finish. That movement seemed not only to silence my auntie but to help me calm down. "Auntie, I was out of control. I was self-destructing. You got me off the streets. You probably saved my life. I came here to say thank you. Thank you for loving me. Thank you for keeping me safe. I truly believe there were angels always sitting on my shoulders protecting me through the tough years after the murders. You, Auntie, were my head angel."

Aunt Ruby, who I had never known to be at a loss for words, hugged me and cried. We talked for about a half hour more. I told her I hadn't even considered what that time must have been like for her. Her sister and best friend had just been murdered by her brother-in-law. She didn't take time to grieve; instead, she chose to take in a family of seven including one very troubled teen. Aunt Ruby and I were close after that. I finally let her become an affectionate mom figure in my life. I was glad I had repaired the Diana-Aunt Ruby connection; it felt good to mend my relationship with my auntie. Mom would be so proud and happy.

* * *

Joe had two sides to him just like Sandra and me: the fun, personable, attractive side and the red-flag side, signifying danger. The problem with noticing the many red flags was they only waved in my face intermittently. Much of the time Joe was a skilled and tender lover. When the sex flag flew, I rarely recognized it because it seemed normal, considering my history. Joe loved to "make love" several times daily no matter how I felt. The feeling of not being in control of my body was a familiar one.

The drunken flag flew quite often. I had the feeling getting drunk was a way for Joe to forget Vietnam, just as I used books as a way to escape. I understood his behavior, but I didn't like it. I thought reading a better tactic. He'd make plans with me and stand me up on a regular basis. His standard excuse was, "I ran into a buddy and we stopped and had a drink." All the excuses involved alcohol. What little money he had, he would spend in the bars. About the time I was starting to view our relationship with a "glass half-empty" attitude, Joe would arrive at my apartment bearing gifts and take me out for a wonderful evening. A thoughtful date night would erase months of drunken behavior, restore my glass half-full view of our relationship, and give me tolerance for a period of future drinking bouts.

Joe was always broke. His financial flag appeared weekly on the exact day I received my paycheck. I earned $42.50 a week. Joe was very persuasive when it came to convincing me to delay paying my bills in favor of lending him money. Because I was in love I let him finagle my finances so he could borrow money on a weekly basis.

I thought Joe was the smartest person I had ever met. We would have the most amazing, deep discussions. He presented his vast knowledge in a calm, respectful manner until, with no warning, he would erupt in anger. The red anger flag would appear out of the blue and slap me in the face with derogatory terms such as "stupid." This usually didn't concern me because I already believed I was stupid.

When Joe and life in general left me anxious and anchorless, I would go to church and visit with Father Ken. He would calmly bring me down to earth and provide me with perspective. Father Ken became a stable force in my otherwise chaotic life.

For the most part, thanks to Father Ken, I was able to weather Joe's storms until one day when Joe took his anger too far. It was January, 1970, and we were engaged for the third time. He knew I was wary of his pattern of rescinding marriage proposals, so this particular proposal had actually come with an engagement ring. We were sitting in my apartment on a faded blue couch that sagged almost to the floor. My animated voice matched my expansive arm movements as I excitedly told him about my great job interview.

"What did you tell them about yourself?" Joe asked.

I proudly answered, "I told them about my skills and why I thought I would be an asset to their company, and of course I let them know I was engaged to be married."

Joe jumped up off the couch and screamed, "You did what? You've got to be the stupidest person I know. What an idiot. They won't hire someone who's engaged to be married and may leave the company." For the most part, my brain's grey matter took in Joe's comments and accepted them as true. After all, they matched the dim view I had of myself. That time, though, was different, because something sparked red in the-matter-of-fact grey. The intelligent, articulate, A-student, college material part of me combined with my queen-of-the-ringers self took control. I calmly and confidently stood up to face him. I took off my engagement ring and handed to him.

I said softly but emphatically, "If I'm that big of a disappointment to you, and as stupid as you think I am, then we shouldn't get married. Please leave."

Joe wore a shocked expression on his face; his eyes were so wide I could see the white around the brown. He was shaking his head slowly as if to say, *I can't believe this is happening. I can't believe she stood up to me.* He opened his mouth, then finding it empty of words, shut it again. He walked out of the apartment and closed the door softly.

The next day, at my job at the printing company, I let it be known I was again single. By that evening I had a dinner date with one of our clients. I had dates every night for the next two weeks. For some reason, most of my dates wanted to take me out for a lobster dinner. Joe called me daily, wanting to talk, but I was so busy I couldn't find time for him.

Due to plans we had made weeks in advance, I relented and let Joe accompany me to one of my cousin's weddings two weeks after our breakup. At the wedding, it became crystal clear I was a free agent and no longer his beck-and-call girl. Evidently, Joe couldn't stand the situation, because halfway through the reception, he blurted out, "I don't want you dating anymore. If you want to get married, we'll set the date." I smiled and nodded a yes, extremely pleased with myself.

I believed I had clearly won this battle. I stood up to him, and then, on my terms, I took action, which accomplished great results. All in all, I'd had a productive two weeks: a new job, a wedding date, and the satisfaction of a point well made. He was wrong about my doomed interview too; I did get the job working for a subsidiary of Samsonite luggage. The outcome would have been truly perfect if he'd apologized for his outburst and name-calling and promised to never do it again. Perfect doesn't happen too often, so I decided to be satisfied with pretty good. I let Joe off the hook. He was a proud man who wasn't very good at admitting his mistakes. He'd already swallowed a bunch of pride, and I felt no need to shove more demands down his throat. He was smart, and I thought he understood my point about his unacceptable behavior. The good Joe was back, and I was fully engaged once again.

I was excited about the wedding. Michael gave me a hundred dollars. Joe's parents bought me a stunning wedding dress and found an inexpensive florist. Everybody brought food to our big old Mexican wedding. We were married on June 20, 1970, in St. Dominic's Catholic Church. The wooden pews held the bodies of our large Latino families and all our friends. The hundred-year-old church was filled to the brim with loud laughter, flowers, and happy faces. My best friend, Louise, was my maid of honor and Jean a bridesmaid.

I asked Father Ken to marry us. He had helped me navigate through some rough waters. I anticipated a future of smooth sailing thanks to him. I wished to honor him by having him share in my special day. Right at the altar in front of the whole congregation, he planted a big, long kiss on my lips, which surprised bride, groom, and congregation. He left the priesthood the following day. Joe told me later Father Ken had offered to take his place should he reconsider marrying me. I found myself grateful for the end of Joe's irritating phase of rescinding marriage proposals.

CHAPTER 11

Double or Nothing

Marriage didn't change the fact I felt responsible for murdering Mom and the babies. Sandra wasn't around because Dad's intrusive presence had faded through the years, and of course I didn't have sex with strangers because I was now married. Despite Sandra's and Dad's absence, though, I knew I was still a stupid slut, a weak, disgusting, worthless person who didn't deserve love. I kept my "real self" hidden and worked extra hard in my relationships, especially my marriage, to prove I was worthy to be alive.

My survival depended on my ability to lead a double life. In my childhood, it was necessary to have a double self to deal with Dad, but now it was all up to me. I knew I was bad, so I had to be the best wife, friend, sister, and employee or I would be exposed as a fraud. To my way of thinking, I needed this duplicity or I would be left with nothing but shame. I was indeed my father's daughter, and this was the only way I knew how to survive.

The first month, our marriage was heaven. I had married a fun, handsome, intelligent guy. It didn't matter that we were broke and living in a small basement apartment, because we were in love. We came home from work, fell in each other's arms, and made mad, passionate love many times in the space of an hour.

"You're beautiful. You're my woman, and I love to show you off," Joe would often say. He bought my clothes: flamboyant, low-cut, and sexy. My childhood saddle shoes and the teen flats were replaced by high heels. He dressed me for our evenings out so I'd make him proud. I was his "arm candy." The phrase didn't reflect the dignified, wifely role I was seeking, but I didn't say anything because I believed that was what I was worth. I was definitely not going to complain. Whore that I was, I was just thankful to have a husband.

When we did go to parties, Joe's ability to achieve the right tone with everyone present astounded me. Everybody liked Joe, and he became the life of almost every party. He seemed to be entirely comfortable in his ever-changing skin. He was an adept chameleon, blending in perfectly with blue and white collars, rednecks, military uniforms and brown-and-green camouflage, dark pants and brightly colored dresses, and black and white tuxes and faded blue jeans. Joe would and could engage with any age and skin color.

Joan and Rod had exposed me to high-society etiquette, the Good Shepherd Home had introduced me to a variety of races and cultures, and of course I felt comfortable in the Latino community. All this was great, but I still didn't feel comfortable in my body. Maybe because I had spent so much time out of my body, staying inside it felt uncomfortable. Maybe I didn't know who I was and didn't want to find out. Maybe I was afraid I would inadvertently reveal my hidden self, which would be a disaster. For whatever reason, I found myself gravitating to some scared girls like me hiding out in a corner of the room. After Joe made his rounds mingling with every soul in the place, he'd find me. He'd coax, nudge, and pull me out of my shell until I joined him in his fun universe. His free spirit was contagious, and I loved catching it.

There were a couple of aspects of Joe's personality I didn't care for. He liked to flirt. When he was drunk, the flirting became laden with gross sexual innuendo, reminding me of disgusting times with Dad. The harsh shades of the flirty drunk repulsed me, but these times were not enough to color over the rosy glow of my marriage.

The other personality trait nagging at me was his black-and-white thinking. I believe once he decided how he felt about something or someone, he would think, *I'm right, and if you disagree, you're wrong.* Since he always thought he was right, he never had to apologize for anything, because in his mind he hadn't done anything wrong. Once he placed a person or an issue in the wrong column, it was almost impossible for it to ever be right in his eyes again. If you crossed him enough, you weren't just wrong; you were the enemy.

Joe also used the words right and good and the words wrong and bad interchangeably. I think he believed a person couldn't be right/good and wrong/bad at the same time. It fit well with my double self. My bad self was real, and my good self a façade. It even worked with how I viewed my family, including Dad; they were all right/good, which meant I was all wrong/bad. I had an inkling even then that each person was a conglomeration of good and bad, right and wrong. I instinctively knew I didn't agree with Joe's black-and-white thinking, but that didn't make him a bad person or even wrong.

Early on in the marriage, I began to notice little changes in Joe's behavior. In reality, it was his old behavior I'd thought would change when we were married but didn't. Much of the time the nice Joe would show up. He'd make comments approving of the way I looked and the dinner I cooked.

A couple of times, however, he came home late in the evening, drunk, and hadn't called because he "lost track of time." On one of these occasions, I teared up, explaining I had cooked him a special dinner and was hurt he hadn't come home. He gently explained if I'd thought to tell him about the dinner ahead of time, he would have made an effort to be home sooner. He also said, as he was kissing me and taking off my clothes, that I was being too sensitive, and he had every confidence I'd be a more understanding wife in the future. There was definitely something very wrong with his argument, but I didn't know what, so I acknowledged his point and vowed to be better.

Joe continued to be a voracious lover. He couldn't seem to get enough of me. Most of the time, his lovemaking was gentle and caring. Sometimes, though, he didn't seem to remember I was there, or he would unintentionally hurt me. At times his sexual appetite was too large even for me, and I would say no. He was sneaky in that he didn't overtly punish me in any way; he just woke me up in the middle of the night for more sex. As a husband, he explained patiently, he had a right to my body any time he wanted, but because of my history of abuse, he'd try to be lenient with me.

Since I'd never had control of my body in the first place, I thought my husband's expectations reasonable. I sometimes didn't like what was going on, but I thought it was just a part of being married. I loved Joe, I loved making love, and I was lucky to be married.

It soon became clear, however, that Joe and I had very different perceptions of what married life should be. My days of flight were over; I was ready to settle down, build a nest egg, and have babies. Joe, on the other hand, was a married bachelor, a party animal who was determined to continue his erratic, irresponsible lifestyle at his favorite bar.

At the age of twenty, I was young, naïve, idealistic, and dedicated to making my marriage work. I felt my job was simple. I had to make coming home so wonderful, refreshing, and exciting that Joe's life at the bar would seem stale in comparison. I became a super wife, devoted to making my husband happy. Even though we both worked, I cooked delicious meals and served them in a timely manner. I did his laundry, ironed his shirts, and made sure every one of his socks had a mate. I kept the house and myself clean and attractive, and I was a willing and affectionate participant in our lovemaking. I thought my efforts were finally rewarded when, to my surprise and delight, Joe came directly home from work one evening. We had a stimulating discussion over one of my finer dinners.

In the morning, after a great night's sleep, we made tender, passionate love three times. "You're so beautiful, and I love everything about you," he said as he left the house wearing his characteristic smirk. When he phoned me at the end of the day just to say he was thinking about me, I knew then my perseverance had paid off.

But I was wrong. Several hours later, he stumbled into the apartment drunk. He screamed that I was a stupid, incompetent bitch because I left my shoes out and he had tripped over them. I knew I was indeed everything he described. How "stupid" to think I was special enough to make him happy. I wondered how Joe could deem me to be a desirable, lovable person in the morning and a hated, repugnant person by the evening.

Sometime early in the relationship, I'm not sure when, I changed my goal from making him happy to doing everything right so he wouldn't get angry. His mood swings were so severe and unpredictable I felt like I was in a war zone; I never knew when a bomb would drop. My mind continually flashed DANGER as my body braced for the next explosive attack.

Buried deep within me was the knowledge I had chosen a man very much like Dad. Joe, like Dad, was volatile. Though he didn't beat me physically, he left welts on my self-esteem by wounding me with his words. I didn't like his anger, but it was familiar, and I was almost certain I deserved it.

Much like with Dad, I frequently felt my only worth to Joe was as a sexual object. Joe was highly sexed, and often we would have sex four or five times a day (one or two of those times would be "making love"). I was married, so it was permissible to make love with my husband, but often when we had intercourse, I still felt like a whore.

After the first year of marriage, Joe began devouring *Hustler* and other hardcore porn publications. Dad's porn was certainly less graphic than Joe's, but both felt bad. Like Dad, Joe thought looking at the girlie magazines would turn me on. Sometimes it did, but mostly I just felt dirty. He added a dimension to the sex play Dad hadn't used, namely reading graphic letters to the editor. I abhorred this material.

"What do you think, Di? Isn't she beautiful? Look at those amazing tits," Joe would say with admiration. "Wow, isn't she sexy?" I'd then grudgingly look at the picture of a scantily clad woman in a provocative pose. Invariably, the woman in the magazine couldn't have looked less like me. She was almost always blonde, tall, leggy, buxom, and perfect. The more Joe pointed out women he considered beautiful, the more the underlying message to me was "she's sexy and beautiful and you're not." Since my only value to Joe was my outward appearance as a sexual object, which he evidently deemed substandard, my already low self-esteem plummeted.

The making love I loved; the just having sex I tolerated; but the rough, kinky sex was repugnant to me. The nightmare of my childhood had begun again. In order to cope with past and now present abuse, Diana #2, my child shadow-side linked to Dad, came back into my life. Her job was to handle Joe's unhealthy, Dad-like perversions.

Just like I had with Dad, I stood up to Joe on occasion. He liked to bite. After telling him numerous times biting hurt and I wanted him to stop, I finally took action and bit him back. Unbelievably, he didn't bite me anymore after that.

I guess I still possessed a tiny bit of self-respect because there were two sexual activities I simply wouldn't allow. Joe thought it would be fun to tie me up. I never let him do it because I didn't trust that he had my best interests at heart. Tied up, I would be entirely dependent on him for my survival. I wouldn't be able to walk away. He would have total control. I would be at his mercy. I shuddered to think what would happen if he were having one of his merciless days. Dad had done a lot of perverted things to me, but he'd never tied me up.

I also said no to anal sex. Since age five, I was terrified of someone putting something in my buttocks. The fear of course came from feeling Dad's erection pushing on my bottom in my earliest abuse memories. Other than these few exceptions, I handled Joe like I'd dealt with Dad: I split myself in two. To the outside world I showed my healthy, feisty, superwoman side, but with Joe, I was subservient and passive. Just like with Dad, it was easier to let him have his way with me than to fight him.

Joe seemed to have an uncanny ability to sense when I was at the end of my rope, so to speak. When he sensed me pulling away, he would transform into the accepting, gentle Joe I adored. When the fun, spontaneous Joe appeared, I was hooked. He'd take me on adventures. We'd explore Colorado forests and rivers. I'd ask hard nature questions, and Joe would almost always have an answer. We'd laugh and laugh and marvel at how good we felt being together.

Four months into our marriage, we went hunting with Joe's dad, John. We stayed at the home of JC, a relative of John's, and his wife, Lucy. They had a cabin in the mountain community of Leadville. It would be a weekend getaway where I would stay in the cabin with Lucy, and John, JC and Joe would go hunting. JC and Lucy had been married for forty years, and I was interested to see an older married couple in action.

JC was a short, solidly built, soft-spoken man. His round face and ruddy complexion made me think of a jolly elf. His wife was a slender, once-attractive woman now hidden underneath the wrinkles of a hard mountain life. JC wasn't the least bit demanding of her, but Lucy, to my surprise, seemed to cater to his every need. She pulled out his chair, served his breakfast, filled and refilled his coffee, cleared his plate. JC seemed to take her servitude for granted. Not I. I was exhausted just watching her. When the men left to go hunting for the day, Lucy prepared a lunch, fetched all his hunting gear, retrieved and helped him on with his coat. Watching this interchange made me curious. When they were out of the cabin, I asked a question Mom would have probably considered too bold: "Have you always done everything for him?"

She shrugged and said, looking up toward a long-ago memory, "Yes, from the time we were first married, I've done everything. At first it was because I was young and dumb. I thought that was what a good wife was supposed to do. Through the years it just became a habit. Now I'm old, and it's too late to change. Don't follow in my footsteps."

I knew I didn't want to be like Lucy, but my self-esteem was low, and I desperately wanted harmony in my marriage. It took having our first child before I finally put Lucy's advice into action.

When I was five months pregnant, we moved into a two-bedroom brick home located in North Denver. This old house was owned by Joe's grandfather, Alfred. He was a widower who had fathered eleven children. Joe's grandmother, Fabriciana, lovingly called Grandma Fabric, used to complain about her husband, saying, "He won't leave me alone."

Grandpa Alfred came often to our house to be picked up and taken to his doctor's appointments. One day, he was sitting at our kitchen table when I walked past. He uncoiled his body and sprang out, grabbing my arms and pulling me onto his lap. To my horror, he started rubbing my thigh.

I had been sexually abused thousands of times in my life. I was pretty adept at taking almost any form of sexual touch in stride. At that moment, however, my brain uncharacteristically registered horror, then anger. My limbs received an urgent message to fight and then run. My limbs did exactly as they were told. I elbowed him hard in the chest, jumped off his lap, ran out the front door, and sat on the steps.

Grandpa came to the screen door and pleaded with me to come back inside. My body was still filled with adrenaline. I was breathing hard, and my fists and jaw were clenched, ready to continue the fight. My anger was so hot my voice hissed like water dropping on a hot stove. "I'm sorry your wife died, but I'm not going to take her place. Do you understand?" His mouth stopped his pathetic pleading, his eyes turned cold, and his face became a wrinkled sneer, but he turned and walked back into the house. I was mad and had fought back! I won!

Joe's grandfather never touched me again, because I didn't let it happen. I was glad I'd stood up to Grandpa Alfred's unwelcome advances, but as was the case with Dad, it came with a cost. After the incident, the dirty old man's words to me were mean and demeaning. He was highly critical of everything I did or said. With Dad, I always eventually gave in and let him have his way with me; not so with Grandpa Alfred. I never once succumbed to his advances, no matter how mean he became. Even so, the constant barrage of abusive comments took its toll. But, just when Joe and I had decided to move again, I was laid off from my job.

So at the end of my seventh month, still living in Grandpa Alfred's house, I prepared our place for our tiny baby. Joe and I had company over for dinner the night my water broke. We went to bed late. I tried to sleep, but the contraction alarm went off every five minutes. I asked to go to the hospital, but Joe wanted to sleep. I acquiesced and let him sleep for a couple more hours until the pain became more intense than the fear of waking him. I nudged him awake. Finally, a very irritated Joe drove me to the hospital. JJ was born after two hours of hospital labor on July 1, 1971. His formal name is James, but from birth we always called him JJ.

Five days after JJ was born, I joined the La Leche League, a group of mothers who believe in the importance of breastfeeding their children until they wean themselves. For the most part, the females in my family circle were fairly supportive, although Jean thought the length of time I was proposing to nurse excessive, and my mother-in-law had to be won over. The male family members had no opinion on the subject.

I thought nursing was extremely important, and I loved everything about being a mother. Staying home with JJ with the support of other young mothers filled me with joy and peace. Holding, snuggling, and nurturing my precious little boy felt as natural as breathing fresh air. My baby's sweet scent, soft skin, and angelic appearance sent my mind back to a magical part of my childhood—taking care of Vincent and Teresa.

Sometimes, though, when changing JJ's diaper, the nakedness of his innocent body filled my brain with monstrous memories of Dad's sexual assault on my body and soul. Just the thought of hurting a child was not only abhorrent but inconceivable to me. On the other hand, maybe I couldn't be trusted. I realized with a start that I was worried I was going to be abusive like Dad. I also knew I was determined not to be like him. *No, I have a choice. I'm a good mom. I'll never, ever do anything to harm a child's innocence! I'll change this horrible pattern now.* This vow was so important to me I efficiently changed JJ's diapers at record speeds. I didn't even want the appearance of impropriety.

When Joe was good, he was very, very good, but when he was bad, he was horrid. There was something about our newborn that didn't sit well with Joe. Maybe it was because my attention was focused on JJ and not him. Whatever the reason, as JJ filled me up, Joe drained me, leaving me bereft and empty. I was sick of his demands.

One evening I was cooking dinner with JJ in my arms. At four months, my little boy's face was alight with animated curiosity. He was my best audience. When I would say something, my little guy would consider my words carefully, then break into a smirk as if only he knew a secret and was holding back great gales of laughter. "JJ, you're wearing your Daddy's smirk..."

Joe's insistent voice interrupted our conversation, the sound traveling the length of the living room through the dining room and into the kitchen: "Di, get me a beer."

I sighed, turned down the beans, grabbed a cold beer, and walked the length of the long house to deliver a beer to my husband, who was lounging on the couch reading the paper. He briefly looked up, made a hand motion to indicate where I should put his beer, and went back to his paper. I'd just turned the beans back up and was opening the silverware drawer when—

"Oh, Di, turn on the TV for me."

"Oh, for God's sake," I murmured under my breath as I headed to the living room to do his bidding. I'd just crossed the threshold into the kitchen when Joe's words hit me from behind, "What a piece of shit. Di, come and jiggle the wires. The piece-of-shit TV isn't working again."

The heat rose in my chest as my angry thoughts burst into flames. I marched purposefully into the living room to confront Joe. I jiggled the wires with one hand while holding JJ in my arms. I stood defiantly in front of the picture on the screen and said in a low, slow voice, "This is the last thing I'm doing for you." My voice got louder as Joe's eyes opened wider. "I'm not your slave. I'm not Lucy." Joe's mouth hung open in shock as I continued my reprimand. "You're perfectly capable of dealing with the TV. Things have changed; we have a baby now. I know how you are. In a few minutes, you'll be mad because I'm late getting dinner on the table." I turned and walked back into the kitchen. I knew my anger, Lucy's advice, JJ, and my new support system had given me the strength to stand up to him. I had temporarily silenced him, but I had a feeling he wasn't going to change in any permanent way. This was a baby step toward taking care of me.

"It's up to me to change," I murmured to my son. JJ's big brown eyes searched my face, and then his little mouth broke into the biggest smile I'd ever seen.

CHAPTER 12

Move, Baby, Move

For the next six years, the flow of our marriage wove back and forth between moving from place to place and having babies. At the end of 1976, we had moved five times and birthed four children. A baby means soft skin, sweet smells, snuggles, and smiles. Moving means hardship, helplessness, horrendous hassles, and headaches. I loved the baby part of my life, but I wasn't too fond of the moving part.

From the first day of our marriage in 1970, Joe's bar tab and our money problems continued to accumulate. Joe had dropped out of school and was, ironically, working for a credit agency. Since my layoff when I was seven months pregnant with JJ, I'd been a stay-at-home pregnant person. Later when JJ was born in July 1971, I became a bona-fide stay-at-home mom.

In January of 1972, when JJ was just five months old, we moved out of Grandpa Alfred's house into a triplex. Joe had to manage the move alone while I spent five days in the hospital with a tubal pregnancy. Several weeks later, just when I was beginning to feel settled in the triplex, Joe and his friend Steve decided to start a collection agency. I was all for Joe's entrepreneurship, but I thought providing for our family a higher priority. Joe, however, thought his career aspirations more important, so money, or lack of it, was always an issue. I was always fairly good with money, but with me not working and Joe not receiving a salary, I began finagling cash Joe-style. My parents called it "robbing Peter to pay Paul." We were beyond poor and forced to move yet again.

On December 28 of the same year, when I was eight months pregnant, we relocated. Oldest brother Michael had purchased a cute little brick house in North Denver with a fenced backyard. My big brother again came to the rescue by offering us a place to live until we could get our feet on the ground. We were to pay a reasonable rent as soon as possible, but until that time, Michael allowed us to run a tab.

This arrangement suited Joe fine because of his vast experience with bar tabs and financial finagling. I was worried we were robbing Michael to pay for Joe's business decisions and bar bill. I didn't want to take advantage of Michael's generous heart. Joe promised he'd pay him his due, so I relaxed a little. We were to occupy the top floor while Michael and his wife lived in the basement.

I was overwhelmed anticipating the actual move. Joe was working, but luckily John, Joe's dad, had the day off because of President Truman's death. The two of us moved out of the triplex and into Michael's house in one day. When Joe came home from work that night, everything was already in its place. Joe didn't seem impressed, but I thought it quite an accomplishment, especially considering my very pregnant body.

Several months after our move into Michael's house, my cousin's ex-wife, Judy, with whom I had a close relationship, was murdered in Aunt Ruby's duplex, the same duplex we'd occupied after Mom died. I was distraught and shaking uncontrollably as I told Joe of Judy's demise; his response was, "Get over it. You take everything too personally." Judy's murder haunted me with memories of Mom's and the babies' murder.

Joe's lack of sensitivity extended past murder to childbirth. He made it clear with three of our babies' births that they and I revolved around his schedule. Therese Michelle, nicknamed Rese, was born fifteen days after the move on January 12, 1973. The night of her birth, Joe insisted on taking a shower at home even though my contractions were two minutes apart. With Gina, who was born on August 20, 1974, Joe asked the doctor at 7:30 a.m., "How long is this going to take? I have an important meeting at ten o'clock." Luckily, Gina was amenable to Joe's schedule; Joe made the meeting with fifteen minutes to spare.

My children were my joy. Dr. Seuss, snuggling, and music filled our days. I'd stay awake at night creating jingles to use as teaching tools. Joe didn't show much interest in me or the children. His interest in me had to do only with how I looked and my availability to have sex. He was constantly commenting about the importance of not gaining weight. How I looked was my worth to him, and having children wasn't a valid excuse to gain weight. He believed me to be stupid and incompetent.

Maybe he thought stupid applied to all females, because he had very little interest in our daughters. He didn't argue with me about how the girls should be raised. He did have an opinion about JJ, however. One of our biggest disagreements was about how to raise our son. I wanted him to be a well-adjusted child who was able to show his emotions. Joe believed in the adage "boys don't cry." I insisted JJ be allowed to be himself; Joe believed my approach would turn JJ into a sissy and a wimp. His way to handle sadness, fear, pain, and shame was to hide those feelings behind a poker face. Making a snowball out of his feelings, Joe would pick up the soft flakes of his emotions, pat them down, cup them in his hands, roll them into a hard ice-ball of anger, and throw them at me.

While life with my children was wonderful, life with Joe was crazy and unpredictable. We were dirt poor. He always had money for alcohol but not for groceries. Many nights he would return home after closing the bars. He would awaken me from a deep sleep, saying, "Get up now; we have work to do." We'd then embark on a major project like painting a room or organizing a storage space. I'd get to sleep at two or three a.m. and then get up with the kids a few hours later.

The inside story was I couldn't count on him. Invariably, he'd miss the kids' games and performances. He would, more often than not, be a no-show at get-togethers with family or friends. I became quick with excuses and lies concerning Joe's absences, which made me complicit in maintaining our relationship and family façade. Joe, however, remained guiltless and drunk.

I thought him extremely selfish. I still thought I loved him, but I didn't like him much of the time. When Joe was home, he wanted me to be by his side. He'd want me to watch TV with him. "I'm not a fan of television," I'd say, "but I'll sit with you on the couch and read." Joe hated me reading as much as I hated him drinking.

He had hundreds of slides of Vietnam. Some nights he would come home with his head deep in a dark jungle. He wanted me to share in the horror of pictures of mangled bodies and people with limbs shot off. I watched until I couldn't stand watching anymore. Even though every shirt was facing the right way and every sock had a mate, Joe still yelled at me. Cora's optimistic theory had been wrong. The steamy jungle tendrils squeezed Joe's brain until the pressure was so great he saw no other choice than to release it in a flash flood of anger.

His mood swings were extreme. Several Saturdays after dinner as I did the dishes, I'd hear his voice from the living room. "Honey, don't worry about the dishes. Come in here and snuggle with me on the couch."

I loved snuggling, but I was raised to get chores done before relaxing. I'd always answer, "I'll be there just as soon as I finish these dishes; I'm almost done."

He'd insist I join him that instant and abandon the chore. I would comply. On these nights he'd awaken me several times to make love. The next morning he would kiss me on the cheek saying, "You sleep. I'll make breakfast."

The first time this happened, I remember thinking what a sweet, considerate, loving man he was. But after that initial experience, things changed. Wide awake, I listened to his footsteps enter the kitchen. I heard the loud clatter of dishes and the clanging of pans; then I heard the screaming. "You worthless bitch. What a stupid, lousy housekeeper you are; you won't even do the dishes."

From the age of thirteen on, I had made some questionable choices that had often turned into crises. In response to these crises, Michael would roll his eyes, chastise me for being irresponsible, and always bail me out. My big brother's existence was the epitome of a stable, fiscally responsible lifestyle. He received reminders from above that his little sister was leading a life that was his polar opposite. Joe's and my constant arguments about money and his drunken rages and middle-of-the-night pounding surely shattered my brother's sleep, peace, and any hope of positive change. I believed Michael blamed me for our situation, but he suffered in a silence. This spoke loudly to me of his disapproval of my life.

Life continued. Joe was rarely home, so I created a happy life without him. Other moms and I talked and laughed while watching our kids grow. In the spring of 1975, I felt settled, reveling in a house full of kids, a garden full of flowers, and a heart full of contentment. I was Mother Earth with roots providing nourishment to my little ones. I breastfed my children until they weaned themselves, much to the consternation of relatives and friends.

My close connection with my children proved to be a great way to nurse myself back to a semi-stable state. I was a very active stay-at-home mom. I became the leader of our La Leche League chapter, which involved helping new mothers with nursing issues. This group provided me with an incredible support system and some lifelong friends.

I was nursing Gina on a late afternoon in June when Joe burst through the door. This afternoon surprise was out of character for my husband, who had a habit of coming home when the moon was up and the kids were down for the night. I focused on his flushed face, anticipating a problem.

"Is everything all right?" I asked, narrowing my eyes, bracing for the blow.

He said simply, "I bought a house. Do you want to see it?" Since unilateral decisions and winning arguments were specialties of Joe's, what could I say but okay?

On the way to the house, Joe explained it was a foreclosure he'd purchased for the lawyer's fees. Joe stopped in front of a dilapidated brick bi-level in Arvada, a suburb of Denver. "Well, what do you think? It was a steal! I got it for a song!"

What did I think? I thought it wasn't worth stealing. I thought linking it to a song was grossly unfair to music lovers everywhere.

The battered front door hanging outside its frame looked like it wanted to free itself from the house. The house kept the door in its clutches by a single bolt. I thought it interesting that the difference between freedom and captivity should hinge on such a small piece.

Joe walked in like we owned the place, which I realized, to my dismay, we did. The first thing that hit me upon entering was the stench of cat urine and feces. The smell travelled into my nose, up my sinuses, and sat down hard on the back of my throat, stimulating my gag reflex. I pictured a hundred undomesticated cats that had never been exposed to the niceties of the litter box roaming freely through this house for years.

What assaulted my senses next were the mountains of rancid-smelling multicolored and -textured trash that filled the interior of our future home. My mind screamed *evacuate the premises immediately* as I pictured a plethora of dangerous insects lurking beneath the garbage.

My scaredy-cat self was tempted to run, but the queen of the ringers held strong. I had no time for cats of any kind. This situation called for the perseverance of a queen, and I was up to the challenge.

It took two months to get the house presentable for a cleaning party. Tons of trash, buckets of cat feces, yards of urine-soaked carpet, shredded curtains, a half-dozen punched-in doors, and blood-soaked mattresses were removed from the premises. The refrigerator and stove each took two days to clean. We provided food and refreshments for our two parties. One was a cleaning party whose purpose was, among other things, to wash down the walls, and the other was to paint. The parties were great fun for relatives and friends and wonderful for the health and welfare of our house and family. For two months, our neighbors observed us, peeking out of their curtained windows and craning their necks as they mowed their lawns and took out their trash. We moved in and life moved on.

The day after we moved in, a neighbor, Judy, knocked on the newly attached front door. I opened the door to a close friendship. Tall, fair-haired, fair-minded Judy bounced into my life. She later told me the neighbors, including her formerly racist husband, had concerns about Mexicans infiltrating their white neighborhood. After getting acquainted, our families socialized often. They remarked about how grateful they were that white trash had moved out and a wonderfully clean Mexican family had moved in to improve property values in the neighborhood.

Three months after moving in, I was pregnant again. I was excited for another child but concerned about our lack of finances. I'd compiled a wish list in my mind of all the things we needed and hoped for the day we would have some spare cash. That day never seemed to arrive. In Joe's view, money was to be spent on his fun toys or pastimes, not on practical family items. As Joe's time in the bar grew longer and longer, so did my list. On my list were some boring basics such as shoes and clothes for the kids, mattress pads, towels, and so on.

Christmas Day that year was especially stressful. We were broke as usual, I was sleep deprived, and I'd just cooked dinner for our large, extended family. In attendance were Joe's whole family, my oldest brother, Michael, and his wife, and my big brother, Paul, and his wife.

The exceptions to my "no crying" rule were my highly hormonal pregnancies; I had no control over the tears. The activities, lack of sleep, and my pregnancy combined to make me feel exhausted, overwhelmed, and emotional. I must have looked exactly how I felt because everyone encouraged me to lie down except for brother Paul, who said, "Di, aren't you going to try out the new hairdryer I got you for Christmas?"

"Oh, Paul, do you want me to try it now?"

"Yup, see how you like it!" he said with his best you-can't-refuse-me-it's-Christmas face.

With a deep sigh, I plugged in the dryer and turned it on. A bill shot out of the dryer and fluttered to the floor. I picked up the one-thousand-dollar bill and burst into tears.

"Oh, Paul, I don't believe you. You shouldn't have," I sobbed. "Thank you, thank you so much!" I yelled and kissed the bill. My wish list was nonexistent for the next two years because my dear, dear brother gave me another thousand dollars the next Christmas as well.

Nine months flew by, and soon it was time for my fifth—counting the baby girl I gave away—labor of love to be born. Mandy took fifteen long, grueling hours to be born. Joe, to his credit or his cosmic debt, was there for every minute. Mandy, to my immense relief, was born on June 28, 1976. One more day and she would have arrived on the thirteenth anniversary of the murders.

The pregnancy had been hard on my body. The doctor recommended I have my tubes tied because of problems with hemorrhaging. I consented so I could stop the bleeding, all the while continuing to bleed emotionally at the thought of having no more biological children after the procedure.

I sat stagnating in my house, wearing my bland, shapeless, frumpy clothes, my face devoid of any makeup. I was grieving the end of my childbearing years. The thought of no more babies blanketed me in a thick, grey, depressive fog.

One morning in July, the sun's rays came streaming through the windows of my mind. The thought of "no more babies" was the same, but the feelings coloring my vision were the vibrant tones of freedom. My body felt light with the thought I would never have to balloon up again with pregnancy.

I bounced out of bed and put on my cutest green shorts and a brightly printed camp shirt. I was young enough not to need blush for my cheeks or lipstick for my lips, but I did accentuate my eyes with velvety black eyeliner and extended my lashes with the latest Avon mascara.

I arranged for a babysitter and walked out into the bright summer day. I'd decided I needed a new look. After getting my first perm, I emerged two hours later a new woman. I was walking near the bank, with a bounce in my step, when a man passed me and did a double-take. He stopped, turned around, caught up with me, and tapped me on the shoulder.

"Excuse me. I just need to tell you that you're beautiful," he said,

I gave a disbelieving gasp but recovered and squeaked out, "Thank you."

The man smiled, nodded, and went on his way.

I stood for several moments, my mouth open in astonishment. I'd been told I was beautiful by men many times in my life, but the comment, at best, was usually laden with sexual undertones. At worst the comment was followed by abuse. This comment came from a stranger with no strings attached. His words were pure in their giving, and for the first time in many years, I actually believed I was, or could be, beautiful.

Me and Fibber McGee

In late August or early September of 1976, I was dealt a crushing blow so severe that at times I thought I might not recover. Gary Gilmore was sentenced to be executed in 1977 in the state of Utah. He was the first person to be executed in the United States in the ten years since Dad's execution in 1967. Colorado's newspapers gave Dad first-page status, while Gary was relegated to the third and fourth pages.

Dad's story and picture infiltrated the media. Everywhere I turned, I came face-to-face with my history. Dad stared at me from the television and newspapers. For the first time, I saw a picture of his grave sitting among the other graves in the prison cemetery. His story and mine went out over the airwaves into my ears and sat in my brain and on my heart. My dreams transformed into monstrous nightmares, endless horror-film footage of Dad abusing me in all ways at all ages. I saw him acting out his perversions in living color night after night. I was afraid to sleep, which left me exhausted.

One rare afternoon, when the kids were all miraculously napping, I took advantage of the opportunity for a short siesta. The sun's rays streamed through the living room window, laying down a pool of warmth on the orange shag carpet. I stretched out on the floor like a cat sunning itself. *A tiny catnap couldn't hurt*, I remember thinking as I drifted off to sleep.

As usual, the second I closed my eyes, I was catapulted into a dream. In my mind's eye, I needed to go to the grocery store, but I was dreading taking all the kids. For some reason, Dad was visiting that day. He was sitting with me on the couch as I explained my dilemma.

"Diana," he said, his golden voice dripping like honey. "I'd be happy to watch the kids while you go to the store. Take your time," he added, and patted my knee reassuringly.

"Okay, Dad, I won't be long," I said as I grabbed my purse.

As I left the house and stepped out into the September sunshine, I felt free and unencumbered. Almost immediately, though, my steps slowed as my floating spirits sank to the bottom of my stomach. I was gripped with an intense feeling I was forgetting something important. I was almost to the car when terror struck. I remembered what was so important: Dad was a pedophile!

I raced wildly toward the house and flung open the door, screaming, "No! Stay away from my children. Get out. Get out of my house now. You'll never hurt my babies."

I woke up panting, screaming bloody murder, sweat pouring down my face. I'd awakened my precious babies, and they were screaming as well. I was relieved to hear their innocent wails. My babies were safe, and Dad was dead.

That was the end of my daytime naps. I'd go to bed exhausted, but I was afraid to sleep. Often when I would succumb, Dad's monstrous ghost would appear, and I'd scream Joe awake. He was gentle and compassionate at these moments, many nights holding me until I fell back to sleep. I was constantly sick to my stomach and had trouble concentrating as Dad continued to invade my life.

At this point, I summoned my shadow-side, Sandra, the part of me that acted out when I was faced with Dad issues. Sandra hadn't been in my life since I met Joe. With her emergence, six years of monogamy ended. She came when she sensed my hopelessness about Dad. She arrived during the first week of the media blitz to see if she could help deflect some of my feelings by acting out sexually. My self-worth started falling into even more pieces.

For the sake of my already fragile survival, I began to have an affair. My paramour picked up each piece of me and patched me back together with words like, "You're so smart. I love the way you think. I love your smile, your voice, everything about you. Talk to me; tell me how you feel. I'm listening."

Joe figured out I was having an affair and decided to try to fix our marriage. Of course, I stopped the affair immediately. Since Joe's work hours were flexible, he started coming home to "surprise" me multiple times a day. Joe, the guy who never seemed to be home, suddenly transformed into the guy who was always home. When he was home, he was home watching me. He shadowed me. He appeared in the kitchen to help with the dishes, and he showed up in the laundry room to fold clothes with me. When I emerged from a shower, he was holding a towel in which to wrap my naked body.

After several days of Joe's daytime home visits, I pleaded with him to give me room to breathe, but he continued to glue himself to my side. Between Dad invading my space by night and Joe invading my space by day, I was suffocating. I needed help! I begged Joe to let me see a therapist. His pat answer had something to do with not airing our dirty laundry in public. I told him the media had already hung me and my family's dirty laundry out to dry. He said, "We can solve our own problems and certainly don't need a stupid therapist in our business."

When I was in elementary school, the whole family would gather round the radio to listen to a comedy show called *Fibber McGee and Molly*. The McGees had a hall closet packed floor to ceiling with Fibber McGee's stuff. In the course of the show, Fibber would inevitably turn the doorknob. Molly would yell no. The audience would hear a good thirty seconds of crashes, yells, moans, protests, and more clanking metal. We'd all laugh, imagining Fibber McGee buried under an avalanche of his possessions. Between shows, I'd imagine him cramming all the articles back in the closet, heaving his body into the door, inching it closed, and with sweat pouring down his face, latching the handle, only to open up the closet the next time. It seemed to be a lot of work just to get a laugh.

My life was like Fibber McGee's closet: stuffed, smashed, jammed into my mind with the door closed and locked. A stranger named Gary Gilmore stole the key and opened the door just a crack. The door swung wide, slapping the wall. I felt like the contents were spring-loaded as a slingshot of smells, sights, sounds, and sensations slammed into my gut. I was pushed down to the ground, buried under a monstrous mountain of memories. The closet scene in real life wasn't funny. I was terrified of feeling. I felt like I'd contracted a bad case of the flu complete with out-of-control vomiting and diarrhea, a mess I could never clean up.

One morning, after a week of arguing with Joe, I finally broke down crying. Five-year-old JJ, who had never seen me cry, said, "I'll help you, Mommy." He promptly took Rese, four, and Gina, two, downstairs. He entertained them for two hours so I could talk with Jean on the phone. He interrupted me only a couple of times to get snacks of juice and crackers.

I was crying so hard, tears were raining down on Mandy. I was holding a sopping wet baby in my arms, but I couldn't seem to stop the downpour. Jean couldn't understand me through the torrent of tears and the gulping sobs. After ten years, the dam had broken. The wall had crumbled, and the water flooded my world. I was drowning. Jean's voice floated gently over the phone line, throwing me a life preserver of hope.

When I got off the phone, I felt better. I would survive this time in my life for my sake and for my children's sake. Dad no longer had the power to hurt or control me. Dad wouldn't win. And Joe didn't have the power to stop me from going to see a therapist. That afternoon, I decided I didn't want to continue to feel this way. I wanted to heal.

After I made that decision, I formulated a plan. I knew it would be much easier if Joe supported my decision, but frankly I didn't care how he responded. When Joe came home from work, I was sitting calmly at the kitchen table drinking tea. I had a cold beer waiting for him.

I motioned to the table and said, "Please, sit. We need to talk." He sat and I talked. "You have two choices. We can stay married and I'll get help, or we can divorce and I'll get help."

Joe said, "We'll stay married, and you can get help."

Diann with her children (l to r) Gina, JJ, Mandy, Rese, 1976.

PART II

HEALING

CHAPTER 14

Sharing My Skeleton Story

I found myself in the office of psychologist Dr. Keller, who worked for Jefferson County Mental Health. Dr. Keller stood about five feet seven inches, and the day I met her she was garbed in a grey skirt and sweater. Her clothes, together with her pale, translucent skin, reminded me of an overcast sky. Her face was all angles: long, sharp nose, V-shaped eyebrows, straight mouth, and dark hair pulled tightly back into a bun. The greyness and the angles mirrored the heavy edges of my mood. I needed to be surrounded by pastels, the soft, light colors of empathy and understanding. I searched her face, and when I found two small brown eyes that exuded gentle warmth, I was finally able to take in a full breath. I exhaled and collapsed in a chair across from her.

"So, Diann, why are you here today? And what would you like to get from therapy?" she inquired.

Since my crying jag with Jean, I had gingerly and painstakingly picked up the jagged pieces of my experiences and stuffed them back into the closet of my mind. If I answered Dr. Keller's question, I'd crack open the closet. I was Molly McGee saying to myself, *No, don't open it up.* The pressure was building. Memories filled with emotions strained to get out. My mind surged toward the knob, and a keyhole's worth of words escaped.

"Well," I said, "I'm not okay." The door then sprang open with a crack. There was a crash, and out gushed a torrent of words. The sentences just tumbled out, flooding the room. "My life is out of control. Look at my hands. They're shaking so hard I had trouble filling out the paperwork. I can't sleep because when I close my eyes, I see my Dad—terrible pictures of Dad. I can't even take a nap. I'm exhausted all the time. I can't think or focus. I have trouble concentrating, and I feel like I'm going crazy. And if I go crazy, I won't be able to take care of my kids, and all I ever wanted to be was a mother. And..."

"Diann!" Her voice, a piercing whistle in the air, signaled me to stop my runaway train of thoughts. I stopped to listen to her faraway voice tunneling through the avalanche of emotions. "Diann, what triggered this intense reaction?"

I was being buried alive. Then, as suddenly as the panic began, it ended, and grey numbed my body. My flattened, frostbitten sentences, severed from feelings, began my story. It felt like I was reading a grocery list as I told her about Gary Gilmore's pending execution, which caused our family to be in the news again. I told her my dad was the last person executed in the United States in the last ten years, and he'd been executed for murdering half of my family. I added to the list as an afterthought, "Oh, and Dad molested me." The skeleton of my story had fallen out of the closet. A grotesque pile of bare-bone facts of my childhood lay on the floor, in front of Dr. Keller, waiting for her comments.

I stopped my detached monotone and looked into the doctor's face. I was afraid I had given her too much information, because her mouth hung open and her eyes had gone wide. She sat, statue still, staring at me for a long time. Her voice didn't speak, but the incredulous look on her face said, *Oh, my God, what am I getting myself into?*

In slow motion, I watched her face change. Her open mouth slowly closed, lips firmly touching, giving an appearance of determination and confidence. The white-edged fear in her eyes dissolved into the soft brown of compassion. She nodded her head in understanding. *My story isn't too much for her. I'm not a lost cause. She knows how to help me!*

I breathed a sigh of relief and waited impatiently for Dr. Keller to give me some urgently needed answers. When the doctor's mouth started moving again, it formed questions instead of answers. She asked me to fill in some gaps in my grocery-list litany. "Your trembling hands. How long has that been going on?"

"Oh, I've had tremors in both hands since the murders. But it's only when I'm really stressed out that they start shaking like this." I pushed my vibrating hands out in front of me. I felt like a schoolchild presenting my detached hands for show and tell.

After getting a better understanding of my background and the specific problem, she asked me a question. "How do you feel about your dad?"

"I love my dad," I answered without hesitation.

"Do you have other feelings about your dad?" she asked.

"I don't know," I replied.

And so it started—six months of weekly sessions where Dr. Keller, with tender tugging, consistent coaxing, and persistent pulling and prodding, helped me begin the healing process. It was the beginning of my salvation.

At first, I was like a skittish, abused puppy, peeking out from my hiding place. I would come out tentatively to taste an offered morsel only to turn and run back to my safe spot. After many sessions, when I finally felt safe and connected enough to Dr. Keller, I got the courage to admit my shameful truth to her.

"I killed Mom and the babies."

The good doctor just sat there calmly and asked, curiously, "Really, how did you do that? I thought your dad murdered your mom and your siblings."

"Well, he did, but I could've stopped him," I stated emphatically.

"How could you have stopped your dad?" she inquired.

"I don't know."

"How old were you?"

"Thirteen."

"You were a child. How much control did you have over your dad?"

Despite the fact that I thought the doctor was leading me to a place I didn't want to go, I found myself thinking about being thirteen, which was thirteen years ago. I'd been a little kid without power to control anything, much less the most powerful person in my family. "None, I guess," I said in surprise.

"So you had no control over your dad. Who killed your mom and the babies?"

"Dad killed them."

"How do you feel about your dad murdering your mom and the babies?"

"Sad."

Just when I was on a roll with my short answers, Dr. Keller changed the subject. "How do your siblings and relatives feel about you?"

"They think I'm a screw-up. They tolerate me because they have to; I'm family. They think I'm bad."

"What do they know about the sexual abuse?"

"They think it happened only once."

"What would happen if you told your story to everyone who is important to you?"

"I don't know. We don't talk about things like that."

"What would be the worst that could happen if you were to share your story?"

"They wouldn't believe me. They'd think I'm a screw-up. They'd blame me for Mom's death."

The wise doctor retorted, "You already think that's what they believe. What would you have to lose?"

"Nothing, I guess."

"So would you be willing to talk to each person?"

"I guess so. Okay."

Dr. Keller was sure the assignment would be a healing process for me. I was just as sure it'd merely reaffirm my badness. Because Michael was my oldest and most respected brother, I thought him the perfect person to prove to Dr. Keller that I was worthless. A week after she handed out this assignment, I called him.

"Michael, would you come over for lunch? I'd like to talk to you about something."

He said, "Sure, when?"

"Now," I said, wishing simultaneously that I'd said *never*.

What had I done? I could call him back and tell him I couldn't talk to him because I had to throw up. I could borrow a move from Joe and rescind my offer. I could run away. I could tell him I was kidding and I had nothing to share.

The insistent sound of the whining phone brought me back to the kitchen, begging me to put it back to sleep in its cradle. I looked at my hand; it reminded me of the movie *The Hand* I'd seen at the home, a detached limb I had no control over. It was trying to squeeze the life out of the phone. I dropped the handset as if it were scorching hot. It fell clattering on the counter. I picked it up and placed it tenderly in the cradle and collapsed into the kitchen chair. I propped my head in my hands, elbows on the table, and watched the door.

Finally I heard the sound of Michael's confident footsteps and his firm knock on the door. "Come in," I said, inviting my oldest brother in to see the real me.

Michael walked into my kitchen, sat down at my table, looked at me expectantly, and said, "What's up, Di?"

Michael had Dad's solid frame, dark eyes, wavy hair, and square jaw. I stiffened when I glimpsed his Dad-like features but then melted immediately into the warm glow of his easy posture and searching face.

I took a big breath and said, "You know Dad sexually abused me the night Mom died, right? Well, what you don't know is that Dad had been sexually abusing me from the time I was five until that night."

Michael's eyes went wide, and in them I could see "when, where, why, and how" questions.

"When I was five, he took me out of bed and into the bathroom next to the kitchen to fondle me. Then he'd abuse me in the attic and in the car when he was collecting papers. When we moved onto 23rd, he molested me in the basement. You know that time he ran away for two months? That was after the first time he had intercourse with me. I told a friend, who told a teacher, who told Father Ronney, who confronted Dad and Mom. He left all of us three days later.

"After he came back, it was intercourse as many times as possible. He threatened to kill me if I told. Every Sunday, in between Masses, he'd molest me at the foot of their bed. When I was thirteen, I couldn't stand it anymore, and I ran away. Aunt Lily and Uncle Tom talked to Mom and Dad. Mom threatened to call the authorities if it happened again. She told Jean to watch out for me with Dad. You know what happened that night."

Michael's open, peaceful face turned stormy. His jaw rippled, his fists balled, his eyes flashed lightening, and his voice thundered. "That monster! How could he? If I'd known, I'd have stopped him. I should've known. I should've protected you. That bastard! If I'd only known, I wouldn't have taken you to see him. I wouldn't have taken anybody. I can't believe we visited him every Sunday. That dirty, filthy, rotten bastard!"

His anger startled me. He was mad at Dad. He thought Dad was bad, not me. He didn't think it was my fault. He thought it was Dad's fault. Twenty-one years of carrying the heavy guilt and shame for Dad drained out of my system. Warm relief flooded my empty spaces.

So, if it wasn't totally my fault, how could he do that to his little girl whom he supposedly loved? For the first time in my life, there was an ember of the unfamiliar emotion of anger directed at Dad. *That bastard*, I said in my brain, because I knew Dad would never allow me to voice profanity out loud.

"Now do you understand why I've been such a screw-up? Why I've been so troubled?" I asked.

Michael stood and gently pulled me to my feet. I fell into his warm embrace. Michael's look and arms wrapped around me. "I love you, little sis. I understand. Thanks for sharing..." His voice began to break, and he couldn't finish his sentence.

I was crying. Michael was crying. We were holding each other as the tears splashed on the floor. "I miss them, Mom and the babies," I whispered. Both Michael and I were sobbing now, releasing years of stuffed tears, finally acknowledging our profound grief and loss. Holding each other, rocking back and forth, we also acknowledged our love for one another. We stood there a long time, encircled by a close family bond and shared history. When I finally took my seat, I sank down in the soft security of my brother's love.

I had more to discuss, so I said, "Michael, sometimes you seem so disgusted with me."

"Di, it's not you I have a problem with. It's Joe. He's fiscally irresponsible. He's never paid one cent of the rent he owes me. He doesn't take care of you or the children. He treats you like dirt. I'm disgusted with him. I've kept my mouth shut because he's your husband. I don't like the guy. You're different. You I love. You deserve more."

"I know," I lied, not yet fully knowing, but for the first time in my life starting to examine the validity of Michael's opinion of Joe. I could see Michael had some legitimate points. But didn't he know that if Joe was all bad, I would have left a long time ago? Michael didn't know the whole Joe. He wasn't aware that several times through the years on my birthday, Joe had gone to great lengths to learn my schedule in order to have a huge bouquet of flowers delivered to me in the middle of the day. He didn't see the good Joe—a loving, caring, spontaneously fun man.

I did talk with Joe that night about the rent we owed, and within a month, we were making payments to Michael. Within six months, Michael was paid in full. My talk, it turned out, had paid off in more ways than one. Speaking with Michael encouraged me to speak with my other brothers and sister.

The organized part of me wanted to share my story with my siblings in order from oldest to youngest. I wanted them to finally know what had happened between Dad and me. Jean should have been next but was inaccessible because she was living out of state. Her husband was in the oil and gas business, requiring their family to move to a different state about every two years.

Al, the next on the list, was constantly changing addresses. He was a lone spirit wrapped up in his own journey and electing to have infrequent contact with his family. In 1976, both Jean and Al lived in California. I thought about calling but then decided talking to everyone in person was more important than order.

Paul was in town, so I'd talk to him next. I knew it would be some time before I'd be able to see Patrick and Lee, my youngest brothers. They were living a remote and isolated existence in a Hare Krishna commune in West Virginia. Patrick, my childhood playground buddy, who was an eleven-year-old at camp on the day of the murders, had admitted he was a lost and lonely teenager. His out-of-control drug use scared him. He started searching for a solution. He found his answer at the age of nineteen when he joined the Hare Krishna movement. This organization provided him with a sense of belonging and a structured, drug-free environment.

Lee, Jean's charge, who'd been only eight at the time of the murders, had not only lost Mom, but two years later Jean, his surrogate Mom, had left. As an adolescent, he was following in Patrick's footsteps. Patrick, concerned about his little brother, convinced him Hare Krishna was the way to go. A year after Patrick became a member, Lee, at seventeen, followed suit. Hare Krishna was definitely not what I wanted or needed in my life, but who was I to judge what was right for my younger brothers? Who was I to judge any of my siblings? All of us were trying to cope with our history in the best way we knew how. I was dealing with it by following Dr. Keller's advice and telling my story.

The following week, I met with Paul. When I told him about the incest, Paul's reaction was very similar to Michael's. He was livid with Dad for abusing me. "If I'd known, I'd have stopped him. I'd have protected you." And then he said the words I craved to hear. "I love you, Di."

Bolstered by the outpouring of love and understanding I'd received from Michael and Paul, I visited Aunt Ruby at her home. Since my apology, Aunt Ruby and I were close, but as close as we'd become, I'd never shared details of my abuse with her. I began my story with, "You know, Dad abused me since I was five. He started with fondling."

"No, I didn't know. Oh, my poor Diana, you were just a baby." At this point I looked up to see my aunt's usual emotional response; tears were streaming down her face.

Her constant waterworks continued throughout our afternoon together. Occasionally she'd stop me in mid-sentence, grab and hug me, and utter words in her typical dramatic style, "Oh, my poor, poor Diana."

It was clear my aunt was very angry at Dad and saw me as his victim, but her constant tears and labeling me as "poor Diana" made me uncomfortable. I was more comfortable with her exasperated "you're a screw-up" look. I even found myself yearning for her to ask, "Why can't you be more like Jean?"

With the story told, I stood up, a little deflated. I was about to leave with my usual parting comment—*Yes, Auntie, I love you too*—when Aunt Ruby said in a serious tone, "I never told you what your mother told me that week you ran away."

I stopped and turned. Barely breathing, I asked, "What did she say?"

"She told me she was going to do something about Lou's abuse. She said she was going to find a way to protect you. She'd been looking into finding a foster home for you."

My ears heard the words, but my mind had trouble processing their meaning. I stood there for so long with my mouth gaping open that Aunt Ruby put her hand on my shoulder and said, "Diana, are you okay?"

My racing mind suddenly caught up with her words, and I felt a warm wash of relief. It was as if the stranglehold of a lie had loosened its grip on my thoughts. "Yes," I said, barely suppressing an out-of-control giggle, "I'm absolutely okay."

For years, I'd made excuses for why Mom hadn't done anything to protect me. One of my favorite justifications was how could a mother sacrifice nine kids for the sake of one? I used to convince myself she had no choice because she was a stay-at-home mom raising ten kids with no means of support. I even kept thinking she believed Dad had stopped abusing me after her last confrontation with him; that she hadn't known it was still going on. Deep down in my soul, though, I was afraid I wasn't lovable enough to deserve Mom's protection. Now, I was hearing words for the first time from Mom that said *I love you so much. You matter to me. I'll do what I can to protect you.*

I hugged my aunt tightly and said, "Thank you so much for letting me know. It means the world to me that Mom was trying to help me." I left the duplex saying with feeling, "Yes, Auntie, I love you too."

On the way home, I sang to myself, *I matter because Mom loved me and wanted to keep me safe.* I repeated this mantra in my head over and over again. At thirteen, I probably would have been furious with Mom for considering foster care for me, but at twenty-six, the thought of her intended actions filled me with gratitude and love.

I talked next to Aunt Lily. Aunt Lily knew a bit more than the others about the abuse because she and Uncle Tom took me in the night I ran away. They were the ones who confronted Dad that night. After hearing more of what had happened, Aunt Lily expressed her anger with Dad and love for me just like everyone else with whom I'd talked.

Aunt Lily, though, kept focusing on the night I ran away. She felt an immense amount of guilt about that night. "Diana, we thought we knew your dad well. It never occurred to us he'd be capable of such a thing. I knew the situation was bad. I just didn't understand how bad it was. If I'd known, I never would've sent you home. I'm so sorry I sent you home."

"Aunt Lily, it wasn't your fault. I didn't tell you about Dad's threats to kill me."

"You told me about the abuse. You begged me not to talk to your parents. You begged me not to send you home. I should've listened, but I didn't. I shouldn't have sent you home. Maybe everyone would be alive today. I'm so sorry."

Aunt Lily wasn't much for mushy sentiments or hugging, but that day I felt she needed both. I gave her a big hug and told her I loved her.

Every week I went to therapy and reported talking to a sibling or a relative. Every session, Dr. Keller would ask, "How did [fill-in-the-blank] feel after you told them your story?"

"They were angry at Dad and loving toward me."

"How did their response make you feel?"

"Glad to hear they loved me and didn't blame me."

"How did it feel to hear they were angry at your dad for abusing you?"

"Good. It felt really good."

"Tell me about your anger, Diann."

I paused here because I knew what she wanted me to say. She was hinting that I should be angry with Dad. I was angry about what the murders had done to my family, but I wasn't ready to talk about it. I didn't know how I felt about the abuse. I hated the incest, but sometimes it felt good. So maybe I'd unintentionally given Dad the wrong impression. Maybe if it hadn't felt good, I would've stopped him.

That was what I thought, but what I said to Dr. Keller was, "Well, for a long time I was angry with Aunt Ruby for trying to be Mom, for telling me what to do and for putting me in the Good Shepherd Home. I was angry with Mother Angela for her strict rules and making my first four months in the home miserable. I was angry with my foster mom for saying I was part of the family but treating me like a nanny." Then I looked at Dr. Keller with a satisfied smile.

"Are you angry with anybody today?"

"Most days I'm angry with my husband. He stands me up. He drinks too much. He's not there for me or the kids. Is that what you mean?"

"We can talk about that if you want. But I'm wondering if there isn't someone you're angry with today, someone connected with your past abuse."

"I don't know."

"You think about it, and we'll talk about it next session."

I was stuck. There were some things I wouldn't or couldn't talk about with Dr. Keller I knew she wanted me to be angry with Dad for sexually abusing me. It had helped that everyone I'd told about the abuse was outraged at Dad. I was angry at Dad for hurting my family, but at some level I still felt responsible. No one had blamed me, but I was still blaming myself.

I was ashamed to tell my therapist that sometimes my body had enjoyed what had happened to me. I couldn't be totally angry with Dad when my body had responded. I couldn't tell Dr. Keller about my alter ego, Sandra. I couldn't imagine saying, *You know, Dr. Keller, I have sex with strangers when Dad invades my dreams or when life's going too well.* I couldn't explain to Dr. Keller that I was BAD and when things were going too well in my life, I had to knock myself down and sabotage myself. I didn't have the words to tell her about the "ugly face" I saw in the mirror before I would act out. I couldn't let her know about Joe's obsession with sex, porn, and strip clubs and that I felt I had to participate in the sexual part of our married life. I wasn't able to confide that the lifestyle Joe and I were leading was reinforcing Sandra's role in my life.

I couldn't tell Dr. Keller about much of my life, but I did want to be a good patient. The doctor wanted me to talk about anger linked to the abuse, so I racked my brain to come up with someone who fit my assignment.

When the light bulb came on in my head, I picked up the phone and called St. Dominic's to locate Father Ronney.

CHAPTER 15

A Reincarnated Catholic

I knew Father Ronney hadn't been the pastor at St. Dominic's for years, but it was a place to start. "I'm calling to see if you know how to reach Father Ronney. He used to be a priest there."

The person on the other end said, "You're in luck. He's here visiting this week. Let me see if I can connect you."

Before I could change my mind, a familiar voice came on the line. "Father Ronney speaking. How may I help you?"

Yes, I'd heard him correctly. The question sizzled through the phone line, catching me off guard. Anger pushed on my temples. *What a joke! Are you actually offering to help me? You're years too late!* I felt like screaming, but I said, "Father Ronney. This is Diana, Lou M.'s daughter."

There was silence on the other end. I finally said, "Father Ronney, do you remember me?"

Father Ronney cleared his throat and said, "Yes, of course I remember. What can I do for you?"

"I'd like to get together and talk."

There was another long silence, which ended in a stilted, unenthusiastic, two-word response. "Of course," he said.

We agreed to meet the next day at one of the church offices. My taut nerves were like guitar strings tightened to the point of breaking. My legs wanted to run, but my brain's determination told my hand to knock on the door.

"Come in," said Father Ronney. I recognized this voice. It matched the tone and tenor of the voice that meted out my weekly penance at my childhood confessions.

I opened the door to see a wrinkled, slightly stooped version of my childhood memory of him sitting safely behind a desk. Time slowed as we both stood facing each other. Tears of pain came, pushing behind my eyes. I bit my lips, trying to keep my emotions at bay. My heart was beating wildly, and all the while my body felt like collapsing. A savage scream crawled up my throat only to be shoved down by a few gulps.

"Have a seat," he said, motioning to a chair across from him. "You're looking well. How are you?"

I had in mind to say fine, but what came out was, "You knew what was going on. You knew what Dad was doing to me. Why didn't you help me?" A staring contest ensued; the man who happened to be a priest stared at me and I stared back, demanding an answer.

I won the contest, for his eyes fell with his voice, a man feeling shame for his behavior. "I'm sorry," he said softly, "but my hands were tied."

His voice then became stronger and more defiant, more priest-like. "I had to follow the Church rules. The seal of confession is absolute."

Before I could stop myself, the words jumped out. "Even with the seal of confession, you could've done something, said something to help me. Week after week, you heard my confession of adultery and you gave me penance. You made me feel like it was my fault Dad was abusing me. You did nothing. You said nothing. You were Dad's confessor too. I know Dad. He was a devout Catholic. He would've confessed to you that he was abusing me. You knew what was going on from both of us. When I thought I was pregnant because of Dad, you talked to my parents but still did nothing to stop it. All that happened was Dad ran away, leaving us destitute. When he came back after leaving the family for two months, you knew from both of our confessions he was still molesting me. Why didn't you tell me to tell someone? You talked to Dad right after the murders. You talked to Dad in prison. You talked to Dad before he was executed. Why didn't you talk to me? Why didn't you help *me*?

Father Ronney looked down at his hands and said, "I'm sorry. I did what I thought was right."

I said to myself, *You weren't right; you were morally wrong.*

I stood up at this point in the conversation and said out loud, "Thanks for your time." I walked out of the church office and Father Ronney's life.

Confronting Father Ronney and seeing a little remorse was satisfying, even empowering. But in the end, it was my anger toward Father Ronney's use of Church doctrine as his rationalization for not helping me that provided the catalyst for change. If the Catholic Church thought the seal of confession was more important than protecting a child from sexual abuse, then the Church was totally failing its people. If the Church, as

I saw it, presented God as a rigid, judgmental, fear-based, pontificating type, then I needed to search for a different view of God. I needed to find a belief system that felt right and would make sense in my life. Just as the Catholic doctrine prevented Father Ronney from helping me, so would my continued adherence to Catholic tenets prevent me from helping myself. I had to find a philosophy I could live with.

Many of the beliefs I lived by as a child didn't even come close to explaining my life. I had a lot of questions for the Catholic Church. Why would a devout Catholic family like mine have to endure so much tragedy and suffering while other, less pious families experience heaven on earth? Why would a church-going family man commit incest with his young daughter? Why would an innocent little girl be sexually abused and then be made to confess the abuse as if it were her fault? Why would any organization think it right to scare a child with the concept of hell complete with devils and fire? What sense does it make to have a system of mortal and venial sins without a way to help troubled people? Why let people off the hook with confession instead of helping them change? Why can't you talk directly to God? Why are Church rules more important than people? How do you explain killing babies or the murder of a little boy so good and loving he gives his toys away at Christmas? How is it possible that my good, religious, loving, pregnant mom could be killed? What kind of philosophy preaches anger and fear instead of teaching love? I set out to find a belief system that would provide me with a new way of thinking.

It seemed like the moment I began my search, Kathy Heller, my friend and mentor from La Leche League, told me about a wonderful lady named Ruby Carter. "She's supposed to be a psychic with incredible insights. It might be fun to visit her one day."

I said, "When?"

The following week, in addition to a La Leche League meeting, a session with Dr. Keller, and my motherly and wifely duties, I squeezed in a meeting with Ruby Carter. Kathy and I knocked on her door in her home in Arvada. A pleasantly plump older woman with greying hair opened the door.

"Come in, come in," a soothing voice said.

Her expressive face was the real invitation. Her smile radiated a sunshine welcome. Her face, filled with the right kind of wrinkles—smile wrinkles, not worry wrinkles—spoke of joy and peace simultaneously. Her eyes made all my skepticism and distrust melt instantly into ease and comfort. The kind, gentle love exuding from those eyes said, *You're safe here.*

Kathy spoke to her first, and then it was my turn. The next half hour was amazing. She knew many details about my family. I thought her insights nothing short of incredible, but it wouldn't have mattered if she had every fact wrong. It didn't matter to me either if her information came from earthly or cosmic sources. What I wanted was a different perspective, a way to view my history in a positive light. I needed a seed of a belief system that would help me grow. Ruby provided everything I needed and more. Her presence filled me with healing hope, and her voice transported me to heaven.

"My, my!" she said in amazement. "You have more spirits in the hereafter than I've ever seen." She paused calmly, observing the scene. "I see a woman with red hair and green eyes, and she's smiling." *Mom!* "She has her hand on your right shoulder. There's a very short woman next to her with a big smile and snow-white hair." *Grandma!* "There are several small children too." *My babies!* "They're all very happy to see you." Her face clouded a bit, and she said in slow, heavy words, "I see a man sitting alone in a room working on a jigsaw puzzle. He's missing pieces to the puzzle. I feel like he's been through life several times and always made the same mistake. This time he won't be able to come back until he finds the missing pieces." *Oh, no, Dad.* She seemed to leave that picture and again become more animated. "I see you have four children. No, make that five, although one of them doesn't belong to you." *She knows about Michelle Therese, the baby I gave up for adoption!* She then went on to describe in detail, and with great accuracy, each of my children's personality traits. *JJ, Rese, Gina, and Mandy!*

I thought these insights were great, but then came the truly incredible part. She talked about how to process the information she'd given me in terms of reincarnation. She told me we pick our birth families before we are ever born. She said we travel through this life many times, and each time we return to life, we come back with all our gifts.

I left that session with a profound interest in reincarnation. For the next several years, I read everything I could get my hands on about the subject. Reincarnation made absolute sense to me. It made sense that I picked this particular family to help me learn the lessons I needed to learn this time around.

The belief that I chose my family catapulted me out of the victim role. Having choices is the opposite of a being victim. I began to formulate a belief system based on choice and free will. I picked my family, and they picked me. We all had free will to change or continue destructive patterns in this life. I guess in the end, Dad chose the destructive route.

From my reading, I even came to an understanding and to a place of peace with the babies' murders. Reincarnation ideology saw the babies as pure souls. They were placed in the family in order to facilitate the tragedy so the seven souls left could learn. What was remarkable was that my siblings and I had no pictures of Teresa and Vincent and only one of newborn Alan. With no concrete evidence of their existence, it felt like they existed solely in our minds to help the rest of us grow.

Mom and Dad and the seven of us were playing out our present karmic life. My brain needed a belief system to latch onto that explained my past and provided a hopeful future. Reincarnation worked for me. I also needed a loving, nonjudgmental God who saw all people as his children regardless of race, religion, or sexual preference. I needed a God who loved all humans equally. I needed a God who was accessible, who I could talk to directly.

Still, I loved the familiarity of the Catholic rituals and all the wonderful music. I had basked in the tenderness and nurturing goodness of the nuns at the Good Shepherd Home. They had provided a safe haven in the tumultuous storm of my teenage years; without that home I probably would have died. Various Catholic charities have helped my family and me immeasurably.

I consider myself a cafeteria Catholic. I see religion as a buffet where I pick and choose what to savor and what to leave alone. I bypass the doctrine of fear-based hell and damnation and confession through a priest.

CHAPTER 16

Superwoman

Gary Gilmore was executed in January of 1977, and thanks to Dr. Keller and my supportive family and friends, I was at peace with the execution. I was definitely relieved to be on the other side of the event. My nightmares were gone. My focus was back. I was leaving therapy knowing I would have "the talk" with my sister, Jean, and my brothers Al, Patrick, and Lee when I could meet with them face-to-face. I thought I was over the effects of my dysfunctional childhood. I was ready to focus on my present life.

I remember my last session with Dr. Keller in that six-month stint. "Diann, you've progressed well."

"Thanks," I said, beaming.

"I wish you the best. As you know, I'm not much for giving advice, but I'd like you to think about something." My ears perked up. Dr. Keller asked questions. She rarely made statements and certainly not statements bordering on advice. "I invite you to be selfish."

To the very end, she could surprise me. "Selfish?" I squeaked out. "Why would I want to be selfish?" I immediately thought of Joe, his unilateral decisions, his absence at important family events, using money for alcohol instead of food for our family. I didn't want to be selfish. I didn't want to be like Joe, but I also didn't want to be impolite, so I listened to Dr. Keller.

"I invite you to start thinking about yourself, to start loving yourself, and to start taking care of yourself physically, emotionally, and spiritually. I'd like you to be able to share all your feelings instead of holding things in. Ask the questions you need to ask. If you become more selfish, you'll be able to love others more completely."

"Okay," I said, not understanding the concept at all. I lived for my children, and there was simply no way I could love them more.

Dr. Keller had helped me a lot, but sometimes she had some pretty crazy ideas, and being selfish was one of them. No, my job, in order to cover up my bad side, was to be the perfect mom, wife, sister, relative, and friend. My job was to be everything to everybody. I fostered the idea that staying extremely busy and playing the superwoman role was the only way to survive, and that was the opposite of being selfish.

*   *   *

In April of 1977, my obstetrician, concerned with continual bleeding following Mandy's birth, insisted I have a hysterectomy. It was the day after surgery, and I was lounging in my hospital room doing nothing when, to my delight, in strolled Joe. His eyebrows were furrowed, but when he spied me, his face cleared. With a grin, he walked up to the bed, planted a big kiss on my lips, and asked, "How are you?"

"I'm a little sore, but I'm fine. I'm glad you came."

"I'm glad you're not reading. I had a nightmare last night that I came to the hospital to see you, but you wouldn't pay attention to me because the book cart was in your room. You were surrounded by books and didn't even notice me." I realized then that sometimes I became so caught up in blaming Joe for everything I neglected to look at my part of our relationship. I vowed I'd be more aware of Joe's feelings.

But after returning home, I began to feel heavy and grey. In the time since Mandy's birth the previous June, I had received three D & Cs. None of the women in my family had ever had female problems. I, on the other hand, had endured severe periods and continual problems since I first started menstruating.

I posed the question to my doctor. "I'm only twenty-seven years old. None of the women in my family have had female problems. Why is this happening to me?" The doctor gave me one of those questioning looks.

"Give me more information, and I may be able to help."

I took a deep breath and said, "My dad sexually abused me from age five to thirteen. He had intercourse with me almost daily for two years. Could this have been the cause of my female problems?"

The doctor's eyes turned down as if he was thinking, but when he raised his head, his eyes were watery. He looked at me and said quietly, "Certainly that kind of abuse to your young body would have caused a good deal of internal scarring. That could have contributed to your problems and your need for a hysterectomy at your young age." This explanation made sense to me, and it was a relief to find out there was a reason for my problems.

After my hysterectomy in June of 1977, we took a family vacation to California. In addition to attending a convention for collection agencies, we made the Southern California tourist scene by visiting Disneyland, Universal Studios, and SeaWorld. While we were at the convention in San Diego, Jean babysat our children at her home in Bakersfield. We picked up the kids and stayed for a short visit. I felt Jean's disappointment with the brief amount of time we spent with her and her family. The tightrope of tension, the tenuous balance of stilted conversation, and the fear of plunging into the hot bed of Jean's anger prevented me from attempting the necessary talk with my sister. I decided to wait for a more opportune time and place.

We left Jean and visited Al in San Francisco. According to my parents, siblings, and all my relatives, Al had always been the independent one in the family. At this point in his life, he was managing a rock and roll band and listening to the beat of his own guitar as well as his own drum. His drum matched the beat of many 1970s drummers who stayed high in their hippie haze of booze and drugs. My serious talk with Al had a different tenor than my talks with Michael and Paul.

Al said in response to my attempt to tell him about the incest, "Hey, Di, I forgave Dad a long time ago. I'm not angry. He told me about the abuse when I visited with him every day the week before he died. I'm over everything."

Al was the other "black sheep" of the family, and I was all right with his detached response. Al was being Al in the 1970s. I was glad, however, that I had talked to Michael and Paul first.

After a fun vacation, Joe resumed his late nights at the bar, having abandoned his smothering tactics of months prior. I was back to disliking my husband. Why did I stay? I was still a Catholic at heart. I made a vow to God to make my marriage work. I wasn't going to run from the relationship just because I disliked the man. I wasn't a quitter. I was strong; I could handle the situation. Joe would have to do something really horrible to cause me to break my vow. I still had hopes he'd change. Besides, a part of me believed Joe when he insisted all our problems were my fault. I was bad. Everything would be better if I tried harder to be good. He drank because I nagged. I deserved the tongue lashings because I was a mortal sinner. I'd committed adultery. Maybe I felt I had no choice. Whatever the reason, I stayed married to Joe.

In November, he was going to turn thirty. "What do want for your big 3-0?" I asked, thinking along the lines of a nice dinner at a fancy restaurant or perhaps a birthday party at home with the family, complete with a birthday cake.

"I want us to go barhopping at strip clubs," he immediately replied.

Accommodating Joe for his birthday, we went from strip club to strip club. I was the only woman at these establishments who had her clothes on and the only woman with her husband. This was my gift to him, but it wasn't fun for me. I didn't understand why he wanted me to be a part of the strip club scene. Sandra, however, understood how demeaning this would be for me and thought the strip club idea a fine one. She was in favor of anything that would carry on the unsavory lifestyle to which she was accustomed. To bring me down when life was going well was one of Sandra's major goals.

By the following year, Joe's collection agency was finally making money, and we were able to purchase a larger house. In May 1977, we moved into a four-bedroom house on a corner lot in Arvada. When spring weather brought out the lilacs and the neighbors, we brought out the volleyball net and set it up on our corner lot.

The combination of a wonderful new neighborhood, a spacious house, and financial security helped our attitude as a couple. Joe was still Joe, consistently inconsistent, but this particular spring and summer he seemed more engaged with me and the kids. When he was good, he was very good, and for three or four months, he'd been super. He seemed to be home more, and I seemed to be nagging less. Every weekend, our friends congregated at our house for fun times, potluck meals, barbeques, drinks, and volleyball. Joe and I became particularly close with a couple, Debi and Bob. We met Bob and Debi through Sandi, Bob's sister, who was dating Joe's brother, Rudy. We all started socializing. When we needed a babysitter for an evening out, I hired Corrina, a neighborhood high school student. She was our kids' favorite sitter.

Corrina had siblings very close in age to my children. On weekdays, Corrina's mother Angie, all the kids and I whiled away our summer days with fun activities: swimming, picnics, playing in parks and on playgrounds. Angie loved Mandy. When I reacted to Mandy's hot temper, Angie had a way of calming me down and at the same time soothing Mandy's ruffled feathers. I loved her steady, laid-back parenting style and tried to emulate it whenever possible.

She was also an incredible seamstress and teacher. She helped me with numerous sewing projects throughout the summer and into the school year.

In addition to the friendly neighborhood and recent financial stability, our home's spacious interior made it possible to realize a dream I'd had since high school. Ever since I was in foster care, I wanted to be a foster parent myself. I thought I could provide an experience different from the one I had as a foster kid. I wanted our foster kid to feel a part of our family. I pictured myself providing affection, encouragement, and guidance to my foster daughter. I'd snuggle with her on the couch while having long, meaningful talks. She'd be expected to pitch in with the family chores, but I'd make sure she never felt like a maid or a nanny. I anticipated she'd love being a big sister and participating in family activities.

After months of endless forms and home visits from the state, my dream of being a foster parent became a reality. In July of 1978, we took in our first foster daughter, Cindy, and her four-month-old son, Jason. Cindy's heritage was Caucasian and American Indian, but with her dark brown, wavy hair and high cheekbones, she looked like she was part of our family way before she felt it.

Cindy came to us carrying her son and heavy emotional baggage full of abuse and neglect from both her family and previous foster care. She came with a sign that read, "Cindy and Jason against the world." When I once suggested Jason's baby bottles of formula would be kept fresher in the refrigerator in the garage, she took offense. She snapped indignantly when I asked her to occasionally babysit the kids. She'd built a fortress around herself on a remote piece of land complete with guard towers and a moat full of snapping alligators.

I was afraid my wish for a wonderful foster mother/daughter relationship would never come to fruition until one day, about a month after her arrival, I spotted her sitting on the couch crying. I sat down next to her. Before she had time to brace, I put my arm around her. Her deep sadness together with an intense longing for connection had, for an instant, crumbled her defensive walls, and she collapsed into my embrace. In a soft, curious tone, I asked, "What's wrong?"

"I'm starting school tomorrow, and I'm worried about getting in with the wrong people again."

"Cindy, I don't think that's going to happen. You're a great mother, and you know your priorities now. You've grown into a different person, a person who will attract the right people into your life, a person who'll make good choices."

She sat up, wiped the tears from her face, and looked straight into my eyes to see if I was lying. "Do you really think so?"

"I know so," I said with my voice, my eyes, and my heart.

She took one more look at me and hugged me hard, like a scared child holding onto her loving mother for protection and reassurance. "Thank you. Thank you so much," she said and hugged me again.

From that time on, Cindy was my daughter, and I was her mother. Even though Cindy thought of me as her mom, she still called me Diann, still afraid of making the closeness concrete and real. If she made it official, she could lose another family.

She slowly connected more and more to us. She participated in all family activities and grew close to her new brother and sisters.

When Joe joined us for family outings, he was the epitome of fun. He came home early one evening and announced to the kids and me he was going to *get* dinner for us. He told us in a pseudo-serious voice we were to sit at the table. When we were seated and seven pairs of eyes, counting Cindy and her son Jason, were fixed on him, he said in the showman voice of a magician, "I present to you the *puzzle dinner*." He paused for optimum effect and said, "And now for your first course."

He rummaged through the refrigerator and pulled out eight pieces of bologna, which included one for himself, and a tube of mustard. He placed a piece of bologna on each plate. He made a smiley mustard face on the lunch meat and said, "You may all eat your seven-of-a-kind, hand-decorated, smiley-faced bologna." It was difficult to swallow our first course because we were laughing so hard. "And now for your berry sweet second course," proclaimed Joe.

He placed a strawberry on each plate, then dramatically sprinkled sugar atop the berries. We ate through eight more courses consisting of a tortilla, carrot stick, apple, glob of leftover beans and rice, banana, cheese, and a piece of bread topped with peanut butter. Each time he added a piece to our puzzle dinner, we laughed. Ten courses later, our stomachs hurt not from the food but from laughing.

After Joe had cleverly pieced together our first puzzle dinner, the kids wanted more. Every few months, the kids and I would request a puzzle dinner, and Joe would usually gladly accommodate our wishes. Joe seemed to comply when I sorely needed a break from cooking dinner or when we had accumulated a bunch of incongruent leftovers. I loved puzzle dinners as much as the kids did.

When he made it to one of the kid's events, their eyes lit up. He was the life of the party. Everyone loved Joe; fun seemed to follow him to all the events he chose to attend. To the outside world we appeared to be the perfect couple raising our perfect family.

Life for the first time in a long time had a more gentle rhythm. I thought I was taking Dr. Keller's advice when I started to do something just for me, something I loved. From the time Dad taught me the waltz and fox trot through my shaking-shoulder days at the Good Shepherd Home, to going out dancing with Joe, I knew dance was in my soul. I started taking modern dance classes. I began receiving comments from other mothers about my new body. "No way you've had four kids. How did you get that flat belly? Why don't you show me some of those exercises?"

I believed I was combining Dr. Keller's selfish idea with my superwoman role. However, I hadn't quite grasped the concept of moderation, so as usual I jumped in with both feet. Despite my aching knees, I took several classes weekly at the Academy of Creative Dance. Joe and I would often go out dancing in the evenings. I also started teaching fitness classes for the North Jeffco Recreation District. I danced my way through the summer and fall as well as taking care of the house, getting the children to their various activities, and cooking, cleaning, gardening, sewing, and reading.

Our family took a break from our normal hectic schedule at Christmas. We had a big family gathering. My brothers Michael and Paul and their families, who lived in town, were to come over for Christmas dinner. Brother Al and his girlfriend Jan came in from New York, and my sister Jean, her husband Barry, and their three daughters arrived from Houston. Both Al and Jean had moved again.

On Christmas Eve, the guys were busy in the living room putting together the play kitchen Santa would give to the girls. Jean and I sat in the kitchen drinking tea. I finally had the opportunity to complete Dr. Keller's assignment of a year and a half ago.

My body felt empty yet weighed down with dread as I thought about beginning the conversation. I was sure Jean would have a different reaction than my brothers. I had so many strikes against me. I had, after all, not even attempted to follow my big sister's straight-arrow path and perfect footsteps. No, my footprints were dangerously erratic, crashing through life's jungle. I'd ruined her wedding by being drunk and having sex with the best man. Then I'd disgraced her by getting pregnant out of wedlock. She'd responsibly married a non-abusive, stable, gainfully employed man. I did the opposite, and as poor as we were, I "irresponsibly" kept having babies. Except for the phone conversation during my Gary Gilmore breakdown, where responsible Jean once again saved me from myself, we'd kept our conversations on the surface. Jean was my heroine and I her disappointment. I thought of our kids nestled snug in their beds while visions of sugarplums danced in their heads. I was stuck in the kitchen while visions of my sister's judgment stomped and screamed in my head.

My sister hates me, I thought, as I said, "I need to tell you what happened to me growing up."

As I talked about the abuse, Jean's eyes filled with tears and soft compassion. Through her sobs, she said, "I didn't know it was that bad.

Mom told me to watch out for you with Dad after you ran away. I'm so sorry. I should've protected you." Still crying, she reached out her fingers, gently cupping my face, and without a word she pulled me toward her and held me, rocking me like a loving mother soothing her precious daughter.

"I'm so sorry. I ruined everything. I ruined your wedding. I'm such a mess. Please don't hate me," I blurted out.

Through her waterworks she said, "Shhhhh. Look at me, Di. I never hated you. I love you so much." We talked into the night. She told me that as a teenager she hated Dad. After hearing my story, she was even more outraged.

"He'd talk dirty to me. I hated it when he would kiss me hard and long on the mouth. But what happened to me was nothing compared to what happened to you." She told me over and over again she wished she'd protected me.

The subject then turned to our respective weddings. She said she didn't blame me at all for what happened at her wedding, but she was very hurt when I didn't make her matron of honor for my wedding.

"I've always envied your incredible beauty, your perfect marriage, and your comfortable life," I admitted.

Jean retorted, "I always wanted your mouth. You have Mom's mouth that curves up. My mouth is straight like Dad's." We started laughing.

"Are you kidding? Never once did I think you'd be jealous of me in any way."

It turned out that Christmas Eve of 1978 was magical, after all. I nestled snug in my bed while visions of purest sisterly love danced in my head. The truth was my big sister loved me no matter what.

*   *   *

By 1979, I was teaching fitness classes daily and taking modern dance classes three times a week. The girls were all in dance classes. JJ was active in sports and taekwondo. For a while, Joe was even taking taekwondo with JJ. He also came up with the idea of designing a monthly calendar complete with clever cutouts denoting our family activities.

The kids loved spending time with their fun, creative Dad, and I loved being with my fun, creative husband. We couldn't relax completely, however, because we all subconsciously knew we needed to be prepared for the volatile, critical person or the guy who might disappear from our lives for months at a time. We were never sure which man would or would not show up.

To further complicate the dynamics, we took in another foster child. Rhonda was a fifteen-year-old with a child, and she wanted to be a teenager, not a mother. She didn't want to be part of our family, preferring to return to her alcoholic mom and permissive environment.

I went to court to testify on behalf of her child. Unlike Cindy, I felt Rhonda lacked the motivation or parenting skills to raise a child. Social services felt differently, and within four months, Rhonda left our family with her baby despite my concerns. I decided perhaps I couldn't save everyone, just almost everyone.

I was feeling increasingly positive about life until one spring day in 1979. I'd been looking forward to spending a day with Joe. He'd taken the day off from work. We had all sorts of fun things planned. We were going to get our picture taken, have a delicious lunch, and take an evening drive to look at a house to buy in the mountains. Outside, the sun was shining and the birds were singing, but on the inside the clouds were heavy with a feeling of impending doom.

The day started with me finding out that a valuable record album Joe was supposed to return to my dance teacher had melted in his hot car. Through the picture-taking and nice lunch, I unsuccessfully tried to shake the "bad" feeling. The feeling was so strong I asked Joe if we could drop in to see Aunt Ruby. She was my go-to person when I needed a mother.

I jumped out of the car and ran to her. "I need a good mommy hug."

She opened her arms wide, circling me with warmth and love. After a long, firm hug, she placed her hands on my shoulders and pushed back in order to look into my eyes. "What's wrong?"

"Nothing really," I said. "Just a bad feeling I can't seem to shake. I'll be fine. Thanks for the hug."

By evening, when Joe drove us to look at a house in the mountains, nothing bad had happened except for the melted album. I was thinking how silly I'd been, worrying for no reason, when we turned left onto a deserted Highway 285 from Parmalee Gulch.

The silly thought turned into a scream as headlights came out of nowhere, bearing down on us. In the middle of the turn, Joe tried to stop and back up, but it was too late as the vehicle rammed full force into the driver's side of our car. I didn't see the other car piercing the night air. I didn't hear the horrible crashing sound of two vehicles colliding. All I remember is hurtling through the air in slow motion, thinking we probably should have been wearing our seat belts. I felt my body slamming hard against something and then nothing.

I'm alive, I thought when I regained consciousness. I was heartened to find my numb, sleeping body didn't hurt, but then I moved, waking nerves that screamed in pain. My eyes took their time adjusting to the dark.

To my surprise, I found myself behind the steering wheel. "Joe," I screamed, panicking. "Where are you? Joe, answer me!"

A deafening silence ensued. Wincing, I crawled out of the mangled car. There he was, his still body lying face down on the shoulder of the road. *Oh, God, no. He's dead.*

"Joe!" I screamed. And then, to my relief, I heard him moan. I collapsed on the ground beside him. Not daring to move him, I gently touched his back and began to pray. "Please, God, don't let him die. Please, God, send help."

God and some bystander had been listening because before I knew it, an ambulance had arrived. The EMTs rushed us to Swedish Hospital.

We were both lucky. I merely had a sprained left ankle, sprained right wrist, and a five-inch bump on my forehead. Joe was lucky to be alive. He was one big bruise, inside and out. We found out later he'd been thrown from the car, and it had actually rolled over on him. Even though he had tire tracks across his thighs and significant road rash, he had no internal injuries or broken bones.

We were released that night. Joe's dad came to pick us up. Getting Joe out of the car was a major ordeal. We couldn't help him because we couldn't touch him. An hour and a half later, he was on the couch, where he stayed for the next three weeks.

Cindy and I played the role of dutiful servants: food, drink, and bedpan duty. Cindy was a rock star. The car, however, was totaled. Fortunately, the accident wasn't our fault; the speeding drunk driver who hit us was cited. Unfortunately, the only other vehicle we owned had a stick shift, which was difficult to drive with my sprained ankle and wrist. I decided only a dire emergency would get me behind a steering wheel any time soon.

An emergency fitting that dire category arrived the day after the accident. JJ fell off a fence, ripping his arm wide open. By some miracle, I made it to the hospital with him. As we entered the emergency room, the EMTs glimpsed my battered face and body. Bypassing JJ, they grabbed hold of me, ushering me toward a bed.

"I'm okay," I insisted. "This happened yesterday. My son needs attention now."

The nurse in attendance gave me a skeptical look and then looked down at JJ, who raised his bloody arm. She shrugged as if to say, *Okay, lady, it's your choice who we treat*, and she took JJ to an examining table.

Joe was laid up for about two months. After he got off the couch, he set up shop in our bedroom. His secretary would come to the house every weekday to help conduct business. For the first time in our marriage Joe was home and dependent on me. The new, stay-at-home Joe gave me the impetus to work harder on our relationship. Because he was home and not spending money at the bars, I was less of a nag, and he was more responsive to the new me.

The new us and our children started attending our neighborhood Catholic Church regularly. Even if I thought of myself as a reincarnated, cafeteria Catholic, I confess I was still a Catholic.

One week we heard the priest talk about a weekend couples' retreat called Marriage Encounter. We decided to give it a try. Marriage Encounter gave us a new way to communicate through writing daily letters to each other. We came away from the weekend totally in love. Even though we had great hope for the future, we ended up writing letters for only about a month.

Joe was more consistent at letter writing than I, but because he also consistently missed the kids' games and performances, the letters didn't help. For Joe's words to mean anything to me, they had to match his actions. Matching word and action wasn't his forte, and within four months of the accident, he was back to his old behavior of spending our grocery and clothes money in bars. I was back to simmering in a stew of resentment resulting in steady, low-grade nagging. But when he bought a red Corvette without involving me, my anger boiled over. "We have four kids and two foster kids with kids. A Corvette is not a family car."

"We have a van; that's the family car," he declared.

Maybe Joe was having fun, but I wasn't, especially when the van was in the shop for nearly a month and I had to use the Corvette for grocery shopping. Our usual one trip to the market became three. I would load up the grocery cart with a Corvette-sized portion of food, pay for it, and walk out to Joe, who was waiting in the Corvette. We'd load the groceries in the car. Joe would then drive the Corvette home to unload while I went back into the store to purchase my second batch, pay, wait for Joe, and so on. We'd each begun playing our old roles. Nothing had changed.

Our marriage was in desperate need of resuscitation. So when Joe booked a trip for two to Hawaii a month in advance of our tenth anniversary, my heart filled with fresh hope. I could see us breathing new life into our relationship by taking some time away for fun in the sun. My chest ballooned with anticipation, but I was sorely deflated when the trip was cancelled due to an airline strike. Because a reworked itinerary would require us to change planes four times and add days and cost to the trip, the Hawaiian holiday was now prohibitive. Our anniversary was still a month away, but the chance for an exotic vacation seemed, literally and figuratively, oceans away.

What I had underestimated was Joe's tenacity and spontaneity when it came to fun. Joe called me on Thursday morning and said, "Hey, they just had a hurricane in Jamaica, and I got a killer deal; the vacation package includes two round-trip, nonstop airline tickets and eight days and seven nights at a five-star hotel. Do you think you can be ready to go by tomorrow night?"

"Tomorrow night?" I squeaked out in panicked excitement. "What do I do with the kids?"

"I already bought the tickets. Find a babysitter." So I did. Joe's parents agreed to watch the kids.

Jamaica was a paradise of fun and rum. Joe was always at his best in a party atmosphere. He was in his element. I marveled at Joe's ability to transform a hurricane disaster into a whirlwind romantic vacation that infused new energy into a stagnant marriage. The attentive, playful Joe who specialized in fun was hard to resist. And so during the eight-day tropical holiday celebration marking the tenth year of our marriage, I fell in love again with my irresistible husband.

Even back home, living our regular life, this lovable side of Joe made an occasional appearance. He'd periodically lead our family on wonderful, spontaneous adventures. The warm memories of the Jamaican sun plus the intermittent presence of the good Joe in everyday life extended the glow of my love toward my husband for months. But I knew from past experience that the irresponsible, volatile, dismissive Joe would return and bleach out my loving feelings. How long would I choose to let this relationship cycle continue? A little while longer.

Shortly after our return from Jamaica, Cindy moved out. She'd graduated from dental hygienist school in July but continued to live with us until late summer when she moved into her own apartment. We were pleased to be invited to her graduation as her honored guests. "My only regret," she said to Joe and me after graduation, "was that I kept my last name. You're my real parents."

A few days after Cindy moved out, we were notified that another foster child was looking for a home. Within a week, Sharon had moved in. She was fourteen and stood 5 feet 6 inches with blonde hair, brown eyes, and an athletic build. She came from a well-to-do family, the only girl in the family, with four brothers. She came to us after accusing her father of sexual abuse.

Because our stories on the surface had many similarities, I had high hopes I might be able to help this teen. Within five minutes of her entering our house, she was calling me Mom. Cindy phoned me in that first week to say hello. Sharon picked up the phone.

"May I speak to Diann?" Cindy asked, wondering who belonged to the unfamiliar voice.

The perky voice answered, "Sure thing." Sharon set down the phone and yelled, "Mom, some girl is on the phone for you."

When I picked up the extension, Cindy's angry voice snapped, "Who is she? And why is she calling you Mom?" After that phone call, Cindy always called me Mom.

As the months went by, I began to think Sharon's story about being molested by her dad wasn't true. Could it be a ploy to get attention, I wondered? This was an alien concept to me. It had never once occurred to me a child would lie about being molested by anyone, much less her father. The thought was hard for me to fathom, but despite my incredulity, I started to doubt her claims of incest; too many pieces of her story puzzled me or didn't fit at all with my experience and knowledge of sexual abuse.

I talked to her social worker about my suspicions. She looked at me and nodded in agreement, but said, "We have to treat all claims seriously."

"I understand. What I don't get is why anyone would falsely accuse their father of sexual abuse. That's sick."

"Sadly, it happens."

But I wasn't ready to give up; after all, I was a super foster parent. Perhaps if I gave her more attention, she'd feel safe enough to be honest with herself. The opposite, in fact, occurred; the more attention she received, the more she demanded and the less insight she seemed to have into herself. Whenever I'd ask any questions about her family or bring up any subject she didn't want to discuss, she'd start to have labored breathing.

I began to believe she brought on asthma attacks at will simply to avoid any confrontation. Everyone was afraid of saying the wrong thing for fear of triggering an asthmatic episode. I found myself spending an inordinate amount of time trying to appease her, though it was clear my efforts weren't helping her improve her life. In my blind desire to be a good foster parent, I'd lost sight of the fact I was beginning to neglect Joe and the kids.

After a couple of months of fostering Sharon, Joe forced me to make a decision. It was either Sharon or him. This became abundantly clear when one day I came home from teaching fitness and Joe had moved all his possessions out of the house and into our motor home.

When I asked him what was going on, he replied, "There's not enough room in the house for all of us. Sharon takes all your time and energy. I'll just live out here until she leaves."

Even though I knew Joe was right, it was not in my queen-of-the-ringers nature to give up. I went into the house and stewed. It was true Joe was still thinking primarily of himself, but by moving out, he'd reminded me that our nuclear family was a priority. I'd known about the importance of family all of my life; after all, I'd been the one who had preached to Joe about it all through the years.

Reluctantly, I called Social Services and spoke to our caseworker. She assuaged my guilt by agreeing that removing Sharon from our home was the best option. The following day, Sharon left and Joe moved back in. Sharon was our last foster child.

Life returned to its normal level of intensity. I made sure every minute was filled with some kind of activity. To me, my worth was measured by how well I performed instead of who I was as a person. My self-esteem was still outwardly directed even as I continued to dip into my great passions of reading, dancing, fitness, sewing, gardening, and being a mom.

When, however, I felt too successful, or when life appeared too shiny, Sandra, my dark side, would appear, usually at dusk. I'd become antsy and unsettled. I felt undeserving of a good life. How could I deserve a good life when I was so bad? All the good I'd done couldn't overcome the fact my core was rotten.

I was able to confirm my badness when I passed a mirror on these evenings and saw my grotesque face. It was like seeing my reflection in a wavy mirror at a carnival, only worse. My face was distorted, elongated like a witch's face, my chin coming to a point. My eyes looked like unpolished stone: hard, flat, and dead. My smile sneered with wicked intent. I'd turn myself inside out and see the ugly feelings about myself in my mirrored reflection.

I would then get a babysitter, call some girlfriends, and have "ladies' night out." Sandra thought the name hilarious because she engaged in the most unladylike behavior. I didn't talk to anyone about my shadow side. My girlfriends never questioned me when I left for a time with a strange man, but I noticed their relief when I returned to the dance floor.

I didn't know whether Joe knew about these sexual escapades, but I certainly wasn't going to tell him. I didn't feel too guilty about keeping him in the dark; after all, it was Joe's voracious sexual appetite, as well as his belief my only worth was my appearance and sexuality, that seemed to spur Sandra on.

CHAPTER 17

The Mustache

In 1981, Joe grew a mustache. Dad was back. When Joe and I were intimate, I'd open my eyes to see Dad molesting me.

"I can't do this. I feel like Dad's here," I'd say.

I begged Joe to shave his mustache. He refused. I began to have the Fibber McGee closet feelings again. Stress began to change into distress. My insides were jittery, and the slight tremors in my hands had become a 7.0 on my Richter scale. In my attempt to outrun Dad, I was teaching sixteen fitness classes a week and choreographing my own dance for a concert. The classes were hard on my body, and my knees were killing me. But hurting physically was preferable to dealing with emotional pain.

Sandra, my shadow side, who'd accompanied Dad's return, tried in her own way to help me deal with the memories by making me out to be just as bad as Dad. She kept me busy by taking me out dancing and having sex with strangers.

On top of all this, I began having an affair with our next-door neighbor, Toby. Sandra wasn't interested in my affairs because they had very little to do with sex. My affairs had to do with my lack of self-esteem. This second affair, just like the first, gave me a sense of self-worth. He gave me things Joe couldn't or wouldn't provide, like attention. He listened to me. He thought I was smart. He liked who I was as a woman.

Joe soon found out about the affair and was furious. "How long has this been going on?" he demanded.

"It just started a week ago," I said meekly. "I'll stop it today," I added quickly.

"You're damn right you will. Diann, you insult me. How could you have an affair with a man who is that ugly?"

I guess Joe wanted me to have affairs with only handsome men. Joe valued two things in relationships: looks and sex. He had no understanding of me or my affairs. But I stopped the affair immediately.

Meanwhile, Joe acted and looked more like Dad every day. When I closed my eyes, I saw Dad everywhere. My life was frenetic. I was unable to concentrate on anything and had trouble completing tasks. My mind moved at warp-speed, ready to crash. Nothing seemed to work.

I couldn't even get my plants to bloom. I'd bought an impatiens plant about six months before this. I cared for the plant. I watered and fertilized it. I encouraged and nurtured it, and when those tactics didn't work, I yelled at it; but still no blooms. Outside, the tulips stood stiffly in the yard, staring up at me with their closed, expressionless faces symbolizing my stuck life.

The nightmares had returned. One specific dream haunted my nights. The dream was a series of scenes. The first scene was a picture of a clear day complete with a vivid blue sky drenched in sun. I watched as five-year-old Mandy played happily in the aqua-blue ocean.

Suddenly, the tranquil turquoise turned to a sea of choppy grey, and the sunlight gave way to a heavy, dark, ominous sky. Out of the rough sea exploded the hulk of a great white shark. Its dead eyes focused on Mandy. Its jagged teeth threatened to tear her limbs apart. Fear for my baby swallowed me whole until a huge black bear lunged into the picture and killed the shark .

Relief washed over me until the bear that had saved Mandy from the shark turned on me. Baring ferocious teeth, the bear threatened to eat me as its giant claws readied to maul me.

I'm dead, I thought. *I'm not going to make it!* I'd wake up sweating. I believed the message meant Mandy would be saved but not me.

It was Good Friday, 1981. I'd made a lunch date with my brother Paul. "Paul, something is wrong with me. I'm losing it. I can't shake this feeling. It feels like Dad's back. Dad's everywhere again. I feel like I felt before Gilmore was executed; so out of control."

"Why? What's happening?" Paul asked.

"It's Joe's mustache! Every time I look at it, I see Dad."

"Why don't you ask him to shave it off?" Paul said.

"I've asked him to, but he won't," I replied.

"What can I do? What do you need?" Paul inquired.

"I don't know. I wish I knew."

"It'll be okay, Di. You'll get through this. You always do."

"I hope so," I said, not believing one word but grateful for his confidence.

That evening, Joe and I attended an After Hours Business event. We were with Joe's brother Rudy, his girlfriend Sandi, and several of our friends. I was jittery, unable to focus, and talking very fast. I was acting so crazed Sandi asked if there was something wrong.

"Yes, there's something definitely wrong. I feel like I'm going crazy." Sandi patted me on the arm and gave me a sympathetic look, but that was all she could do. I felt like I was beyond help, a bomb ready to explode. Who would pick up the pieces?

We'd left JJ, almost ten, Rese, who was eight, Rese's friend Carly, Gina, six and a half, and Mandy, five, at home with a babysitter. On the way back from the party, Joe stopped at a 7-Eleven near our house to get cash change for the babysitter. The last thing I clearly remember was getting out of the car.

The rest of my ordeal consisted of nightmarish-quality flashes until harsh fluorescent lights assaulted my eyes and the loud sounds of people speaking and moving inundated my ears. I tried to sit up but found I couldn't move. My arms and legs felt like they were glued to my sides. I was lying flat on my back on some kind of surface. My claustrophobia intensified, and I thrashed like a trapped wild animal, my eyes wide, darting around.

"Help me. Get me out of here!" I yelled.

I heard a voice on my left. "Hey, sis, it's me, Paul."

"Paul? Paul, I can't move. Where am I?" I was paralyzed with fear yet at the same time thrashed my head back and forth, struggling frantically against the bonds that held me.

I heard Paul's faraway voice say, "You're in the emergency room at St. Anthony's."

"I'm in the hospital? What am I doing in a hospital?" I screamed. "I can't move. Paul, you've got to help me!"

"Take it easy. Calm down," he said, patting me. "You'll be okay, Di. It's okay. You're in a straitjacket. You freaked out. You thought Joe was Dad. Joe's here. He wants to see you."

"No! Paul, do you hear me? Don't bring him here. I don't want to see him. Get me out of here!"

At this point, some heavy-duty drugs must have taken effect because I don't remember anything until the next morning. I woke up in another room in a strange bed. The room was quiet, Paul was gone, and the sun was streaming in through a window. I tested out my range of motion by practicing a few snow angels in the bed. I was no longer restrained. The dark, heavy curtain of life had lifted. I felt light and giddy.

I laughed out loud. "It's over. The worst is over," I shouted aloud to myself, or at least I thought only to myself.

"Yes, I do think that is an accurate assessment," a voice said.

I jumped. A man was sitting in a chair across from my bed. "You startled me. I didn't know anyone was in the room."

A handsome, blond-haired man dressed in a white coat was sitting comfortably, arms and legs crossed, observing me.

"I'm Dr. Peterson, a psychiatrist. You're in the psych ward at St. Anthony's, and you've had quite an ordeal. What do you remember?"

"Just bits and pieces, like getting out of the car. I remember my husband opening the front door and thanking someone for bringing me home." My voice curled up in embarrassment as I said, "I remember lying on the floor in a fetal position in the corner of the basement whimpering."

When the psychiatrist kept the same impassive expression on his face, I continued, "I remember a little of the emergency room. My brother Paul was there. That's all I remember." To fill in the silence and in order to hopefully be discharged, I added, "I feel much better now. I feel like a great weight has been lifted. What happened?"

The psychiatrist said, "Well, from what I could piece together from talking to both your husband and your brother about your history, something triggered you to revert back to the time of the murders. I understand you were thirteen. Oftentimes, with severe trauma, there'll be a triggering event or a series of events that send you back in time. Many times this lets the victim replay the trauma on their terms.

"In your case, you saw your husband as your abusive father and threatened to kill him. After running around the house brandishing a kitchen knife, you ran down to the basement. Your husband corroborates your memory. He reports he found you in your basement curled up in a fetal position."

Oh, Lord. I couldn't believe I'd acted like a crazy person in front of the children. How awful for them. And to make matters worse, Rese's friend Carly had witnessed my bizarre behavior. I'd have to explain to Carly's parents what had happened. My behavior was horrifying and embarrassing to me. Why couldn't I deal with my past like a normal, rational human being? I just wished I could remember. I hated losing time.

"Do you know what triggered you?"

I did know that much. "Yes, for the past couple of months I've been having nightmares about my dad. I think this was because of my husband's mustache. With a mustache, Joe looks a lot like my dad. A lot of weird things have been happening, like looking in the mirror before going out with my girlfriends and seeing myself as an ugly, bad person."

For the first time, Dr. Peterson's calm face changed expression. He looked shocked as he said, "Ugly? That's hard to believe."

Again, much like the stranger's words after my perm years before, his reaction made me believe maybe I wasn't ugly after all.

Before I was released, Dr. Peterson asked me if I was up to seeing my husband. "Yes, of course," I replied, relieved Joe, mustache or not, wasn't Dad anymore.

Joe picked me up, and in the car on our way to buy Easter goodies for the kids, I asked him a few more questions. "Tell me about what happened last night," I asked.

"Diann, I didn't know where you were. You were gone when I came out of the store. I looked for you and couldn't find you. So I went home. Half an hour later a person from our neighborhood saw you wandering and brought you home. The neighbor rang the doorbell and explained who she was. Before she could say a word, you started screaming at me. You thought I was your dad. I was so relieved to see you, I reached for you. You started pounding my chest with your fists. You were screaming, 'I hate you, Dad! I'm going to kill you.' You shoved me hard. You ran into the kitchen, got a knife, and ran screaming through the house. I ran after you saying, 'Diann, I'm Joe. I'm Joe. I'm not your dad.' You would have none of it. It seemed like forever. Finally I stopped trying to reason with you. I found you later in the far corner of the basement in a fetal position. I was so scared. That's when I called 911."

I believed him. "I'm sorry I put you through all that. But I'm better now." I examined my husband's mustached face. "I could be a lot better, though." Joe gave me a curious look, so I added with a smile, "It wouldn't hurt my feelings if you shaved that mustache now."

Joe's face became obstinate. With a serious expression, he asked in a challenging voice, "If I shave it, what'll you shave in return?"

My smile faded with my good mood. I was relieved Joe was no longer Dad, but a harsh reality slammed me down to earth: Joe was still Joe. This was a typical Joe statement, and I wasn't surprised.

Having just gone through a major breakdown, however, I didn't have the energy or inclination to fight. I answered in a flat tone, "Whatever you want. Just shave it off." This seemed to appease him because he hugged me and told me he loved me. Later that day he shaved his mustache.

When we entered the house, I found myself in the middle of four hugging, kissing children. I immediately sat my children down and said to four pairs of wide eyes, "That must have been really scary for you." Four heads nodded vigorously. "I'm sorry I scared you. I had to deal with some bad things that happened in my childhood. But I'm all right now.

Rese, my inquisitor, asked, "What bad things happened to you, Mommy?"

"Well, I was kind of reliving the night when I was young when my mom and some of my brothers and my little sister died. This made me mad and sad." The explanation satisfied them.

Later that day I spoke in person with Carly's parents, telling them in greater detail what happened. They were very understanding and promised to talk to Carly.

Next, I called Jean. After her tears and many questions, she came up with a "big sister" plan to help me. "Di, I think you need a break. Why don't you come to Louisiana and visit me?"

The last time I visited Jean, she lived in California. I'd love to see her new place in Louisiana.

The idea of a break appealed to me, and I eventually decided to make a trip to see not only Jean but my younger brothers, Lee and Patrick, in West Virginia as well.

The next day was Easter. I rose and was greeted by a day radiating sunshine and warmth. I laughed out loud as I spied my impatiens plant in full bloom, its delicate fuchsia and white petals smiling in the light. Outside, the tulips with their beaming faces of red, yellow, purple, and pink announced the arrival of spring. The light of the universe showing off its brilliantly colored blooms promised I would never again fall into the kind of deep darkness and despair I'd experienced.

The next two weeks were spent at home waiting to get a decent fare on an airline ticket. I had many conversations with Joe during these days about our relationship. He wanted to know what he could do while I was gone to understand me better. I told him the best way to understand me was to listen to the lyrics of Barry Manilow songs. When I returned, I told him he could attend my dance recital and understand me through my dance.

Finally the time came to embark on my two-week vacation. My first week's plan was to visit Patrick and Lee, who lived on a commune owned by the Hare Krishna called New Vrindaban, West Virginia. The second week's plan was a visit to Jean's home in Lafayette, Louisiana. The thought of seeing my younger brothers and older sister felt like a warm fire on a cold night. I needed a break from my life in Arvada—Joe, the kids, my dad's memory, everyday pressures, as well as thinking constantly about my dance recital. Part of me wanted to run away from everything, and part of me wanted to run toward something. Dad, sick as he was, had always stressed the importance of family. In a strange way, I was honoring his memory by running toward the solace of family. I was also validating myself by planning to talk about the abuse with Lee and Patrick.

As the plane began to soar through the air, so did my spirits. Sinking down into my seat, I opened my book and tried to read. I was giddy with the prospect of two whole weeks of delicious freedom. But to my chagrin, I couldn't relax enough to make sense of the words on the page of the book I was reading. An irritating inner voice kept buzzing in my head. "You just had a major breakdown, and now you're going to spend a week on a Hare Krishna commune with no amenities? Do you know what you're getting into?"

In my brief phone conversation with Lee, who now went by Ganendra, I'd made it clear I wasn't interested in converting to the Hare Krishna life. Ganendra promised, for himself and Patrick, now known as Ambarish, that they'd go easy on their big sis. I wasn't worried they'd criticize me for my breakdown or the sharing of my history. I'd never been judgmental about their Hare Krishna lifestyle, so I expected no criticism from them in return.

Indian names or not, they were still my little brothers. So why was I so anxious? The answer came with the flash of an Indian feast my brothers had put on in Denver several years earlier. My memory conjured up the revolting scent of curry, which reminded me instantly I hated Indian food. Then, the image of me trying to sleep on a hard floor, my starving stomach screaming for beans and tortillas, popped into my brain. Would I be able to survive the commune even for a week? The idea of questionable food, no beds, no electricity, and no plumbing was a little overwhelming. And what about the bugs? I hated insects, especially hornets. *Stop it*, I said to myself when I realized I was wasting my precious relaxing time worrying.

My thoughts then turned to my upcoming dance recital. Each dancer had to choreograph her own routine. We were to interpret a color through dance. I chose grey. I had the color, but I couldn't seem to come up with a routine until one day, after my affair with Toby had ended, Joe accompanied me to the dance studio. The fog lifted, and I realized I'd chosen grey because it exemplified my relationship with Joe. I wanted Joe to understand I saw the world in "ifs and buts" while Joe saw the world in black-and-white. So I choreographed a dance depicting white, then black, to represent Joe's extremely rigid thinking. Then I danced my own thoughts representing the more moderate "ifs and buts" of grey. My dance was a creative way to explain to Joe who I was.

Post-breakdown, however, the color grey took on a new meaning. I realized my world had been heavily colored with ambivalence. My ghostly grey past haunted my present feelings about Dad, Joe, and myself. Lost in a thick fog, I'd been unable to distinguish between my past and my present. I decided after this vacation I'd visit Dr. Keller again in order to gain some insight into myself.

Suddenly, our rough landing bumped me out of my clouded thoughts. We taxied into the Pittsburgh airport, and as I walked off the plane, I spied Ganendra (Lee) waiting for me. He was smiling and, after a big hug, led us to our transportation, a beat-up Ford Maverick that belonged to the commune. New Vrindaban was located in a remote area of West Virginia, about an hour and a half from the airport. As soon as we began to drive out of the city and into the rolling hills of the countryside, my tension lessened.

After miles of friendly chitchat, Ganendra asked me about my breakdown. I told him about the mustache and about ending up in a straitjacket in the hospital. This led me directly into telling him about my sexual abuse, which culminated with the story of Dad going berserk on June 29, 1963.

Ganendra kept his eyes on the road, his wordless mouth open. The silence was unnerving as I waited for his reaction. He finally turned to me and said in a soft voice, "I was a little kid when Dad killed everybody. I never understood any of it. Nobody ever talked to me about that night. For the first time in my life, things are starting to make sense. I still don't totally understand, but you've answered some of my questions. I'm so sorry, Di. I'm so sorry about all of it—the breakdown, the abuse, the murders. I love you so much, and I'm so glad you're here."

Then his voice became louder. "How could he have done that to you? That bastard!" he said, surprising even himself. The validation felt good.

The conversation then meandered through an array of subjects. He talked about how early he had gotten into sex. As his eyes glazed over, he said, "I was a wild man, getting into drugs and sex."

What was it about our family and sex? It was true. Lee's first child was born when he was seventeen. What I knew about the others led me to believe everyone in our family had a strong libido.

The gently rolling hills mirrored our conversation, and my heavy worries lifted into the greenish-blue hills of the countryside. When we turned onto the two-thousand-acre parcel of land called New Vrindaban, the road changed, becoming more of a bumpy path. How odd that the sight of the poorly maintained entrance to the commune seemed to heighten my sense of adventure rather than dampen my spirits.

The little Maverick, sometimes losing its footing, climbed slowly over the narrow, rutted road. Several times the car lost power as Ganendra navigated the steep slopes, but it didn't break down or even get stuck. The Ford snaked through a dense forest until suddenly we broke through the thick canopy of trees into the light. In front of us lay a vast green valley dotted with simple shacks.

The beauty of the land rushed in to fill my heart. I knew I was in the perfect place to heal. Having traveled my own rutted, frenzied, dark path for so long, I was also ready to experience the light. My mind traveled to the not-so-distant future, when I would visit Dr. Keller again and admit I wasn't done with therapy. I'd have her help me make this breakdown into an incredible breakthrough.

"We're here," declared Ganendra with a grin. "Let's go see Ambarish (Patrick). He's tending to his precious cows."

Ambarish was in the barn, milking a cow, but upon hearing our footsteps and seeing our shoes through the cow's udders, he quickly jumped to his feet. He stood there smiling with his arms wide open, ready to embrace his big sister into his life.

"Di, how are you?" he said as he hugged and kissed me.

"I'm better now I'm here," I said, sinking into the familiarity of my little brother's love.

After meeting some of the cows and a having a short chat with Ambarish, Ganendra and I left. Ganendra took me to his house, where I'd be staying for the week. We walked toward a dilapidated, unpainted, two-story building.

Ganendra said proudly, "We have the lower floor. I'm in charge of keeping the fire stoked. It's our only heat."

As we approached, my stomach lurched as I noticed hornets had built a big hive on the side of the structure. Ganendra pushed the door open. The inside space consisted of an open room with a brick-lined hole in the corner. There were cold ashes in the bottom of this primitive fireplace. There was no furniture. The plywood floor was dotted with three sleeping bags.

Ganendra pointed to the bag that was to be my bed. A small cooler held food for breakfast and lunch. The dinner meal was served in a communal dining room a short walk from the house. Behind a partition was the bathroom, complete with a hole in the ground for the toilet and a spigot for a water supply. Through the haze in the room I could see a form I recognized as my brother's wife, Bhakti-Nidhi. I greeted her and thanked her for letting me stay.

"Where's Partha?" I asked, looking for their nine-year-old son.

"He's at the school with the other kids," said my brother.

"At school on a Saturday?" I inquired.

"He lives there." Ganendra then went on to explain that all the kids over the age of three lived together at the school. This was so the parents won't be distracted and could concentrate on their jobs. In response to my incredulous look, he said, "Don't worry. I see him every day at least once, sometimes twice. After I show you around, we'll go to see him."

The tour took only minutes as there wasn't much to see. Soon we were off to visit the school and Partha.

Partha spied his dad and me and came running. We hadn't seen each other for a couple of years, but Partha gave me a big smile. He recognized me for two reasons. Ganendra had told him his aunt would be coming from Denver. He also knew who I was because I looked out of place in my non-Indian garb.

Partha and I had just started a conversation when a kid about Partha's size came up and kicked me in the leg. Seeing this, Partha growled and pummeled the boy with his fists. The adults all stood around staring. As far as I observed, there were no repercussions for either boy. Later, Ganendra told me he thought the kid had kicked me because my strange clothes frightened him. I bought a sari the next day from the commune's store where Ganendra worked.

A few days into the visit, I found an opportunity to talk with Ambarish and continue my therapeutic journey. I wasn't surprised when he reacted like all my other siblings, except for Al, to the news of the breakdown and my childhood abuse. Like the others, he was angry with Dad and supportive of me.

"Di, I can't help but think if I hadn't been away at camp, I could've stopped him."

"It's not your fault. You were eleven. What could you have done?" Ambarish listened to my words, but I don't think he was convinced.

Ambarish had two wives. His first wife, Vigia, was unable to bear children. Being a father was important to him, so he married Pitambar, and they had a son. When I arrived at New Vrindaban, their baby boy was just three months old. I'd been looking forward to meeting his baby and second wife.

Since Ambarish was with the cows, I went alone to visit my new nephew. Pitambar greeted me at the door with a smile and a hug. She was a few inches taller than I and dressed in a colorful sari. Her warm brown eyes welcomed me. In her arms, she held Nitai, my new nephew. My mouth open, I stared into the precious baby face that was the mirror image of my brother's.

As I entered their home, I noted their living quarters were just as sparse, but even smaller than Ganendra's place. Almost immediately, Nitai let it be known he was hungry. Since my La Leche League days, I'd been very interested in breastfeeding, and this seemed to be something Pitambar and I had in common. As Nitai nursed, I began to ask her questions. "Are you getting enough to eat? I remember when I was a nursing mother I could eat all day long."

"Well, I don't have much food in the house," she said with a soft voice and downcast eyes.

"Doesn't Ambarish make sure you have food?" I inquired.

"Sometimes he brings me food. But he eats at the school with Vigia, his other wife."

I could feel the heat of anger engulf me as I began to comprehend their simple yet complicated life. In a loud voice that caused both Pitambar and Nitai to look at me with wide eyes, I yelled, "You need more to eat than this. I'm going to get you some food. I'll be back."

I ran out the door, briefly glancing back to see an open-mouthed Pitambar watching me. I was furious with Ambarish and muttered angry words to myself all the way to the store. Feeling and voicing anger was new for me, but the breakdown had evidently opened up new pathways of expression.

At the store, I bought nuts, fruits, vegetables, and cheese and took them back to Pitambar. After I stocked her cooler with food, I went in search of my brother. I found him tending to his precious cows.

Ambarish looked up and smiled, but before he could greet me, a torrent of angry words assaulted him.

"Shame on you!" I yelled. "How could you not provide food for your wife and baby? I don't care that you have two wives, but if you do, you damn well better provide for them, especially the one who has your baby."

Ambarish's initial shocked expression turned sheepish as he comprehended my words. As it was lunchtime, he took me to the school to see Vigia, and she served us a delicious stir-fried meal with spinach and fresh cashews. In between bites he said, "I'll be better about providing for Pitambar." We left without a morsel of food for wife number two, making me wonder if my anger had made any difference.

My week went by quickly. The routine was simple. We got up at three a.m. to chant. We ate breakfast. Ganendra and I walked to the store. He worked while I practiced my dance routine in a room in the back. At the end of the day, we ate at the communal dining room as I talked and laughed with my brothers. After a week with nary a hornet's sting, I felt glad to have come—and glad to leave. I felt somehow more pure and cleansed.

Next stop was Lafayette, Louisiana, to see Jean. Ganendra steered the Maverick over the now-familiar bumpy road. I arrived in plenty of time to catch my direct flight from Pittsburgh to Lafayette. This vacation was certainly one of extremes. My brothers had no amenities; Jean had every amenity. I stayed in a luxurious guest room with an adjoining bathroom complete with a bathtub/shower combo. Jean's plan for my recovery was to totally pamper me. Sleeping in as late in the morning as I wanted to in my comfy bed, I awakened to a big breakfast each day. The week was filled with lying out by her swimming pool, shopping, laughing, and visiting with her friends.

I returned to Denver a revitalized and reenergized woman. Upon entering my house, JJ, Rese, Gina, Mandy, and even Joe swarmed around me with kisses and hugs. During my absence, Joe, in an attempt to understand me better, had listened to my Barry Manilow tapes. He wrote me beautiful letters referencing lyrics from those songs. I appreciated his efforts and felt our marriage might be back on the road to recovery.

Even though we'd struggled in our relationship, it happened behind closed doors, so most of our friends and family thought ours was the marriage to beat. They wanted their marriages to be like ours. Ours was the home where everyone congregated. We were the couple in whom others confided. We were the life of the party, but I no longer cared to continue my frantic lifestyle. I no longer cared about how Joe and I appeared to the world. Joe became a second priority. I'd just experienced a breakdown. I needed to simplify my life in order to truly heal, but first I needed to finish a project I'd started. I needed to dance the color grey.

Finally the day of the recital arrived, and I danced a perfect dance. I danced for me. I danced my thoughts and feelings. My dance was gracefully grey. My movements were fluid and free, a dance to release me from the heavy, unforgiving chain of thoughts holding me to my past. I danced against the rigidity of black-and-white thinking.

My dance of grey was a springboard to the possibilities of colors in my life. I was, it turned out, getting to know myself, and expressing that knowledge through dance. Joe said my dance helped him understand me better. Maybe it did, but mostly it didn't matter what Joe understood.

I think he truly wanted the marriage to work, but on his terms. He was supportive if it meant he would maintain power and control over the relationship. I think he and I both knew his mustache was only one minor way in which he resembled Dad. I think he was scared that any part of me could stand up to my dad. This might mean one day I'd be able to stand up to him. For the first time in my life, I felt free to focus on me. I was aware of Joe's ambivalence, but I didn't care.

True to my goal to simplify my life, the grey recital was my last. I stopped taking dance classes and cut down my fitness teaching schedule. I let go of my frenetic life. I believed God's promise to me that the worst was over. I also believed I had to do my part on earth to prevent not just "the worst" from reoccurring but all future breakdowns. From that time forward, I was determined to have a Dad-free, breakdown-free existence. I wanted to do life differently. To reach this goal, I needed new tools, which led me directly back to Dr. Keller.

CHAPTER 18

Learning to Be Selfish

W hen I entered Dr. Keller's office, before I even sat down, I said, "I'm back. I had a breakdown and ended up in the hospital in a straitjacket."

She didn't seem surprised. "Welcome back. Why don't you tell me what happened?"

So, in my characteristic Fibber McGee style, I flooded the office with a torrent of words, ending with, "The mustache brought my dad back in full force. He was back to being my puppeteer, pulling all my strings… And when I had my breakdown, I felt so stupid and embarrassed. I made a fool of myself. I scared my children and Joe. Why can't I handle my past with some level of maturity? I feel like I regressed big time, and I don't even remember most of it."

When I stopped to take a breath, Dr. Keller jumped in. She had a knack for helping me corral my runaway thoughts. I was relieved she wasn't asking her characteristic series of questions. She seemed to know I needed grounding. She did this by clarifying and normalizing what happened during and after the breakdown.

"The way you acted during the breakdown, although you thought it embarrassing, was not unusual behavior for the severity of your trauma. When your dad came back via Joe's mustache, life became so overwhelming the only way you were able to handle the distress was to dissociate. Your dissociative state allowed you to express and release pent-up rage from your childhood. Definitely, you have nothing to be ashamed of."

I must have looked skeptical because she kept trying to convince me. I'd been so used to identifying myself as a bad, stupid, crazy person it took the entire first session to let go of the shame and guilt associated with my breakdown.

Finally, only after being buried under a mountain of evidence proving my behavior was okay, I began to believe her. After all, both Dr. Keller and the psychiatrist at St. Anthony's had similar explanations. They both couldn't be lying just to make me feel better about my behavior, could they?

The next two or three sessions dealt with the meaning of the breakdown itself. She said with admiration, "Diann, this breakdown was an extremely big and important step in being able to get angry at your father."

"It might have been important, but I don't even remember much of it. The one that got angry with Dad was my thirteen-year-old self. She did all the work."

"True, but she must have felt fairly sure that you, the thirty-one-year-old, could pull her through the confrontation alive. You were ready to release all those feelings or it wouldn't have happened. Your anger toward your dad was finally stronger than your fear. Because you stood up to him, he'll no longer have control over your life, and you can begin to heal."

The words seemed to puncture a hole in my self-esteem, causing my defensiveness to rise. "The Gary Gilmore breakdown amounted to nothing? I thought I was healed then. I thought I was done with therapy! Now you're saying I'm just beginning to heal? I don't think I can survive another breakdown!"

"Diann, your progress has been remarkable, both times." Her words were as soft as goose down. My tense body melted in relief as I sank into the soothing sound of her sentences. She began to talk about how I had courageously shared with my family about Dad's secret life with me. She said I was breaking the pattern of abuse for my children and for generations to come. Telling my story had been an important part of my healing and a springboard in taking the next step in my process, namely, getting in touch with my feelings about what happened. I had, through this last breakdown, successfully battled Dad's ghost and won my freedom. I was now at liberty to discover me—what I believed, how I felt, and who I was.

She went on to say it hadn't felt safe to explore my feelings as long as I was still connected to Dad. She called the connection between Dad and me "trauma bonding" and said that with this last breakdown, I'd broken that bond. I listened to her with my ears, but I heard her in my heart. I knew what she was saying was true.

In the next couple of sessions I started talking about my successes. I told her, proudly, that I'd finished her assignment and had talked to all my siblings. I told her in sharing my story, I'd found empowerment. This was the first time talking about the abuse had caused healing in my life, not disaster. I discovered my family found me lovable.

I told her since embracing the concept of reincarnation, I no longer felt like a victim. I'd chosen my family in order to learn valuable lessons. I talked about Easter and blooming, dancing, and simplicity. After about five sessions, we both decided the crisis was over. My life was full again, but not frenzied, and I felt ready to venture out on my own, complete with my shiny new set of tools.

In the last session, she again encouraged me to be selfish. This time, I understood her meaning. She said part of being selfish entailed getting a support system, beyond family and friends, who could help with personal growth and healthy expression of feelings.

I was way ahead of her on that one. I already had my perfect support system. I said excitedly, "I don't know if you are familiar with the Women's School Network, but I teach fitness classes there. They offer classes that are geared to women. I plan on taking many of their self-help, self-esteem classes."

Dr. Keller smiled and pushed me out of the nest, knowing I was ready to fly.

So, for the next couple of years, I went on a journey seeking to find the real Diann. Because I taught fitness classes for the Women's School Network, I was able to take many of their personal growth classes for free.

As far as self-help classes were concerned, I walked in the door a scared, vulnerable baby with baggage. I was a small seedpod seeking an environment in which to grow. It was clear the first day of my first class I'd come to the right place. I immediately found two Diann-affirming mentors, Nancy and Rosa.

Nancy, the head of the organization, was my Mother Earth. Solid and grounded in her beliefs, she showered me with her warmth and wisdom. She had all the time in the world to watch me bloom and grow. Even though in my life she often played the role of a mature, wise, nurturing mother, we also had a reciprocal relationship. We both felt comfortable sharing almost everything happening in our lives. We had much in common, including one big vice: We were both smokers. We'd sit for hours, talking and smoking. Nancy would boost my confidence, and I'd go home feeling lighter than air.

At home, Joe would deflate my "stupid, crazy" ideas of independence and self fulfillment in a split second. I'd arrive in Nancy's office the following morning crying. Nancy's wise words would soothe my wounds. As I began to change and grow, Joe felt more threatened and intensified his verbal attacks.

In true queen-of-the-ringers fashion, I developed calluses to protect me from Joe's stinging words. For the most part, I was able to ignore his hurtful assaults. I was a woman on a mission, and nothing could stop me now. I still was unable to fight him, but occasionally I thought if I kept honing my skills, I would once again be a strong, unstoppable force.

My other mentor was Rosa, a short, petite, Italian powerhouse exuding a lust for life and learning. Her self-esteem classes were full of pearls of wisdom such as, "Please don't identify me with the things I've done that were unskilled responses to life situations" and "I will love myself without conditions, not when, if, or because."

I began repeating these and other affirmations over and over. Due to the affirmations and Rosa's inspirational classes, I found myself halfway believing I was an authentically good person. The other half of me, however, knew I was bad, only pretending to be good, which made me a fraud. The core of me was still rotten, and positive affirmations didn't apply. Joe was right: I was fatally flawed and undeserving of love. Nancy and Rosa didn't know the real me.

One day after class, Rosa approached me. "Diann, you've done so well in my classes, Nancy and I have been talking about what might be the next step in your healing. We know your story and agree that expressing your anger might be it. We're co-facilitating a one-day anger workshop, and we'd love for you to participate. What do you think?"

Instead of thoughts, flashes of scenes rushed through my consciousness: nightmares of Dad chasing me, a picture of me screaming, my thirteen-year-old self trying to kill Dad, me in a fetal position, me in a straitjacket. These movie clips led to a thought process that yelled, *Heck, no! I'm healing just fine, thank you very much. Dealing with anger and jumping off a cliff are synonymous. Too dangerous.* No, I definitely didn't want another nervous breakdown; I might not come back to the real world this time. I'd believed the worst was over, but what if I was wrong?

Even if I didn't have another breakdown and didn't have to be institutionalized, there was the problem of being found out. At the Women's School, I'd successfully hidden my true self. I wasn't looking forward to revealing my rotten core. An anger class most certainly would expose me as a fraud. It'd be in my best interest to continue what I was doing—namely, safely and slowly elevating my self-esteem. Esteem boosting allowed me to take the Fifth; I wouldn't be forced to incriminate myself.

I'd made up my mind. "Rosa," I said, my eyes lowered to avoid an unnecessary confrontation, "thanks so much for asking, but I've already gotten mad at Dad, and I don't think…"

Just then a gentle palm cupped my cheek, which made me turn my face and look up. I saw, behind gentle brown eyes, the kindest of souls. Rosa's warm, impish smile snuggled me with a message of safety and hope. "Okay, I'll do it!" The words had defiantly marched out of my mouth, and there wasn't a dang thing I could do about it.

When Rosa exclaimed, "Good for you!" and hugged me, I knew I was committed. My negative side thought, *Yeah, hopefully not to a mental institution.*

The next Saturday, I walked into a large room scattered with pillows. Several couches were arranged in a circular fashion. I saw four other women who looked as apprehensive as I felt.

Then my eyes fell on Nancy and Rosa, and my stomach started to calm. Nancy's large, powerful frame filled the room with empathy. She addressed the class, saying, "We wanted to provide you with a safe environment both physically and emotionally. Pillows are safe, don't you think?" The audience, including me, nodded our heads and tittered nervously. "As far as emotional safety goes, Rosa and I are here to make sure things won't get destructive or out of control."

There was an audible sigh of relief at this statement. Nancy went on to say, "Women sometimes have difficulty expressing anger because of our traditional, nurturing, noncombative role. Women tend to be relational peacekeepers. We, on the whole, tend to view anger as destructive. Often this belief stems from abuse experienced in the past. Woman also tend to stuff their anger and are sometimes afraid if they let the monster out, it'll be so big and strong, they won't be able to control it. The fear is they'll become destructive themselves. Does anyone relate to these statements?" The head-nodding was almost violent. "So, why do we need to deal with past anger?"

Rosa quickly jumped in. "Releasing your anger is important in order to move through this world as a whole human being. Past anger tends to keep you stuck and is often stored as resentment. It's a secondary emotion compressing the other feelings, including joy and happiness. It doesn't matter how many self-esteem classes you take or how many affirmations you make, if you continue to hold onto anger, I believe it's almost impossible to achieve wholeness. The pillows in the room are to be used freely as punching bags. We invite you to growl, scream, or use any other sounds that help you to release. We'll be here to support and guide you as needed. One by one, please introduce yourself, tell the group why you're angry, and the group will help you express it. Who'd like to go first?"

That wouldn't be me.

I listened as the other members of the group released their anger: one woman over being abandoned by her mother, another woman who had been cheated on by her husband, a woman who had been struggling with drug abuse her whole adult life because of the physical abuse she received as a child, and a victim of domestic violence. I watched them successfully get angry and was buoyed by their courage. I happily cheered them on and felt release when they were finished.

As usual, I chose to go last. I always chose this position because of the sensational nature of my story. I didn't want anyone ever to feel their experience wasn't important. On the other hand, I wanted the group to view humans as resilient, able to survive and heal from even the most horrendous traumas. I was also aware my pain wasn't even close to the atrocities committed against humanity in third-world countries.

What noble reasons I came up with! Maybe the real reason I always went last was I was a big scaredy-cat, afraid of my own shadow. Maybe things really weren't that bad; maybe I was exaggerating circumstances just to get attention. Whatever the case, I realized all eyes were on me, waiting for me to say something.

I took one large gulp and started my story. "I'm angry at my dad because he sexually abused me from the time I was five years old until I was thirteen, at which time he was caught. Instead of facing the consequences of his actions, he elected to murder my very pregnant mother and three of my younger siblings. My father was executed in the gas chamber and died before any of his children expressed anger toward him for his actions. I wasn't able to show anger at him until my breakdown a couple of years ago when I reverted to my thirteen-year-old self. That doesn't really count because I only remember bits and pieces."

The group's eyes were deer-in-the-headlights eyes, big and unblinking. Nancy seemed unperturbed because she said calmly, "Okay, Diann. That's the story. Now what are you angry about?"

"Well, I didn't like what he did to me. I didn't like living with shame my whole life because of the choices he made for me."

Then Rosa said, "You didn't *like* it? Come on, Diann, get angry. Just let it go."

Rosa started the group chanting, "Let it go! Let it go! Get angry! Get angry!"

Nancy yelled, "What are you angry about, Diann?"

With trepidation I said, "I hate you, Dad. I hate what you did to me. You killed Mom and our babies. You took the chicken way out by asking to be executed."

Nancy said, "That's a start, Diann. Now feel it. Let's hear you. Scream it."

"Dad, your last words to me were so trite. What did you mean, don't let what you did to me affect the rest of my life? It has affected me every moment since then. You chickenshit! You bastard! Yes, I'm swearing and there's not a damn thing you can do about it! I hate you for murdering Mom and the babies! How crafty of you to die before you had to feel your children's anger. I hate you! I hate you for taking away my innocence, my childhood. I hate you for raping me for years and making me feel like it was my fault. I hate you for taking away my children's grandparents. I hate you for the pain you caused me and my siblings."

And then I began sobbing uncontrollably. All the air in my body was gone, deflated by my blistering anger. My legs could no longer hold me up, and as they started to crumple, I began to fall.

I fell into the strong, supportive arms of six women. They held me up, whispering in my ears "good girl," "you did it," "you're so brave," "way to go," "you're safe." In my crumpled heap, I felt simultaneously drained and fired up. My newfound expression of anger was exhausting and energizing at the same time.

For many years, to deal with the mountain of frozen feelings, I had covered myself in a glacial coating of numbness alternating with a blizzard of frenzied activity. The anger workshop had changed things; my icy emotions had melted into a molten, red flow of rage. I was happy the heat of my anger had burned away my sickly subservient connection with Dad. I was concerned, however, that this anger would continue to burn, finally incinerating all the love in my heart, leaving me with only ashes of hate.

I liked the power being mad at Dad gave me, but hate had me in a claustrophobic chokehold. I knew I didn't want to be stuck, period. I didn't want to shut down or run away from my feelings, but I also didn't want to stay only to fight if it meant feeling hate and shutting out love. I didn't want to go back, but I didn't know how to move forward.

After a couple of months of hating Dad, being critical of Mom, and being judgmental of the people in my life, including myself, I decided I needed a new outlook. I was sitting alone outside of the Women's School watching the graceful, grey swirl of cigarette smoke stretch skyward and then dissipate into blue. I was thinking I'd like my life to be fluid and lazy like smoke. No, perhaps I wanted to feel light and billowy like clouds. I had more questions than answers. I was asking myself what my next move was in this healing process and who would help me find the answers when a familiar voice floated into my consciousness.

"Diann, how are you?" Gentle yet strong words of concern pulled me back to the world. I looked up to see Rosa's smiling face.

"I'm doing fine." My wide grin attempted to underscore my sentence. Since Rosa, in reincarnation terms, was an "old soul," she seemed to bypass the words riding on my smile to look through my eyes.

"You may be wondering what your next step should be."

"How did you know what I…"

She had an impish look on her face that said, *Let's not waste time! I know you.*

Loud voices inside me told me it wasn't safe to share, but for some reason I trusted her. To my amazement, I told her about my needs and wants. "I need help! I want to get out of this anger/hate phase I seem to be in, thanks to your workshop." What I didn't say was that I was feeling vulnerable. I still felt the need to protect myself.

Her eyes sparkled as she said, "You did amazing work with anger, but it sounds like you're feeling stuck. Am I hearing you're ready to let go of the anger and resentment but you're a little afraid of what will happen if you do?"

My inside anger, still in control, snapped, *You're damn right I'm scared.* My critical voice took over. *Swearing again, huh? You and your filthy thoughts are out of control. You're weak. You're unstable. You're a big baby! What are you whining about? It wasn't that bad.*

What I said out loud, in the calmest voice I could muster, was, "You're right. I'm afraid if I really let go, I'll feel powerless again. I don't know if I'm ready. I don't like the anger, but it does make me feel powerful and protected. If I let go, I'm afraid of drowning in all the tears and pain. What if I can't handle it? I hate nervous breakdowns with a passion. I won't go back there!"

Rosa's voice was gentle but firm. "Diann, you were afraid your anger work would cause a breakdown. How did you feel after the workshop?

"Relieved…strong," I said weakly.

"You've told me you believe everything happens for a reason. Maybe there's a reason we're talking about this now." I nodded slowly.

"It sounds like you want help in letting go of your anger. I'm teaching a weekly class on forgiveness. I think it might give you the tools you need in order to move on."

"Do I have to forgive him?" I blurted out, feeling like a kid.

"No, of course not. You're in charge of your process."

Rosa said exactly what I wanted to hear: *I'm in charge. It's my choice.* I found myself looking at the ground as my kid voice continued to ask more questions. "If I forgive Dad, does it mean I think what he did to me and the family was okay? Will I be letting him off the hook?"

Rosa, voice light as angel wings, lifted my face up to gaze into her kind eyes. "I'm quite sure you'll choose to do what's right for you." She paused before stating her views on the subject. "It's my belief you're not condoning your father's behavior or letting him off the hook if you choose to be free of the hold he has on you. He can't hurt you physically or sexually anymore, but it sounds as if he still invades you in the form of anger and pain. I see forgiveness as the process of letting go of those negative feelings about him in order to truly be in control of your life." She stopped, as was Rosa's way, to let things sink in. Then, in total Rosa style, she gave me a zinger. "And, of course, the process involves forgiving yourself!"

I didn't know if this forgiveness idea would work, but I knew I needed and wanted to try. Dad's words pushed down hard on my heart: "Try not to let what I did to you affect the rest of your life." *Well, Dad, if I'm able to forgive you, you'll no longer have any control over me. I'll always remember what you did, but you won't be able to affect or violate my peace and happiness ever again. I'll be free to be who I choose to be for the rest of my life.*

"Where do I sign? When do I start?"

With notebook in hand, commitment in my brain, and hope in my heart, I entered the class. Lessons one through five covered everything from communication, including communication stoppers, to belief systems and how they interface with emotions. I learned such gems as "guilt requires payment in pain" and "when negative experiences are confronted, they lose their power." Lessons six through nine involved structured journaling and sharing thoughts and emotions with the class.

Journaling was a powerful tool because it allowed me to concretely see the thoughts and feelings I'd always bottled inside. It validated those feelings in a way talking never had. As I wrote, the sleeping thoughts and feelings from the past awakened.

At first, an anxious chatter ensued, electrifying my nerves, which felt like my muscles were racing down my arm and into the hand holding my pen. The words spilled out onto the page of their own volition. They seemed to mirror my mind, gushing out in an erratic, seemingly senseless fashion. But after a while, the pressure of all the stuffed feelings began to diminish. The raging flash flood of feelings transformed into a rushing mountain stream of thoughts, which became a meandering brook of words, strung together in sentences, pooling in serene reflections. It was such a relief to let the past out of my body onto paper where I could examine it objectively. The material wasn't new. In fact, it'd been old for a long time. What was new was holding it still, turning it over, examining it from a different angle, and viewing it with a detached curiosity. My answers to a series of questions led me to the peace and freedom of forgiveness.

First, I wrote about my mother, which was, I noticed, just as much about me as it was about her. I wrote, *I craved love, attention, a feeling of specialness and worth, but instead I was labeled bad—felt bad—was bad.*

I wrote that *what I wanted and didn't get was protection from my father.* I felt Mom couldn't or wouldn't make Dad stop abusing me because she thought I was making it all up. Looking back, thinking Mom didn't believe me was the precursor to feeling like I was a fraud.

I resented the fact Mom didn't have time for me. In order to survive, I had to try to be the perfect helper. I went on to say, *I'm so afraid to believe that in all those years (5-13) that I wasn't important enough to her to get her protection.* In hopeful contradiction to that thought, I said, *I'm beginning to suspect she did the best she could for the times. How do you put the rest of the family in jeopardy for one child (me) when there are so many others to consider?* Incest wasn't out in the open then—she didn't have anyone to talk to about it. I'd have been scared, too, with so many mouths to feed and no skills.

I wrote about Dad, saying, he had all the power. He controlled me through punishment and gifts. He dominated my feelings; most of my pain, happiness, sadness, and positive strokes came from him. *For me he was the FORCE. There was no way I could fight his power. I always felt guilty about my weakness in giving in.* I went on to explain his affect on my self esteem. Because of incest, I viewed myself as a whore. For years I was promiscuous, believing my only asset was my sexuality.

What I wanted from Father and didn't get was a "normal" father-daughter relationship. I had no choice but to dutifully play the role of his wife, confidant whore, possession, and scapegoat. I simply wished to be a daughter. I resented Dad's perfect family-man image because I knew differently.

I then wrote about how I could respond to my traumatic upbringing. I decided it was possible to become a whole, productive person by letting go of the pain and hang-ups of my childhood. If I decided to lie to rest the bad feelings of the past, I could grow beyond my hurt and self destructive patterns. I could choose to learn to grow into a healthy human being. The choice was both exhilarating and frightening. I had so many unknowns and questions that scared me; who would I be if I made all these changes? Would I recognize myself? Would I like who I had become?

The forgiveness phase of the journal came next. I pictured Mother with an encouraging smile on her face but a bit of apprehension in her eyes. I think she worried that I may have difficulty forgiving her for not protecting me., It was true that since becoming a mother, I better understood her actions, but I still wished she had done something to stop the abuse.

To the question of how I thought Mom felt about life in general, I wrote she felt trapped. I went on to say, *Dad was such a controlling person who gave you no room for independent thought. Momma, how did you put up with it all? You must have known about the affairs, and you certainly knew about me. How horrible for you not to have had a choice. I hear your cry of desperation for your life and your plea to me to understand. I do, Momma! As a wife and mother, I can imagine the kind of pain you must have suffered with Dad.*

Empathy for Mom's situation brought me to the conclusion that she loved and protected me to the best of her ability considering the times and circumstances. I had thought she didn't help me because she didn't love me. I now realized she truly loved me, she simply didn't know how to help. I guess, I couldn't accept Mom's love because I didn't feel deserving of love. I felt unlovable.

Mom, I do forgive you. It especially helps knowing you were doing something to help me before you died. I love you, Mom. Thanks for being with me so often now. Thank you for the great foundation you gave me.

I tackled forgiving Mom because she was the easiest. With Mom forgiven, I took on Dad. In my mind's eye, I saw a pain-stricken, pleading look on my father's face. I was relieved to see his expression devoid of the arrogant smirk he usually wore. *Dad, I don't see any evil in your face. No sign of power. You look defeated.* It seemed as if for the first time in my life, I had power over Dad. He was begging for my forgiveness and I could choose to say no. This time I was in control. I chose to ask him some questions. Even though he was very tense, I made him wait for my decision. *Do you think I can forgive you? Do you think I will? Are you going to run away if I don't?*

Dad ran away from all of his problems. I was pleased I was finally seeing Dad through a different lens. The little-girl perception of Dad's omnipotence and strength was gone. Dad wasn't strong; he was a coward. He molested me and killed Mom and the babies because he was too chicken to face the consequences of his actions.

In my journal, I talked about how he probably felt as a husband and a father, saying he *felt confident, strong, in control of the situation. He had his wife and children totally under control.*

In a lot of ways, he was a great father. He taught us how to be a family.

I answered the question, "How do you think he feels about his life as a whole?" *I think in the end the only real accomplishment he felt was his children. He made a good mess of everything else. He must have had lots of trouble living with himself because of his double life. He was never financially successful, but he had seven self-sufficient, healthy, intelligent, and independent children.*

He must be saying, "Please forgive me for all the hurt I gave to all of you, especially you, Diana. I love you Diana, please forgive me. Understand, for me, it was something I really couldn't control. Diana, you've had a taste of that kind of lack of control." He was doing fairly well until the comment about me. I was mad! Yes, I acted out sexually and put myself in danger, and I have forgiven my promiscuity. I'm fairly sure, I wouldn't have been promiscuous if it hadn't been for your abuse of me, Dad. The fact I whored around falls squarely on your shoulders. I understand that at the time there weren't many resources to help you with your problem, but murdering Mom and the babies because of your shame was a horrible solution. I sought help so my children wouldn't suffer. I did the work with the result that I do have control of my sexuality. I am very different from you Dad because **I didn't ever molest children.**

Dad needed to know some things before I went to forgiveness. I told him, *I'll try not to hate you for what you did to me.* I did hate what he did, but I was choosing to let go of hating him as a person. So in the end, my response was, *Dad, I do forgive you and I do love you. I will try to get through the rest of my life without feelings of hate for you. I will try to forgive the ugly things and remember the good things about you. You were just a part of the puzzle of my life; a large piece, to be sure. I think you really did love all of us. And I think you did the right thing by leaving this world.* By choosing to be executed, he saved my children/grandchildren from having to personally feel their grandfather/great-grandfather's legacy.

I finally came to this conclusion: *Yes! I can look at my parents as people, individuals with the same kind of flaws, worries and emotions that I have.* This much was true; Dad was responsible for so much loss: the loss of my innocence, Mom and my babies, my home, and my self-esteem. Dad took much from me, but he also gave me things. He nurtured in me a love of God, a love of family, and a passion for music and dance. So in the end, I decided to let go of the loss and focus on his gifts to me.

Forgiving Mom had been fairly straightforward. I could totally empathize with her plight because, after all, I was living her life. She'd been as dependent on Dad as I was on Joe. Having ten children and being pregnant with the eleventh when she died left her with limited choices.

I could, however, look at her choices from a different angle. It was her choice to marry Dad. She chose to stay dependent on him by continually having kids, not working outside the home, and not learning how to drive. I realized, except for knowing how to drive, my life was eerily similar. I had a bunch of kids; I was a stay-at-home mom. I was dependent on a husband who was obsessed with sex, and we were always broke. Forgiving Mom also meant forgiving the part of me that subscribed to a dependency and poverty mentality. I chose to keep the good stuff about Mom—her laugh, her fun spirit, and her love of children.

I ended my forgiveness journal with these words: *What could happen if I were to truly forgive? I could have more capacity for love. I could feel better about my life as a whole. I would feel free. I could think of my childhood with a smile, instead of with sadness. I could dwell on the good things instead of the bad.*

The process of letting go was also about forgiving myself, which seemed to bolster my sense of self-worth. The year of 1982 was the year of letting go. It was also the year of taking back—taking back the good traits I had inherited from my parents and taking back my power.

CHAPTER 19

Mom the Cat

Early in February 1983, a cat showed up at our house. She was a Russian Blue with large green eyes. I shooed it away. I'm not a cat person; in fact, I'm highly allergic to cats. The next day, when I returned from taking the kids to school, the cat was back on the front porch. This pattern continued for several more days, and I shooed it away each time.

One evening while we were eating dinner, the green-eyed cat showed up once again. She strutted along the windowsill outside our kitchen window, peering in.

"Dumb cat! I'm taking care of this once and for all," I said. I picked up a broom and went outside, headed for the cat. "Go away! Go away!" I hissed, swinging the broom.

She hissed and arched her back. Her fur was standing straight up. Her spitting and ferocious green eyes scared the bejesus out of me. I immediately screamed, dropped the broom, and ran back into the house. I was panting, and my eyes were wide as I said, "It was like a big tiger!"

Joe and the kids burst out laughing. The cat was here to stay. That night I fed it, and that night Mom began to visit me in my dreams.

These dreams lacked the nightmare quality my dreams of Dad had. Far from being scary, these dreams were more of the persistent variety. Mom's message was always the same: "It's been twenty years since our deaths. It's time to get the family together and talk about what happened. It's time for all of you to heal and move on with your lives."

I'd talked to each person individually about my abuse, but we hadn't shared our thoughts and feelings as a family. Through my dreams, Mom kept emphasizing the importance of the meeting while the cat played an irritating, nagging role by day.

As the dreams progressed, she became more specific. "I want the meeting to occur this coming May. I know I can count on you."

Meanwhile, the cat made her way into our lives. The ethereal quality of this cat, with her green eyes so like Mom's, was a persistent reminder of my responsibility to gather the family together. I was tempted to name her Nora but finally decided to let the kids name her. They named her Snoopy. Joe wanted to get rid of her. "You know I hate cats. Snoopy is no exception."

I disliked cats too, but this cat, at least in my mind, was somehow indelibly linked to my mother, so she stayed.

Getting the whole family together seemed impossible. Michael and his family were in Vera Cruz, Mexico, and couldn't be contacted. Jean told me she couldn't possibly come, with too many activities in the month of May. Al was still on his independent, disengaged, alcoholic streak. He adamantly stated he'd talked to Dad daily the week of his execution and had nothing to discuss. Paul had trouble believing Mom had initiated a meeting but said he would show up if I could pull it together. Patrick and Lee were still ensconced in the Hare Krishna commune and wouldn't commit.

I was discouraged, but Mom, night after night, kept encouraging me. And day after day, the cat kept looking at me with those pleading eyes.

In February I'd reached a low point. Despite my best efforts, this meeting didn't look like it was going to happen. On February 10, the doorbell rang. I opened the door and was startled to find Ganendra standing on my front porch. I had no idea he'd left West Virginia. "Hi, Di, I'm home. Can I stay with you for a while?"

"Well, happy birthday, brother. Of course you can stay. Come in. It's cold outside."

He came in and looked down as the cat rubbed against his legs. "You own a cat? How did this happen?"

"She wouldn't leave," I said.

"Pretty eyes. What's her name?"

"Snoopy," I said, not wanting to explain.

Discouraged with the Hare Krishna community, he'd decided to come home. Upon arriving in Denver, brother Ganendra returned to his given name. The kids didn't adopt either name; they affectionately called him "UG".

Lee's return to Denver brought new energy to my efforts to see Mom's wish granted. To me he renewed hope the family would somehow come together. The weeks went by, and I held on to a strong belief it would happen. Since in my dream Mom kept insisting the meeting be held in May, I scheduled it for Friday evening, May 20. I couldn't guess who'd be there.

In April Jean called. "Di, you won't believe this, but I had a dream about Mom last night. Mom wants us to get together. She told me to come to your home. It's still a terrible time, but I'll make it work. I'll fly in on Thursday night, May 19, and leave on Saturday, May 21."

Two weeks before the scheduled date, Michael and his family returned from Vera Cruz. I told him about the meeting, and he assured me he'd be there. He also volunteered his home as the meeting place. With Michael back and the other siblings falling in line, Paul told me he'd definitely come as well.

Around that same time, Ambarish called and said that he also would be there. He told me he was feeling a strong pull to be home for the meeting. He took a bus from Pittsburgh and came in just for a long weekend. The only sibling who refused to come was Al. He was still isolating himself from the family.

So the meeting was held at Michael's house. Mom had been specific that she wanted only her children to attend. Spouses were to be included after the initial meeting was over. Some of the spouses were upset with this arrangement and felt they had a right to be included, but all six of us agreed initially it just needed to be us. We sat comfortably in Michael's family room. Michael, Jean, and Lee sat on the couch; Paul was lounging in the La-Z-Boy; and Ambarish and I sat on the floor. The cat, having completed her assignment, was at my house sleeping in Rese's room.

I started the meeting by saying, "Mom brought us here today so we could share face-to-face what happened to us twenty years ago. I've talked to all of you individually about what happened to me. But we've never shared our thoughts and feelings as a group. Mom wants us to share so we can heal."

At this point, the silence became deafening as every one of us traveled back in time to the year 1963. We all became kids again. I began. "You know I blamed myself for the murders. I believed they were my fault because I thought I could've stopped the abuse. I ran away the week before and talked to Aunt Lily and Uncle Tom even though Dad warned me he'd kill me if I told anyone."

When I took a breath, Jean piped in, "No, Di, it was my fault because it never would've happened if I hadn't told him I'd tell Mom."

"Hold on, everyone. I'm the oldest. I should've been the one to stop him. I should've protected you, Di," Michael said.

"No," said Paul. "I did something bad that day. It was God's punishment. It was my fault."

"I was only a little kid, but I remember that night like today. It was horrible. I rode in the ambulance with Jean and Di. I never felt responsible, but I sure felt bad," said Lee.

We all looked at Ambarish. His head was down. He said softly, "I wasn't even there. I didn't know anything had happened. Michael and Jean picked me up from camp the next day. I knew something was wrong then. Aunt Ruby told me when I got back to Denver. If Dad had carried out his plan, I would've been… Oh, God, I would've been the only one left. If I'd been home, maybe I could've stopped it." Ambarish let out a sob. All of us were crying, flooding the room with twenty years' worth of released guilt.

Then Michael's strong voice filled the room, pushing our cries away. "We were kids. We weren't responsible; Dad was!"

"At sixteen, I hated Dad. I hate him now for what he did to you, Di. No, the truth is, I hate him for what he did to all of us," Jean declared. "By asking for the death penalty, he took the chicken way out."

"He died with the love of his children intact. If he were still in prison, he would've had to face our anger," I said.

"And hate," added Jean.

"What I despise is the execution part. If he'd just been locked up, we wouldn't have had to deal with the media. He left us to deal with his mess, and all of us boys carry his name," said Paul. "We can't get away from the media. He died, and even after twenty years, we're still living with his execution."

"I was only eight when Mom died. What I can't believe is that we went to visit Dad every Sunday for four years. Why didn't anyone say anything?" Lee said.

"I'm not sure," I said slowly, "but I think even though he did terrible things, even though he changed our whole lives, Dad was the only thing we had to hold on to from our old world." Everyone nodded in agreement.

Lee continued, "He was executed when I was twelve, and I'm still dealing with what he did."

"Good old Dad. He left us with one final trauma, one final indignity—his execution," I said.

The tension had drained from the room as we sat encircled by sibling love and understanding.

"Despite everything, we're a great family who loves each other," Michael said, looking around the room. Noticing a vacant spot, he added, "Al will come back to us one day."

"Mom wants us to move forward with our lives and leave the pain of twenty years ago behind," I said.

At this point, everyone stood, and we hugged each of our brothers and sisters. It seemed everyone felt the relief of finally talking about Dad and the murders after all those years of silent suffering. Did it help? Immensely. Did it take away all the pain? No way!

*   *   *

A couple years earlier, Joe had decided he was tired of the collection business. "I want to be on the happy side of money," he said. He sold his business to his brother, Rudy, and went to work for a mortgage company.

By 1983, he was doing quite well financially. Once again we were bursting at the seams; we needed a bigger house. We'd been looking at houses for a few months. We'd toured about forty houses and hadn't yet found the perfect fit. I knew what I was looking for and had a clear picture of my dream house in my mind.

Three days after "Mom's meeting," I went to a potluck with some women friends. I entered the hostess's home and knew within two steps she owned my dream house. After a tour, I had no doubt. The problem was her house was not for sale. I told Joe about the house, and we searched her neighborhood for the same model, hoping to find one for sale. By the first week of June, we found our perfect house, put in an offer, and the offer was accepted. We were going to own our dream house!

On the Fourth of July, exactly twenty years after Mom was buried, we moved into our new home, and it was clear the house was a gift from Mom. She was thanking me for getting her family together. *And thank you, Mom, for this magnificent home.*

Just then I felt a ripple of soft cat fur on my legs. Allergic as I was, I reached down and picked Snoopy up. I snuggled with her and whispered in her ear, "Thanks for being so persistent." I held her out to look into her green eyes. To my astonishment, Mom's spirit was gone; her job done, she'd moved on. Two cat eyes returned my stare. "My, my, Snoopy, you're just a cat again, aren't you?"

Snoopy didn't feel the need to respond.

CHAPTER 20

Shift Happens

Joe's roller-coaster life was chock-full of ups and downs. Life had enough peaks and valleys as it was, and I didn't understand Joe's need to create more. I preferred being on level ground where I could walk, skip, dance, and occasionally leap.

Due to the extraordinary gift from Mom, my life was looking up. Living in my dream house was heavenly. In addition to being a great space to raise four kids, it was a perfect party home. For the next two years, we hosted not only large family gatherings but many all-occasion parties as well. One of the highlights of our party-giving experience was a neighborhood Halloween party in which the whole house was lighted only with candles.

To complete my dream home, we adopted an ideal dog. He was a five-year-old Dalmatian whom we christened Gandalf, from the book *The Hobbit*. Gandalf definitely had my best interests at heart. He slept outside my bedroom door by night and was my constant companion by day. Our quality time together included a daily five-mile walk through the neighborhood.

Gandalf loved everybody, and the kids and I loved him back. JJ felt especially close. Gandalf was a well-mannered, respectful dog. He was a people pleaser but not the irritating, too-eager type. He gave family members their space. Though it went against his natural instincts, he always obeyed our commands. When we were eating, he'd lie down about five feet away. His polite non-begging garnered him unhealthy table scraps from the whole family. Only under extreme circumstances would he ever consider breaking a rule.

Joe and Gandalf had a tenuous relationship because they were both vying for my attention. There were many times when Gandalf was my clear choice. Gandalf, unlike Joe, seemed to know exactly what I needed no matter what my state of mind, whereas Joe ridiculed my periodic crying jags. Gandalf, wet with my saltwater shower, showed me deep and loving acceptance.

Snoopy despised Gandalf and took to walking the perimeter of the house just to avoid him. I had a hunch Snoopy looked for ways to get our dog in trouble. One evening, the family, already very late, hurriedly exited the house for an event. We left, among other items, a tub of butter in the center of the kitchen table.

Returning three hours later, we opened the front door to find Snoopy waiting for us. We were all surprised to see her there because she'd never, ever met us at the door. She gazed up at us with an air of superiority. Her expression seemed to say, "Follow me. You're not going to be happy with the dog." Her tail up, she slowly, deliberately walked to the kitchen, knowing we'd follow. There was a bloated Gandalf and an empty butter tub, both lying on their sides. Snoopy expected the dog to receive a severe reprimand, and when it didn't happen, she left in disgust.

I remembered my remorse after eating the entire bag of pistachios at the Good Shepherd Home. Sister Euphrasia had decided she didn't need to discipline me because I'd punished myself enough. Gandalf was of the same ilk; he had such a hang-dog, conscience-stricken expression on his face that I instantly forgave him. His stomachache was punishment enough, and his gas was a potent reminder to put away all the food regardless of the circumstances, especially with Snoopy around. Gandalf remained the family protector, my shadow, Joe's nemesis, Snoopy's arch enemy, and JJ's best friend for as long as he lived.

In the center of our dream home was our spacious living room, which was large enough to hold biweekly fitness classes. Dana, one of my students, and I became fast friends. Over time, as we shared our life stories with one another, I discovered she was a writer. Dana was so intrigued by my story she decided to write a synopsis of my life, which she hoped might become an outline for a future book.

Over the next several months, I talked and Dana put my life in written form. In the past, telling my story to my family and Dr. Keller had helped me heal. This project seemed to be one more way to mend myself. This synopsis was a validation of my survival, and for the first time my focus was to share my story to help others. I wanted the words to march out into the world and tap mothers on their shoulders and say, "Pay attention to your precious children. Watch for signs of abuse." I wanted my words to wrap themselves softly around those who had been sexually abused and give them hope.

*   *   *

From 1981 through the middle of 1984, Joe was doing well in the mortgage business. The interest rates were reasonable, and home sales were booming. Sadly, by the end of 1984, interest rates went through the roof, and the bottom fell out of the mortgage business. In an effort to beef up his business, Joe changed companies a couple of times. Instead of increasing business, however, each move seemed to have the opposite effect.

With our dwindling income, I was forced to get a nine-to-five job. This was a sharp departure from my stay-at-home-mom status. I'd worked side jobs for spending money or benefits. I'd taught dance and aerobics for the Woman's School Network in exchange for being able to attend classes and taught bi-weekly fitness classes in our home for extra cash. I resisted for as long as I could getting a real job, but being a pragmatist, I realized my family needed my financial contribution. After fifteen years of staying home with my children, diving into the work force was daunting, so I waded in slowly by starting at a temp agency.

I was soon hired full-time by an oil and gas company. My employer liked my typing skills but was more impressed with my ability to multi-task and to stay calm in stressful, chaotic situations. I guess being a mom of four kids and a wife to an erratic husband provided me with the right skill set. I was also valued, I was told, because I was smart, efficient, and dependable. The more self-assured and independent I became, the less Joe seemed to like me and the less I believed him when he called me stupid.

Alas, our combined income wasn't enough to sustain living in our dream house. None of us wanted to leave, but all of us did what we had to do. I was fairly resigned leading up to the move, but my tear reservoir was building. I was stuffing my feelings again, Fibber McGee-style, and the closet was about to burst open.

In the end, it wasn't the move that pushed me down into the black hole; it was Gandalf. He was suffering from a severe case of hip dysplasia. I was suffering from intense guilt knowing his hip pain was partially due to his nightly snack of table scraps. We didn't have any money for surgery, so we put down my dear, sweet boy the day before the move.

My immense grief over Gandalf, coupled with the devastating loss of our dream house, found me in my bedroom sobbing for a whole day. After the day of release, I emerged from the bedroom weak and drained but ready to start stuffing again until the next balloon burst.

We found a patio home in the same general area in order to keep the kids in their respective schools. We were all sad to leave our beautiful house, but at least we knew one family in our new neighborhood. Jackie, a Realtor who worked with Joe, was a single parent with four children similar in age to my kids. She lived just a few blocks from us.

Jackie, I soon learned, was an absentee mom. Because work and social events were Jackie's priorities, her kids—Ryan, Dena, David, and Jamie—became part of the landscape of our home. My eleven-year-old daughter, Gina, and fourteen-year-old Ryan seemed particularly bonded. I thought they were just very good friends. Gina felt differently. As an adult she told me she thought Ryan liked her as a girlfriend but was going out with other girls until she was old enough to have sex.

One day in the summer of 1986, left again to their own devices, Ryan and the girl he was seeing, along with all his siblings, were walking in an adjoining neighborhood when another teenager whistled at Ryan's girlfriend. Incensed, Ryan and Dena went home and armed themselves with knives and a machete. They returned to confront the whistler. Ryan proceeded to slice the boy's heart in two with the knife while his siblings watched.

The murder profoundly affected our whole family. It felt as if this event shot each one of us in the heart with a stun gun. When the immediate shock began to wear off, we were left with a confused numbness. JJ, Rese, and Mandy experienced times of anger and sadness but were able to resume their lives. Joe as usual wouldn't or couldn't express his feelings, and I as usual stuffed mine.

Gina was unreachable. I tried to coax her back into our world, but I couldn't get any response. I decided she was probably in shock and just needed some time and space. She was so quiet and withdrawn we paid little attention to her in the following weeks. We were focused on mobilizing our resources to help with the trial. We were supportive of Jackie even to the point of accompanying her to court. Ryan and Dena were eventually found guilty and sent away to juvenile facilities. Jackie sent the other kids to a relative out of state. When it became apparent Jackie had no intention of mothering any of her kids, I severed the friendship.

By the time I refocused my attention on Gina, she was in a tailspin ready to crash. From things she said and didn't say, I gathered both that she had a severe crush on Ryan and she was severely crushed by the murder. She was in trouble and inconsolable. It was as if *she* had been stabbed in the heart.

When school began, my straight-A student began receiving Cs and Ds and skipping school. By the second month of school, her acting out began in earnest. She abruptly changed her group of friends. Gina's behavior in particular concerned me because it was so similar to mine as a teenager. She was exhibiting the behavior of a sexually abused child. I attempted to find out what was going on, but Gina was not talking. My sweet girl became belligerent, and I didn't have the tools or the time to focus on her. I knew I'd been an excellent mom when the kids were little, but I was at a loss as to how to parent teens.

To add to my distress, JJ was being a typical teenager, getting into minor scrapes at school. Joe, when he wasn't at the bars, was often terrorizing us at the dinner table with his erratic behavior. When I was out in public with Joe, he was often embarrassingly drunk, loud, and lewd. The black hole of depression threatened to engulf me again. My life felt like it was going down the toilet.

The only people who didn't seem to be draining me were Rese and Mandy. Both loved school and seemed fairly content with life. One day, ten-year-old Mandy rushed into the house bursting with excitement.

"I want to be Donald Duck for the Disney Spectacular. My teacher said I could! The whole fifth grade gets to be in the show. But Mom, I need a Donald Duck costume that really looks exactly like him. Can you make it? Can you?"

"I'm glad you're so excited. It sounds like a fun show. I don't think I have the skills to make your costume, but I know who does. What about Angie?" Even though we'd moved, Angie and I had kept in contact. Our families visited each other frequently.

"Angie! Angie can do it. She'll make it look just like him." I smiled and nodded. "Call her. Call her right now." And I did.

When I told Angie about Mandy's show, she started laughing hysterically. When she caught her breath, she said, "Mandy will be a great Donald Duck. The character fits her temperament perfectly." I had to agree. Mandy was spectacular because not only did she fit the character, but Angie's costume was a perfect fit in every way.

My work and my book project also energized me, keeping me afloat. By March of 1987, after working on it on and off for about four years, Dana had completed a twenty-one-page synopsis of my life's story, which she entitled *Dead Center*. Upon reading it, my adopted daughter of my heart, Cindy, said, "Mom, you should send this to the *Oprah Winfrey Show*. This is just the kind of stuff she likes."

I responded, "Who's Oprah Winfrey?"

With an exasperated sigh, Cindy explained, "She has a wonderful talk show. She's on TV every day."

On a whim, Dana and I took Cindy's advice and sent the synopsis to the *Oprah* show in March. I then promptly forgot about it. I believed Cindy about the excellence of Oprah's show, but I worked full-time and had no opportunity to watch her in action.

That August, we took a family vacation. We arrived home on a Thursday to a note on the kitchen table written by our neighbor, who'd been feeding Snoopy. The message read, "Call Oprah Winfrey."

Surely this was a joke. Why would Oprah contact me? I read the note a second time more slowly. It was then I remembered the synopsis. I read the note a third time, and then what did I do? I started screaming, "Oprah Winfrey called!"

Joe and the kids came running. The kids were jumping up and down, their excited voices tumbling over each other. I held up my hand for silence, and as they watched, I picked up the phone and called the number for the *Oprah Winfrey Show*. I spoke to one of her producers, who wanted me on the show airing the following Monday. I mouthed "Monday" to my shocked family. I set down the phone and collapsed into a chair. Four laughing kids piled on top of me as a beaming Joe watched from the sideline.

A whirlwind of activity ensued. I overnighted two photos to Oprah, one of me sitting on Dad's lap and a portrait of the whole family taken before Alan, Vincent and Teresa were born. I called Dana to tell her the exciting news. I alerted family and friends and asked them to notify people. I made arrangements to take more time off work.

On Friday, the doorbell rang. It was one of my co-workers. My office mates had taken up a collection so I'd have money to buy a new outfit for the show. Everyone at work was really excited. A TV was to be brought to the office so everyone could watch me on *Oprah*.

Suitcase packed complete with new outfit, parenting duties for Joe listed, kids kissed, family notified, I boarded a plane in Denver bound for Chicago. My seat belt was securely fastened, the flight attendant had talked about what to do in case of an emergency, and the plane was in the air. I finally had time to think, and my thoughts terrified me.

Yes, this was indeed an emergency. I wanted off the plane. Sure, I intended to help other victims, but being on *Oprah* was a little extreme. Why had I sent her my story? It was full of the intimate details of my life. The synopsis talked about not only what happened in my childhood but also about me as an adult. Besides, I hadn't even been able to watch her show. *What if Oprah doesn't understand or is disappointed in me?* What was I doing? This was crazy. My new outfit wouldn't help a bit because I'd be naked in front of millions of people. What would my co-workers think of me after I talked about the sexual abuse, murders, and execution?

No, if I was honest, I was worried about what everybody would think of me after I told about my acting out sexually and my breakdowns. *Not much,* a critical voice screamed. *Who do you think you are, anyway? I'll tell you exactly who you are. You're a promiscuous sinner and an unstable person. No one will like you when they hear about the real you.*

A strong, soothing voice responded, *Calm down, Diann. Your co-workers will be supportive. They like you. You're strong. You're resilient. Oprah called you for a reason. She believes you have an important story to tell. You want to help. This is your chance.*

"Yes," I whispered. "Oprah thinks I have an important story to tell. Maybe I do."

I arrived at Midway Airport and was greeted by a limousine driver holding up a sign with my name on it. Detached from my body, I felt like I was floating. This surreal sensation, I told myself, had to be just one of my many vivid dreams, but the limo driver sure looked and sounded real! Even though he drove me to a solid-looking luxury hotel located near the studio in the heart of downtown Chicago, I still couldn't believe what I was experiencing.

Dan, a Denver friend who'd moved to Chicago, brought me back to earth. He picked me up at the hotel and took me to his home to have a delightful dinner with his wife and children. Back at the hotel room, I felt small, alone, insignificant, and wide awake as I tried to sleep in a king-sized bed, in a luxury hotel, in a strange city.

The sun's rays finally put an end to the long, dark night. I dressed and joined the other scheduled guests in the lobby. We were picked up by another limo and driven to Harpo Studios in order to participate in a show entitled "Sole Survivors." All the guests, including me, were placed in a spacious dressing room. The makeup artists were trying hard to create a natural effect. The tension in the room was thick and heavy. I certainly felt like a sole survivor.

When Oprah entered the room, the heaviness vanished and the air smiled. I watched in amazement as she briefly talked to the other guests. In an instant, shoulders relaxed, closed postures opened, frowns smoothed. But then she turned toward me, and I froze. Sitting down across from me, she took my hands in hers. I melted as her face held my eyes and created a space of well being for me. She said with her eyes, *I understand you're scared. You're safe. No one will hurt you when you're with me.*

Her voice enfolded me with warm words as I remember her saying something like, "We're going to be doing things a bit differently today. I'll bring you out on stage by yourself for the first segment. The others will join us later." Since I'd never watched her show, I had no clue what she meant, but I believed all would be fine. I learned later that, at the beginning of the hour, she usually brought on an entire panel of guests to interview throughout the show.

Makeup applied and important instructions received, I was led on wobbly legs onto the stage. Oprah began, "When my first guest's father realized he risked being publicly exposed for sexually abusing her, he then calmly decided to kill his family one by one. He murdered his wife and three of their children, leaving my first guest and the rest of her brothers and a sister alive."

Before I was aware of what was happening, I was being introduced to the audience. I was alone on stage with Oprah, telling my story. We sat in barrel chairs close together. They were angled slightly toward the audience to let them eavesdrop on our conversation. It felt as if I were in a comfortable living room having an intimate talk with a dear, empathetic friend.

She turned her warm, compassionate face toward me and said, "I know this will be a hard story to tell. Just reading it was difficult."

With that we were off, with Oprah asking questions, leading the way through my story. I felt so supported it seemed like she was holding my hands through the entire interview. Later, after watching the tape, I realized this wasn't true. When we were on the air, my hands were sitting in my lap, but I know she held my hands throughout all the commercial breaks. The tape also revealed as I talked about my "very close, loving, large family," the family photo I'd sent flashed on the screen behind me. When I told Oprah about Dad's "great flaw," the photo of me at the age of five sitting on Dad's lap was shown.

The time passed quickly. By the first break, we'd covered my incestuous childhood, Mom and Father Ronney knowing about the abuse, Dad disappearing for two months, the frequency of intercourse, sex being the lesser of two evils, and me running away a week before the murders.

When we came back on the air, Oprah gently guided me through the night of the murders. I nearly lost control when I talked about learning of baby Teresa's death. At this point in the interview, Oprah reached across me to grab a tissue just in case either of us needed one. Neither one of us did.

"I know it's difficult and I don't want to exploit what happened to you, but later in your father's confession, he explained how he killed the family and why he did it. And the reason was what?" I realized then I had felt exploited by the media for twenty years. Not once had any reporter or interviewer been sensitive to my feelings, not until Oprah.

I talked about Dad's flawed thinking, the murders, Alan saving us, and our family's disgust with the media.

Oprah's first question after a second break was, "How did you cope?" She immediately added "People cope in different ways." She had by this comment invited me to share any answer I wished to share as well as preparing the audience for whatever strange answer I might give.

To my surprise, probably due to Oprah's safe, soothing demeanor, I felt comfortable telling the world about my foibles.

When I presented my sexual promiscuity as a coping tool, Oprah normalized my behavior by saying, "That is what happens to a lot of people who are involved in incest and abuse," I could have kissed her.

Oprah had an uncanny ability of validating my feelings while simultaneously using my story to educate. She told the audience that my feelings of being alone, flawed, bad, and undeserving of good things were all normal responses to being an abuse victim. She went on to say sexual abuse was quite common. She got a laugh when she stated, "It happens in homes that everybody is acting like they're Beaver Cleaver." *Amen,* I thought. We continued our chat, covering the myth "all daddies do this," my stay at the Good Shepherd Home, visiting the prison every Sunday, and the execution. Before I knew it, another break occurred, which signaled the end of my interview. I stayed on stage for the second half of the show while the rest of the guests told their stories. A trauma expert from Seattle talked for about two minutes. Walking to the limo, my mind took flight. *I'd made it! I'd survived my childhood and endured the pain so I could help others. I talked and people listened. Oprah believed my story and thought it important. Oprah thinks I'm valuable. Maybe I am valuable.*

In the limo ride back to the hotel with the other guests, the expert expressed his anger at me, saying I dominated the show. He felt his two minutes of talk time was an insult. For an instant, I reverted back to my old feelings of not being special enough to take up so much time. The moment passed quickly. I smiled as he continued to rant and rave. I didn't feel guilty; it was, after all, Oprah's call.

After arriving at the hotel and bidding farewell to the other guests, I hastened to my room to pack my things. Riding down in the elevator to the lobby, I felt a pair of eyes staring at me. Feeling uncomfortable, I asked, "May I help you?"

"Excuse me for staring, but weren't you just on *Oprah?*"

"Yes, I was," I said, not knowing what else to say.

"Your story was heart-wrenching. You're so courageous," the woman with perfectly coiffed hair and makeup said.

"Thank you," I replied, thinking it wasn't about courage; it was just about doing what I *had* to do. No, I was doing what I *chose* to do. There was a difference.

A limo was waiting for me as I exited my hotel. As soon as I was comfortably seated, the limo driver said, "Test to see if the car phone works. You will be receiving a call."

I checked the phone, thinking, *Who'd be calling me?*

When the phone rang, I jumped. With a nervous giggle, I answered, "Hello."

"Diann, this is Oprah. I wanted to thank you again for coming on the show. Your story touched me."

We talked the entire forty-five minutes to the airport. She wanted me to think about the possibility of doing an exclusive interview with her and making a movie about my life. She said she'd like to buy the rights to my story. We ended with me saying I was interested but that I wanted to talk to my siblings first because it wasn't just my story. She promised to call again. She'd have her lawyer send a contract.

A beaming Joe picked me up at the Denver airport. It appeared he and everybody I knew were very proud of me. When we arrived home, the kids surrounded me. "Mom, you were great," said both JJ and Rese.

Mandy piped in, "Mom, I saw you on the TV. You looked a little funny but still like my mom."

Gina broke through her uncommunicative stance and said, "I could always tell when you were going to talk about something sad, Mom, because you'd laugh or smile." I hadn't been aware I had done that, but on reviewing the tape, I realized my insightful Gina had been right.

Cindy, who arrived at the house about fifteen minutes after we did, peppered me with questions about Oprah. "What was she like?"

I smiled, remembering her, and said, "She was one of the most incredible people I've ever met."

"I told you she was great. I've seen her show a bunch of times." Cindy then salted me with praise for my performance. "She never does that, Mom; she never brings just one person on. She let you talk for so long. You were so good!"

Monday night was usually a fairly calm evening at our home, but not this Monday. The phone wouldn't quit ringing. People I hadn't heard from for twenty-five years began calling. A typical conversation went something like this: "I had the TV on when I was doing the laundry. I heard Oprah interviewing someone named Diann. Then I heard your voice. I'd recognize that voice anywhere. I raced out into the living room yelling, 'It's Diana.' You were so great. Oh, I had no idea. How are you?"

It was wonderful reconnecting with old friends. Buoyed by all the praise, I called Jean. "Jean, what'd you think?"

"You were good," she said with forced enthusiasm, sounding flat.

My stomach constricted into a prickly ball. "What's wrong?"

"Nothing, really. It's just you didn't tell me about the pictures. I wasn't prepared to see the pictures. The whole show was harder than I thought it would be. I thought you were great, though. I'm proud of you."

"Oh, Jean, I'm so sorry. It all happened so fast. I had no idea what they were going to do with those photos."

Jean had given me a sneak preview of what I should expect from my brothers. As anticipated, their comments were equally subdued. Ambarish and Al didn't count because they missed the show. Michael and Lee were mildly impacted by the photographs. Paul had an adverse reaction not only to the pictures but also because his name was mentioned on air.

All my siblings seemed to be proud and supportive, though, and later on in the week when I mentioned Oprah wanted to buy my story, the comment from every sibling I asked was to do what I wanted to do.

The next day, I wore my "Oprah outfit" to work. As I was walking into my building, I was stopped two or three times. "Weren't you the woman on *Oprah*? Didn't I see you on the Oprah show? You look exactly like the woman on *Oprah*, same outfit and everything."

I entered my workplace to tumultuous applause. Everyone wanted to give me a hug. They were all talking at once. Words such as "courage," "proud," "great," and "wonderful" circled around me and lifted me up like a hero on a sports team. I'd made the right choice. I felt empowered.

Every time I chose to tell my story, I was loosening Dad's stranglehold on my life. I was standing up for all the sexually abused children in the world. My fears of hearing comments like "promiscuous sinner" were unfounded. Going on *Oprah* was a validation of my life. *Oprah* was setting the stage for "living," not merely "surviving." I was building strength to say no to all kinds of abuse. I was getting ready to say no to Joe.

Life returned to a semi-normal state. A month had passed since Chicago. One afternoon at work, I received a call from Oprah. Her voice came over the wire and sat in the room with me holding my hands. "Have you thought any more about our discussion?"

"Yes," I said in a clear voice. "I've thought about it quite a lot. I'm interested, but there are a couple of things I feel strongly about. I don't want to see the murders on the screen. I don't want any blood. I don't want my story to be sensationalized. I want the story to be told in such a way that it takes into consideration the feelings of my siblings. I want you to change the names of my brothers and sister who are living."

I finally took a breath, which gave Oprah a chance to reply. She said she understood my concerns and all my wishes would be honored. She also told me if she were to purchase my story, she wanted her writers to write the script. I felt a stab of disappointment at this news because Dana was a friend and had worked hard on the synopsis.

My spirits lightened when she offered me a sum of money for the story that would make our financial worries vanish for a long time. She said I'd be receiving a contract from her lawyer, and she looked forward to working with me.

I received the contract a week later. After a little back-and-forth with her lawyer, I was ready to sign. I was just about to make phone calls to my siblings to make sure they were okay with the arrangements when my brother Paul called.

"Hey, Paul, I was just about to call about the contract."

"Let's have lunch tomorrow and talk," said Paul. We agreed to meet at one of our favorite Mexican restaurants.

"Paul, I'm really excited…" I started to say, but before I finished my sentence, he hung up.

I didn't think much more about our conversation until I saw Paul the next day sitting at the table with a serious expression on his face. I sat down slowly.

"What's wrong?" I asked, not really wanting to know.

"I've been thinking about this contract of yours, and I've decided if you go through with it, I'll change my name, move to Hawaii, and never speak to you again."

Tears welled up. "You'd disown me?" I said through sobs. "You feel that strongly?"

"Yes, I do," he said, his face stony.

My heart was broken. My sweet, generous brother Paul, who'd given me a thousand dollars two Christmases in a row, and who'd sat with me in the hospital during my latest breakdown, might never speak to me again! Together, my siblings and I'd seen so much tragedy and experienced so much loss. Dad had instilled the importance of family. My siblings had supported me through my dark times. I would not lose another sibling if I had a choice in the matter.

"Then I won't do it. I'll tell Oprah no," I said with tears streaming down my face. Paul looked relieved.

I cried all the way home. I entered the house still crying about our conversation and holding a soggy speeding ticket, a gift from a friendly policeman. I called the lawyer and told him why I couldn't sign the contract.

At a family gathering about six months later, Paul said to me casually, "Hey, Di, about that Oprah movie idea, I've changed my mind. Go ahead and sign the contract if you want to."

I knew my brother. He would first respond emotionally to a problem, then later he'd calm down, think more rationally, and come to a different conclusion. It would have been great if he'd come to his conclusion about the Oprah deal half a year earlier. Alas, that didn't happen, and by the time he reevaluated his decision, I felt that the opportunity had passed. My life's tale on the big screen simply wasn't meant to be.

I believe strongly everything happens for a reason, and the reason is always positive. I couldn't imagine what gem of wisdom I could possibly learn from turning down Oprah. I didn't have a clue as to what the positive outcome would be. I tended to see my life in terms of reincarnation. I was pretty sure it wasn't time for my story to be told Oprah-style because I had more lessons to learn. I was fervently hoping the lessons would get a little easier as I aged.

Way back in a far corner of my mind was the tiniest spark of an outcome I might even be able to achieve in the future. I imagined I could be actually living an adapted version of a fairy tale's dream of happily ever after. Most of my brain, however, was still stuck back in my thirteen-year-old attitude that true happiness for me would be as elusive as trying to catch a rainbow. The most I could do was to see life through a lens colored with optimism. I knew at the time making a movie was the least of my concerns. I was now dealing with teen rebellion and, as it turned out, the beginning of the end of my failing marriage.

I felt I was headed in an empowering direction, though, because being on *Oprah* had given me confidence that I could not only share my story, but I could help others by doing so.

When my old neighbor Beth asked if she could give my name to a therapist she knew who worked in the prison system, I immediately gave my consent. I agreed to speak to a group of convicted pedophiles and rapists who wanted to hear the victim's side of the story. My presentation was to take place at the prison in Cañon City.

Consenting to speak was one thing, but actually going back to the prison where Dad had lived and died was another. I convinced myself returning to the place I'd visited as a child every week for four years and where Dad had been executed wouldn't bother me. I was a visitor performing a different role with an entirely different mission.

On the appointed day, the familiar drive down to Cañon City was actually enjoyable. I found the conversation stimulating and Pikes Peak breathtaking as usual. I was doing well all the way up until the time of the mandatory frisking. At the entrance to the prison, my brain understood the requirement, but my body hated it. *I'm being violated in order to enter a prison to help violators understand what it was like for me to be violated as a child? I don't think so. Not going to happen. You touch me again, and I'll kill you. I'm going to be sick.* I said these things to myself, allowed myself to be frisked, and followed Pam into the prison.

The place hadn't changed in the twenty years I had been away, but I had: I was much stronger. I hoped that experiencing motherhood, two breakdowns, therapy, classes on self-esteem, anger, and forgiveness and being on *Oprah* had armed me with the knowledge, compassion, and wisdom to talk to this audience.

We entered a room bordered by walls of grey cement and filled with about twelve inmates sitting in chairs, all staring at me. It was like standing in front of a dozen Dads. In an instant, under their scrutiny, I transformed into a young, weak, unarmed child named Diana. I shook my head, attempting to shed the fear trying to freeze my brain.

I cleared my throat and mind and began speaking. "My name is Diann, and I was sexually abused by my dad from the age of five to thirteen."

The second I heard myself say *Diann*, my power was back, my voice was strong, and my message was clear. I continued. "Dad, for fear of being publicly exposed, murdered my pregnant mom, two brothers, and a sister. He was convicted of murder and resided in this prison for four years. In 1967, he was executed here in the gas chamber. I'm sure you knew him or know of him. I'm here to tell you how it felt to be abused. I want to let you know how what he did has affected my life."

That was the easy part. I had told my skeleton story many times. Now for the hard part: spilling my guts to pedophiles and rapists, spilling my guts to Dad.

I went deep inside myself and began sharing the heart and soul of my story. "Let me tell you what my dad, the man who was supposed to love and protect me, taught me. He taught me my body wasn't mine; it was his to be used for his sexual gratification. My body had no worth other than that purpose. Because I thought my body was worth nothing, I believed I had no value. He began teaching me these lessons when I was five years old. He fondled me when I was a little girl still sucking my thumb. He told me at first that all daddies did this. Then later, it was 'you do this or you get the belt, you can't see your friends, and your life will be hell. If you tell, I'll kill you. By the way, it's your fault I'm having sex with you. Because of your seductiveness, I can't help myself.'

"I learned when I was eleven, twelve, and thirteen years old, when he was having sexual intercourse with me daily, that I was a whore enticing him to molest me. So when he murdered my eleven-month-old baby sister, Teresa, my four-year-old baby brother, Vincent, and my six-year-old baby brother, Alan, and Mom—my very pregnant mom—for fear of being exposed, that was my fault too."

At the mention of my babies, the tears started flowing. I swallowed hard, willing myself to continue. As I paused, I looked out into the audience. To my surprise, most of the men were crying, which caused me to cry even harder. I took some time to compose myself and continue. *I'll get through this.*

"I believed if I hadn't been such a slut, or if I'd been stronger, or if I'd kept my mouth shut, he wouldn't have killed anyone. He taught me I was responsible for the murders; I killed Mom and the babies. What he did colored every aspect of my life, all my choices. For a long, long time, I made very bad choices. I spent years in therapy trying to undo what Dad did to me when I was I child. What I know now is that Dad was sick and wrong. Today I'm still learning that none of what happened to me was my fault, my body is mine, and I'm valuable."

By the time I was finished with my presentation, everyone in the room was crying, including Pam and me. I don't know what my talk or their tears meant to them. I'm not sure if any of the inmates attempted to make amends to their victims. I didn't have a clue if a single other survivor was helped by what I did. I just know it helped me. I felt empowered. I was heartened to see horror on their faces and tears in their eyes as I recounted how it felt to be sexually abused. It was my fervent hope some of these men heard in their hearts what they had done to their victims. *Were you listening, Dad?*

During the next two years, I accompanied Pam two more times to speak to similar groups of inmates convicted of sexual crimes. All three visits were incredibly healing and empowering. The frisking, however, never got any easier.

I also went several times with Pam to the women's prison in Florence, Colorado. Florence was about ten miles south of Cañon City, so the drive from Denver was a familiar one. On my first trip to the women's prison, as we passed Cañon City, I exhaled a huge breath of accumulated anxiety I hadn't even been aware I was carrying. I inhaled the refreshing air of hope. I realized even though I felt empowered by my talks to a population of pedophiles and rapists, I didn't hold out much hope they would or could change.

If you were living, Dad, I'd still want you locked up forever. If you were free, you would have continued to molest children. You couldn't stop. After me, it might have been Teresa, and maybe a new baby girl. You'd have had access to all your girl grandchildren. Except for mine! I would have never let you touch

210

my girls, the mother bear part of me screamed. No matter how much a pedophile or rapist teared up at my presentations, I was glad he was locked up. I didn't trust that type of male inmate no matter what they said or how hard they cried.

I was certain speaking to a female audience would feel different. I was aware some of these women had been convicted of very serious crimes, murder being one of them, but prison officials also said being incarcerated for rape or pedophilia was a fairly rare occurrence in the female population. I thought, however right or wrong, if a female inmate wasn't a rapist, pedophile, or serial killer, there was hope she could change. I believed this because, if circumstances had been different, I might have resided within these grey prison walls myself. Guardian angels had protected me and allowed me a safe passage to adulthood.

Upon entering the women's prison, I still didn't like being frisked, but it was more tolerable because it wasn't linked to Dad. The voluntary gathering of inmates, numbering about twenty, were sitting in rows of chairs chatting with each other but abruptly quieted when Pam and I entered the room. Twenty sets of eyes stared at me. I looked back at the group, but instead of seeing a dozen dads, I saw me in all of my various shapes, sizes, ages, and attitudes.

I shared my story. My experiences, which had been deemed sensational by many of my friends and acquaintances, were a familiar narrative for this audience. Many of these women understood my story perfectly, for it was similar to their own. I was filled with compassion as I looked at the faces of the inmates. *"There but for the grace of God go I,"* I repeated to myself over and over.

When I spoke, I spoke to twenty individuals. "I don't know what happened to you as a child, or what brought you to this place. All I know is in many ways you and I are alike. As a kid I felt I was bad and every bad thing my family experienced was my fault. I acted out my badness by making destructive choices. I'd have continued on this path except my aunt placed me into the Good Shepherd Home, a Catholic home for troubled girls.

"At fourteen, I was incredibly troubled and very angry. My aunt's actions got me off the street and gave me a safe place to grow and change. I was given the chance to begin to learn about myself, to learn I actually had choices. When I decided I wasn't bad, I also decided I might be somewhat lovable. With that possibility, I was able to let love in. Most of my family and friends were very loving and supportive. It's a long, ongoing process: lots of talking about my thoughts and feelings, therapy, and self-help workshops. I was a tough case, but eventually I came to the conclusion I'm not a bad person and what happened when I was a child wasn't my fault. I learned my traumatic history doesn't define me. Nobody gets to decide who I am or who I'll be in the future except for me; I have a choice."

The pressure was building in my body, making tears well up behind my eyes. I wanted each person to know they could choose love. A tear trickled down my cheek, and my voice caught as I declared, "Nobody gets to decide who you are or who you'll become except for you. You get to choose."

I looked around the room to a sea of tearful emotions, which started my waterworks in earnest. With these prison presentations to both men and women, I was certainly bursting my thirteen-year-old, no-cry vow in a big way. I decided it was worth it for the sake of the inmates. In my mind's eye, I could picture God, an amused expression on his face, mouthing the words "For whose sake, Diann?"

Okay, okay. I was crying for my own sake and my own healing.

CHAPTER 21

Me and Myself

With interest rates sky high, the mortgage business dwindled to nothing. Joe would often have jobs in the evening and on the weekends fixing and cleaning up foreclosed houses in inner-city Denver. The kids and I dreaded going with him to help because of his constant criticism.

"Can't you do anything right? You're so stupid. That's not what I asked you to do." Inevitably, he'd bring us to tears.

Home wasn't any better; it seemed the kids and I were always bracing for an outburst from Joe. We never knew which Joe would come through the door: Dr. Jekyll or Mr. Hyde. He could be in a fantastic mood upon arriving home and within seconds could turn hostile. He'd hit us hard with verbal punches almost daily. His favorite punch word was "stupid." His favorite punch sentence was, "Can't you do anything?"

Nevertheless, on the weekends, Joe and I often went out as a couple. A Friday evening staple was going to happy hour at the Paramount Café. It was Joe's routine to secure us a corner table outside the café so he could observe the women as they walked by.

"Wow, Di, look at that nice ass. Those tits have a nice jiggle to them, don't you think?" he'd comment to me in a conversational tone.

After the Oprah show, Joe's comments became excruciatingly repugnant to me. For the first time, I couldn't seem to numb myself out. The reason I'd fallen for Joe the first week we met was that he seemed to accept me not only after I told him about Dad and the murders, but also when I informed him I was pregnant. I was convinced, then, that nobody would accept me if they knew the full story.

Well, it felt like I'd told a good portion of the United States my full story, and Oprah, my peers at work, friends, and strangers seemed to accept me. Many people even considered me courageous. I'd acknowledged my promiscuity on television, and I received understanding and compassion. I was beginning to believe I didn't deserve this degrading treatment, and neither did any other woman. I was coming close to no longer being able to tolerate his demeaning objectification of women, whether he was demanding I look at porn with him or discussing the physical attributes of other females on our date nights. I was shifting. I was getting stronger. I was building up the courage to confront Joe, but I wasn't ready yet.

Around the time of my thirty-eighth birthday, Joe went out of town for a week for a possible employment opportunity. What a fun and peaceful week we had. Mealtime was so relaxed that the kids and I sat talking and laughing for hours. The heavenly week brought home a fact I already knew but didn't want to admit, which was that Joe was a huge contributor to our family's distress. We all realized we didn't miss him when he was gone.

Joe called one evening and asked how I wanted to celebrate my birthday when he returned. I immediately replied, "I'd love to go dancing at a legitimate nightclub where I can keep my clothes on." Upon his return, his birthday surprise was to take me to PT's, a strip joint in town.

In February, Jeffrey, a friend of ours, generously offered to take us out for drinks and dinner. We gladly accepted. Snow clouds blanketed the night in frigid temperatures as we made our way into the warm atmosphere of an Old Chicago restaurant.

Joe, who soon became quite drunk, started flirting with our redheaded waitress. When he grabbed her butt and asked, "Does the rest of the hair on your body match the hair on your head?" I'd had enough. I walked out of the restaurant to our car where I sat steaming and freezing, like dry ice. My body and emotions were frozen in anger. I felt coldly distant from Joe. It was clear I couldn't take much more abuse. After what seemed like an interminable length of time, Joe came out of the restaurant screaming obscenities.

He drove home like a maniac as my anger turned to terror. Snow pelted the windshield in white rage. Inside the car, Joe's face radiated heat: red rage. His eyes were opaque lumps of burning coal, devil-eyes not of this world, not a part of my husband. I wanted to scream like the tires.

The car's headlights bounced off of the black-wet and slushy-white streets. I could see the blurry shadows of snow-covered fences and flocked trees as knife-like flakes slashed sideways through the black night. I never thought this would happen in my lifetime, but I actually wished to see the gyrating blue lights of a cop car in the rearview mirror. I wanted him to get caught for a DUI, I wanted him to be taken away in handcuffs, and I wanted him in detox. *Stop drinking, stop terrorizing me, and for God's sake, stop being a madman!* My racing thoughts swirled as the car lurched to a stop in the driveway.

Once in the house, fast as Dad was with a belt, Joe grabbed my blouse and yanked as he attempted to rip me and my clothes to shreds.

"You fucking bitch," he said with bared teeth and wild eyes. "Move, you stupid broad," his words snarled as two hands shoved me toward the stairs.

I stumbled but caught myself just in time to feel another rough push on my back. He pushed three or four more times until I was up the stairs and through our bedroom door. I felt his hands squeezing my arms, his fingers digging into flesh. I didn't say a word as he threw me onto the bed, screaming, "How could you embarrass me like that? Jeff had the nerve to lecture me on how I treated you. I'll treat you how I want to treat you, you bitch."

A conglomeration of all my worst memories and present fears had ganged together for an attack. I was about to be crushed under the weight of Dad's and Joe's sexual and violent acts. I was being gang-raped!

This thought hammered me as Joe proceeded to do the unthinkable, one of the few sexual acts I refused to do. As he raped me anally, my insides exploded in agony. For a second I curled in on myself, small and helpless, lost and anchorless. Then from far away, I heard Horton the elephant's mantra, "A person's a person no matter how small." Deep within me came an animal growl; it gained momentum and when it reached my throat, it formed two gigantic words: "NO! STOP!" I roared. He didn't stop. When he was done, he rolled over and fell asleep beside me.

Violated and raw, I lay awake in the dark. At about two a.m. I got up. By day's dawning light the sunrise looking red and bruised like me, I had already scoured the kitchen and bathrooms, done two loads of laundry, dressed for work, and made my decision. I was calmly standing, arms crossed, at the foot of the stairs as Joe descended the steps to the main floor. He slowed when he saw me.

"I want you to leave," I told Joe, my voice strong and clear. "I want a divorce. Last night you raped me. You know my background, and yet you raped me. I'm in control of who touches my body. I said *no*, and *no* means *no*. You aren't allowed to touch me like that ever again. I'll never be a victim again. Get out! Leave! I'm going to work, and I want you gone by the time I get home. Oh, and Joe, see the kids get to school."

I turned and walked out of the house. Joe, who knew he had pushed me too far, didn't say anything. By the time I arrived home from work he was gone.

That night I sought the counsel of my mentor, Rosa, who had deftly guided me through the rough waters of anger and forgiveness. Rosa must have seen the agony in my face because her hug circled my pain, rubbing salve on my wounded heart.

She welcomed me into her office. "Come in. I've been expecting you." Her words, sitting in silence between us were, *Yes, I knew your work would lead you down this path to this very spot. Dealing with your husband is your next step.*

As soon as I sat down, I began. "I can't live like this anymore. Being with Joe is not healthy for me." I told her about the rape. "I'm through being a victim," I said.

She agreed wholeheartedly with my resolve, bolstered my spirits, and validated my feelings and actions. When I left, I knew I was on the right path. I walked out of her office and into my new life.

The following week, Joe called me daily, apologizing profusely and pleading to come home. "I was drunk. I'm sorry I hurt you. I promise not to do it again."

My answer was, "Drunk is not a reason. You made the choice to get drunk. You knew what you were doing. I'll never accept drinking as an excuse again." I'd accepted his excuses that he was drunk and sorry a zillion times before, but no more. I'd put up with his demeaning remarks, his volatile rages, his disrespect of me and the kids, his drunkenness and lewdness, but I'd changed. I was done.

I soon realized I'd always essentially been a single parent. Joe was often absent due to "workaholism" and alcoholism. As far as the day-to-day operations were concerned, the only major change was the lack of stress. Gina was still acting out, but at least I didn't have to cope with Joe too. Emotionally we were much better off. The kids didn't seem to miss Joe because I'd been the stable and present parent all of their lives. When he was present, the kids and I walked on eggshells. It was a relief to not worry.

Joe moved into his brother's office. He called us quite often, always using his "nice" voice. The "good, fun" dad chatted with the kids. He had conversations with me about the children and specifically about how to help Gina. He seemed to be a better dad and husband when he wasn't living with us. When he informed me in one of our phone conversations that he was sleeping on his brother's desk, I began to feel a little sorry for him, but I held to my resolve.

Joe was still unemployed and told me he had to use the little money he acquired from side jobs for his living expenses. I quickly realized even the meager amount of money he'd been contributing made a big difference when it came to our mortgage payment. Because Joe wasn't giving us any money, we once again were forced to move.

Magically, by the end of March 1988, I had found a spacious house in the same area as our former patio home and for less money. It was ideal for us, sporting a big yard butting up to JJ's and Rese's high school. It had a large country kitchen, five bedrooms, four bathrooms, and an enclosed patio looking out onto an ample backyard. I did need help moving, and Joe quickly volunteered.

I had an argument in my head for and against his helping, but in the end, I accepted his offer. *I'm tired of fighting him. It won't hurt to let him help just this once. Besides, he needs to get his stuff. I think he's finally learned his lesson. I think he's changed for good this time.*

Are you nuts? He raped you! You open the door to your heart a crack, he'll come into your life and break it again. He'll help you now only to hurt you later. You're a fool if you think he's changed. It was hard enough getting him out of your life in the first place; it'll be even harder later. You think you're tired now; just wait until he burrows his way back into your life.

What a negative skeptic you are! He's family, the father of your children. He's a good guy who just wants to help. You're making way too much of this.

We moved on Easter weekend, and after the move, we went, as a family, to Easter dinner at Joe's parents' house. Joe's parents were very upset about our separation. They loved me like a daughter, and I called them Mom and Dad. I think Mom took the separation very personally. She blamed me for leaving the family.

After a scrumptious meal, Mom Cora cornered me. "How could you leave my son? Don't you think over the years I got mad at John and wanted to leave? But I didn't. Marriage is difficult. You need to work it out with Joe."

I looked at her and said, "Did Dad ever rape you? Because that's what Joe did to me." I paused there, remembering that night. "You know my background, Mom. I can't go back to being a victim again."

Cora didn't expect this comment, for her eyes went wide with shock, then softened and began to tear. Her mouth opened to say something, but just then some of her noisy, rowdy grandkids entered the room. The moment was lost and the conversation over.

It might have been the warm, familiar family gathering. It might have been Joe being on his best behavior for two months. The good Joe was fun and delightful. It might have been Mom Cora's lecture activating my Catholic guilt or maybe even her sadness over our separation. It might have been because I felt sorry for Joe, as he was alone and sleeping on his brother's desk. It might have been that I still felt undeserving of a non-abusive relationship. It might have been my laziness; it was just easier to give in. It might simply have been that it was a nice, beautiful Colorado day and I felt magnanimous.

Whatever the reason, when we left Joe's folks house as a family that Easter afternoon and arrived at our newly rented house, Joe stayed the night. That night turned into a week. The week turned into a month, and before I knew it, Joe had moved himself and all his belongings back into our lives.

While Joe's actions indicated he wanted to be a part of our lives, Snoopy's and Gina's behavior suggested the opposite. Snoopy had issues with changing locations. Her goal had been to nag me on behalf of Mom about the family meeting. After the meeting, we were able to find our dream house. Snoopy disappeared for two weeks when we moved in. And then later, when we had to move again, this time into the patio home, she disappeared for a month. Maybe she felt she no longer served a purpose in the family because with the last move, Snoopy checked out the place and then left for good. The kids put up *Lost Cat* signs around the neighborhood to no avail. I imagined her sticking her paws into another unsuspecting family's business with her usual goal of making life an interesting challenge.

That May, fourteen-year-old Gina started to run away regularly. It seemed like she, just like Snoopy, no longer wished to be a part of our family. My daughter was in the deepest of trouble. The trouble felt familiar because I'd experienced it; this I felt in every inch of my being. I remembered sharply my own rebellious, fourteen-year-old self. Gina's behavior mirrored mine so closely it spooked me. The ghostly wisps of my body's memories filled me with dread for Gina. She'd been sexually abused, I was sure of it. My brain dug deep, always going back to the time when Ryan murdered the boy and Gina's behavior changed. I kept recalling jagged pieces of the puzzle of that time, turning them over, examining them for clues, but I couldn't see the answer. Gina wasn't talking, but I knew she needed help.

I didn't know the specifics of what happened to Gina until many years later. As an adult she told me she'd been raped by three Mexican boys when she was eleven. It was on a day when she'd skipped school shortly after Ryan murdered the boy. Looking back, my little girl's subsequent behavior made perfect sense to me. She never told me about the rapes at the time because she had misbehaved by ditching school and she thought I'd be mad. In the months and years following, shame coated her heart and infiltrated her mind. Her horror about being raped translated in her mind to "I'm bad." The mistake she'd made by ditching became "I'm a mistake." She didn't dare talk because she thought the rapes were all her fault. I'd failed, after all, in my efforts to protect my family from sexual abuse.

Though my salary wasn't great, my mental health benefits were good. I looked over the list of in-network providers and chose the service I thought would address Gina's behavior the best. I enlisted the services of a counseling center named DAPA, Drug Abuse Programs of America. Gina, my resistant teen, went kicking and screaming to counseling.

Concretely, I knew I'd done everything I could think of to do as a parent, but to me DAPA wasn't nearly enough help to keep my baby safe. I looked up into the heavens and admitted I had very little control over Gina's life. I called on the angels that had helped me as a teen and were still helping me get through tough times.

I'm doing okay. Now would a few of you please help Gina? I smiled despite the gravity of the situation as I pictured a couple of competent, veteran angels with kind faces sitting on each of Gina's shoulders. She definitely wouldn't like them hanging around, especially if she knew I'd sent them. I was confident, however, that she would be oblivious to their existence; I was at her age. I then immediately called Aunt Ruby, the head of all my earthly angels, and reiterated again how sorry I was for causing her so much grief!

After working with Gina for a couple of sessions, the counselors, James and Susan, a husband-and-wife team, recommended we send her to a treatment center in Houston for a month. We wanted to place her in different surroundings, thus significantly reducing the unhealthy influence of some of her friends. We made this decision to ensure her safety and hopefully provide healthy help and support, much like Aunt Ruby did for me when she sent me to the Good Shepherd Home.

For a month, a huge weight was lifted from my heart knowing Gina was safe and getting help. Sadly, an even angrier Gina came home and picked up where she left off. The counselors at DAPA reassessed the situation. They suggested Gina's acting out was but a symptom of a greater family issue, so Joe, JJ, Rese, Gina, Mandy, and I all entered family therapy.

Some of the sessions were quite informative. The particular session that stands out in my mind was when our counselors had the kids draw the family tempers on a blackboard. As a group my children drew Joe's temper as a continuous set of spikes across the board. The kids saw Joe as a person with constant volatility. Their depiction reminded me of jagged shark's teeth. Yes, from his temper to his obsession with sex to his appearance even without the mustache, I had indeed in many respects married my dad.

My temper appeared on the board as a straight line starting from the far left to the far right, with a large spike reaching all the way to the top of the board and back at the end. My kids understood I had a long fuse, but when I blew, you didn't want to be around. Yes, from my temper to my busy, child-filled life to marrying a sex-obsessed man to my appearance, I was a lot like Mom.

After seeing the family for a couple of sessions, our counselors told Joe and me in a gentle, tactful way that we might be the problem. It was true that when the relationship was good, we were a very good couple. But when the relationship was bad, we were horrid together. Joe and I began marriage therapy.

Therapy was difficult because Joe showed no emotion. Our arguments were circular in nature. I'd bring up an issue, he'd redefine the problem as my fault, and I'd accept some of the blame. When I brought up his drinking, his reply was, "If you hadn't been such a bitch, I wouldn't have spent those nights at the bar." And because I'd yelled about his drinking and because of my affairs, I took some of that on too.

I was working full-time and we were struggling financially, so I brought up Joe's lack of employment. "Joe, we're barely surviving. I think you should get a job. Work at McDonald's if you have to—anything to bring in money. The kids need clothes; we need to eat."

He thought the suggestion was insulting. He said I didn't understand and wasn't being supportive. Joe said indignantly, "How dare you criticize me? What about all the years you were a stay-at-home mom?" He had a point.

Back at the house, the good Joe disappeared as he reverted back to his old behavior. I'm not sure what he did all day, but whatever it was, it didn't seem to benefit me or the family. He spent some time rearranging the kitchen in a way that made no sense to me. When I arrived home from a full day of work, even if we'd made previous plans, he'd often be gone, only to come home drunk at two a.m. or later. If he was home, he would stand over my shoulder when I was cooking dinner and tell me how to cook.

After a couple of days like this, I turned around and said, "You poor person. How sorry I am you've had to put up with such lousy cooking for the past eighteen years. How have you even survived?" I can be really sarcastic when the need calls for it. That time, Joe stomped out of the room. I was so angry I didn't care.

One morning in August, Joe said, "Let's do something tonight. I'll be home by six."

That same day my friend Oksana called me at work and asked if she and her new baby, Tatiana, could come for a visit that evening. I said yes without hesitation, knowing the probability of Joe's being home by six was next to nil. Oksana and Tatiana arrived about 5:45, and we were visiting in the kitchen when Joe came home.

Ignoring Oksana, whom he knew well, he said to me, "I told you I'd be home by six so we could do something. Why do we have company?"

I looked at Oksana to gauge her reaction. As I predicted, she was staring daggers at Joe, her brows furrowed and her lips tight. Oksana was one of my few friends who knew what went on behind the scenes of our outwardly happy marriage. She was definitely on my side, which bolstered my courage.

I responded, "Why would I believe you'd be home at six tonight just because you said so? You usually don't show up when you say you will. Why would I believe today would be different? We have developed a life without you because you're gone so much. I'm not dependent on you to fill my time. When Oksana called and asked if she could come over, I didn't hesitate to say yes. I figured you'd go to the bars. That's your normal routine."

At that, Joe stormed out of the house, shouting, "I'm moving out."

My words followed him out the door, "Good. And this time, don't plan on coming back."

I heard a rumbling engine and the angry screeching of tires. I spied Joe's red-hot Corvette streaking away, leaving behind a beautifully peaceful Colorado evening.

Oksana, Tatiana, and I enjoyed a delightful time together. That night as I snuggled contentedly alone under the covers, I made a decision. I decided, on principle alone, never to date another alcoholic, volatile Sagittarius who owned a Corvette.

The next week Joe called daily, apologizing, wanting to come home. I was finished. There was no more Joe coming home. We went to our last counseling session as a couple, and I announced we'd decided to get a divorce.

The words hung in the air for a split second. Recognition of the meaning of the words fell over our therapists' faces. The shadow of concern left them, and I saw a look of joy in their eyes. Then something happened I will never forget: James and Susan started to clap in celebration of our decision. I felt validated. Joe's face grew cloudy, offended. They explained they thought divorce was a good idea; they believed the marriage had become destructive to us and our children.

Their words seemed to bounce off Joe as his face turned from stormy to stony. He stood up and said, "I guess that's it, then," and walked out of the therapy session.

I remained seated. The first thing Susan said after he left was, "We've never seen anyone with less emotion than Joe."

"He can get pretty angry," I said with conviction. They laughed in agreement. They then suggested I stay in therapy to work on my childhood.

I smiled. "Oh, I've already been in therapy. I've already dealt with my childhood abuse."

They smiled back, knowing I had additional work to do, and then suggested I might benefit from a new therapy technique called Inner Child Work.

It was true I'd done a lot of work already. I had told my story, I'd adapted my Catholic belief system, I'd gotten in touch with my anger, I'd forgiven my parents, I was now standing up to Joe, but I'd never shown understanding or compassion to little Diana. I had never connected to my child self.

After viewing the *Oprah* tape, Susan and James gave me my first assignment: to tell my story without a laugh, a smile, or a smoke. The idea was to eliminate my defenses in order to feel my feelings. Boy, could I feel them; sadness, guilt, shame, pain, confusion were all there, but mostly there was fear.

My therapists explained that when I was a child my parents hadn't protected me. Inner child work was a process, through imagery, that the adult/parent part of me could use to connect with little Diana and protect her.

"So, Diann, close your eyes and think of a time little Diana needed your adult part to protect her," said Susan.

The second I closed my eyes, she was there in living color: her dark brown bangs and long hair, the flushed red cheeks, the zigzag of confusion etched by dark brows on soft skin arching over wide, terrified, green eyes. I could see the "oh" of surprise on her pink lips. There she was, my six-year-old self, in the attic, standing on Dad's project table after practicing Christmas carols. My thirty-eight-year-old self teared up. Diana looked so vulnerable. She was so young and innocent. I could see the back of Dad in the picture, his hands beginning to lift up her dress.

In my mind's eye, I rushed into the room and, pushing Dad aside, I lifted Diana off the table and held her in my arms. My voice was soft and strong as I said to her, "It's okay, I'm here. You're safe with me. I'm not going to let him hurt you." She clung to me, burying her head in my shoulder as I brushed past my shocked father without saying a word to him.

I took her to the library. She loved books, and she felt safe among them. She was safe with me. Nobody was going to ever hurt her again, not on my watch!

Suddenly I was aware of James' voice saying, "When you're ready, you may open your eyes." I lingered a few more moments with my little girl, then slowly raised my eyelids to see two therapists' large smiles.

My smile matched theirs as I proudly announced, "I did it! I protected Diana from Dad, and there wasn't a darn thing he could do about it."

He no longer had any power over me. I had the power to protect Little Di from Dad.

For the next several months, I went on a magical journey. I used my adult mothering instincts to nurture and heal my inner child. For the first time in my life, I saw the real little Diana: precious, valuable, vulnerable, innocent, and lovable. I found, to my astonishment, that there was absolutely nothing wrong with the child within me. I wasn't fatally flawed. I wasn't bad; on the contrary, I was inherently good.

James and Susan thought I might benefit from some twelve-step programs like ACOA, adult children of alcoholics, or CODA, codependency anonymous, to deal with my dysfunctional family patterns. I didn't feel I fit into these groups because often my story seemed too big to share. In many groups, a few members seemed to dominate to the point where others weren't able to speak.

James and Susan also wanted me to attend a twelve-step group for sex addiction. I didn't believe I was a sex addict, but I had to admit having sex with strangers had been a problem. Sandra, my shadow side, lurked in the wings during and after my marriage, waiting to have sex when life swallowed me up.

Since doing inner child work, however, my relationship with Sandra was changing. I used to have sex with strangers when I was feeling too good about myself. The healing inner child work seemed to coat my insides with the warm contentment of self-acceptance. I was better able to stop myself from feeling bad about feeling good.

I knew I wasn't a sex addict when I attended a twelve-step meeting of SAA, Sex Addicts Anonymous. I walked into an all-male group of sex addicts, most of whom wanted to take me under their wings and show me the ropes.

I decided quickly that the ropes they had in mind would only tie me tighter to my destructive patterns. Sex with strangers had been a result of my abuse and feeling bad about myself. I certainly didn't crave inter-course with strangers; in fact, I hated it. I didn't desire a sexual relation-ship with anyone in the SAA group, either.

CHAPTER 22

With a Little Help from My Friends

I was no longer riding on Joe's emotional roller coaster. He could live his highs and lows, have his temper tantrums, and drink alcohol to his heart's content without my interference or comments. He'd so distanced himself from me and the kids that I was left with the unfamiliar feeling of detachment toward my husband. I remained separated because I couldn't actually afford to get a legal divorce.

Though I was happily divorced emotionally, the physical world kept us attached. I was surrounded by his stuff. I solved that problem by having a garage sale over Labor Day weekend. A few days beforehand, I told Joe to take anything he wanted and the rest would be mine.

Being free from the emotional tentacles was one thing, but the many financial obligations of providing for four kids were squeezing me like octopus arms. I was broke. While Joe loaded up some of our life's possessions as he was leaving, I timidly asked him if he'd be able to help financially.

His answer was an emphatic, "No! I supported the kids for the last sixteen years. It's your turn now." True to his word, I never received a penny from him for support. In addition to not being able to pay for our living expenses, creditors were hounding me to pay the bills accrued when we were still married. Most, I felt, were Joe's responsibility, but because the creditors had my phone number, they called me. With the help of an organization called Consumer Credit Counseling, I formulated a plan to pay the bills, and I could answer the phone without bracing.

A month after pronouncing he wouldn't contribute financially in any way, he called me. "Di, we have to talk. There are things I want to share with you."

Hoping Joe had been overcome with a sense of financial responsibility to his children, I met him at a restaurant for lunch. His face was light and animated as he proudly related, "I've been reading some of the books you recommended. I just finished one of John Bradshaw's books about the inner child. I've come to the conclusion our breakup wasn't totally your fault. I have some problems too. I think a lot of my problems stem from the fact my mom potty-trained me at thirteen months. I've more insights too. I think we should get back together. We should try again."

Sitting across from him wearing one of my favorite green dresses, I decided to give Joe a little test to see how well he really knew me. "Joe, what's my favorite color?" His shoulder shrug gave me the answer. I liked the way things were going, so I asked another question. "What jungle animal do I love?"

His face clouded over. This conversation wasn't going the way he had pictured it. "What kind of stupid questions… I mean, what do your questions have to do with our relationship?"

I looked at the man I'd lived with for nearly twenty years. I was sad he'd never really taken the time to know me. I said softly, "I'm glad you are learning about yourself, but it's too late for us. We weren't good for each other." With that I placed some money on the table for my lunch, stood up, and walked out of the restaurant. So much for thinking Joe had a guilty conscience.

Many evenings while riding on the bus to the Park & Ride and then driving the few miles home, exhausted, thoughts would balloon up in my mind, and my chest would constrict my breathing. *I shouldn't even be driving; I don't have car insurance. The choice is between insurance and food. How will I feed my kids? I have to drive; I have four kids. I should try to take mass transit that would drop me off a couple of blocks from home. I love to walk. It'd probably do me good. It would add hours to my day; I don't have enough hours as it is. Will we make it?*

I was working as hard as I could. In addition to my day job, I was making burritos and selling them at work, doing data entry for the Women's School Network, and giving haircuts and perms. In short, I was doing everything I could think of to bring in more money. Still, after paying for the bare essentials, I'd have approximately eighteen dollars left per week for groceries for the five of us.

One night, after work, I had all but given up. We had no food in the house. I was a creative cook, but I didn't even have staples like flour to make something from scratch. My mind was a whirlpool spiraling down, spitting out doubts as to my capabilities as a provider. I wasn't even able to feed my children.

As I turned into the driveway, I glimpsed something on the front porch. My first thought was that the kids hadn't picked up some of their things. When I got closer, I saw a couple of bags of groceries. Somebody had given me flour, rice, sugar, and beans as well as fresh fruits and vegetables. I sat down on the porch to sort through the groceries. Halfway between crying and laughing, I gingerly picked up a package of cookies. Standing up, I hugged the food as I walked into my bare kitchen with enough supplies to feed us for weeks. Who was my angel? I didn't know. In the months that followed, it seemed that whenever I reached a new low in supplies and emotions, groceries miraculously dropped down from the heavens. This happened no less than three times.

The food angels seemed to be watching over me pretty consistently, but I guess the responsibility angel thought I should be more law abiding because one evening, driving home from the Park & Ride, I was stopped for having a burned-out brake light. Of course, the officer asked me for my license and proof of insurance. The license I could produce; the proof of insurance I could not. I was issued a court date. I cried a little, but I knew the situation was my fault and responsibility. "No mistakes, only lessons," a friend had told me. Well, I was darn sick of all the lessons. I wanted a break!

The next month I worked like crazy to come up with money for insurance. At the time of my court appearance, I'd amassed $250. I was almost sure I could plead my case, receive a minimal fine, purchase my car insurance the following day, and still have money left over for Christmas.

When I arrived at traffic court, I sat down with a large group of people. Thinking this would take all day, I was pleasantly surprised when the bailiff announced everyone who was there for lack of insurance was to come into the courtroom. The entire crowd stood and entered as one. I was again pleased to see the judge was a woman who might be sympathetic to my plight. This was my day!

When we were all seated, the judge addressed the group, saying, "There are no extenuating circumstances and no excuses. You each will do forty hours of community service and pay a $250 fine. Go to the clerk and pay your fine. Next case."

Fifty pairs of wide, shocked eyes looked at the judge. Dazed, people got to their feet and slowly walked out of the courtroom. I sat on the bench a minute longer. I put my face in my hands and cried. Panic rose up inside me as I thought, *Oh, crap! This is all the money I have in the world.*

I went to the clerk and paid the $250. They asked if I'd purchased insurance yet. When I said I hadn't, they confiscated my driver's license until I could show proof of insurance. I called a friend who picked me up. When I arrived home, I made arrangements to get my car towed to the house. The next day, deflated, I took the bus from my house to work, which added an hour to my daily commute. In the coffee room, I lamented to my friends about my run of bad luck. They were all empathetic, which made me feel better.

After a sleepless night, I arrived at work the following morning still not knowing what I was going to do about insurance or Christmas. As I approached my desk, I saw a note. The familiar handwriting was from my friend Twyla. Warmth spread through me as I picked up the note and read, "Have a nice Christmas." Out of the corner of my eye I glimpsed another piece of paper placed beneath the note. With shaking hands, I picked up a check made out to me for $250. I held the check to my heart, and with tears of gratitude rolling down my cheeks, I whispered, "Thank you, my friend Twyla. Thank you so much."

Even with Twyla's generous gift, I entered the Christmas month with my usual heavy heart. Since the age of seven, Christmas music made me cry because the familiar melodies conjured up memories of little Diana being sexually abused. Even as a child, though, the Christmas carols laden with my tears couldn't tone down the magic feeling of Christmas. At age twelve, when life with Dad was grim, the sound of Santa Alan's ho ho ho's had lightened my holiday spirit. Vincent's and Teresa's excited squeals of laughter brought happy music to my ears.

The month of December had begun weighing me down in the year 1963. The dead silence of my first Christmas without Mom and the babies was horrible. Christmas after that was never the same. Out of all the Christmases after the murders, there was only one I liked: the Christmas of 1978, spent with Jean.

As an adult, I was hopeful the magic of December might return with the sweet, gleeful voices of my children, but Joe's attitude usually did a great job of drowning those joyful sounds out. In my married life, during this grey month, the pattern was always the same. Inevitably, we entered the holiday season broke. Joe turned a deaf ear to my requests that we save and plan for the purchasing of gifts for relatives and kids. Ordinarily, he'd agree to go shopping with me on December twentieth "just to look." We never bought any gifts on these reconnaissance trips. The buying trip would be late evening, December twenty-third. In a surly mood, he always started a fight after buying the gifts and left in a huff for the bar. He'd holler back at me while running out the door, "I can't stand you around the holidays." Every year Joe conveniently returned just as I finished wrapping the last present.

But midway through December 1988, I sensed a slight difference in my attitude. I still didn't much care for the holiday music, but I did feel lighter. Two weeks before Christmas, I jumped in my recently insured car and headed to the mall for some serious but limited gift buying. For the first time in years, the kids' presents were wrapped and under the tree, the family gifts were ready, the house wore its finest holiday garb, and everyone seemed relaxed and happy weeks before Christmas. I felt so bighearted I even invited Joe to join us for the opening of gifts on Christmas morning.

Christmas morning found the kids waiting with anticipation for their dad to arrive so they could open their gifts. All the kids were there, including Gina, who had decided Christmas was one day worthy enough to dispense with her bad behavior. When Joe arrived, late as usual, we commenced with the opening of presents.

The children opened all my gifts first. Gifts were generally practical in nature, but I did manage to buy a special surprise for each child. It was then time for the kids to open Joe's presents. JJ, Rese, and Mandy said their polite thank yous as they opened their boring, practical gifts from Joe. When Gina opened her gift, she screamed, "Oh, just what I wanted. A leather coat!"

The other kids' mouths hung open. They were in shock at the injustice of it all! Then, through gritted teeth, Rese said, "No fair!" mirroring the other kids' sentiments. Joe ignored his three angry children and beamed at Gina as she twirled around the room in her plush new leather coat. To the rest of us, it seemed as if she were being rewarded for her bad behavior. Gina had spent the last couple of years causing nothing but havoc and pain.

Later, talking to Joe, I said, "What were you thinking? I could've used that money for food and gas. Gina didn't deserve that coat."

Joe's reply was, "Lighten up, Di. Don't be such a bitch. I bought the jacket because that's what she said she wanted." *I remember why I'm not with you, Joe. We were having a drama-free December until you showed up today. Maybe I can't give the kids a lot of expensive presents, but I'm getting my priorities straight.*

Shortly after the holidays, in January 1989, my forty hours of community service started. My job was to waitress on Sunday mornings for brunch at the American Legion. I was delighted to find that, even though I didn't get paid for waitressing, I could keep my tips. I guess the management liked me because they asked if I would waitress at their Friday night steak dinners as well. As soon as I hit my forty hours, I was able to get paid for all my time.

The community service ended up being a blessing in disguise because it afforded me another avenue for making money. Although I believe many of the people at the Legion drank heavily, they were all very nice to me. Some of the men wanted to date me. Usually they left me alone when I explained I didn't feel comfortable dating men from my workplace. One man, however, was extremely persistent. "Come on, just one date so you can get to know me."

"Before I make a decision, I need to ask you some questions."

"Sure, ask me anything."

"What is your astrology sign?"

"Sagittarius."

"I don't date Sagittarius men."

"Oh, come on." The all-too familiar, loud, slurred, speech of a drunk assaulted my ears. "That isn't fair. If you'll give me a chance, I'll take you for a ride in my Corvette," he said in a cajoling voice.

"I don't date men who own Corvettes."

The man's face turned beet red as he spat, "You're just a stupid bitch. I don't want to date such a closed-minded bitch, anyway."

I thought to myself, *Your angry name-calling is the final reason I'll never date you*, but I said, "Okay, I guess we've made the decision not to date."

* * *

While the finances were improving slightly, life with four kids was an ever-changing daily adventure. My oldest and my youngest were pretty easy to be around. JJ, a junior, was a straight-A student who seemed to excel in everything he tried from music to sports. He didn't date and, to my relief, didn't get into much trouble in other ways either. My sweet Mandy was absolutely a bright spot in my world. She was my elementary school angel.

At sixteen Rese was, as far as I knew, one of those teen daughters a mother dreams about. Good grades, good friends, good clean fun in wholesome co-ed group activities was my daughter's modus operandi. Early in her sophomore year of high school, she acquired a part-time job on the weekends at Denny's for spending money. Usually Rese made good decisions, and rarely did I worry about her.

Except for one time. One day, after a shift at Denny's, she ran in the house, her face flushed and her eyes dancing. She announced to me in an uncharacteristically defiant tone, "I'm changing my clothes and going out on a date." Her eyes warned, *Don't screw this up for me; you've always said I make good decisions, and I've decided to date this guy*. She then nodded her head and glanced behind to indicate said date was walking up the sidewalk. "Mom, his name is Mike. Talk to him. I'll only be a minute."

Tall, dark, and handsome, Mike was a man with a deep voice and enough facial hair to warrant a daily shave. The keyword in this case was "man." Suddenly my mother bear instincts reared up. No sexed-crazed older man was going to screw with my sixteen-year-old daughter.

"Hello, Mike. I'm Rese's mother. How old are you?"

"Twenty-three," he answered rather proudly.

"Rese is sixteen." At this information, Mike's mouth fell open, and his eyes began to bug out. "Yes, that's right, she's a minor. I'll let you take her to lunch. I want you back in two hours. If you touch her, I'll prosecute you to the fullest extent of the law."

One-and-a-half hours later, Rese returned home. When I asked her how her date went, she said, "Boring. He was really nervous and kept looking at his watch. I think he's too old for me. We had nothing in common."

"Really?" I said, feigning surprise and inwardly sighing with relief. That was the end of problems with Rese dating older men.

That night, sitting on my bed, my mind traveled back to my great mom day. I smiled with satisfaction knowing Rese's *man* friend hadn't stood a chance after I loomed large in my mother bear stance. I'd saved my sweet peanut butter cup—a frequently used nickname of Rese's she barely tolerated—from being eaten alive. *A sixteen-year-old girl has no business hanging out with a twenty-three-year-old man. What was she thinking?* I chuckled, answering my own question: *She was thinking thoughts very similar to mine as a teenager.* With that, I tucked myself in, safe and sound, snuggling deep under the covers. That night I slept like a baby.

I woke with a start. My mother bear technique had worked on Rese but had so far been ineffective with Gina. I needed to focus on my daughter who was in trouble, the daughter who reminded me of my teenaged self. Fourteen-year-old Gina's situation was becoming dire. She continued to run away. Sometimes I wouldn't hear from her for weeks at a time. With these disappearances, I lay awake at night sick with worry. In the daytime, I felt like a pressure cooker ready to blow because I had to keep up a good front for my other three kids. I plastered on a smiley face at work at the oil and gas company in order to stay employed.

In March, Gina started living with some friends: Aaron, Bill, and their female cousin Sheila. The only adult in the house was Harry, Aaron's dad. I immediately went to the house to scope out Gina's living situation and meet her housemates. I was relieved to see she had her own room. The kids seemed okay.

Harry, however, made my blood freeze. I couldn't put my finger on the reason for my intense negative impression. Harry was short, skinny, and rather scrappy looking. Maybe it was simply that Gina was living at his house instead of home with me. *Yes, that must be it,* I thought. I didn't like the situation at all. My pedophile alarm was ringing, but I ignored it. I was so relieved and grateful that I at least knew where she was.

After Gina had lived there a couple of months, I received a call from a psychotherapist named Jane. The therapist said she was seeing Harry and was concerned for Gina. Harry was having sexual fantasies about my daughter. She recommended I remove Gina from their home as quickly as possible.

Fear grabbed me around the neck and shook me, body and soul. This was my absolute worst nightmare. This couldn't be happening. I dropped the phone, jumped in the car, and drove as fast as the car would go to rescue my baby. I explained to Gina that Harry was a dangerous guy.

She thought he was "creepy" too. "I don't like the way he looks at me," she said. To my surprise and relief, she collected her things and came with me without a fight.

Against my better judgment, I called Joe. I felt obligated to let him know because he was Gina's dad. Upon hearing the news, he came to the house, grabbed JJ's baseball bat, and screamed, "I'm going to kill the son of a bitch!"

I pleaded with him to stop, but my words just hit him in the back as he bolted out the door. Soon he returned. Harry had called the police. The cops had persuaded Joe to leave by threatening arrest. He came in our house and unleashed his anger on Gina.

"You God-damned whore. You slut! I can't stand to look at you."

Gina looked at her dad as if he had cut her heart out with a knife. Her face said, *I thought I was bad, and now my own dad is confirming it.*

I was so angry with Joe I could've used the baseball bat on him. I paused, looking at him with my fists clenched. I resisted the temptation to hit him. I rushed to Gina's side as Joe stomped out of the house. In the few seconds I wasted being angry with Joe, I'd lost my connection to Gina. The hurt and vulnerability were gone. There was a blank expression on her face, tinged with defiance.

That night was one of the blackest nights of my life. I felt I was an utter failure as a mom. Being a good mom when the kids were little was the only sure accomplishment I'd made in my life. When the kids had become teens, I hadn't known what to do. I allowed my Gina to live in a house with a pedophile so I wouldn't worry. I was despicable. I plummeted down a hole so deep, so dark, all light was snuffed out. For a brief moment, anchorless, hanging in space, drowning in despair, I contemplated suicide. As the scenes floated through my mind, flashes of two parallel stories surfaced.

In my mind's eye, I watched little Diana sponging up all the shame while being abused. I pictured her acting out her badness. I saw snapshots of a troubled Gina acting out and running away. I watched an enraged Dad hitting me with a belt, coupled with pictures of an irate Joe holding a baseball bat and calling Gina names. Flashes of Mom appeared, overwhelmed, helpless to save me. My breath caught in my throat as I pictured myself immobilized, not knowing how to help my daughter. *Gina is better off with me dead; they all are. I don't deserve to live.* I then screamed a raw, guttural scream as I saw Mom, Alan, Vincent, Teresa, and Dad—all dead.

Suddenly, the light of my children's faces swam into my consciousness. No, I wouldn't kill myself. I wouldn't leave my children with that kind of trauma. I couldn't possibly do to them what my father had done to me and my family.

I looked up to the heavens and prayed, *I know I requested a couple of angels in the past, but I need major reinforcements. I'm desperate. We have a crisis on our hands! Since I've decided to stay around and fight, would you please send in an army of angels? If possible, could you give her twenty-four-hour protection to keep her safe? When she leaves again like I know she will, please let me know where she is.*

In the morning, I went downstairs and hugged my children one by one. Gina even let me hug her. She stayed for about a week. One day I came home and she was gone. After that, she would come and go. God must have heard my prayers, though, for after that night, she did keep in constant contact. Thankfully, she didn't go back to Harry's, but she didn't stay home either.

I continued to grow and change for the good. Sandra packed up her overwhelming and undeserving feelings and moved out of my psyche. With her left my promiscuous behavior and any inclination to have sex with strangers. Her move coincided with Joe's final departure, and the arrival of my no-victim stance. I hoped both moves were permanent. They felt permanent, but one never knew for sure.

Mostly, I filled in the holes of my self-esteem with healthy decisions, but I wasn't ready to abandon all my harmful habits. I was still a smoker. I'd smoked cigarettes off and on since I was a teenager. Smoking seemed to be the only sure-fire way to calm myself when I was feeling overwhelmed.

I was dating a number of men. One of the most persistent men in my life was Stan. He was our company's UPS agent and appeared out of nowhere when I needed help. He was eight years younger than I and not classically handsome, but he had his own charm. He was short, standing five feet six inches, and he was skinny. His hair and eyebrows were light brown with red highlights and had a bushy quality to them. When he smiled, which he did often, it accentuated a major overbite.

Due to his impoverished, neglectful, uneducated beginnings, he lacked social skills, and I tried to help him with these aspects of his life. He wasn't well read and would often mix up words, but he was very good with numbers. He loved to apply his gift to sports statistics. One habit of Stan's that made me cringe was that he swore like a sailor even though he'd been in the Air Force. He tried to curtail the filthy language in deference to me, but often he'd slip.

He was incredibly friendly. When we went on a date in downtown Denver, which encompassed his UPS route, everyone knew him. "Hi, Stan" and "How's it going, Stan?" I'd hear twenty or more times an evening. What was even more amazing was that Stan would know all twenty people by name.

"My, you're a popular guy," I said after a couple of dates.

Stan's face had an "aw, shucks" expression as he said, "It's simple: I love my job, and I love people."

Despite his outgoing, friendly demeanor, I found out early in the relationship that he was uncomfortable with any form of physical affection. When we first dated, he couldn't bear to be touched. Even my most gentle of touches would cause him to wince and say things like, "What are you doing? That doesn't feel good. Stop it; that tickles. I don't like being touched."

I replied, "Stan, this should feel good. What happened in your life that makes my touch feel bad?"

Slowly, haltingly, the stories crept out, but he was ready at a moment's notice to retreat once again into silence. He'd never talked to anyone about the horrendous physical abuse inflicted on him by his father or about being brought up in a family who never lovingly hugged or kissed.

Stan's childhood stories helped both of us to understand his reactions, but it didn't help to significantly change his behavior. After dating for about a month, I literally decided to take matters into my own hands. "I'm a touchy person," I told him. "If I can't touch you, I don't know how this relationship is going to work. One of the ways I show love is through touch."

To Stan's credit, he put his trust in my hands and allowed me to begin massaging his scalp. At first, he could tolerate only a few minutes of it. While my hands were caressing his head, my voice would try to soothe his fears. My mantra went something like this: "This doesn't tickle. This doesn't hurt. This feels good. You don't have to be afraid." As the weeks went by, Stan let me touch him more and more. Eventually, I was able to massage his head for hours at a time. His head, for whatever reason, was full of indentations that I called "craters."

My hands would often touch the recesses of his mind. Out of memory holes would emerge recollections of being abused by his explosively angry, alcoholic father. "When I was a kid, Dad would hit me a lot. He was one mean, fucking drunk!" At the swear word, my body tensed and my hands stopped moving. Stan realized his mistake, saying, "Sorry."

I continued my massage, and he continued his story. "Most of the time, I didn't have a clue why he was mad at me. I remember one time, when he was drunk, he pushed me off his truck. He was still really mad, so he threw a beer bottle at me. It hit me hard in the head, right where you're rubbing." We continued on this healing journey, using Stan's head as a road map. The process was healing for me too. I loved being able to help heal Stan's traumas through the healthy use of touch.

Despite some shortcomings, Stan's positive, outgoing personality, his politeness and respect, the kindness radiating from his beautiful blue eyes, and his stability made me feel secure. I continued to keep my options open, however. After nearly twenty years of a destructive marriage, I was going to take my time. Besides, I was just too busy keeping my family afloat to consider a serious relationship.

While my debt load was decreasing, my rent was increasing, so I decided to move the family once again. I began the process of de-cluttering the house to make our move easier. The easiest place to start was Gina's room because she rarely came home. She kept in touch, but I couldn't touch her with my words or actions. I had no idea what was happening in her life. As I entered my fourteen-year-old daughter's room and sat down on her unused bed, a deep sadness permeated the room, pressing in on me. A shiver went through me, urging my body to move so as not to be sucked down the black hole of depression.

I decided I'd better start packing, so I picked up some notebooks lying on her nightstand. Gina's handwriting beckoned me, and to my dismay, I found myself in the middle of a sordid tale of drugs and sex. I was disgusted and repulsed and didn't want to know about my daughter's degrading escapades, but I couldn't stop reading. The earlier heavy, cold, grey feeling suddenly flamed red and hot. Seething, I called Joe.

"Are you still sleeping on your brother's desk?" Without waiting for a reply, I said, "I have a bed and bedroom furniture for you. Gina isn't living here. She isn't using it. You need it, so come and get it before we move."

Joe came for the furniture. When Gina learned I'd read her journals and gave away her belongings, she was furious. But her anger at being betrayed didn't even come close to matching mine.

Throughout the drama created by Gina and Joe, my therapists, James and Susan, had been a lifeline. One day they left DAPA without notice. They sailed away from me, pulling up my anchor of security. It felt like they left me adrift without so much as a life preserver. After my anger ebbed, I realized I was still afloat, holding on to some buoyant tools I'd discovered in working with these gifted therapists. The inner child work alone had helped heal my early wounds. There was no way I was going to abandon little Diana; I wasn't going to quit therapy. I would drop my own anchor. I was queen of the ringers, and I'd grab my healing process and hold on. I was a woman on a mission, but little Diana was resistant and seeing red. The adult in me won, and I joined a DAPA therapy group. The new group was led by Jim, a short, balding, older man who specialized in addiction, and Kathy, a woman about my age who sported curly, shoulder-length blonde hair and a big smile. She specialized in inner child work.

The group was an inner child and shame reduction group based on the work of John Bradshaw and Pia Mellody. The truth about inner child work for me was that once I shifted my perspective to include little Diana, I had much better insight into my behavior. Sure, I understood little Diana, just like Diana #2 and Sandra, had been a part of me, but by separating the child part from my adult part, I was able to honor myself more fully.

As far as therapy was concerned, my inner child was mad at James and Susan for leaving. In my new group, little Di sat sulking and distant. She wasn't in the mood to talk. I, as an adult, also felt uncomfortable sharing my story, but not for the same reason. My story seemed so big, I was afraid the other people in the group might feel overshadowed. I didn't want to do that. I was wary and withdrawn.

Both parts of me felt stuck in icy feelings and frozen thoughts. With Susan and James gone, little Diana and I needed to discover if this new group was safe and a good fit. So all of me sat and listened. As the months passed by, I felt myself slowly beginning to thaw.

One night in group, Kathy announced she'd just experienced a severe personal trauma. She thanked us for our understanding and told us not to take her possible inattentiveness personally. She explained she was struggling with many emotions and didn't mean to lose focus on us.

Her self-disclosure made her human and created for me a kinship with her. After carefully watching her do inner child work with other group members, I began to trust that she might be able to understand and accept me. With the help of the therapy group and friends, I felt relatively stable, but just in case something drastic happened in the future and I needed to talk to a professional on an individual basis, I decided I'd call Kathy.

No matter how well my life was going, the monstrous arms of the month of June always pushed me down. It held my head under the heavy pillow of history, trying to suffocate me. I hated June like I hated December. The murders, the execution, Dad's birthday, Father's Day, and my marriage to Joe all happened in June. Early June of 1989 found me still broke, having to move again, angry and depressed about Gina, and experiencing the usual misery and dread of the month. Stan and friends helped me move into a small, three-bedroom townhouse in Arvada.

Even with the wonderful warmth and love extended, I couldn't escape June's jail-like feeling. I felt frustrated and disgusted with Gina. She didn't have a room in our new house because she didn't deserve a room. Finally, though, JJ's graduation and the fragrant lilac blooms of summer filled my lungs with the freshest of air and forced June to release its stranglehold on my heart. JJ had reached his high school graduation effortlessly. He immediately got a job working with a friend laying concrete. Knowing my son, I suspected this type of job wouldn't be challenging enough for him. I also knew he'd figure things out when he was ready. Since I, as a single mother and sole breadwinner, hadn't quite figured out my career path either, I was glad to have JJ still living at home. The money he contributed to the rent was a big help. June of 1989 didn't end so badly, but I still welcomed July.

CHAPTER 23

The Last of Dad's Legacy

By the time the summer flowers faded and September ushered in its crisp air and golden aspen leaves, my life was feeling as settled as my life had ever been. With Dad and Joe gone, the negative energy of those two abusive men who had invaded my life for so long had all but disappeared from my thoughts. For the first time in my life, I was having fun trying out my social wings, and dating several different men. Stan was becoming my main man, but I wasn't ready to choose.

It was during this time I was notified one day that DAPA had abruptly closed its doors. I was disappointed our group didn't get to say good-bye to each other, but I felt I was ready to leave the nest and test my emotional wings. If down the road I needed the support of a therapist or a therapy group, I had Kathy's number, but for now life was good and I was coping fairly well. My life, of course, was still my life. I was incredibly busy. Even though I was working full-time plus Friday nights at the American Legion, I still struggled financially. Despite the fact my teenagers continued to challenge me, I began the school year with high spirits.

Life certainly wasn't perfect, but it wasn't dominated by crisis like my life of old. I was making dinner one evening and thinking how very grateful I was for the relative normalcy when the phone rang. It was Pitambar calling from Pittsburgh.

"Diann." Her voice was shrill and clipped and very different from her normally soft voice.

"What's wrong? Are the boys okay?" I asked. Since I had visited New Vrindaban in 1981, Pitambar and Ambarish had added two more sons to their family: Acarya, six, and Ananda, four. Nitai was now eight. Six months before the call, although still practicing Hare Krishna, the family had left the commune and Ambarish's precious cows and moved into the city of Pittsburgh. Maybe, I thought, the boys were having trouble adjusting.

"No, no, it's Ambarish. He's been talking crazy. I finally had to call 911 when he ran through the neighborhood naked. He's in a hospital psych ward in Pittsburgh. I don't know what to do."

"Pitambar, what do you need? Do you have food?" I asked. After she reassured me she and the boys were fine, I told her I'd talk to my siblings and get back to her soon. I hung up the phone, feeling a crescendo of crisis rising in my throat.

Jean and I were the only two family members who could get away that following weekend. Michael wanted me to go, so he gave me money for the plane ticket. We converged on Pittsburgh, Jean from Houston and I from Denver. After taking a cab directly to the hospital, we entered the locked-down psych ward and were ushered into Ambarish's room.

Ambarish was lying in the hospital bed and welcomed us with a crooked little smirk. "Hey, my two favorite sisters. How are you?"

"More important, how are you?" we both chimed together. Ambarish looked at us with a subdued expression. Jean and I both rushed toward our little brother and hugged him tightly for the longest time. I think we were both afraid to let him go.

Finally he pushed away and said in a matter-of-fact tone, "I think I'm doing better. The psychiatrist put me on Lithium. He thinks I'm bipolar. He thinks the medication will help stabilize me. So far, it kind of makes me feel numb."

Then with a sheepish grin, he added, "I was feeling and acting kind of crazy. I suppose Pitambar told you that I ran through the neighborhood naked; kind of crazy, huh?" We both nodded.

"What brought this on?" I asked. Since I had perhaps the most experience with breakdowns in our family, I suspected the answer had something to do with Dad. Unfortunately, I was right.

"Well, I guess I'm not cut out for city living. I've been under a lot of stress. My head started spinning with crazy thoughts. I started feeling like Dad. I was afraid I would hurt my wife and kids." With this statement, he started shaking his head back and forth and began to tear up. He looked at us, his green eyes pleading for us to help.

"Look at me," I said gently, stilling his head in my hands. "You're not Dad."

Jean touched his shoulder. "That's not who you are. You have a choice. You don't have to be like him."

"Sometimes it feels like I don't have a choice," he responded. "Maybe this medication will stop my crazy thoughts and mood swings." With the phrase mood swing, his low, melodic voice abruptly changed. The next sentence came out in tight, high puffs. "You know, if he'd carried out his plan, I would've been the only one left." I could see an eleven-year-old's look of horror on my thirty-seven-year-old brother's face.

"But Dad didn't kill us all. It didn't happen," I said.

"We love you," said Jean. "Di is right. You need to let it go."

We stayed through the weekend. We left before he was released from the hospital. Both Jean and I felt he'd heard us and seemed to be doing better. I knew, though, from personal experience, how Dad could permeate a life. I'd never felt I could hurt my kids like Dad hurt us, but I did understand about feeling crazy and having breakdowns. I hoped Ambarish would get help in addition to the medication. I vowed to keep in contact. I called weekly. It did appear the medication was working because Ambarish seemed to regain some of his old optimism.

When I called in October, he excitedly announced he and his family had moved back to the farm. "I'm home. I don't know why I went to the city in the first place. Well, it doesn't matter now because I'm home. I'm a simple farm guy. Except for the last seven not-so-great months, I've lived on the farm for almost twenty years. Things will be a lot better. You'll see."

On November 7, 1989, I called to wish him a happy birthday. "Happy 38th Birthday, Brother. You're old, but you'll never catch me."

His voice came from far away, originating from the deepest, darkest hole imaginable. His words were whispered over the telephone wire. The message slugging me in the stomach was loud and clear: "My family would be better off if I were dead."

"That's crazy talk," I said. "Your family loves you."

He said, "They won't. I'm just like Dad."

"No, you're not," I screamed. "No, you're not." I pleaded. "Don't talk like that. You're scaring me."

"Yeah, I'm a scary guy," he said in a flat, matter-of-fact tone.

"Are you taking your meds?

"Nah, I didn't like the way they made me feel. They weren't helping, anyway. Living in the city was the problem. Moving back to the farm was the solution."

"Please go back on your meds. They were helping."

"I don't think so," he said. "Do you know if Dad had carried out his plan, I'd have been the only one left? How can I live with that? Oh, well, it doesn't matter, because I'm just like him."

We talked for a long time. My words seemed to have no effect. He couldn't hear me, but I sure heard him. The monstrous part of Dad had my brother in his grip. Ambarish's words twisted my stomach into tight knots, crawled up my skin, and grabbed my throat, choking off my breath. "Damn you, Dad," I hissed. "You're not going to win."

I immediately called all my siblings. "Ambarish is in trouble. I've never heard him so depressed. I'm sure you were going to call him for his birthday. Please don't wait. Call him now."

One by one my siblings called me to report their impressions of Ambarish's mental health. Each agreed he was very depressed. No one had been able to make any inroads into his psyche.

The days passed at a snail's pace. I jumped every time I heard the phone ring. As it had been a couple of days since I'd talked to Ambarish, I decided to wait and give him a call on Sunday. My mind kept trying to tell me no news was good news and things would be better. I rationalized that my weekly call would find a new and happy person on the other end. My brain was trying to convince my body to relax, but my body wasn't buying it. The electricity coursing through my nerves made everyday life almost too intense to bear. As I worked waitressing at the Legion Friday night, the noise was too loud, my thinking too disjointed, and my mind was spinning too fast. *Please be okay, my little brother* was my mantra. My sleep was restless, but I arose to the glow of the sun warming the earth. It was a Saturday sunrise, and all was well.

Breakfast had been made and eaten. The kids were occupied with their various activities. I was relaxing and cleaning up the dishes after an exhausting night and week when the phone rang, piercing my eardrums. The second ring caused my body to jump. With shaking hands, I fumbled for the receiver. "Hello," I said, somehow sensing Pitambar on the other end.

"Diann, this is Pitambar. Ambarish hanged himself today, and he's dead."

My scream of grief and outrage was long and loud. It seemed to go on forever, vibrating in my body, ballooning out my mouth, and echoing out into the universe. After what felt like an eternity, I came back to earth. I looked up to see eight wide, scared eyes staring at me. I lifted my hand and mouthed to my children, "Just a minute and I'll tell you." I turned my attention back to Pitambar.

"Where, how, tell me."

"He hanged himself from a tree outside the house. I didn't see him, but Acarya and Ananda did. Di, will you call everybody? I can't do it."

"Okay, Pitambar. Okay."

"Good," she said and was gone. I hung on in shock, the dial tone of finality ringing in my ears.

I slowly clicked the phone off and sank down into a chair as my kids surrounded me. "Your uncle Ambarish is dead. He committed suicide this morning." They stood there wide-eyed and open-mouthed, not sure what to say or how to help me. After "oh mom" and "so sorry," I looked at them with soft eyes. "I'm okay," I said, waving my hands, telling them they didn't have to stay with me. "I need to call your aunt and uncles. Pitambar asked me to."

I called Michael first. When I told him what had happened, he immediately started crying, howling with pain. I called Jean next. She was devastated and sobbed her heart out. I then called Paul and Lee. Both of them cried hysterically.

Al's number was the only one I didn't know by heart. I looked it up and dialed, afraid I wouldn't be able to reach him. He was isolated and detached from all of the family except for Ambarish and Lee. In the past few years, Al had visited Ambarish at the farm on a number of occasions. He liked talking with Ambarish because he, too, believed in the tenets of Eastern philosophy.

I dialed, and to my astonishment, Al picked up after the first ring. "Di, what's wrong? Is it Ambarish?"

"Al, oh Al, he's dead."

Al let out a bloodcurdling wail. He was crying so hard, he couldn't speak. The more he cried, the more I felt I had to remain strong. I talked softly, giving him the details, and made tentative plans to meet in Pittsburgh. Michael, even in his grief, had already taken care of buying a plane ticket for any family member who couldn't afford it, namely Al and me.

I'd just hung up the phone with Al when Michael, Paul, and Lee came through my front door. Hugging, swaying, sobbing, my siblings clung to me. I didn't cry. I couldn't cry. I had to be strong for my brothers. Between the howls, they expressed their anger toward Dad for causing the pain leading to Ambarish's suicide. We were all angry with Ambarish for leaving his family with the same legacy Dad had given us.

"He could've come to us. We loved him." Short sentences were spoken between hugs and wails of agony.

"He had choices. He hanged himself where his boys could find him. How could he? How could he?"

When my brothers were spent, they left to pack and make arrangements to leave for West Virginia the next day. I sat in a chair, staring out the kitchen window seeing nothing, hearing nothing, feeling nothing.

The ring of the doorbell jolted me. At the door stood my cousin Bob sobbing uncontrollably. Bob, Aunt Ruby and Uncle Frank's son, had been through a lot with our family. We'd moved in with him and his family after the murders. Uncle Frank, his dad, had died two months earlier.

I could tell this news had put him temporarily over-the-top when his normally cadenced, deep-toned male voice became speedy and high-pitched. "Mom told me about Patrick. Oh, my God! Oh, my God. Di, what are we going to do?"

My response to this crisis reached a crescendo as it felt like everyone around me had broken down. My insides were definitely building up for some sort of breakdown, but I just couldn't let that happen. I was the one member of my family who had gone to therapy. I had tools to handle crises. *It's my turn to be strong. My family has been there for me through my tough times; they can cry on my shoulders for once. I won't cry. I can't cry.* To my relief, my voice came out with whispery soft words of comfort for Bob. He seemed to respond. I wondered how Bob got the news so quickly; evidently, Michael had called Aunt Ruby.

Later that afternoon Stan called and wanted to know if he could see me. I told him what had happened. He was silent for a minute, then he said, "I'm so sorry. Do you want me to come over?"

"Yes," I said simply.

When he arrived, he suggested we go out to his car and talk. We sat in his 1968 Impala, and I told him about my brother.

When I was through, he looked at me tenderly and murmured, "I'm so sorry," and handed me a sympathy card. That did it! Stan's kindness and the thoughtfulness of the card pushed me over the edge. I looked at the card, but instead of crying, my throat started to close up. I couldn't breathe. I was gagging, gasping for air.

"I gotta go," I choked.

Wordless, I looked at Stan, pleading with him to understand. He nodded. "It's okay. Call me if I can help."

I sponged up his gentle words, but they seemed to make things worse, filling my already clogged airways. I jumped out of the car and ran through our front door and into the living room. I forced enough air through my starving lungs to scream, "Kids, I need you." Four teenagers heard the panic in my voice and came running. "Hold me," I gasped. Eight arms of love and security embraced me, and I was finally able to cry. I sobbed uncontrollably for what seemed like a long time. My kids held me together as I fell apart. Finally, with a shuddering sigh, I gave my precious children permission to let go.

"Okay, I'm better now." The love of my kids gave me the strength to cry and to breathe again.

I slept fitfully that night because I was busy dreaming, revisiting scenes from my life with Patrick. I saw Patrick and me on the playground. I heard Patrick singing with the voice of an angel. I saw Patrick coming back from camp and saw his tortured face after finding out about the murders. I then saw him turning into Krishna's Ambarish. There was Ambarish with his precious cows. Ambarish saying he was like Dad. The nightmare started then: Dad killing Mom and the babies; Dad killing all of us. Patrick the only one left; Patrick floating through space swinging from a tree.

"No! No!" I woke up sweating, remembering I was here and alive, but my dear brother Patrick was really dead and gone.

The following day Michael, Paul, Lee, and I boarded a plane to Pittsburgh. We had a layover in Chicago and were surprised to hook up with Jean, who was waiting for the same connecting flight. Al would meet us in Pittsburgh at the airport.

The flight felt surreal as time warped, speeding up and slowing down. Temperature and temperament fluctuated. I was hot and cold, anxious and numb, sad and angry. The plane ride seemed to take days or only seconds.

As we disembarked, we spied Al, slump shouldered, standing alone. My heart swelled with emotion. It was so good to see my wayward big brother again and so sad our reunion was under these circumstances. After much hugging and more crying, we piled into a rental car and headed to New Vrindaban, West Virginia.

We went directly to Pitambar's house. She met us at the door with Nitai, Acarya, and Ananda plastered to her side. Upon seeing six big adults peering in through the open door, the kids clutched Pitambar's sari even tighter. Nitai broke away first as he recognized Ganendra (Lee) and Al. Nitai let Ganendra and then Al hug him. He then shrugged and let us all hug him. The little ones, taking a cue from their older brother, soon bravely began to talk with the big group of very affectionate aunts and uncles.

That night we held our own wake. For hours we laughed and cried, remembering our life with our brother. We all rode the emotional roller coaster late into the night. The reason for the gathering made the night hard, but the fact we were gathered as a family made it a healing time.

The next day a Hare Krishna funeral was held, a ceremony that filled the air with chanting. Ambarish's cremated remains were placed in an urn on the altar along with a picture of him. The Hare Krishna mantra was chanted to the tune of "Amazing Grace" as one by one we each went up and threw flower petals at the base of the altar. All of us—Michael, Jean, Al, Paul, Lee, and I—cried throughout the ceremony. Afterward, the community, along with my family, walked in procession to a nearby pond, where we lovingly scattered his ashes.

After buying Pitambar and the kids enough food and clothing to last for a good amount of time, we said good-bye. We drove away and left our brother behind in West Virginia, resting peacefully on the farm he loved with his cows grazing nearby.

The plane ride back found me smoking, literally and figuratively. I smoked about a pack of cigarettes every day, but I smoked even more in times of stress. This indeed was a stressful time, so I went to the back of the plane and opened my pack of cigarettes. I also found myself smoking with anger.

I lit up as red-hot thoughts sizzled through my brain. I was angry as hell. Patrick was another one of Dad's casualties. Dad had murdered another sibling. Would this nightmare never end? Would his power over us never cease? *I'm mad at you too, Patrick. You had a choice. You chose not to take your meds. You let Dad win.*

A steely, calm, cold feeling entered my heart. *You're not going to win with me, Dad. This is the end. This is the last of your legacy in my life, Dad. I'll do whatever it takes to improve my life and the lives of my children. I have control of my life. I'll never be at your mercy again.*

At that moment, I made a choice to move from scarcity to abundance. I decided to go back to school. After Mom's death, I'd found out she had graduated with an associate's degree from Barnes Business College before her marriage to Dad. She'd never done anything with it. I would be different. I registered at her alma mater the following Monday. I started college in January, the same week I turned forty. I intended to climb the pay-raise rungs as I pursued an associate's degree in accounting with a minor in computer science.

My already-busy life whirled by. Four kids, a full-time job, a part-time job working Friday and Sunday at the Legion, going to school three nights a week, and a social life kept me spinning. My vast experience with death and loss and my view of death as being part of the human condition allowed me to go on.

After Patrick's death, I talked to Stan, as I had once talked to Joe, and explained that when I died, I wanted to be cremated. I didn't want anyone to have to deal with an open casket. After viewing dead bodies in open caskets too many times in my life, I was adamant in this regard.

Stan wholeheartedly agreed. "I definitely don't want a big religious burial," he said, wrinkling his nose. "For sure I want to be cremated." After a moment of silence, he added, "I have a will, you know."

"No, I didn't know."

"After the Air Force, I came to Denver. I didn't know anybody. A couple on my UPS route took a liking to me and invited me over for dinner a lot. They became my second family." He smiled then. "I had a crush on their daughter, Tanya." Frowning, he said, "But she liked me like a brother. So, as a brother, I asked her to be the executor of my estate, and she said she would. I don't have a lot now, but I'll just keep on plugging away. You never know, I may be rich someday," he said with a grin. "Anyway, having a will and somebody I trust to handle things when I'm gone makes me feel better."

I looked at Stan's wiry, fit body and said, "Well, you won't have to worry about that for a long time." I knew death was a part of life, but I also knew our family had experienced more than our fair share of the premature, violent type. I was hopeful that from here on out, the people I knew and loved would die of old age. Old age or not, I, and now Stan, had decided we preferred cremation. We were two people in this universe who didn't like the tradition of an open casket.

*   *   *

In March, I received a notice my meager salary would be garnished due to an overdue optometrist bill. Panic gripped me because we were barely making it as it was. Although I was working two jobs and going to school full time to improve my plight, I was still on shaky ground financially. This garnishment would change the feeling of already big financial tremors into an earthquake of devastating proportions. I was reluctant but finally called Joe in desperation. Although he'd been absent from our lives and hadn't contributed a dime, he'd run a successful collection agency. I believed he had the expertise and connections to solve the problem.

In my best diplomatic voice, I explained the situation in a long string of words ending with, "So with your background, I thought you might be able to help me."

"You thought wrong. The answer is no. I won't help you." And to add finality to his answer he hung up, stinging my ears with a dial tone.

"What the hell am I going to do?" I picked up the phone and talked to my brother Michael, who'd consistently been my savior in dire situations.

Michael listened, as always, to my tale of woe, making mild noises, such as, "Hmm...yes." When I got to the part where Joe wouldn't help me, he said "totally selfish" and "ridiculous!" When I'd finished, Michael asked, "Why haven't you divorced him?"

My answer was succinct. "I can't afford it."

"It's time, Di. I'll pay for the divorce. I'll talk to an attorney friend of mine. I'm sure he'll be more than happy to help. Don't worry about the bill. I'll take care of that too. It's a loan, of course; you pay me back when you're able." Another crisis averted; back to life as usual.

On June 4, 1990, almost twenty years to the day from our wedding, I went to court to dissolve my marriage to Joe. Joe sauntered into the courtroom and sat next to me holding a legal pad and a self-righteous grin. He pointed to the paper and stated emphatically, "Here's a list I've compiled of our outstanding bills. Maybe you haven't thought of this, but before the divorce can go through, we need to take care of these bills."

"Let me see," I said, reaching for the pad. He handed it to me with a smirk, which faded quickly as I went through the list checking off the items. "I paid this and this and this…" When I was through with the entire list, there was one bill left. "This is a bar bill you accrued after you moved out. I'm not paying for this."

"You paid all these bills?" he asked incredulously.

"Yes, and I'm going to school full time majoring in accounting with a minor in computer science."

Joe just stared at me, stunned. The smugness had been replaced by an expression I had never seen and didn't know how to identify. To my astonishment, out of Joe's mouth came words of admiration. "Wow! You really are smart, aren't you?"

I smiled and thought, *Yes, Joe, I'm not only smart, I'm free. So sad you never really knew me.* I walked out of the courtroom and into my life as a single woman. I would date—I might even consider having a serious relationship with Stan—but I was not inclined to get married anytime soon.

The usual joyless June that weighed my mind down with horrible anniversary dates was giving me a slight reprieve. Thoughts of my divorce let my mind dance with abandon, light on its feet. Sunshine and a stable Stan filled my days.

Although Stan still had an apartment, he spent much of his time at our new townhouse. From early on in our relationship, Stan not only knew my favorite color was green but also that my favorite animal was an elephant. Stan, who was a collector at heart and had an impressive beer stein collection, decided I needed a collection of my own. Soon, thanks to Stan's generosity, I had the beginnings of a decent elephant collection.

Stan was generous financially, and I began to relax a little about money. I no longer believed I'd end up on the streets. Stan accepted me and loved me. My worth wasn't based on my appearance, although he would often say he liked the way I looked. He was safe, and I, in turn, safely and lovingly touched his life. This was the first time in my life where I was not only in control of who touched my body but also in control of a sexual relationship. I taught Stan the mechanics of feel-good physical intimacy. I noticed that by taking control of my body and my relationships, I no longer needed to lead a double life. Dad, Diana #2, Sandra, and Joe seemed to be gone for good, and I was free to be me.

JJ, as I predicted, decided a job as a concrete man didn't provide the solid, well-paid career he'd anticipated. A couple months before my divorce was final, he joined the Navy. He made his mother proud by placing in the top five percent in the nation on his civil service exam. His primary purpose in joining the military was to further his education, which he did, first through the Navy and later through the GI Bill. I missed my son and the girls missed their brother, but I think JJ was more than ready to learn to navigate this big planet.

As a smaller family, we carried on. I snuggled with Rese and Mandy every day. I snuggled with Gina, too, when she was home and if she'd let me. Our family had our issues, as most families do, but we presented a much more positive environment for Stan than he'd ever experienced. He was used to feeling unloved and terrified; now he felt cared for and safe.

Through my experiences living in many different environments, I'd picked up some tips on etiquette and decorum. Stan, who had never been exposed to polite society, was open to my suggestions on proper manners and grooming. In short, we began to provide an environment for each other that allowed both of us to heal.

As safe as we both felt, we still had very little in common. He had his passions and I had mine, and they didn't intersect. When I would bring up any subjects outside of his interests, his eyes would glaze over. With Stan, I missed the stimulating adult conversation that challenged me to learn and grow. Stan, like Joe, was very uncomfortable with feelings. Stan didn't like my laugh, so I'd try to stifle it when he was around. Because feeling safe with a man was unprecedented in my life, I decided to suppress my concerns. Stan was a very good man, and I was probably being too picky. I was expecting too much out of a relationship. I rationalized that I had friends who could fulfill my needs.

For the time being, things were stable and the kids seemed content; we were exhibiting all the outward appearances of a happy family. Rese and Stan liked each other, but Rese was in her junior year of high school and not in need of a father figure. Gina was in and out of our lives. Stan and Gina were civil but distant. Mandy, fourteen, was in desperate need of a dad, and Stan yearned for a tomboy daughter with a quirky sense of humor.

Mandy and Stan became great buddies. They talked, played games, and watched movies together. When Stan discovered Mandy liked Donald Duck, he kick-started and financed a substantial D. Duck collection. As is normal with even best-buddy/stepfather/stepdaughter relationships, they had their issues. When Mandy would leave the lights on or wet clothes in the washer, Stan would tape the offending switch or appliance shut.

As always with teenagers, even with the happiest of family scenarios, there were challenges. Sometime in the summer, Gina, who had been living elsewhere for a while, called me at work one morning and asked if I'd meet her for lunch because she had "something very important to discuss."

She showed up with Aaron's friend Bill. Both Aaron and Bill were living with Aaron's dad, Harry. As soon as we sat down, my earnest fifteen-year-old got right to the point. She announced in a breathy, long, run-on sentence, "We're in love and want to get married and live together, and we need your permission."

I, an earnest forty-year-old, got right to the point also. "You're too young to get married, so I won't give my permission."

Gina and Bill tried their best arguments to no avail. Finally, Gina shrugged and gave me a look that said, *I thought you'd say that, but I wanted to give it a shot.*

"I'm hungry," she said. "Let's order lunch."

I chalked up this little incident in the win column for me as a mother. Yes to lunch and no to the marriage of my fifteen-year-old daughter seemed like a responsible adult decision. Gina probably gave herself a positive point for the effort extended in meeting with me and getting a free lunch for her and her boyfriend.

Meanwhile, sixteen-year-old Rese continued to be the "good girl" of the family. She got good grades and participated in some of the school's extracurricular activities, including chorus, which she loved.

Mandy was a delightful kid at home but a different story at school. She started middle school and immediately connected with a group of troublemakers. The first school-sponsored dance found her and some of her friends drunk and in the principal's office. The school called Michael because they didn't have my number at the American Legion.

When Michael arrived at the school, an inebriated Mandy followed him meekly to the car. She was mortified her esteemed uncle had witnessed her drunkenness, but it wasn't enough to keep her from using drugs and alcohol for the rest of her school days.

Stan continued to be a presence in our lives and started to stay overnight. I graduated from Barnes Business School in December and promptly put in for an open position in accounting at the oil company where I worked. I received the position and a seven-thousand-dollar-a-year raise. I was still working Friday nights at the Legion. Stan would usually show up at the Legion to visit every week, order a Long Island Iced Tea, and sit and chat with the Legionnaires. I always looked forward to his visits, and so did everyone else. A whole legion of people loved Stan, and he loved them back. I felt as if life were beginning to flow. Things were definitely getting easier with nary a crisis on the horizon.

One evening in February of 1991, Gina popped in the kitchen while I was cooking dinner. She sat down at the table and watched me. This behavior was not typical of my outspoken, impatient, opinionated daughter, so I looked up and asked, "What's up?"

Gina looked down for a second, took a deep breath, squared her shoulders, looked me straight in the eyes, and said, "I'm pregnant."

Heat hotter than the hottest jalapeño pepper started in my gut and radiated out through my limbs to my balled fists. I looked at her, the silence deafening. Finally I said, in whispered hisses, enunciating every word, "I… would…suggest…you…leave…the… kitchen…right… now."

Gina sprang out of her chair and ran out of the room. I wanted to hit; I wanted to slice Gina up with my words. I exploded in rage, slamming kitchen cabinet doors and throwing pots and pans in the sink. I stopped my frenzied fury long enough to catch my breath, and in that instant, I heard the front door close. At least Gina had made one good decision; she'd left the house. I definitely needed time to cool down.

For two days, I stewed. The anger heat in my body was quickly replaced with an icy-cold worry. How were we going to manage? How could I possibly handle Gina's pregnancy financially or emotionally? I definitely didn't want to be a grandmother at the age of forty-one. I had too much on my plate and couldn't imagine handling a baby at this time in my life. Why hadn't she been more careful? Why wasn't she more responsible? Didn't she care about herself enough to protect herself from pregnancy? I didn't even know who the baby's father was.

On the other hand, who was I to judge? I suddenly understood the negative responses from Aunt Ruby, Michael, and Jean about my unwed pregnancy. When I remembered how misjudged I felt, compassion for

Gina filled my body. *We will, indeed, cope with her pregnancy. A baby is always welcome in my life. I'll be "Nana" again, this time as a grandmother.*

That weekend I picked up the phone and called my daughter. "I love you, Gina. I'm disappointed you're pregnant. You're too young to have a baby, but we'll cope. You're my daughter, and I'll support you."

Gina sighed, her voice soft. "I love you too, Mom. Can I come to the house and talk?"

About fifteen minutes later, Gina was home. The talk was soft, tear-filled, and connected. I found out the baby's father was not Bill, whom she'd wished to marry, but Aaron, Bill's best friend. She was gone again the following day, but I hoped this little one would change my relationship with Gina and our lives for the better.

My past rearing its ugly head, combined with that old churning feeling in my stomach, nudged the synapses in my brain to think maybe I could still use some help. I called Kathy and went back into therapy by way of a group.

Kathy's group fit me better than the DAPA group. It met every two weeks, which worked well with my hectic schedule. It was a much smaller group than DAPA, and for the first time in group therapy, I felt comfortable sharing my day-to-day frustrations and dilemmas. It was still very difficult for me to express emotions, especially my tears, but the group seemed to understand me. They were encouraging and sometimes downright pushy, but in a playful way.

* * *

Stan liked family life, but our place didn't provide enough space for one of his biggest passions: restoring vintage vehicles. He was always scoping out potential spaces to work on his cars. In short, he was looking for garages with attached or detached houses included. So on April 21, his birthday, his express wish was to cruise my neighborhood streets with me in his vintage 1968 Impala looking for a garage to purchase.

While cruising, we spied a house for sale sitting in the center of a large corner lot. His eyes popped out of his skull when he saw the house came with a two-car attached garage plus a one-car detached garage. Stan's exuberance was catching. I chuckled to myself, thinking Stan loved working on cars as much as Patrick had loved his precious cows.

The house looked average in size from the street. Looks were deceiving, however, because when we entered, we walked into a spacious, three-bedroom, three-bathroom house complete with all the amenities. Stan was sold. We immediately went back to my townhouse and called Michael, who was a Realtor. Stan put in an offer that same day. What a birthday present! The offer was accepted; the closing was set for the first week in June.

I was in the process of writing JJ a letter about the move when he called. It was the first Saturday in May.

"Mom, remember Barb, the girl I brought home last Christmas?"

"JJ, how great to hear from you; I was just writing you a letter."

"Great, Mom," he said distractedly. "Do you remember Barb?"

"Of course," I said with an exasperated sigh.

"What did you think of her?"

"I liked her."

"What would you think if I married her?"

"Really, JJ? How exciting. When do you want to get married?"

"That's the thing. We've decided to get married here in Chicago next Friday," he said in an excited voice.

My heart sank at this news because I knew I couldn't be there. "JJ, I don't think I can afford the time or money on such short notice."

"I know, Mom, but scheduling these things in the Navy is tricky. This is what we both want. Maybe we can celebrate in Colorado when we're on leave in September."

"Maybe," I said without conviction.

"Gotta go. Love you, Mom," my son said and hung up the phone.

I held the phone in my hand. Tears were dripping off the receiver and onto my spirits, which lay in a soggy heap on the floor. I was beyond sad. I wasn't going to be able to attend my son's wedding.

I was also mad. I was mad at JJ for being so cavalier about things. I was mad at my parents, Joe, the world in general, and myself for forever being poor. I was mad I cared so much.

Maybe, I thought, my spirits lifting a little, *I could throw a wedding reception for JJ.* My spirits plummeted when I asked myself the next logical question, *How am I going to afford such an extravagance?* The answer to my financial concerns didn't come until two months after our move.

Rese, Mandy, and I moved into Stan's house in June of 1991 with all my belongings. Stan had bought the house, and I furnished it. Stan loved all my furniture and was especially ecstatic about my king-sized bed. We promptly sold his single at a garage sale.

We settled into a routine. Stan loved routines, and so did I. To my delight, Stan enjoyed doing some of the household chores I thought tedious. He liked cleaning bathrooms and doing laundry because they had a calming effect on him. His best-loved household chore was ironing. Ironing was in Stan's top five greatest stress relievers. Since ironing was definitely not one of my favorite pastimes, not having to perform this odious task was a stress reliever to me. He'd learned to iron in the Air Force and now ironed everything from his UPS shirts to Mandy's and my pants and blouses. Stan thought the most thrilling household item I contributed to the new abode was my ironing board.

The month of June was changing its tune. Not only were we back in a spacious home, but Rese graduated from high school a week after we moved in. JJ had been talking to Rese through her senior year about joining the Navy. Rese decided to give it a try. Three months after graduation she followed in her brother's footsteps, joined the Navy, and moved to Florida in August for basic training.

The answer to my financial concerns came in the form of a windfall the same August Rese joined the Navy. I'd been in a car accident the previous year and had been going to the chiropractor five days a week for a year. One evening while I was still at work, I received a call from the insurance company for the other driver. They offered me $6,500 to close the case. Not being savvy in these types of cases, I agreed immediately and thanked my lucky stars. With that money, I was able to pay all my bills, throw a wedding reception for JJ and his new wife, Barb, go to Rese's graduation from boot camp in Orlando, Florida, purchase a very used car for my pregnant Gina, and buy a trampoline for Mandy. Or I thought the trampoline was for Mandy, but in reality, Stan and a bunch of Mandy's friends used it as much as she did. What a rich and wonderful summer we enjoyed!

Another highlight of the summer was a visit from Uncle Fernando. He'd breeze into town every couple of years to visit the entire family. He brought with him a breath of refreshing family love. He represented the best of Dad. He was the person Dad could have been. This particular year he couldn't stay long, but he made sure to visit all of us who were in town: Michael, Paul, Lee, and me.

Shortly after he left, Paul came to visit me. He had a funny look on his face like he had something in his mouth he needed to spit out. I knew my brother, so I waited. Finally he said, "Di, I asked Uncle Fernando why he thought Dad abused you. Do you know what he said?"

Yes, I thought to myself, *I bet Dad had been sexually abused as a child,* but I said, "No, what did he say?"

"He said there was an older woman in the apartment building where Dad lived with his foster parents. He said Dad was this woman's sex slave. Dad was sexually abused for many years." I nodded because I knew Dad had told Uncle Fernando the truth. I was almost certain Dad had been molested; I just didn't know the details. These facts didn't excuse his behavior; they just explained it. I thanked Paul for validating what I already knew.

In October 1991, gambling casinos opened in Colorado. I was fortunate to be offered a position at the historic Teller House in Central City in their human resources department. In order to be able to accept the job, I needed a reliable car, but my credit was still not the best because of my years with Joe. I was grateful to Stan for agreeing to co-sign on a loan. True to my word, I paid for everything concerning my Chevy Cavalier and never missed a payment. I loved my job, the pay was good, the people were great, and the work was challenging and fun. Life was truly looking up, and the heavens were answering. I felt like I was being well taken care of.

Stan came home one day and announced he had purchased $75,000 of life insurance. "Diann, I made you the beneficiary. It isn't much, but if I die, you'll have some money."

"You're not going to die, but I'm honored you chose me as your beneficiary," I said and kissed him. That same month my first granddaughter, Alexandra, was born. Gina moved in with us shortly thereafter. It was wonderful to have a baby in the house again.

Sometime in 1992, I recognized my relationship with Stan was not the happily-ever-after life I'd envisioned. Stan was the safest, kindest, most stable man I had ever known. He was great with my kids. Mandy adored him, and he adored her. I felt security and love, but I was unfulfilled. His interests were limited and included only UPS, cars, the lawn, slapstick comedies, sports, and his dog. All our conversations seemed to revolve around these subjects. I missed the stimulating and thought-provoking conversations I had with Joe.

I also wanted someone who was emotionally available. Like Joe, Stan had trouble talking about his or anyone else's feelings. Listening to my feelings inevitably led to his hearing shutting down and his eyes glazing over.

Stan, after all this time, still felt uncomfortable with my big laugh. When I'd get together with family and friends, invariably someone would say something I thought to be hysterically funny. When I laughed, Stan would leave the room. After discussing this in group, my fellow members encouraged me to keep talking about my feelings with Stan. I remember saying, "I'm sick of just surviving. I deserve to live, right?

"Right," they said in unison and clapped.

I picked an evening I felt was conducive to "the talk." I poured my heart out, leaving nothing unsaid. I talked about how we had so few interests in common. I talked about how unfulfilled I felt. I told him I felt I made all the concessions on entertainment. It was what he wanted to do or nothing. I talked about my love of music and dance and how he never entertained the idea of going out dancing with me. I continued spelling out my deepest felt needs and wants.

All this time, Stan didn't say a word. I stopped talking to take a breath, nearing the end of my soliloquy, and looked at him. His face was blank. He said, "Do you know where my tool belt is?"

"No, Stan, I don't." I'd had it. His nonresponse validated my frustration. I wasn't quite ready to leave, but I knew in my heart it was only a matter of time. I loved Stan very much, but I wasn't in love with him. I deserved more, and so did he.

One evening, I convinced Stan to sit down and watch a movie of my choosing. I chose Disney's *Beauty and the Beast*. The movie transported me to another world, a world where dreams come true. Magic filled my soul as love filled my heart. I cried for all the years I hadn't known I deserved happiness.

After the movie, Stan, who hadn't noticed my tears, said good night and headed up to bed. I watched the movie one more time and cried even harder.

After the movie, between my jagged sobs, I spoke out loud to make my statements real. "I deserve to live!" I said softly. A little louder, I stated firmly, "I deserve to be happy." On a roll, I shouted, "I deserve a wonderful relationship!" For my grand finale, I spoke in my loudest, clearest voice, enunciating every word: "I deserve my own Prince Charming!"

Stan slept on, not hearing a word.

Diann and Fred on their wedding day, April 12, 1996.

Part III

Living

CHAPTER 24

Saying Good-bye

"I watched *Beauty and the Beast* and came to the realization I deserve more in a relationship," I told my therapy group. "I'm ready to fall in love and be swept off my feet. And, in order to do that, I need to leave a very good man. I'm struggling with the guilt of hurting a man who's never done anything to hurt me." The group responded by validating my right to honor myself. They encouraged me to listen to my inner self and to follow my heart.

As strong as my feelings were, my responsibility to my daughter was stronger. I chose to put my relationship with Stan on the back burner because Mandy was returning from summer vacation the next day.

Mandy had spent the last two summers with my foster daughter, Cindy, and her family in Atlanta. Her sophomore year had ended with Mandy receiving an award for excellence in geometry but with less-than-stellar grades in the classes she'd consistently skipped. She had left for the summer with a defiant attitude but, to my relief, came home with a new-found resolution to stop ditching school and smoking pot.

Thank you, Cindy, I thought as my daughter told me she would attend all her classes, even the ones she didn't like. Cindy's influence on Mandy seemed profound, and I sent my daughter off to school confident her junior year would be much better for both of us.

Mandy's first day saw the collapse of all her heartfelt promises. Upon entering the school, Mr. Lewis, the vice principal, spied her, and with a superior smirk on his face, said in a loud voice that carried down the hall and into the ears of her peers, "Uh-oh! Trouble is back."

That did it. An angry, hurt Mandy ditched school that day and proceeded to consistently ditch for a couple of weeks. I started receiving calls from the school, and at the end of two weeks, I was done.

"Mandy, I give up," I said. "If you think you can make it in this world without an education, then you can start today. I'll call the school tomorrow and take you out. You're sixteen now, so you can legally quit school. You need to get a full-time job to pay your way. Also, you're grounded until you get a job. This isn't a vacation. Once you get a job, you'll start paying two hundred fifty dollars a month rent. You'll also be responsible for your own shampoo, conditioner, tampons, etc. You can eat at home when you're here, but you'll contribute to the groceries. And since you're still underage, you'll continue to abide by the house rules."

Surprisingly, she agreed and got a full-time position at a nearby McDonald's the next day.

The following week, Stan left for his annual trip to Maine to see his family. I took the opportunity to throw myself a slumber party. I called fifteen of my closest girlfriends for this all-night extravaganza. We did everything but slumber. We ate, laughed, partied, and talked.

"I've invited you here for selfish reasons," I said when there was a lull in the action. "First of all, I need to ask your opinion on something, and second, I just need a good night of laughter." I shared my feelings about my right to have a Prince Charming. I told them I was thinking of leaving Stan.

Their comments ranged from, "What's taken you so long?" to, "You two have never been a good fit," to, "We love you and will support you no matter what you choose." I received unanimous permission to follow my heart.

Stan returned from his vacation, but before I had a chance to share my new insights, he brought up the subject of our relationship. A couple days after his return, he'd come home in a huff after visiting Debi and Bob, the couple Joe and I were friends with back in Arvada. When Joe and I divorced, they were very supportive and stayed in contact with me and the kids. When I became involved with Stan, they became close to him too. Stan often used them as a sounding board.

I was busy cooking the family dinner when he stomped into the kitchen and announced, "I provide everything here. I provide the house. I co-signed for you on your car. I pay most of the bills. You haven't contributed anything. I'm just not happy."

Even though I'd made up my mind to leave the relationship, his words stung. His statements weren't entirely true, and I felt I had to confront him, so I responded by saying, "I'm grateful for everything you've done for us. And I realize you pay most of the bills. I've always contributed what I can financially, and when you asked us to move in with you, you knew my financial situation. To say I haven't contributed

259

anything is wrong. Because of me, you now have a family. You've learned from us what a loving family is all about. I've helped you learn how to eat and act in polite company. I've helped you learn how to pick out clothes that flatter you. Before me, you were essentially a virgin. You're now a most competent lover. Most of the friends we have were my friends before we got together. I cook all the meals. I do the majority of the cleaning. You're right, I don't contribute as much financially as you do, but what I do contribute is important to this relationship."

Stan's mouth hung open, and his eyes blinked fast as if to repel my words. He wasn't saying anything and I was on a roll, so I continued. "I understand you're not happy, and I need to let you know I'm not happy either. I think we've gone as far as we can go together in this relationship. I've decided to move out. I love you, but I'm not in love with you. There's too much we don't have in common. I love to laugh out loud. I love to dance. I love to have long conversations that mean something. I need you to know this has nothing to do with you and everything to do with me. I've changed. You're a wonderful person, and I will be forever grateful to you for many things, but especially for showing me what it feels like to be totally safe with a man. Because of you I'm learning to trust men."

Stan's mouth hadn't moved; it still hung wide open as if frozen. His eyes had stopped blinking and now also stood wide open, matching the frozen appearance of his mouth. It was as if I'd shot him with a stun gun. He struggled to find a response; finally he spoke three words laden with emotion and desperation: "I can change." I told him I didn't want him to change. I told him he was wonderful just as he was and he'd make someone a wonderful husband someday, just not me.

"I'll learn how to dance," he said, either not hearing or not believing my previous statements. I responded with an exasperated sigh. We talked into the night. He was like a dog with a bone, valiantly holding on. I was calm but firm. Finally I told him it would take me a bit of time to rent a place and asked him if I could stay for a couple of months. I told him Mandy, Gina, Alex, and I would move on January first. Stan agreed, believing this would give him enough time to convince me to stay.

My decision, although difficult, was the right one. I spent the next couple of months feeling a lightness in my step and a tendency to laugh out loud for no reason. The laughing abruptly stopped when the dreaded month of December arrived singing its seasonal songs. I was sick of my past encroaching on my happy mood. I was tired of the depressing hold Christmas carols had on my life.

One evening, I had the house to myself. I took our trusty dog, Lady, a husky mix Stan had given me the previous Mother's Day, and retired to my bedroom. I had lots of old Christmas music on cassettes I'd carted around, Christmas music I loved but was unable to enjoy. I sat on the floor cross-legged with Lady by my side, put on the Christmas music, and cried my eyes out. I cried for the loss of my innocence, I wailed for all my hurt, pain, and shame the abuse caused me, and I sobbed for all the world's abused children. I cried for all the lost years of not being able to enjoy this music I loved. I thought of my mother, whose birthday was in December. I missed her and wished I could talk to her one more time.

After hours of crying, I felt renewed. Lady, sensing a shift, opened her eyes and wagged her tail. My heart was brimming with joy. "Do you want to dance?" I asked her.

She barked a gleeful yes, and I cranked up the music. I grabbed Lady's front paws, and we were off dancing to Michael Jackson's distinctive voice. It was just my dog and I dancing our celebratory dance. When Stan entered the room, his mouth fell open. To him I must have looked like I'd lost my mind. I released Lady's paws and fell over laughing. I shared with Stan what the evening meant to me and why we were dancing. He listened, but in the end I think he still thought I was a bit crazy.

I moved on New Year's Day into a small, compact house in Westminster. It had three bedrooms and one bath. Gina, her fourteen-month-old daughter, Alex, Mandy, and I settled into our new digs. There were a few downfalls and challenges to the new space. The tiny house couldn't accommodate all my belongings and, sadly, didn't allow dogs. So, Lady continued to stay with Stan with the understanding that when we found a place that would accept my girl, Lady would live with us.

The bathroom situation was a new hurdle. Our family had never had to deal with sharing only one bathroom. But instead of it being a stressful situation, the single bath provided many great giggles and stories. To add to the chaos, I invited Janet, an adult female co-worker, to stay at our house temporarily until she could find another place to live.

Stan had agreed to let me store about half my furniture at his house until I could afford to rent a storage facility or move into a larger place. He helped us move and continued to visit us daily, bringing Lady along with him. I was grateful for his help and companionship. I wasn't dating anyone, and my Prince Charming hadn't appeared on the horizon yet, so Stan's continued presence wasn't a problem. I was a little worried about the prince's arrival because I truly didn't want to hurt Stan.

On January 13, I turned forty-three. This birthday, above all others, was scary for me. My mother was forty-three when she died. A dark storm cloud of impending doom hung over me. I couldn't shake the feeling a bolt of tragedy would again strike my life.

The positive aspect of a looming catastrophe was it made each day more precious and each decision more important. While driving to Golden on an errand, I was thinking about just how valuable my friends were to me. I decided I'd drop in on an old neighbor and friend I hadn't seen in years. Fortunately she was home, and as always with my friend Angie, we picked up our relationship as if no time had passed between visits.

"Are you sewing?" Angie asked.

"Yup, when I have time. I use all the tricks of the trade you taught me. You helped me so much."

"We had such fun. I miss those times."

We talked about our respective lives, relationships, and health. She told me she was scheduled for an angioplasty the following week. "I'm glad you told me. I'll call and check on you, mainly to see if you're behaving yourself and following doctor's orders. I may have to visit and straighten you out," I said.

"Please, not another visit. I'll be good." Angie laughed.

The conversation turned to our kids. We reminisced about the fun our families had when we were neighbors. "How's Mandy?" Angie asked.

"She's fine," I said. "In fact, she still has the Donald Duck costume you made her in fifth grade. She's still collecting Donald Ducks. She certainly loves Donald. I think she relates to him."

Angie laughed and said, "Donald Duck fit her perfectly. As I recall, she did have quite a temper."

"She still does, but she rarely has a full-fledged Donald Duck meltdown anymore," I said.

Angie laughed and said, "I love that girl." As I was leaving she called after me, "Thanks so much for coming by. Let's get together soon."

I had relished every minute of our visit and resolved to keep in better touch. While in the kitchen making dinner, I told Mandy about our visit. "I totally remember her, Mom. She was the best. I'll be right back." A few minutes later Mandy returned from her room wearing her Donald Duck costume. "It still fits and I'm keeping it forever."

A week after my visit with Angie, Stan left unexpectedly for Maine because his father was seriously ill. He left professing his love for me and still confident I was his lady. I, on the other hand, was confident I'd made the right decision to move out of Stan's house, but I still cared deeply about him. He wasn't my Prince Charming, but he was still my best friend. He kept in touch, calling me when he arrived in Maine and again the following morning. He promised to call me again that evening.

I went to work a little concerned about Stan's dad but feeling foolish for my unease. I put my feeling of impending disaster out of my mind and concentrated on work. Midday the phone rang. I thought it might be Stan missing me so much he'd called early.

It wasn't Stan; it was Angie's daughter. Her voice cracked as she said, "Diann, this is Corrina. Diann, Mom's dead. She died on the operating table while having an angioplasty."

"Oh, God, no, not Angie! I'm so sorry," I gulped. My throat constricted, and the tears pushed hard against my eyes. When I hung up the phone, I was numb. I can't remember how I got through the rest of the day. I soothed myself by thinking, *I'll be okay. Stan will call tonight. It'll be all right when I talk to Stan.*

Gina and Mandy were both at the house when I arrived. I told them about Angie. Gina was sad and Mandy devastated. Mandy clutched her Donald Duck costume and cried. For a few hours Mandy and I consoled each other, which took my mind off Stan's silence. That night when the sun left the sky, taking all its light, and when the phone refused to ring, a stifling sense of dread enveloped my body.

I didn't sleep that night, alternating between *No, Angie, you can't be dead. I just saw you a week ago. I'm glad for our visit, but Angie, you can't be dead* and *Stan, why aren't you calling? You said you were going to call and you didn't. This isn't like you. I need to talk to you. Where are you? Please call me.*

I went into work the next morning exhausted. In one long, run-on sentence, I told my office mate, Claudette, about Angie's death and that Stan was supposed to call last night and he hadn't and it wasn't like him to forget.

After expressing her condolences about Angie, Claudette attempted to reassure me about Stan. "There's probably a good explanation for him not phoning. I wouldn't worry."

"You're probably right," I said, still worrying.

The "good explanation" came a couple of hours later, via a phone call from Stan's mother. "Diann, Stan was in a car accident. There's no hope; his brain stem was crushed."

I screamed and screamed. Claudette came running, a concerned look on her face. "A car accident," I gasped. "Stan's brain stem crushed. I've gotta go. I have to get to Maine. Money! I don't have money." Claudette grabbed my hands and led me to my boss's office. Between sobs, I told my boss, Tammy, what had happened and that I needed to find a way to get to Maine right away. "I don't have any money. I don't know where I'm going to find the money."

"I'll see what I can do," Tammy said, walking out of her office. I sat there in her office, frozen. I don't know how long she was gone. She came in quietly and tapped me gently on the shoulder. Her touch felt harsh, like a karate chop, and it catapulted me out my chair and out of my skin. "The president of the company has agreed to lend you the money for a plane ticket."

"I could kiss you," I said. "Thank him for me. I'll pay him back. Thanks so much." I then called Mandy. She picked up on the first ring. "Mandy," I said, swallowing a sob. When she heard my voice, she sounded alarmed. "Mom, why are you calling from work? Is it about Angie's funeral?

"No, honey, it's something else." Just then I heard voices in the background. "Who's at the house?"

"I knew you wouldn't mind. I just didn't want to be alone today. I wanted someone here to take my mind off Angie, so I invited Danny and Stuart over to hang out at the house until it's time for me to go to work."

"Mandy, listen to me," I choked. "Stan was in a bad car accident. His brain stem was crushed. He's not going to make it. I'm coming home to pack. I'm flying out to Maine tonight. Cancel work, honey; I'll be right home. Mandy, is Gina there?" Silence met my ears. "Mandy, are you there?"

My little girl's voice crawled through the telephone line and sat in my ears, curled up small and vulnerable. "No, Mom, not Stan. I want to go see him. Come home. I don't know where Gina is. Bye."

A red-faced, puffy-eyed Mandy fell in my arms as I entered the front door. We held each other and sobbed. After what seemed like a long time we let go. I looked around the house. "Where…?" I started to ask.

"I freaked out and sent them home," she said. "Mom, you gotta let me go. I have to see him. What are we going to do without him? What are we going to do?"

I don't know, my mind cried out, but what I said was, "We'll be fine." Not feeling the least bit fine, I hugged my youngest and whispered, "We'll miss him terribly." After a long pause, I further crushed my Mandy's spirit by explaining my dire financial situation. "Honey, I had to borrow the money even for my ticket. If I could afford it, I'd take you. I'll call you every day. I don't know how long I'll be there." As an afterthought I added, "Janet will be at the house to handle any problems."

Just then Gina came in holding a sleeping Alex. She stopped in her tracks, looking shocked at my tear-streaked face. "Mom, what's wrong?" There was panic in her voice because Gina to my knowledge had seen me cry over Angie and only once or twice before that. The last time I cried in front of my kids was when Patrick committed suicide but crying definitely wasn't in character for me.

When I told her, she slumped down on the couch, "Oh, Mom, no!" She placed her sleeping baby gently on the floor, stood up, and hugged us both hard. "I'm so sorry," she said over and over. Even though she wasn't very close to Stan, she knew Mandy and I were.

A few hours later I was on a long flight to Lewiston, Maine. Because I purchased the ticket at the last minute and Stan and I weren't married, I had to pay full price. The good thing about paying an exorbitant price was being given a seat in first class. This was the only time I ever flew first class. As I sat in my comfortable, cushy seat, I thought back to the last couple of days. My premonition of tragedy had come true.

It was hard to remember what life was like before Stan. It felt like he'd been a friend forever, but in truth it had been since 1985. He started out as my UPS delivery person. I chuckled to myself, remembering him visiting me every day and announcing to me weekly he wanted to find and date a woman "such as yourself." We started dating in 1988 after Joe left. We started overnights in 1990, and the kids and I moved into his new house in 1991. Even after Stan and I separated and I moved the family into our small house, we saw each other daily. I couldn't imagine a life without him in it.

I was filled with a profound emptiness. Mom, Teresa, Vincent, Alan, Dad, and Patrick dead, and Stan was dying. The loss seemed almost too much to bear. A sick feeling gripped my stomach as I realized I needed to add one more person to my list. *Oh, Angie, I'm so sorry I'll miss your funeral. I won't be able to say good-bye to you, my dear friend, because I must say good-bye to Stan.*

I was a little apprehensive about going to a strange hospital to watch Stan die. I relaxed when I remembered Stan's mother, Martha, and his family would be there. *I won't be alone, and we'll be able to comfort each other.*

During a layover in New Jersey, I bought a couple of Louis L'Amour books to read to Stan. I don't much care for these Western novels, but I knew Stan would love them. The last leg of the trip was a short commuter flight to Maine, then a cab to the hospital and up to Stan's room.

As I entered, my eyes focused on my young, strong Stan as he lay in a bed hooked up to all sorts of life-support machines. He didn't look injured; his face had a few minor scratches, but there were no obvious wounds. *He'll be okay; he is just sleeping peacefully*, I thought. I had a strong urge to rush to his side, shake him gently, and tell him it was time to wake up. I started toward the bed but stopped midstep when I suddenly became aware the room was filled with his large family.

I saw, then heard, Stan's mother, Martha. She looked even thinner than I remembered. Her angular face was distraught, and behind her dark-framed glasses sat puffy eyes. Her hollow cheeks were tear stained. She was weeping. I walked directly toward her and embraced her. We held onto each other and cried as Stan's seven siblings watched.

I expressed my condolences to the rest of the family, and we sat in stunned silence together in the hospital room staring at Stan. Other than a few uttered sentences, the only sound was the respirator helping Stan to breathe.

Hours had passed, or maybe just minutes, when the doctor entered the room. His voice pierced the silence competing with the sound of the respirator. "I'd like permission to take Stan off life support. His brain stem was crushed, and thus there is no brain activity." He looked at our blank faces and explained exactly what that meant. "He'll never recover. There's no reason to keep him on life support," he stated emphatically. Maybe in response to our grief-stricken faces, he softened his voice as he continued. "Each organ in his body will shut down one by one. Because he's young and strong, even after taking him off life support, it might take as long as a week for his heart to stop." We all looked at Stan to confirm to ourselves that, indeed, he was still young and strong and the only thing wrong was a crushed brain stem.

I wanted to plead with the doctor, *Please just repair his brain stem. I don't know how I'll live without him.* But I said nothing, and we all followed the doctor, zombie-like, into a conference room where Martha, with a gut-wrenching sob, signed the necessary papers.

By late afternoon, Stan was moved to a private room, and while the family was saying their good-byes, I sought out a nurse and asked her if she could direct me to an inexpensive hotel close by. I told her about my life with Stan in Denver. She started to talk about hotels but then stopped. She must have seen the desperation in my eyes because she touched me on the shoulder and said, "Honey, there might be a possibility you could stay in the old nurses' quarters next door." She came back a few minutes later with the good news. I was welcome to stay in the old wing.

She escorted me through the hospital into a dimly lit narrow tunnel connecting the two buildings. I followed closely behind, the sounds of our shoes echoing loudly on the concrete floor. The lights seemed to flicker, whispering ominous warnings as we passed. I felt like a character out of a Stephen King novel—trapped and at the mercy of sinister forces. A part of me wanted to scream and run back to Stan's room or at least beg the nurse to hold my hand. The other part shamed me out of it

The corridor became more surreal when we arrived at an old elevator shaft with an ancient pair of accordion metal doors. The elevator shuttered and creaked up to the fourth floor. It opened onto a narrow hallway with bedrooms on either side. Sandwiched between the rooms was a communal bathroom. The nurse cheerfully showed me my room, told me to make myself comfortable, and said she had to get back to work.

I whispered a tight little thank you, afraid if I opened my mouth wider, I'd scream. I was the only person on this floor in this haunted vacant building, and there was absolutely no way I could make myself comfortable. I was positive I was never going to sleep there at night by myself.

I didn't even know if I could cope with the place in the daytime. Remembering the horror movies I'd seen and the terrifying events often occurring in showers, I took the quickest shower I'd ever taken. I dressed and jumped in the elevator, ran down the ever-darkening hall and into the new hospital wing. I arrived in Stan's room panting. The nurse who'd shown me to my quarters looked up as I entered the room. She noticed my heavy breathing and said, "Is everything all right?"

Before I could stop myself, a small, squeaky voice escaped. "Scary. The nurse's quarters are scary." The nurse smiled kindly, handed me a blanket, and motioned to a La-Z-Boy chair in the room. There I stayed in Stan's bare room. When a patient has a crushed brain stem, there's no need of a telephone or a television.

When Stan's family came to visit, I'd let them have time with him. This gave me the opportunity to eat something and smoke. I slept in a chair in Stan's room by night and made the long journey to my room in the light of day for a quick nap, shower, and change of clothes. The second day, when I arrived in Stan's room, Martha was there.

"Where're you staying?" she inquired.

"The nurses are so nice; they found a room for me in the old nurses' quarters in the old hospital," I replied.

Her face immediately became stony. "Stan told me all about you. You really don't have any business being here. You left. You broke his heart."

"Stan and I were still seeing each other before he came to Maine. He still believed we were together. I know he'd want me to be here," I asserted.

Her jaw clenched and her eyes flashed as she said, "I don't want you here. He was my son."

From that point on, I was treated like the enemy. I slept in Stan's room the next couple of nights. As Stan's body deteriorated, Martha's pain transformed into animosity toward me. I heard from the nurses that Martha loathed my presence and I wasn't welcome. She told the entire staff not to tell me anything about Stan's condition. She didn't want the doctors to speak to me at all. Evidently she had told her children about me, because several of them had attitude shifts as well.

A cold front ascended on the state of Maine, chilling me to the bone as the blustering weather swirled around me both outside and inside the hospital. The flickering lights, the scary abandoned nurses' quarters, Stan's mother and several of Stan's siblings coldly looking through me as if I were invisible intensified the sensation of living in a nightmare.

But it wasn't all bad. Stan's favorite brother, Mike, and his sister, Cindy, talked to me, which I appreciated. The nurses were kind. They saw how very much I cared for Stan. They watched as I read to him, talked to him, and bathed him. I often took over their nursing duties.

Still, even with their support, I felt totally alone. The nurses and doctors were forced to honor Martha's wishes and not tell me anything about Stan's condition. Even though I craved the professional medical opinions, I could see for myself the deterioration of Stan's body.

It was my second afternoon alone with Stan. My blue, icy-cold insides were cracking. I felt deep fissures and wounded feelings floating on the surface. Chasms of emptiness filled my soul as I listened again to Stan's deafening silence.

I was reading to Stan from Louis L'Amour. I'd just read, with expression, an exciting shoot-em-up scene, the kind Stan loved. I looked up, expecting to see those sparkling blue eyes bright with appreciation and his big smile lighting up his face. My ears wanted to hear his deep, strong voice with its Maine accent. But Stan's eyes remained closed and his mouth was a tight, straight line, and the only sound was that of his labored breathing. I held his face gently in my hands and kissed his cheek. It was then I noticed the bruises—blues, purples, browns, and oranges. Bruises of all shapes and sizes floated on the surface of his skin, shouting out, telling me the extent of hurt in the body below.

"Oh, Stan, I'm so sorry." I started crying, not only for Stan, but also for me. "I'm so, so alone. Someone help me."

I found a pay phone down the hall and called my therapist, Kathy. My hands were shaking so hard I could barely hold the receiver to my ear. With every ring, I said the same fervent prayer: *Please, pick up*. Every time I'd called Kathy before this, my message had gone to her voicemail. This time, to my astonishment, she answered. She was trying to call out while I was trying to call in my despair, panic, and pain.

"Oh, Diann, I'm so sorry," she said after I told her my story. "But you're definitely not alone. Your family, your friends, the group and I are with you. We're all here. You're surrounded by people who care about you. You're doing the right thing. Stan feels your love. He senses you're there."

"But Stan's family hates me. I'm the enemy because I left him. I need someone here on my side."

"Call the people who'll remind you you're not alone," Kathy said.

I started making calls. I called Mandy, Jean, and Michael. Every call bolstered my spirits.

On the third night, Martha came in the room and stated, her icicle words dripping with animosity, "From now on I'll be sleeping in this room. And, incidentally, I called Stan's friend Hal in Denver and told him to change the locks on Stan's house. Oh, and Hal is going to keep Stan's dog, Lady. You've no rights. You gave them up when you left Stan," she hissed.

"All the furniture in Stan's house is mine except for the new living room set he just purchased," I explained.

"Yes, I know about the new furniture, and I can't believe you took the bed and left him sleeping on the couch," she sneered.

"Martha, the house was furnished with my furniture. The bed was mine. Stan and I had been shopping for a new bed for him. The little single bed he had when we moved in together was sold at a garage sale. Stan had offered to keep, and use, my furniture until I could get a storage facility. And Lady is my dog. She was a Mother's Day present from Stan!"

"He's my son. You hurt him. You lost all your rights when you left him," she said and walked out of the room.

"I can't believe your mother, Stan," I said, looking at Stan. As my eyes rested softly on his bruised body, I decided I'd deal with this later. Saying good-bye to Stan was my first priority. I really did understand why Martha wanted to take her pain and sorrow out on me. I didn't like it, but I understood it.

"But Stan...why Lady?" I asked, but he didn't answer.

I went down the hall to the reception area and used the phone. "Michael, I feel so alone here. I'm in enemy territory. If only there was just one person here on my side, I think I could handle it. I know there's not much you can do..." Michael, my big brother, the problem-solver was silent. I said nothing because I knew the silence meant the cogs in his brain were whirring.

When he finally spoke, the words squeezed out slowly as out of a toothpaste tube. "Di, I'm just thinking out loud. Al…he lives on Cape Cod; he's the closest to Maine. If I can get ahold of him…he's kind of hard to get ahold of…if he's able to spare the time, I'll send him the money for a bus ticket."

"Oh, Michael, thank you. Just knowing you're on my side makes me feel better," I said.

The days and nights blurred together as my time at the hospital continued. By night, I slept in a room adjoining Stan's, much to Martha's chagrin. By day I bathed him, sponging out all my feelings, tears raining gently onto his injured body. As I rubbed his feet, I poured out my soul, explaining again why I needed to move; it had nothing to do with the person he was but rather the person I'd become. I covered his body with lotion as I covered all the thoughts I ever wanted to convey to him. I held his hand and he held my heart as I talked about our love and shared memories. I touched his face, all the while facing the fact I'd miss him terribly. Having no more words of my own, I read to him. When the nurses came in, I'd ask if there was any duty that had to do with Stan's care I could perform. They seemed to sense my need to physically care for him and, as much as they were allowed, let me be his nurse.

On the morning of the fifth day, I was sitting alone near Stan's bed. The only sound was Stan's ragged breathing and my heartbeat pulsing through my body. I hadn't had a good night's sleep for four days, and I was questioning my decision to continue my vigil in this toxic environment. How much longer could I survive in enemy camp? I closed my eyes to rest before the next battle.

It was dark, and I was a small child yelling and pounding on the closet door to get out. At least Jean was there with me. Then Jean disappeared and the closet turned into a locked chamber with backlit glass openings. There was a loudspeaker attached to each opening. The faces in the window were enemy faces—Martha and each of Stan's siblings who hated me. They were all yelling terrible things about me. I tried to yell back, but they couldn't hear me. The noise was deafening. I held my hands over my ears. I was at my breaking point when the screaming stopped. The sound was replaced by loud footsteps and a knock at the door. Startled awake, my body stiffened, preparing for Martha and her crew. I squared my shoulders and faced the door. In walked a miracle.

"Hi, sis, how are you?"

"Oh, Al, I can't believe you're here." I ran and jumped into my brother's arms. I collapsed, shaking and crying.

Just then Martha and some of Stan's siblings entered. I immediately stopped crying and braced myself. Al kept his arms around me. He looked straight into Martha's eyes, stuck out his hand and said, "Hi, I'm Al, Diann's big brother. You must be Martha, Stan's mother. I've heard a lot about you."

Martha's jaw tightened. She opened her mouth ready to spew some hateful comment but then looked into my bigger-than-life brother's eyes that said, *Don't you dare hurt my sister in any way.*

"I'm glad to meet you." Martha's words dropped like rocks out of her clenched mouth, hard and heavy. She didn't dare attack me with Al around. My hero merely nodded in acknowledgment, not in agreement.

I had someone on my side. I was no longer alone. "Let's go, Al. I'll show you around." As we walked down the hall, I said, "You sure handled that well."

"Yeah, Michael filled me in," he said in a serious tone. And then my dramatic brother said with a sparkle in his eyes, "I really came because I couldn't wait to see the haunted nurses' quarters. I love ghosts, unlike my scaredy-cat little sis."

For the first time in days, I laughed. "Oh, Al, you truly are my hero. Thanks for coming. We'll get to the ghosts after lunch and a cigarette."

After a leisurely lunch, I did show Al the old nurses' quarters. My brother, it turned out, was very comfortable with the haunted accommodations. He wasn't a bit afraid. And, with him there, neither was I. We chatted for most of the afternoon, and after spending more time with Stan, had a great night's sleep. Martha and her kids were much more subdued with Al there.

My big, healthy Stan was wasting away. On day six, I knew the end was coming soon. I called my friends Bob and Debi to give them an update

Debi, who worked for Frontier Airlines, said, "Diann, I purchased four tickets with my discount, and we're coming to Maine to say good-bye to Stan and to be with you."

"Four tickets?" I asked.

"Yes, Bob, his sister Sandi, Mandy, and I will be coming in on Saturday."

I couldn't speak. The lump in my throat was full of tears. "Thanks for coming. Thank you so much for bringing Mandy."

I hung up, hoping Saturday wouldn't be too late. It would be Stan's eighth day off the respirator. For the past couple of days, I'd been talking to Stan about dying. "Stan, I think you're hanging on because you're worried about us. It's okay if you need to leave. Mandy and I will miss you terribly, but we'll manage." On this night, though, my talk had a little different tone. "Stan, if you can hang on a bit longer, some special people will be coming to see you to say good-bye. They'll be arriving tomorrow afternoon."

The afternoon of January 30 arrived, and so did the Denver crew. They walked into Stan's room and stopped. His emaciated body was such a shock to see. Mandy gasped, gave me a quick hug, and rushed to Stan's side. She kissed his sunken cheek and said, sobbing, "Oh, Stan, I love you and I'll miss you."

Bob, Debi, and Sandi surrounded his bed, touching him, holding his hand, telling them they loved him. The room was quite crowded with Martha and her family, Al, me, and the four from Denver, so I leaned over and whispered in his ear, "They're all here, Stan. It's okay now. I'm going to leave for about ten minutes, and I'll be right back." I left to the background of quiet crying and Stan's halting, labored breathing.

After ten minutes, I returned to louder sobs surrounding a quiet Stan. He was gone. He had waited for Mandy, and he had left this world when I stepped out of the room. Stan was a considerate gentleman to the end. "I love you, Stan," I whispered.

Mandy and I held each other for the longest time, and then we let go to hug Al, Bob, Debi, and Sandi. Martha was staring at me with hate in her eyes.

"He'll have a Catholic burial in Maine. He'll be buried near our family who loved him."

She enunciated the word "loved," extending it out. Emphasizing it, she looked pointedly at me. Al stepped in beside me and looked pointedly at her. She lowered her eyes enough for me to gather my courage to speak for Stan. "Stan wasn't a religious man. He told me he wanted to be cremated."

"He was my son, and I'll bury him the way I choose," Martha responded.

I was spent. I didn't have any more energy for a confrontation with Martha. I knew then I'd go back to Denver and have my own service for him.

Al looked at me, took my arm, and said, "It's time to go." Al, Sandi, Debi, Bob, Mandy, and I all filed out of the room. Cindy, Martha's daughter, caught up to us.

"Diann, I'm so sorry about everything. Mom is sick with grief and…"

"I understand, Cindy, I really do."

"Good," she said. "She's been hard on you." I nodded in agreement. "Thanks for understanding." All I could manage was a nod and a hug.

The whole crew followed me to the haunted nurses' quarters. As I was walking down the corridor with Cindy, something occurred to me. I suddenly remembered why Stan had driven to Maine in the first place; his Dad had been hospitalized with pneumonia. I was embarrassed I hadn't thought to ask.

"Cindy, I can't believe I haven't asked until now. How's your dad?" Martha and Stan's dad had divorced many years before.

"Oh, yes, thanks for asking. He's doing much better. It's been hard going from hospital to hospital, but he'll be released soon." Cindy's eyes started to water, and she said in a shaky voice, "It's funny how life happens." I squeezed her hand but was too choked up to say anything.

As we exited the hospital, I breathed in a sigh of relief and a mouth full of snow. We had walked out of the storm into a blizzard.

After leaving the hospital, Al, Debi, Bob, Sandi, Mandy, and I jumped in a rented SUV. Bob gripped the wheel tightly as we all looked out the windows into blinding nothingness. The vehicle seemed to crawl, steering us through an alien world to the local Comfort Inn. The hotel lobby was light, warm, and welcoming, but my insides remained cold, numb, and empty of feeling. We headed to our rooms in silence. I fell into bed exhausted, wanting sleep to blot out the nightmare.

Sunday morning brought more snow. The television weather channel was reporting the worst storm in twenty years. Outside the snow piled up, pressing in on the building, as a blizzard of thoughts about Stan swirled in my head.

This Sunday happened to be Super Bowl Sunday. We all gathered in one room and passed the time talking about a number of subjects, not wanting to be alone with our thoughts as we waited for the game to start. Every subject, no matter what it was, seemed to lead to Stan. How could a football game between the Buffalo Bills and Dallas Cowboys go on with Stan, our sports statistician, dead? Why'd he have to die? How could the world keep on turning?

The unanswered questions piled high on top of one another to create a mound that filled the room with heavy, unbearable grief. Al, seeing our pain, suggested he'd be available to give us each a massage. We all looked up, temporarily snapped out of our reverie. "I'll even throw in some gentle chiropractic," he said, and to top off his sentence, he added, "for free." Al certainly knew how to break the tension.

My ears recognized the sound of my own laugh as it joined the other chuckles. I stopped my laugh immediately when I realized Stan would be very uncomfortable with this scene. He would probably have left the room. I'd give anything for him to have left the room and not the world. I excused myself. I went into the bathroom and cried. When I returned to the room, the game had started. I usually liked watching the Super Bowl, but instead of watching the game, I was focused on the comments about Stan. "Stan would've loved this game."

"Yes, and he would've known all the stats and background of each and every player."

My sports fanatic was gone. I excused myself again. I went back to the bathroom to let my tears flow. I spent very little time watching football; most of my day was spent locked in the bathroom bawling.

On Monday, all of us stepped out into the continuing blizzard. Debi, Bob, and Sandi jumped into their rental car and drove to, it turned out, a severely crippled airport. Al left in a taxi headed for the bus terminal.

Our last morning in Maine greeted us with thirty inches of snow and a rough ride to the airport. As I boarded the plane, my tight shoulders began to loosen and my jaw unclenched. I wouldn't miss Stephen King's beloved Maine. I wouldn't miss the weather, the ghosts, Martha, or most of her family. I'd miss Stan, but in the last eight days I'd said everything I needed to say to him. I had said my good-bye.

As I passed my seat in first class and joined my daughter in coach, I knew I was bringing Stan's spirit with me back to Denver. As Mandy and I talked, a plan for Stan's wake crystallized in my brain. "Mandy, Stan would've hated having a Catholic funeral. I'm going to try to put together a memorial service for him this weekend if I can." Thinking about how popular he was and how all of downtown Denver knew and loved him, I said, "I think I'll put some flyers in the shop windows downtown. The downtown newspaper may even write an article about him." On a roll, I said, "And Stan loved the Legion, and the Legion loved him. Maybe the Legion will let me hold his service." The thought of honoring Stan in this way cheered us up considerably. Both of us could actually feel Stan smiling down from the heavens.

I hit the ground running as soon as we got home. I'd missed more than a week of work. My bosses were very understanding while being demanding. On work time, I was focused on work, but during lunch and breaks, I was on the phone organizing Stan's memorial. To my delight, the editor of the *Downtowner* not only wrote a tribute to Stan but also mentioned the memorial we were having at the Legion on Saturday.

The memorial was well attended. Many of Stan's customers and Legionnaires came, along with members of my family and some friends.

Bob and Debi attended. Bob gave a moving eulogy and brought tears to my eyes when he said, "I knew I would love Stan because Diann loved him." There was a bar at the service, and people were encouraged to toast Stan.

Stan's "second family" was also there, the family who'd adopted him when he first came to Denver. He'd made Tanya, their daughter, the executor of his estate. Tanya's parents took me aside and told me they felt it was improper and in poor taste to have a memorial to Stan in a bar. To this criticism, I retorted, "Stan came here every Friday night while I worked, and these people were his friends. I lived with him and knew him better than you; he'd have loved this venue."

The next week I heard through the grapevine that Martha was aghast. That was fine with me as I'd been aghast at the way she'd decided to memorialize him as well. I just knew Stan was there in spirit and loved every minute of it. I could picture him with his buck-toothed grin saying, "Thanks."

CHAPTER 25

My Prince Charming

S tan's spirit settled in Denver. Mandy and I saw him everywhere. I'd be at a stoplight and look over at the driver of the car in the other lane. Looking back at me smiled a replica of Stan with his bright blue eyes and his toothy grin sitting in his old Impala. When this happened, I'd hold my breath, my heart beating wildly in my chest. For an instant my mind believed Stan was alive. The moment would flee and leave an empty spot still warm with hope.

Mandy, who was still working at McDonald's, would come home at least once a week and say Stan had come through the drive-thru. With bright, wet eyes she'd state, "I looked up, Mom, and this guy looked exactly like Stan." I'd then recount the Stan look-alike I had seen. We both knew it was Stan's way of watching over his girls.

His spirit, however wonderful, couldn't unlock his house so I could retrieve my things. His ghost couldn't spirit back my dog, Lady. Martha, true to her vindictive word, had Hal change the locks on Stan's house and dognap Lady. I called Hal, begging him to return Lady. He said he wasn't going to give her back, finally saying, "I gave her away; I don't have her anymore."

My household items, tools, and furniture were sitting in Stan's house and garage waiting to be rescued. Finally, Mandy and I drove over and did what we always had done when we were locked out; we wiggled the sliding-glass doors and entered our old home through the master bedroom. We took small items that would fit into my car. We took back my pots and pans and some cooking utensils Stan had borrowed until he got around to equipping his kitchen.

I took a large gulp of air as the world pressed in when I glimpsed my ironing board leaning against the laundry room wall. *Oh, Stan, what'll I do without you?* A lot more ironing, I thought, as I carried the ironing board and iron to my car and drove home. I parked my loaded car in my driveway, walked in my house, picked up the phone, and unloaded on Michael.

"Martha changed the locks on Stan's house, and I can't get my things out. Michael, they stole my dog! Lady is mine."

Michael had a solution, as always. "Let me call my attorney friend and see if he can help." And, as always, Michael's solution worked, but only partially this time. I'd be able to retrieve my things, but no one had been able to locate Lady. "Well, girl, I couldn't have kept you at this place anyway. Good-bye, girl. I love you," I whispered to the night.

The attorney called me to give me a time and date to pick up my stuff. The court order said on February 15 between the hours of noon and three p.m. I could go to the house and remove my belongings.

I called Michael again and in a panic said, "I have three hours on Sunday to get a houseful of furniture and a bunch of other items out of Stan's house. The kids can help me, but I don't know what I'll do about a truck."

Michael said, "You remember my friend Fred Kissell? He has a truck. Let me call him and see if he can help."

"Of course I remember one of your best friends," I replied. Fred and Michael had been close since 1963 along with another friend, Dick, who rounded out the "three amigos." Fred had started out as Michael's boss at the *Rocky Mountain News*, and later their careers paralleled each other's.

I woke up on February 15 anxious and overwhelmed. I dreaded this moving day. I felt a strong aversion to seeing Stan's mother, Martha, who had flown into Colorado from Maine that week, and Tanya, whom Stan chose to execute his will. The task of moving so much stuff in a mere three hours seemed insurmountable. But as I stepped out into Colorado's balmy February weather, its sky of soothing blue and its sun's rays warming the earth, it immediately calmed my nerves and melted my frozen feelings.

So it was with high spirits we arrived at Stan's house at 11:45. With me were Mandy, her boyfriend, Danny, and another friend, Stuart. About five minutes later, Aaron showed up with Gina driving a pickup truck. "Thanks for bringing a truck. We can start loading right away," I said to a smiling Aaron.

We all stood in a line facing the garage at high noon as Martha, with Tanya standing beside her, slowly opened the garage door. My peaceful mood suddenly faltered. It was Fibber McGee's closet all over again. My belongings had been tossed haphazardly into giant piles reaching up to the ceiling. Unloosed by the movement of the door, an avalanche of familiar items rolled, clanked, and crashed onto the driveway. I closed my eyes and covered my ears. When the worst was over, I looked down to see Lady's metal dog bowl clattering to a stop at my feet. I reached down to pick it up. Clutching it in my hands, I whispered with tears in my eyes, "Oh no, I can't do this!"

Mandy and Gina were at my side, patting me on the back, saying, "It'll be okay, Mom."

Just then I heard sounds of laughing and turned to see Martha and Tanya standing to one side of the garage sniggering and pointing at me. The kids grabbed my hand and pulled me to the other side of the garage.

"Come on, Mom, don't let them bother you. We need to start loading the truck; we don't have much time."

We'd almost finished emptying the garage when Fred Kissell arrived with his truck. "Do you still need help?"

"Absolutely," I said. "We've emptied most of the garage, but would you come with me to the house? I'm still missing quite a few of my things."

"I'd be glad to," he said.

As we approached the house, Martha and Tanya blocked the doorway. "You're not allowed in; there's nothing of yours in this house," Martha sneered.

"I have to do all the work on the estate, and I get nothing. You get all the good stuff. It's not fair," Tanya whined.

"It *is* fair. I lived with Stan for two years. I loved Stan. You never returned his affections." In case she wanted specifics, I added, "He had no furniture. What little he had we sold at a garage sale when I moved in." Tanya scowled.

Martha looked at Fred and decided it would be best to let us pass. An entertainment center and a couple of bookshelves later we were out of the house. I tried to persuade Martha to let me look through the other garage for some lawn furniture and tools I knew were in there, but when it got to be three p.m., I let it go.

We drove back to my place and unloaded everything into the garage. And then Fred and I stood out in the driveway leaning against my Bronco and talked. I told him about Stan, and he talked about being burned twice by his ex-wives. His first wife had left him for another man after twenty-eight years of marriage. His most recent marriage had lasted a year and a half.

"She left fourteen days ago on February first," he said, choking a little on the words. "It's been tough."

"Stan died on January 30. I watched him die for eight days. I can't believe he's gone."

We talked about everything: kids, family, life, work, truck maintenance, and our pain. I was attracted to this man—his slight build and handsome face with expressive brown eyes and deep dimples. But more than his looks, I was captivated by the conversation. It was nothing less than miraculous: heaven on earth. It was music, dance, the color green, the smell of lilacs, my love of elephants, Dr. Seuss, and jalapeños all rolled into one. We had an incredible exchange of feelings. He not only listened, he also heard me. His eyes didn't glaze over even once. He did something I hadn't believed a man capable of: He reciprocated with feelings and stories of his own.

We stood there in the glorious Colorado weather and talked like old friends. Three hours later, we reluctantly said our good-byes as I thanked him for all his hard work. The next day I called him to get a referral for a garage that could work on my Bronco, but really I called him so he would hear my voice once again. I was presently too raw to entertain a relationship, but I felt a connection and wanted him to remember me in the future.

Months passed. I wasn't coping. I thought I was going crazy because one minute I'd be laughing, the next minute crying. There were anxious times when my heart was beating so hard I was sure I was having a heart attack. At these times, I couldn't catch my breath. I was exhausted all the time because I wasn't sleeping. My temper was uncharacteristically on a very short fuse and would frequently flare up at my kids. My hand tremors were so fierce I had trouble performing simple tasks at work. I decided I didn't have time for another breakdown, so I called my M.D., Dr. Simon, for some medication that would allow me to function. He prescribed Xanax.

Even though I felt better with the drugs, I went to see Kathy for a private session. The group sessions usually provided enough support and were much less expensive, but I wasn't going to take any chances. I had an aversion to nervous breakdowns and wanted to take every available precaution to avoid them.

I told Kathy on the phone that I thought I needed to do some more inner child work. Even though all my therapy experiences had been beneficial, the inner child work had been the most effective tool in dealing with my past. Kathy responded with, "That sounds like a great plan. After all, you are the expert of you."

Maybe I did know better than anyone else what I needed, but I had no clue why I was asking for inner child work to deal with Stan's death. Maybe Kathy would be able to figure out the puzzle.

Kathy's blue eyes and big smile welcomed me into her peaceful office. I sat down in a blue swivel chair. I told her in detail about Stan's death and his mother turning on me. As I talked, I found myself sinking lower and lower into the chair, suddenly heavy with grief. It wasn't just about Stan, my most recent loss. It was all my losses: Martha and most of Stan's family treating me like an enemy; my dog, Lady; the death of my friend, Angie; Patrick, my sweet brother; Gandalf, my devoted dog; my dream home; the baby girl I gave up for adoption; Dad, Mom, Alan, Vincent, and baby Teresa. That didn't even count the more intangible losses like my childhood innocence.

A single tear trickled down my cheek as Kathy's voice mirrored my thoughts. "So many losses; almost too much grief for one person to endure."

My heart spiraled down, burrowing deep into a vast void, filled to the brim with the kind of emptiness only profound loss creates. Just as I was ready to fall, feeling-first, into the abyss, a thought grabbed me by the scruff of my neck and brought me back to hope. I'd be okay because I believed strongly that everything happens for a reason. And in the end, the reason was always positive. I was sure, too, that I was put on earth this time around to learn and grow from my mistakes made in a past life.

I puffed myself up and said to Kathy, "It's a lot to deal with, but I've come this far. I have a strong spirit. I know I'll be okay. I'm going through all this pain to get to a good life. These are only lessons I need to learn."

Kathy's expression was one of admiration. "You're amazing. I agree, you'll get through this hard time and have the life you want."

Part of my brain was listening, and the other part was busy guessing what terrible things I must have done to be the recipient of so many tough assignments. "I must've been one of Hitler's henchmen because it seems the lessons keep on coming," I said with a laugh, attempting to cover an ocean of tears. Kathy's soft, sad smile acknowledged the laugh but followed my sadness. My tears were building up in my chest and coming dangerously close to spilling into the room.

I was trying hard to plaster on my brave, impassive face, but I don't think it was sticking because Kathy observed, "Your face is showing a lot of emotion. I'm curious; what are you feeling?

The best I could do was to come up with one-word statements: "Sad, heavy, anxious, overwhelmed, guilty, confused. There's a whole bunch of feelings. I hate feeling this way; I feel so out of control."

"Maybe it would help if you close your eyes." When I closed them, it did help to shut down the flood of emotions. Kathy's voice washed over me in gentle waves. "Notice the sensations in your body." My eyelids blanketed my eyes as I peered inside. "What are you noticing?"

I'd done so much therapy that my answer was immediate. "My stomach is empty and churning. There's a lot of pressure behind my eyes and tightness in my throat because I feel like I'm going to cry but I don't want to. My heart hurts and I'm having trouble breathing. The rest of my body feels stretched tight and numb."

"Good awareness, Diann. It sounds as if you've felt these sensations in your body before."

I nodded. Yes, these were very familiar feelings.

"Keeping your eyes closed, go back to a time when you were a child and you had similar sensations in your body. Can you see yourself?" Kathy's words came slowly, resting between sentences. "How old are you?" The sound of her voice seemed to drift in on air from a faraway place, but when it arrived, it was filled with nonjudgmental compassion.

My voice pushed itself up through water. "Young, maybe thirteen," I choked.

"Can you see her?"

I couldn't speak, so I just nodded.

"Noticing her from your adult perspective, what do you think that little girl is feeling?"

"Too much; she's doubled up with grief and guilt. She's not mad; she's sick to her stomach. Dad just murdered half her family, but she thinks she caused it to happen; she thinks she killed them. She shouldn't have run away; she shouldn't have talked. If she'd let Dad continue to molest her, they'd be alive. She wants do-overs. She wants her babies back. She wants her mommy."

"I want you, the forty-three-year-old, to go up to her and introduce yourself. Tell her you weren't there when she was growing up, but you're here now and you can see she's feeling horrible."

Kathy continued, "I'd like you to give her some messages. Tell her you love her very much. Tell her you're so glad she's alive. Tell her she doesn't have to be afraid anymore because you're there and you'll never leave her. Tell her you'll protect her and keep her safe. Tell her you'll take her to a safe place right now. Ask her where she'd like to go."

"Library. She wants to go to the library."

"Safe in the library, ask her if she'll let you hold her. Will she let you?"

Tears were streaming down my cheeks as I nodded yes. Diana fell into my arms, her body shaking and convulsing in great, jagged sobs.

"Tell her you have all the time in the world to hold her. You'll hold her until she's ready to let go. How's she responding?"

I felt hard tension melt into the softness of a snuggle. The shaking stilled and the cries quieted. "She was crying, but she's starting to relax," I said with relief.

"Look at her. Is there anything wrong with this child?"

"No, nothing. She's precious."

"Yes, the truth is she's a great kid. She's a good girl. You're right. There's absolutely nothing wrong with her, but there was something wrong with her environment. Tell her you're so sorry she was molested. Tell her she did absolutely nothing to cause the molestation; none of what happened was her fault. She wasn't responsible for any of her dad's actions; he was. He was a sick man, and she was an innocent child. Does she believe you?"

"She's listening. She has a half smile of hope. She's beginning to believe."

"Diann, how are you different from little Diana's parents?"

"I'm not abusive, and I have time to snuggle."

"How's she feeling now that you're there, listening, understanding, and taking care of her?"

"She's happy. She's laughing."

"Great! Now I'd like you to shrink her down to about the size of an apple and put her in your heart. I want her to hear your heartbeat. I want her to know you love her and will always be there. I want a cord going across your chest. That cord is your communication line to this child. I want you to make it a color that's both peaceful and powerful. You can make it two colors if you want."

I thought I knew for sure what my cord color would be; green had been my favorite color since childhood. I looked at the color of the thick, braided cord of peace and power. To my astonishment, it was a rich, vibrant, shimmering shade of turquoise. The color filled my heart with healing light. It radiated out, touching every part of my body. I was turquoise.

Kathy was saying, "Call into the cord. Can she hear you? Have her call back. Can you hear her?"

"Yes, we can!" I said as a laugh of relief and joy bubbled to the surface. "She feels so free and happy."

I opened my eyes to a new life—a turquoise life. I said, "This was great, but I thought I'd already dealt with my past. I thought I was done."

Kathy smiled. "It's a process. Stan's death triggered the memories of past losses. I'm thinking little Diana never processed her feelings about the murders because she didn't have any adult she trusted enough to tell. Today she does—you! You're the only one who can truly understand her and her feelings. Only when she's connected to you can she feel safe. Healing can't happen without safety."

My adult had done a lot of healing; I'd just forgotten to include little Di in the process. But the important part was that I was connected to her now and felt whole and safe.

As with most important breakthroughs, progress was intermittent as the turquoise thread of hope wove in and out of my life. Even though I knew better times were ahead, before I embarked on my new life, I had to finish the old. It wasn't the losses of my past weighing me down; it was grieving my latest loss, Stan.

I knew with every fiber of my being I should completely finish saying good-bye to Stan before finding my Prince Charming. My knowledge, however, didn't prevent me from reverting to some unhealthy habits. I stayed incredibly busy for the next two and a half months. Sadness, pain, and cigarettes were my constant companions when I was alone. To avoid feeling sorry for myself, I went out dancing with my friend Claudette two or three times a week. When she wasn't available, I went dancing alone. I also dated a couple of men in a futile effort to out-run my grief.

On April 6, Fred Kissell called me at work to ask if I was available to go out to dinner that night. "I'd love to, but I have a previous engagement. Please be persistent and call me again."

And so he was. I got a call on Wednesday and Friday but had to give him the same response. Friday's invitation was to attend the inaugural game for the Colorado Rockies baseball team. I would have loved to go, but I had to work. I did tell Fred I was keeping myself incredibly busy after Stan's death and to give me a little more notice. I could sense his discouragement and hoped he wouldn't give up.

The following Sunday was Easter. We celebrated the holiday at Michael's home. "So has Fred called you yet?" Michael inquired after dinner.

"Yes," I answered. "Three times last week he asked me out, and three times I had to turn him down because I was busy. I really want to go out with him, but I'm a bit concerned because he's eight years older than I."

Michael said in a serious tone but with a sparkle in his eyes, "If it's any comfort to you, Fred is the oldest of my friends, but he's the youngest at heart."

"Thanks! That *does* help," I said.

The next day I left work early because I wasn't feeling well. I had three engagements that evening, and I wanted to rest before I went out. I was talking to Jacky, an employee, while waiting for the shuttle when I saw a navy blue Isuzu Trooper drive up. Inside was Fred. He rolled down the window, and before he could say a word, I asked, "What are you doing here?"

He laughed and said, "I was in a poker tournament in Blackhawk and thought I'd come and give you one last chance to go out with me."

"Well," I said slowly, "I was just leaving, but you can take me to my car."

As we drove to my car, I told him, "Since you've been so persistent, you can follow me to Golden and buy me a drink if you want." We went to Señor Frogs, and I told him right away about my three engagements that evening. "I can only stay for one drink." We then proceeded to talk the night away. He remembered meeting me when I was thirteen and thought I was a cute little kid..

"I remember meeting you. You and Dick came by when we were outside playing bases. You and Dick were just two of Michael's friends. You were old," I said, laughing, "as old as the hills."

"I love your laugh. And yes, I was rather mature." His face suddenly turned sober. "I met your parents only once. It was on the day I met you and your whole family." With tears in his eyes, he choked, "The murders happened only a few weeks later. I remember hearing about that horrible night as if it were today. I was a district manager for the *Rocky*. Tony, my partner, called me the next morning to tell me to expect three down routes because Michael's dad had killed his wife and three of his children. I felt like I'd been hit by a truck; I can't even begin to imagine how you must've felt." He looked at me, his dark brown eyes glistening with compassion.

Maybe it was because he was a good friend of my brothers' and knew about our family history or maybe it had to do with the tears in his eyes, but for whatever reason, I began to tell him about my childhood. I shared with him about the years of sexual abuse, the murders, and thinking for a long time the whole tragedy was my fault.

I felt no reticence in sharing my entire story, which was truly amazing. I explained to him, without shame, that for years after the murders, I punished my "bad" self by having sex with strangers. I was interested in pursuing a serious relationship with him and intuitively knew if we were to have a future, I needed to be open and honest from the beginning. We hadn't physically touched; he hadn't even held my hand. But as I told him about my sordid past, his eyes held me in a warm embrace and his lips kissed my wounded words. It truly was like talking to my best friend.

As it turned out, we already knew quite a bit about each other's lives through Michael. We also discovered we had a lot of wonderful things in common, from our love of family to similar values and religious beliefs to our mutual interest in sports, books, and movies. We learned we both had daughters who had children out of wedlock, which left no room for judgment on either side.

There was a time about two and a half hours into the conversation when I courageously brought up the subject of his birthday.

"Fred, may I ask a serious question?"

"Of course," he replied.

"What's your birth date?"

"December 5," he replied.

"Oh no, you've got to be kidding. That makes you a Sagittarius."

"Is that a problem?"

"Yes, a major problem. I vowed never to date a Sagittarius man again."

"Well, I vowed never to date a smoker, so I guess we're even."

"I guess so," I said, laughing and at the same time thanking the universe I had found this man. Five hours later, which seemed like no time and yet a lifetime, I realized I'd blown off my other plans and recognized my priorities had forever changed. As we stepped out into a night bright with stars, I said through gales of laughter, "I guess I'm not going to make my three engagements after all."

"Did I tell you I love your laugh?" he said.

"Yes, you did. Actually, I like it too," I said, laughing.

The following week was magical. The talk that changed my life happened on Monday. Wednesday we went to a Colorado Rockies baseball game, and Friday we went to see *Auntie Mame* at the Country Dinner Playhouse. Fred was planning on taking me home right after the play because he had some down routes and would be getting up very early in the morning to deliver newspapers. I asked him if I could help him. A wide smile crossed his face, showing off his dimples, which I took to mean yes.

Upon entering the main level of his home, the first and only thing I noticed was a small, glass, dining room table with four chairs and two healthy-looking plants. It was true this place with its electricity and indoor plumbing was a vast improvement over Lee's and Patrick's commune, but the barrenness of the room seemed eerily similar.

"I like the plants, but we may have another problem if you're against furniture," I said with a frown.

"I'm basically pro-furniture, but my ex won the fight. I did get the pool table though," he said with his dimpled smile. "Would you like to see the man cave?"

"Of course," I said, following him down into the basement, all the time dreading the descent. To my relief, I stepped into a friendly, inviting, safe man cave with a protective man who owned a pool table. After a rousing game of pool and blatant, suggestive, flirtatious remarks from me, Fred Kissell, the consummate gentleman, finally decided to kiss me.

We kissed for the first time and the second and the third…then he took my hand and we ascended the stairs. I noticed as we passed the unadorned and furniture-deprived main floor and began to climb the stairs to the upper floor my knees made their usual protest. I also noticed the pain's sharpness had been reduced to whispers, blunted by my joy. Still holding my hand, he led me to his bedroom.

"So this is where you keep your furniture," I said as my eyes rested on a king-sized bed and a bedroom set. His wide smile and dimples answered in the affirmative.

We toppled onto the bed laughing. I felt light-headed, twitterpated, like Thumper the rabbit in Disney's *Bambi*. I was a little nervous and instinctively glanced down at my hands to check my embarrassing tremor. A huge intake of breath followed by a whispered "unbelievable" escaped my lips because I was witnessing a miracle. The tremor in my hands that had plagued me since the murders was gone. I laughed out loud with joy as I thought, *Fred Kissell, you shook my world and stopped my shakes. I have indeed found my Prince Charming.*

A wisp of thought crossed my path. *You hardly know him. Slow down; get to know him first. What if you're wrong about him?*

My spirit answered, *I know him. I know in my heart and soul the goodness of him.* I felt irrepressible bubbles of happiness erupt throughout my body as I saw our faces in the dresser mirror. *His goodness mirrors the goodness in me! He's a gift from the universe so right and true.* There was nothing left to know.

We made wildly gentle, passionate love, and then, as in a dream come true, we snuggled. *So this is what a healthy, intimate relationship feels like!*

The following morning, I smiled all the way home. Walking in the door, I yelled, "Girls, we're going out to dinner tonight. I have an important announcement to make." I assume they came running not out of curiosity about the announcement as much as the promise of going out to eat.

Mandy, now almost seventeen, expected to see the post-Stan furrowed brow and clenched teeth. She did a double take when she ran smack-dab into my huge grin. "Whoa, what happened to you, Mom?" Mandy asked.

"Happiness happened," I said. Mandy looked at me strangely and was about to say something when Gina entered the room.

"Why are you smiling like that? You're being kind of weird," my nineteen-year-old Gina commented.

Alex just babbled as I said, "Just wait until dinner."

At the restaurant between the salad and the main course, I told my girls, "I met the man I'm going to marry. I met my Prince Charming." They were very happy for me, as much as teenagers can be. Mostly I think they were pleased there was every indication I wouldn't be so snappy and irritable with them. Usually strapped for cash, I this time sweetly suggested dessert, a suggestion they loved.

Rese, JJ, and Jean were excited when they received my news via phone. I talked to Michael in person. He immediately noticed my glow. "Congratulations; I guess you and Fred finally connected. I'm so happy for you, sis." I thought I'd let the rest of the family find out in due time.

I spent Monday ending relationships and tying up loose ends. I talked to Claudette and said I wouldn't be going out with her anymore. She was happy I'd found my true love but sad about losing her best dancing friend.

My regular group therapy session was that week. I excitedly told the group, and my therapist, that I wouldn't be coming anymore. Because I had worked so hard to become healthy, I felt I'd been able to attract my Prince Charming, and my life was moving in a wonderful new direction. They all agreed and clapped.

Finally, I talked to Stan in heaven: *I'll carry our love for each other in my heart always. I wish you hadn't died but because of your death, I was able to know and love Fred freely. I never wanted to hurt you. If you had to die, I'm glad you died at a time when I was still your girl. Thank you for loving Mandy and me and watching over us while we healed. Thank you for releasing me to love and live a full life. I'm grateful for all you have given me.*

I then thanked the universe for providing me with such a wonderful gift. I'd spent many years getting healthy in order to be at a place where I loved myself. The universe had given me my gift for completing the journey. I talked to God, saying, *I know Fred is a gift from you, God, a gift to reward all my work in healing myself.*

As with all gifts bestowed by the universe, I was called upon to do my part; it was clear doing my part was to quit smoking. As a child I'd given up my main self-soothing tool of thumb sucking for Jesus' sake at the age of seven. Now I knew I had to give up my adult self-soothing tool of smoking for the sake of the relationship. I believe one should never take gifts from God for granted.

So a couple of weeks into the relationship, I went back to Dr. Simon, this time to get a prescription for the nicotine patch. Fred hadn't asked me to quit, but I could tell he was just putting up with my dirty habit. Frankly, I was sick of my smoking also. I was tired of having to brush my teeth after each cigarette so Fred wouldn't have to kiss an ashtray. Having to give up time with Fred to go out on the deck to smoke was getting old too.

"How are things going?" Dr. Simon asked with a concerned tone. "Are you here for more Xanax?"

"No!" I exclaimed. "I don't need it anymore. I met my Prince Charming, and he's not a smoker. So I'd like a prescription for some nicotine patches." I then told him all about Fred. He was very happy for me. He'd been my doctor for many years and had been a part of my journey.

The patches worked very well and I quit smoking, but I had to figure out what to do on my thirty-nine-mile, three-cigarette commute to work. I decided to replace the cigarettes with playing great music on the radio and singing nonstop, at the top of my smoke-free lungs, all the way to work.

In the following weeks, I visited Fred at his house every day. The fullness of our relationship contrasted nicely with the emptiness of his house. The place was so bare, I felt it my duty to sneak in a few elephant figurines. Fred found it humorous that I felt the need to adorn all his cubbies and ledges with elephants.

Within about a month, a good deal of the herd had migrated to Fred's house. One day as I followed Fred into the master bathroom, he looked up at the windows above the tub and spied a new family of elephants. He turned to me and said, "When did you bring these elephants over?" As I started to speak, he gently placed two fingers to my lips to quiet me and said, "You know, when I gave you the key to my house, I wanted you to visit. I didn't know you would move in...with a herd of elephants."

"What can I say? We're a package deal," I said, laughing.

Fred said, "And it's a package I can live with."

I seemed to find magic everywhere: clothes folded neatly on the dryer, a surprise bouquet of flowers blooming in a vase, a repaired gadget I'd broken, a look, a laugh, a gentle touch. But the most miraculous of all were our conversations. We talked under the sun and stars, we sat and talked, we ate and talked, we played and talked, and we walked and talked. We talked about everything and nothing. We talked about the past, present, and future. Our words danced to the music of our souls. We talked about feelings.

"Fred, I want to tell you about my anger."

"Are you mad at me?" Fred wore a panicked face, his eyes darting back and forth, searching for a sign in my body language.

"Nope, I'm not angry, and if I were, it certainly doesn't mean our relationship is over or even in trouble."

"I'm not great with anger, but I'd much rather you express it than just walk out of my life. Promise me you'll talk to me when you're mad."

"Okay," I said, taking him up on his statement. "I'm getting frustrated that, right now, you're not letting me explain." Fred stopped talking. "Starting when I was thirteen and through some of my adolescence, I was mad at the world. Today, I don't get mad very often, but when I do, I revert back to that teenager. When this happens, I have to stop talking and walk away in order to get my thirteen-year-old under control. I'll return as an adult, and then we'll be able to have a reasonable discussion." Fred was wearing a concerned little-boy face, so I said, "When I walk, I'm not abandoning you. I'll be back."

"My teenager will get really mad if you don't come back," Fred said with a grin, and that was that.

We settled into a routine. I went to my house each evening after work and made sure there was food for the girls when they got off work. Then I'd meet Fred for dinner. Sometime later I'd go home for the night. To change things up, I decided to invite Fred to my house for dinner. I was making a special Mexican dinner for my special gringo. The dinner consisted of my homemade tortillas, beans, pork green chili, and potatoes.

Fred and Mandy were kidding around with each other when he noticed me struggling to peel potatoes with one of my dull knives. He excused himself and was out the door saying he'd be right back. He drove home to retrieve his special knife sharpener. When he returned, Mandy and I watched as he proceeded to sharpen every knife in my kitchen. Cooking was a lot easier with sharp knives. Fred loved my cooking and said any time I wanted to make tortillas, he'd gladly play a supportive role by eating as many as I wanted to cook.

Even though my life with Fred was exquisitely happy, Stan continued to watch over Mandy and me. We were now seeing Stan look-alikes about every two weeks instead of every couple of days. In early May, an envelope arrived in the mail. I ripped it open to find a check for $75,000 from Stan's life insurance company. A shower of thoughts poured from my brain as I looked at the check. *Oh, Stan, thank you so much for loving us and taking such good care of us. With your estate settled, I'll be able to relax and enjoy what you have given me.*

I had exactly one day to enjoy the check. The following day while at home cooking with my sharpened knives, I was greeted by a process server who handed me a summons to appear in court. Tanya, Stan's executor, was suing me for my car. I stuck my sharp knife into the potato I'd just peeled and called Michael. "Michael, I have a problem."

"You and Fred are still together, aren't you?"

"Absolutely, but Tanya, the executor of Stan's estate, is suing me for my car."

"You made all the payments, right? You have records of everything, right?"

"Right," I said.

"She hasn't a leg to stand on. I don't think you need an attorney for this. Just tell them the truth." Michael advised. "Oh, and Di, I'm glad that things are good with you and Fred."

"Michael, things aren't good. They're great!"

I did go to court. Tanya's tearful, dramatic appeal to the court went something like this: "Your honor, as executor I had to do all the work on settling Stan's estate. Diann left Stan before he died, but she got everything and I got nothing but the headaches. I had to sell the house, and she got $75,000 in insurance money. I think I'm entitled to the car."

At this point the judge gave Tanya a look that said, *I can't believe you're wasting my time.* The judge said out loud, "I think I've heard quite enough."

Then it was my turn. I stated calmly that Stan had co-signed on a car loan for me, but the car was mine in every respect. I'd made all the payments and paid for the insurance, gas, oil, and maintenance for this car. "I have all the records with me to prove I made all the payments, Your Honor." With this the judge looked at me and said it was clear the car was mine and then adjourned the case.

My heart was light and my step bouncy as I left behind a sulking Tanya and all the issues surrounding Stan's death. I stepped into the Colorado sunshine, and I jumped into *my* car and drove toward my new life with Fred. A herd of elephants couldn't keep me away, especially since the herd now resided at Fred's house.

Life just kept on getting better. It was Mother's Day, Sunday, May 9, when I received a most precious gift from Mandy. I was in the loft and happened to glance down into the dining room. There sat my sixteen-year-old and Fred talking. Both were leaning in, engrossed in conversation. It appeared each was trying to capture and hold onto every word.

Mandy's animated face, as well as her expressive hands, connected with Fred, and he connected back.

Fragments of sentences floated up to the loft, and the sound lighted gently in my ears. "I felt sad when…my boyfriend said…I thought…" I realized my daughter was sharing personal thoughts and feelings with him. Love filled my body and spilled over, for nothing could contain the joy I felt knowing Mandy and Fred and I were going to become a close family.

At the end of May, we decided to have a family party. Mandy, Gina, and Alex attended plus Fred's three daughters, Wendy, Kelly, and Kristy, and their five kids. Fred's grandchildren entered the house. Eight-year-old Mark, whom I had met briefly, said, "Hi, Diann. Come on, guys. Let's go play in the basement."

All five grandchildren disappeared. Fred's and my kids were left. They tilted their heads and smiled shyly. Fred's girls' eyes flitted around, noticing a change in the place. It was true his house was still devoid of furniture, but I think the whispers were about not recalling their dad's affinity for elephants. There were women's touches in the kitchen and noticeably softer touches throughout the house, such as several new plants in the windows. Kelly, Fred's middle daughter, followed me to the master bathroom. After noticing the face creams, lotions, and open cosmetic bag on the counter, she said in a perky voice, "Are you living here with Dad?"

Not knowing what response I'd receive, I said cautiously but firmly, "Mandy and I are not totally moved in yet, but we will be soon. I love your Dad already, and he loves me too."

I needn't have worried. Kelly skipped down the stairs, and I heard her lilting voice saying to her sisters, "Yep, we're right. She's almost moved in, and she's here to stay." I was pleased as she repeated my statement as fact. "And she loves Dad and Dad loves her too."

The lease at my rented house was up the first of June. I decided to use part of the insurance money from Stan to buy a townhouse. The purchase seemed like a good idea for two reasons: a prudent decision tax-wise, and a great place for Gina and Alex to live. The grey, cocoon feeling of June had morphed into beautiful, happy wings of freedom. My new life had taken flight as I found my place in the world. I moved one last time. I had come home.

I smiled as I remembered my happy little brother Alan's "Mr. Clean" commercial. I could hear his sweet voice singing along with mine as I belted out the lyrics, "Mr. Clean, Mr. Clean." I had decided to make a fresh start by cleansing my life of every item from my marriage to Joe. To create my clean slate, I had a garage sale and got rid of many old wedding gifts: dishes, silverware, and utensils. I sold all my furniture, releasing most of the items for a song. I gave away a $3,000 dining room set because I was starting my life anew. What I didn't sell I gave away to charity. Mandy and I moved into our new life with our clothes, a few plants, and yes, the rest of my elephant collection and many Donald Ducks.

Everyday living with my close-knit little family seemed almost perfect until one evening when Mandy began to unravel. I was cooking dinner when she came into the kitchen. She stood there watching me, her big brown eyes holding back a bucketful of feelings. "What's up?" I said, putting down my knife and turning my full attention to my daughter.

"Mom, I don't know what to do. I really like Fred," she said, wet with tears. "He talks to me, he listens, he cares about me, but I'm scared to love him."

"Oh, honey, why?"

"Because," she said between anguished sobs, "because if I love him, I'll be disloyal to Stan. Stan loved me. We played together. He gave me most of my Donald Ducks and taught me how to drive. Mom, I'm afraid to get close to Fred 'cause every time I have gotten close to a 'dad,' he leaves me."

I took my hurt little girl in my arms and said, "Oh, Mandy, I'm so sorry you're hurting. I know how much you loved Stan." My sixteen-year-old melted in my arms and nodded her head vigorously in a little-girl fashion. "It has to be confusing for you. You love Stan at the same time you're having loving feelings toward Fred. I understand. Would you like to talk about this with someone other than me? Maybe a therapist can help you sort out your feelings."

"Yes," she said, blowing the tension out of her body with a big sigh, "I'd like that."

The next week she met with Kathy. Returning from the session, she bounced in the door and announced in her usual strong voice, "Mom, I'm home."

"Hey, honey, how did your session go?"

"Great! Everything's going to be okay," and she gave me her big Mandy smile. "Thanks, Mom," she said and went out to the garage to talk to Fred.

Later that month, Fred and I took his tent trailer and went camping at Tarryall Reservoir in the Colorado Rockies. Camping in the rough was fun with Fred until the third day when I stepped in a gopher hole while playing Frisbee. My twisted knee immediately swelled to the size of a melon. We drove to the nearest phone and called Dr. Simon, who advised us to get to his office right away. We drove the hour and a half back to town and his office. As the good doctor was draining the fluid from my knee, he looked over at Fred and said, "Funny, you don't look like a Prince Charming."

Fred looked at him quizzically and said, "What was that?"

Dr. Simon said, "Well, Diann came into my office a couple of months ago and told me she'd met her Prince Charming."

Fred's flushed face looked at me in embarrassment. "Di...?"

"He's my doctor," I said, shrugging, "so I had to tell him the truth. But Fred, not to worry; sometimes doctors are wrong." There was a moment of silence, and then we all burst out laughing.

CHAPTER 26

A Reason to Believe

A fter the prince and I left the doctor's office, we were allowed to resume our camping trip with the condition I stay completely off my leg and said prince would take care of my every need. I sat relaxing in my lawn chair with my crutches by my side and let Fred wait on me while also tending to the cooking and cleanup. I felt loved, cherished, dependent, and uncomfortable with this turn of events.

My discomfort became literally and figuratively heavier and heavier as the weeks went by. When I'd started to date Fred, I was at my best physically. I'd lost some weight because of Stan's death and was in good shape because of dancing at least three times a week. But the combination of quitting smoking and the knee surgery, occurring about two weeks after the camping trip, weighed heavily on both my mind and body. I'd gained forty pounds in a matter of months.

I wondered if subconsciously I was testing Fred. "Will he love me if I'm fat?" I wondered, too, if I hadn't gained weight so men wouldn't find me attractive and I wouldn't be tempted to stray. I wanted nothing I could control to negatively affect my relationship with Fred. Looking back, I'm not sure gaining weight was the healthiest or the best strategy to ensure a successful relationship. Fred never said anything critical about my weight gain, just "Diann, you're beautiful inside and out. I love you just the way you are."

Living with Fred was truly living. It wasn't about surviving my childhood pain. It wasn't even about healing from it. It was about sunshine, snuggling, safety, living, loving, and laughter. It was bouquets of flowers for every occasion. All of life's little struggles like my knee surgery, my weight gain, and Gina's and Mandy's teenage rebellion were simply bee stings in life's rich garden.

Life was just about perfect, but he even agreed that our living quarters could benefit from a feminine touch. I brought my womanly decorating prowess to bear. Together we furnished his house, which included buying a couch, coffee table, a couple of end tables, and lamps. Plus we filled Mandy's bedroom with a new king-sized waterbed in her favorite color—black.

Furnishing the house was one thing; decorating was another. I'm against bare walls. In addition to holding up the house, I think walls should be decorated to reflect the inhabitants' loves and personality. The problem was the whole interior of the house needed painting. My stomach knotted and my muscles tensed as I realized that painting meant "project time."

As Fred and I got the tape, paint, brushes, and rollers out, my nerves felt like a rubber band stretched to the breaking point. I readied myself for the demeaning comments. The word "stupid" came to mind. I braced, but I bravely, and tentatively, shared my ideas about the project. I painted and taped alongside Fred, waiting for something bad to happen.

Nothing ever did. In fact, Fred seemed to be having fun. Having fun with a male partner was a new concept for me. I became a little calmer when I realized bracing was indeed "stupid." So with each stroke, I covered my anxiety with a fresh coat of confidence. After the project was completed, I said to Fred in my little girl's voice, "Thanks for not yelling at me."

Fred's eyes went wide with surprise. "Why on earth would I yell at you?" My eyes answered his question by filling up with unshed tears. There was a look of understanding, then compassion, as his eyes filled up to match mine. He opened up his arms to me and gave me a gentle hug, dissolving all the years of Joe yelling at me.

I had never experienced teamwork in an intimate relationship before. My heart filled with gratitude, as I placed a dried-flower arrangement composed of flowers from all the bouquets of love Fred and I had sent each other on the newly painted wall.

So when June came, I wasn't bracing when I was hit with bad news. I could either take a twenty percent cut in pay and move my hours from Monday through Friday to Thursday through Monday or take a layoff. My boss, clueless about Prince Charmings, was married to her job. She wanted me to be the same.

I fought back. "I have a wonderful life. My boyfriend is off on the weekends, so with the days and hours you are asking me to work, I wouldn't see him."

Her response was, "I guess it's a layoff then." Even though in my head it was clear to me my boss wanted me to live to work, and I wanted to work to live, the layoff found me lying immobilized on the couch for a week, empty, sluggish, and insignificant.

In the middle of the fifth day of being a couch potato, I looked up and out the windows, wanting to be inspired by a clear blue Colorado sky. Instead, a grimy pane clouded my vision. That was when I jumped off the couch, grabbed my window-washing paraphernalia, and began working with my hands to clear my head.

I spent the next couple of months spring cleaning, organizing, and recovering furniture. Like Stan, I found hands-on manual labor a great way to decompress. Fred, noticing my newfound energy, had my sewing machine repaired so I could re-cover the cushions in the camper. Wanting to make full use of Fred's gift, and still having trouble with the concept of moderation, I went on a sewing rampage.

Fred's comment that he felt like "a seamstress's widower" finally guilted me into leaving my machine behind and going on a family camping trip with his and my girls. The days warmed by the sun and the Milky Way of stars by night showered magic upon us. I thought it a perfect weekend.

As the terrific trip was drawing to a close, Mandy tapped me on the shoulder and waited for my attention. "What's up?" I asked.

Mandy whispered her reply. "I'm pregnant."

My blood froze as I remembered hearing these very words before, another time and place, a different daughter. This time there were no kitchen cabinet doors available to slam. Anyway, I felt I'd moved past that kind of behavior. But since *my* thirteen-year-old was still in charge of my anger, I held up my hand to Mandy and walked away. After kicking up the dirt and scaring a few birds, I walked back to her, sucked in a bunch of fresh air, patted my heart several times, and with tears in my eyes, I said, "I'm very disappointed, but you have my support."

"Mom, there's more." I was silent at this point, so Mandy continued. "Tony wanted me to get an abortion. But I don't believe in abortion, so I said no. He doesn't want to have anything to do with me now, so he dumped me. At first I was bummed, but I'm over him. Oh and Mom, I've been thinking…" *Not very much*, I thought. "I can't continue to smoke pot and work at McDonald's if I'm going to support a child. I think I'll get my GED."

"Sounds like a good plan," I said, thinking, but not adding, *Except for getting pregnant in the first place. I'll believe it when I see it.*

It turned out both Mandy and I were ready to become productive members of society. After months of glorious time off, I secured a job as a secretary at Rocky Flats, a nuclear facility in Golden, outside of Denver. Mandy seemed to grow up as the baby grew in her womb. She sat for her GED test at Warren Tech, an alternative school in Lakewood, knowing she had someone else to think about other than herself. Even though she took the test cold, she scored higher than any student in Warren Tech's history; in fact, she scored in the top four percent in the United States. Who would have thought such an irresponsible act would motivate Mandy to use her intelligence and become responsible?

Charlee, Mandy's daughter, was born in February 1995. "Oh, Mom, isn't she beautiful? I love her so much. I am going to start college as soon as possible. I want to be the best mom ever."

Along with the birth of Charlee, the other exciting news in my life came in a March phone call from Rese saying she wished to marry her longtime boyfriend, Daniel.

"Mom, can you hear me?" Rese's faraway voice threaded its way from Guam across several continents to land smack-dab in my telephone earpiece.

"Yes, honey, go ahead."

"I can't talk long…too expensive. Daniel and I want to get married this June in a Catholic Church in Denver. We'll take the pre-Cana classes here. We can get a week off for the wedding. I know it's a lot to ask, but could you make all the wedding and reception arrangements? Mom, are you still there?"

At this point in the conversation, I felt the need to sit down. "Congratulations, Rese. I'll do my best."

"Thanks a bunch, Mom."

"Oh, Rese, would you like me to make the bridesmaid and flower girl dresses?" Just as soon as the words popped out, I wanted to bring them back in and ponder their merits at length.

"It would be great if you could, Mom. I'll have my wedding dress made here. I'll let you know about the invitations. Thanks again, Mom. I've got to go." Rese was gone, leaving me with an enormous task.

My first challenge was finding a Catholic Church to marry my daughter and her fiancé. The first churches I contacted didn't allow couples to be married there unless they attended the premarital classes in their church. After trying four or five churches, I finally found one, Spirit of Christ Catholic Community that would perform the ceremony.

I met with Father Bob, who was very accommodating, and after we'd set the date and made the arrangements for Rese, he asked me about myself. I told him I'd been married for twenty years, had four children, and then divorced. I smiled as I recounted living with Fred, which made me incredibly happy.

After asking about the reason for the divorce, he said, "Are you ready to get an annulment and stop living in sin?" For a moment I couldn't comprehend what he was talking about. These were words not on my radar screen—foreign, flying in the face of my values.

I finally found my voice and said, "No, I'm not." My comment seemed to shock the priest, as his eyes opened wide. I further flabbergasted him by saying, "I don't feel like I'm living in sin because Fred is a gift from God. Besides, an annulment after twenty years of marriage would feel like I was invalidating my children."

I guess I made my point sufficiently because the priest didn't bring up the subject again. I know he was just following Catholic doctrine, but I really don't like it when Church rules seem to discount direct gifts from God.

There were months of long-distance correspondence with Rese about the millions of little details that make a wedding. I so wanted to make Rese's wish list a reality, but I was having trouble getting motivated to make the dresses. I told Aunt Ruby about my lack of motivation. My eighty-five-year-old aunt, still sharp as a needle and an accomplished seamstress, offered to help me sew. "Thank you, Auntie, that won't be necessary, but I think it would help if you'd sit with me while I sew."

My aunt kept me company in my sewing room, rocking baby Charlee in a rocking chair. The time was filled with hilarity and good conversation, and somehow the four bridesmaids' dresses and two flower girl dresses materialized too.

June arrived, and true to their word, so did Rese and Daniel. On the day of the wedding, Rese was beautiful, as was the church, wedding party, flowers, and cake. I was in dire need of sleep. Happy the wedding was over, I was ready for the kids to return to Guam and, after some rest, grateful for life getting back to normal. To Fred's dismay, the new normal now meant me spending an inordinate amount of time in my sewing room making decorative items for the house.

The happily-ever-after life with my prince, who'd gradually transformed into a regular guy, was good except for one thing: I wanted to be married. Fred and I talked about tying the knot, but in order to tie the knot with me, he felt like he needed to untie his stomach knots caused by two failed marriages. He didn't want to reexperience the hurt or pain.

My desire to be married wasn't about security or money. It wasn't even about love, although I loved him with all my heart. I just didn't want to go through what I'd experienced with Stan's death.

"If something happened to you, I wouldn't have any rights again," I told Fred. "I know your daughters love me, but I also know what happens to people when their loved ones die. And I won't—no, I can't—go through that again."

Our fears from the past were colliding; I was pretty sure Fred's love for me would win out. But I also wished he would hurry, because my patience was wearing thin.

The black storm clouds that had seeped into my skin and hovered low over every June and December of my past had vanished. Ever since Fred, I'd been living under a protective arc of rainbow colors and light. June had been the month of moving into Fred's house, and December was filled not only with my favorite Sagittarian's birthday but also with music and miracles. Our children were having babies: Fred's six grandchildren and Gina's Alex, Mandy's Charlee, and JJ's Breanna and Gray. The holidays were filled with the magic of children's giggles, Santa Claus, and a whole lot of family love.

The joy of the holidays finally loosened and unknotted Fred's stomach because on Christmas evening, 1995, Fred pulled me to him and with tears in his eyes said, "Will you marry me?"

I responded with my usual calm demeanor by squealing, "Really? Of course I'll marry you."

We decided to get married on the third anniversary of our first date, April 12. This was exactly three years from our five-hour-long first "just going to have one drink" date. Our plan was to have a simple ceremony and celebrate in June with a big party after Rese and Daniel returned from Guam.

The week before the big day, Mandy began to act strangely. She was arriving home later than usual and seemed a bit "loopy." I didn't smell the aroma of pot or alcohol on her breath, and she was being her normal attentive self with Charlee, so I decided to keep quiet. I did, however, file the information away in my brain. JJ, who'd moved back with his family to Denver the previous March, was also acting strangely. Just before leaving for the ceremony, JJ handed Fred a balloon and said, "Here, you might need this."

After Michael and his wife, Erlinda, stood up for us in a private civil ceremony, all four of us went to dinner. The topic of conversation was about what mischief our adult children were planning. Figuring something was up, we asked Michael and Erlinda to accompany us to our hotel. Our kids had arranged for us to stay in a fancy honeymoon suite for a night. We entered the hotel lobby with mild trepidation.

When we signed in at the front desk, the desk clerks saw our names and turned to each other and snickered. This was not a good sign. The clerk then handed us a wrapped box and said to open it when we got to our room. We entered our palatial suite, where a stunning sight greeted us.

A bank of windows presented to us a breathtaking view of Denver's sparkling city lights. The living room was filled with flower arrangements and champagne. The tension melted away as I said, "We were worried for nothing. This is lovely. The kids…" I stopped talking, spying a sign on the bedroom door. The four of us stepped up to the door. The message was written in bold letters. It said, "STOP! DO NOT ENTER UNTIL YOU OPEN YOUR GIFT BOX!" One to follow instructions to the letter, I opened the gift to find a box full of quilting pins.

Fred, Michael, Erlinda, and I looked at each other with question marks emanating from our heads. Fred said, "Pins? What are these for?"

This scene was becoming more surreal with each second. Everybody froze, afraid to move, but finally I, with Fibber McGee abandon, opened the door. An avalanche of rainbow-colored balloons bombarded us. I couldn't catch my breath, I was laughing so hard. I could occasionally glimpse Fred's, Michael's, and Erlinda's heads bobbing above the sea of balloons. We were neck deep in balloons. The balloon flood seemed to fill every space in the hotel room.

I instantly understood the use for the box of pins in my hand and swam to my compatriots to arm them. Minutes of pin-happy poking ensued as popping echoed through the room. In the din, I used my best breaststroke to get to the phone and call each of the kids, holding the handset aloft so they could hear the popping noises in the background. When I talked to JJ, he said, "I hear you got our gifts. Great idea, huh? That was mine, Mom. We blew up a thousand balloons. You guys have everything, and we didn't know what to get you. We thought this would be fun."

Mandy added to the story, saying, "Didn't you think I was acting strangely, Mom? I was high from blowing up balloons. We didn't think to use a pump until the last day."

After taking a few pictures of Fred and me standing on the bed with only our faces peeking out, Michael and Erlinda left us to our honeymoon. *Thank you, my children, for making our wedding day so memorable,* I thought as I drifted off to sleep.

In the middle of our honeymoon night, I was awakened by a rowdy party outside our room. So at about two a.m., I jumped out of the bed and made myself useful by picking up balloon fragments and placing them in a wastebasket.

I'd finished gathering up everything in the living room, which made a nice-sized pile of colorful scraps, when I felt a hand on my shoulder. True to my scaredy-cat nature, I jumped. I turned to see Fred's sweet smile.

He said, "Di, hand me that wastebasket, please." When I handed it over, he promptly threw the basket in the air, and the balloon fragments scattered all over the floor.

"Why'd you do that?" I questioned.

"This is our honeymoon, and you're not allowed to work."

I laughed and said, "I love you, Fred Kissell, but sometimes you're very annoying."

CHAPTER 27

Full Circle

A fresh coat of honeymoon magic covered my busy life. The past forty years seemed to belong to a different person. I was so filled with happiness and hope I felt little resemblance to the person I was before my life with Fred.

Detached though I was, I knew my story had relevance and a potential to help change lives. JJ and Mandy each took college classes dealing with the subject of capital punishment. They both elected to give speeches about the death penalty using their grandfather as an example. I began giving talks whenever I was asked.

My theory about truly changing a life became a reality when I gave a talk to my niece's class at her alternative high school in January of 1997. The subject of my talk was my life story, incorporating my feelings about the death penalty. After my lecture, a young man with long dark hair approached me. He walked slowly toward me, his head down and his hands making balls in his pockets. When he reached me, however, he lifted his face and with his startling brown eyes looked straight through my eyes into my soul. His voice, surprisingly clear and heavy with emotion said, "Thanks for coming. Your talk really helped me." He swallowed a couple of times, brushed his hands across his face, and blinking back tears, he continued, "I've seriously been thinking about committing suicide, but after listening to you, I realize I have other choices."

I grabbed his hands, and with tears in my own eyes said, "It's never as bad as it seems. And you do have choices. Thank you for sharing with me. And good luck."

This one young man validated my life as so many people in my life's journey had done before him. In the big picture, the craziness of my life made sense if it meant that out of all my pain emerged a greater capacity to understand other's experiences. If I could help just one person move from despair to hope, the pain had been worth it.

I left the classroom energized. *Yes, it was worth the pain. It's never as bad as you think it is. You do have choices.* The words "pain," "bad," and "choices" formed a word cluster in my mind: "the pain of bad choices," which took me down a dark path of heavy thoughts dead-ending with Patrick's suicide.

Patrick, you had a choice. Why was I able to help this young man choose life instead of death when I couldn't prevent you from committing suicide? Then my thoughts turned to the brother who was living but remained, by his own choice, isolated and detached from our family. *Where are you, Al? I worry you're making bad choices. Are you in danger? Why won't you let me help you? Please, God, keep him safe.*

As is often the case in my life, my unspoken words were sent into the universe and flew on the wings of angels, landing safely at the very hospital in which my brother Al lay. Al called the house several months after my talk. Fred picked up the phone and listened to my big brother Al's decision to stop drinking. All I could see was Fred mouthing the word "Al" to me. As he listened, a broad smile crossed his face, and he gave me the thumbs-up sign. I realized I'd been holding my breath in anticipation of bad news. After I began to breathe again, I tuned in to Fred's voice. "Okay. Okay. Sure. Okay. We'll send the money. See you soon. Bye."

I gave Fred one of those exasperated but curious looks. "Honey, I knew you'd agree with a decision to help your brother. He called from the hospital and couldn't talk long." Fred filled me in. "He ended up in the hospital because of his drinking. Al admitted to being alcoholic. He asked us to please send him a one-way airplane ticket home. He told me if he didn't come home and stop drinking, he thought he'd die. He asked if he could live with us until he gets on his feet. He told me he'd been hiding his alcoholism from the family his whole life. He said he'll explain it all to you when he gets to Denver."

"Oh Fred…" I started. Then emotions overwhelmed my words. With tears of relief and hope, I fell into my husband's arms. Finally finding my voice, I said, "Al's coming home. He's making a choice to live!"

Al lived with us for six months. He went to an A.A. meeting the day he came home and has been sober ever since. He admitted he started drinking wine as an altar boy. His first drink, he confided, made him feel fantastically normal, and getting high became his purpose in life.

Having Al present and engaged completed our family circle. Even though the credit for turning his life around went to Al, being able to help my big brother in his time of need felt wonderful.

The warm fuzzy feeling I continued to get by sharing my experiences with others was also very rewarding. This feeling, however, starkly contrasted with the triggers of the experience itself. In September of 1997, the capital punishment issue, which I lectured about, raised its ugly head again. Fred was sitting at the breakfast table perusing the *Rocky Mountain News*. He looked at me with a pensive gaze, saying, "Di, have you read the paper today?"

"No, of course not. You know I don't read newspapers," I said, looking at my husband with suspicion. "What's going on?"

"It's Gary Lee Davis. He's going to be executed the second week of October here in Colorado."

Suddenly, cold gripped my body as a seventeen-year-old mind revisited the play-by-play description of Dad dying and the media frenzy surrounding our family. Then my mind fast-forwarded ahead to me at age twenty-six, having a nervous breakdown and drowning in the media coverage when Gary Gilmore was executed; and now, more media. I wouldn't be able to stand our family name being smeared across the news. *I hate it, I hate it, I hate it*, I thought, gritting my teeth and balling my fists.

Warmth then spread over my body, and I opened my hands as it dawned on me that when Davis died, Dad would no longer be the last person executed in Colorado. This gave me hope the thirty-year degradation of our family name would end. Our family would at last, finally, be free. When I came back to the table, Fred was looking at me with a concerned expression on his face. "How're you doing, Di?"

"I don't know yet," I replied, and with that Fred stood up and enveloped me in his arms.

That evening, Fred came home and told me Gene Amole, a local columnist for the *Rocky Mountain News*, had asked him if he thought I would talk to him. I hate the insensitivity of the media, but Fred thought he was a good guy, so I told my husband to give him my work number.

When I got a call from Gene the next day at work, I was ready for him. He wanted to hear my thoughts about the impending execution and maybe write an article.

My quick reply was, "I'd be glad to tell you my thoughts off the record. I don't think my family would appreciate me giving an interview."

"Well, if we're not going to do an article, then it's really not necessary for us to talk. But I'm curious; what do you think about the upcoming execution?"

"I have real mixed feelings. I'm still not a straight-across-the-board proponent of the death penalty, but I'd be lying if I said I wasn't feeling relief my family will finally be taken out of the spotlight. I don't have anything against this man personally, but part of me is really happy he's going to die."

Early on the morning of October 14, 1997, the date of Gary Lee Davis's pending execution, I woke up to Fred's huge grin. "Tonight after work, we—Steve, Marcy, you, and I—are going to a movie. Not just any movie. We're taking in a hilarious British comedy, *The Full Monty.*"

"You sound like an advertisement," I said, laughing. At work the execution briefly crossed my mind, but more than anything, I was anticipating our evening of laughter with Fred and my friends. *The Full Monty* was everything it promised. My full-bellied, Mom-like laugh filled the theater. Unlike Stan, Fred was delighted with my big laugh and was pleased his plan had worked. It had, as he'd intended, totally kept my mind off the execution. And as I'd hoped, Gary Lee Davis's death kept the media's mind off our family's story.

One day as the end of the century was approaching, my former therapist Kathy called and asked if I'd be willing to spend an hour telling my story once or twice a year to a class of counselors who wanted to learn about trauma. In every class I taught, I felt there was at least one person who received inspiration from my story. This, in turn, gave me validation. The talks always seemed to boost my self-esteem and reenergized me, refilling my coffers with hope.

My helium-filled self-esteem lifted my confidence high enough for me to quit my job of six years working at Rocky Flats and go out on my own. With Fred's total support and love, I started Diann's Designs. I set up shop in my basement. My specialty was custom embroidery and sewing, which included making wedding dresses, and I also did alterations. In the whir of machines, I would often hear my grandmother's excited voice: "Felicidades," she would say in Spanish, which in English means, "Congratulations; I'm so proud of you."

I contracted wedding dress alterations through a local bridal shop. The owner was a petite, attractive, middle-aged Swedish woman named Hilga. In her slightly accented English, she'd been very helpful in passing on her expertise in wedding dress alterations to me. Her biggest pearl of wisdom, spoken with European fervor, was, "The only thing you really need to do wedding dress alterations is trust in your own skills." Shortly thereafter, she asked me to alter a $2,000 wedding gown made of heavily beaded raw silk. As I was exiting the bridal shop with the dress, she said sternly, "Remember, when you leave with this dress, you're responsible for it. If anything happens to it, you're liable." With this caution, her pearls of wisdom, along with my own confidence in my skills, took a dive.

For two weeks, the dress hung in my family room with a half dozen other dresses, glaring at me, just daring me to touch it. Three days before the appointed fitting, I decided I could no longer procrastinate. With trembling hands—not a great sign for an accomplished seamstress—I took the dress off the hanger and stared at it. It stared back at me. In an attempt to not let an exorbitantly expensive dress intimidate me, I begged for help.

Immediately the smiling faces of my grandmother, my mother, and Aunt Ruby appeared. *Bring me your skill and nimble sewing fingers while I work on this dress,* I prayed. They answered my prayer, because the alterations turned out perfectly. From then on, I learned to call on them whenever I found myself in a sewing dilemma. Aunt Ruby was big in my prayers but even bigger in real life.

In the winter of 2002, dear Aunt Ruby was placed in a rehab/long-term care facility. Luckily it was close to my home, and I was able to visit her daily. Since I'd cut her hair for the past twenty-five years, I wasn't surprised when she called one morning and said, "Help! I look like George Washington. I need a haircut. Bring the scissors."

That was my funny, white-haired auntie for you. She died in April 2003 at the age of ninety-two. When I gave her eulogy, I recounted many of her hilarious stories and told of her accomplishments as a person, seamstress, and cook. I admitted the greatest compliment I'd received in my life came from her. One day, Auntie, whom I revered as the tortilla queen of the universe, said, "Diana, you make the best tortillas. They're so thin! Would you teach me?" I looked at her expecting to see mischief in her eyes and a smirk on her face to indicate this was another one of her many jokes, but Auntie's face was dead serious.

I'd learned so much from my aunt, but this was the one time I was able to teach her. Aunt Ruby was a precious gem in our family. She was a mother when we lost our mother. She was a mentor and a friend. When I think of her, she makes me laugh.

Alas, as my joyous emotional being was expanding, my physical body was deteriorating. By 2003, my knees were so bad I walked like Quasimodo. If it hadn't been for the daily ingestion of anti-inflammatory medication and painkillers, I'd have turned into Quasimodo couch potato. Finally, I saw a specialist who insisted it was time for a knee replacement. Unfortunately, both knees were equally bad. After X-rays, Dr. Miller took Fred and me into his office for a chat.

"Tell me about your knees. When did they first start hurting you?"

His question took me back to my two surgeries and the gopher-hole incident with Fred and back further to teaching fitness and my dance recitals when I was married to Joe. Then I suddenly had a vision of the

Good Shepherd Home and standing on the second-floor landing, waiting for the pain in my knees to subside.

"I've been in pain many times. I had arthroscopic surgery on my
right knee in 1993 and on my left in 1995. In my twenties and thirties, I
was very active with dancing, which was at times painful. But I guess the
first time I really noticed the pain was age fourteen."

The good doctor didn't look a bit surprised. "Your story is consistent
with my findings. You have a couple of externally rotated kneecaps, probably from birth. It sounds like you've made good use of them throughout
the years." I nodded in agreement, feeling a little weak in the knees
because I wanted more information but dreaded hearing it in equal measure. "You'll need both knees replaced. I strongly suggest you have them
done one at a time."

After this advice sank in, I begged my doctor to allow me to do both
knees at once, saying, "I have my own business, and if I'm going to be
down for an extended period of time, and if I'm going to be on lots of
meds, and if I'm going to be in a lot of pain, then I'd prefer to do this
only once."

He reluctantly agreed, saying it was a highly unusual request and,
ultimately, it would have to be approved by the anesthesiologist. The
surgery on both knees was eventually scheduled for November 4, 2003.
The week prior, I was told to stop taking any anti-inflammatory and pain
medications.

I was convinced having the surgery was absolutely the right decision. Mentally and emotionally, I knew getting off the drugs in order to
have surgery was a small price to pay for a new knee life. But I forgot to
let my body know. When I stopped taking the meds cold turkey, my body
went into painful, paralyzing, debilitating shock. My body was already
slumped and bowed from resting its weight on crooked knees, but without the drugs, I folded in on myself, crippled with pain. My determination was temporarily bruised and broken.

"Fred," I said, "when I try to move, everything hurts: my shoulders,
my hips, my hands, my head, my back, my ankles, and of course my
knees. I had no idea those drugs were helping so much. I know I can
make it, but…"

Fred put his fingers to my lips. "More than anything on earth, I hate to
see you hurting. But it'll be worth it. Hang in there, baby. You'll make it."

And I did.

After a five-hour operation, I woke up to my sweet husband's face.
"You made it. The surgery was successful. You're the proud owner of two
brand-new knees. How do you feel?"

"It hurts and…"

"Hey, Mom," Mandy and Gina said in unison.

My fuzzy, drug-hazy eyes slowly focused on the smiling faces in the room. Faces belonging to people I loved. To my amazement, I began crying. I don't know if the downpour was caused by my excruciating pain, by the fact I had no control over my emotions, or from my heart being deeply touched by their support and overflowing love. It was my guess this was a bona fide combination cry.

The second night of my eight-day stay in the hospital took on a nightmarish quality. It was late. My visitors had all left, and I was lying flat on my back, alone with my agonizing thoughts and pain. I hadn't thought this surgery through. I was now in a place of total dependency. I couldn't do anything without help: take a shower, wash myself, go to the bathroom, or get up and walk across the room. *I don't have a leg to stand on*, I thought, chuckling.

I cut my laughter short because if I jiggled too much, I'd be hit with a tidal wave of agony. As I gazed out through my pain to the black night of my thoughts, it occurred to me I'd been in this place before: down in the basement with Dad. Little Diana knew this feeling. Dependent on Dad, Diana had been alone, frozen in hopelessness. Her efforts to stand up were knocked down by Dad's harsh consequences. My heart filled with memories as I walked through the scenes of my life. I saw Dad pushing me down, burying me in shame. And then I saw myself brushing the dirt off and standing in the sunshine. I saw Joe shoving me into a hole and stomping on my self-esteem. And then me getting up and standing on my own two feet. I glimpsed my nervous breakdowns I used as a catalyst for my breakthroughs. And finally, I witnessed myself turning off my tears in order to feel in control of my emotions. I couldn't do that now. I wasn't in control of anything.

I was wrenched out of my reverie by a rumbling in my intestines, followed by a great pressure in my bowels. I needed help. I immediately pushed the panic button, praying a nurse would come quickly. I concentrated as hard as I could on keeping my bodily fluids inside, but by the time the nurse arrived, I was covered with foul-smelling fecal matter.

"I'm sorry. I couldn't hold it any longer," I lamented.

The nurse rolled her eyes, wrinkled up her nose in disgust, sighed heavily, threw the covers off of me, and recoiled at the sight of the mess I'd made. The feelings of shameful Diana, which had been dormant for so many years, welled up. "I'm so sorry. I didn't mean to," I said, my eyes stinging with tears of humiliation.

I was awake most of the night, partly because of the pain and partly because I was stuck, still lying in the lingering stink of shame.

The night shift was over, and a morning nurse entered at the same moment the sun's rays lit up my room. "Good morning," she said, with soft, kind eyes. Used to my sunny disposition and seeing my troubled face, she looked at me with concern, and said, "How are you?"

"I had kind of a rough night. I had an accident," I blurted out. As I told the story, the nurse listened with compassion.

"Your accident was totally normal. It happens all the time. And it's definitely not something to be ashamed of. This is part of our job, and she acted unprofessionally. You can request she not be your nurse again."

"Thanks. That makes me feel better." Later that evening when I called for a nurse, the nurse from the night before responded. When she came in the room, I told her I wanted a different nurse to help me. When she asked why, I told her, trying not to get emotional or embarrassed, that it was because she'd shamed me. She left the room, and thankfully I never had to see her again. By standing up for myself, I'd reclaimed my dignity and wiped clean my humiliation.

I decided then by choosing to get both knees operated on at the same time, I alone was responsible for putting myself in this situation of total dependency. I could fight to keep control and when I lost it respond in shame, or I could accept the help and love of others with grace and humor. So when Fred came in the next morning, I asked him if he'd help me wash my hair.

In my physical state, nothing was easy. We laughed through the awkwardness of Fred's newfound role. I ended up with the sweet-smelling feeling of being cherished and a headful of clean hair. I asked my daughters, through those eight days, to accompany me to the bathroom and "treat me like your little ones in diapers." I kept telling them it would be good practice for my old age. I learned to ask for help, and my family and friends lovingly obliged.

As far as turning off my tears, the pain was too intense, and I no longer had any control, so I joked we needed to Velcro a Kleenex box to my wrist because there was no end to my waterworks.

Words I'd stuffed in the closed closet of my mind while being careful not to be an interfering mother or sister had been pried open by my hospital experience, and the sentences now tumbled out. I gave voice to my opinion about JJ and Barb needing to get a divorce, since they had both been in other relationships for some time. I talked to Lee about his marriage. Surprisingly, the sound of my sentences landed softly and sensibly in their ears, and, to a person, they responded with love and acceptance. I wondered if Mom would think me too bold. I decided she'd be proud of me.

About five days into my hospital stay, the doctor performed a routine procedure to remove the drainage tubes from my knees. The tube in my right knee came out easily, but to his and my distress, the tube in my left knee had adhered to tender new tissue. He kept apologizing as he tried to pull the tube free, saying, "I'm so sorry. This has never happened before."

I just screamed. I'd already been experiencing agonizing pain. This pain was over the top; it was intolerable. It swallowed me whole and took my breath away. It was, without a doubt, the worst physical anguish I'd ever experienced in my life. The morphine sat in my system, impotent in its ability to provide me with even a modicum of relief as ever-tightening hands of pain attempted to squeeze the color from my existence. I loved my life with Fred; I loved my family. I didn't want to die. I just wanted the pain to stop. But even as my spirits spiraled downward, I was certain this was simply another gift from the universe, a lesson to be learned. I'd been hoping for a much gentler approach.

As day collapsed into night, so did I. I was completely worn out. My resistance was gone. And so in that early morning grey space between sleep and wakefulness, the dam I'd erected around my heart at the age of seventeen crumbled and burst open. Tears of grief flooded my body, spilling over into the room. For hours, I sobbed for the loss of my family: Mom, my babies, Patrick, and Dad. The frozen emotional pain I'd held in for so many years melted into tears and flowed out of me.

As I let my sorrow go, I heard a whisper of a voice from far away. It was feather-soft, and as its warm words brushed past my ears, it felt more like a feeling than a sound. The words swaddled me in the soft, pink edges of dawn. I scanned the room searching for the owner of the voice, but, alas, I was the only one in the room. Maybe the voice was merely a figment of my vivid imagination. One thing was true: This wasn't a dream, for my eyes were wide open, and my ears strained to hear the next words.

There it was again, a little louder this time. The sound surrounded me, soothing and sure, saying, "You're good. All is well. Your circle is complete. You've reached a higher level of enlightenment." The voice paused then, and maybe to make sure I fully understood the implications, added, "You know, enlightenment, just like Oprah Winfrey." I loved and admired Oprah so I took in the statement as a supreme compliment.

Sure, the voice could have been the drugs talking, or me talking to the pain, but its ethereal quality wrapped me in the warmth of truth. I had indeed, come full circle. "Try not to let what I did to you affect the rest of your life," Dad had said.

I'll remember what you did, Dad, but the amount of love I have in my life dwarfs the shame and pain you caused. From that night on, I knew I could handle anything that came my way. I'd walk through this experience into a life rich with color.

Once again the physical pain flexed its muscles, but the emotional suffering had vanished into the morning sky. After my hospital stay, I was moved to the rehab facility that had been Aunt Ruby's last residence. It was like a reunion. I knew many of the nurses and knew my way around. My body, through the years, had learned to compensate for, and adapt to, my bum knees. With my new hardware, I had to relearn, in baby steps, to stand and walk upright. I was released ten days later when I managed to walk up and down three stairs—life's stairway to heaven.

CHAPTER 28

Giving Back

L ife's garden was rich, full with the lush beauty of love. Fred and I considered ourselves truly blessed by our blossoming family and the freshness and fragrance of friendships. The threads of my life were woven together to make a perfect tapestry. Our family was expanding yearly with the gifts of grandchildren. I had a great group of friends whom I met with daily, first at exercise class and then afterward for coffee. My business was thriving, and I loved the women who worked for me.

After years of struggling, I was on solid ground financially. I wanted to pay forward the generous gifts I'd received along the way. With Fred's new venture into real estate, combined with Stan's insurance money and proceeds from my business, we were in a position where we could begin to give back. In the year 2000 on a Catholic Church-sponsored trip, Fred and I went to Juarez, Mexico, for a week to build a home for a needy family.

The colorless, dusty border town of Juarez reminded me of an old, bleached-out, black-and-white photo. The town, after years of being beaten by the sun and wind, had an anemic grey pallor to it. Our group's task was to build on its monochromatic coloring by erecting a grey brick-and-mortar house.

Our first day involved being a part of a human conveyer belt hoisting five hundred thirty-pound cinder blocks to the proper location. By the end of four days, we'd framed in a house complete with two doors, two windows, and a plywood roof.

Our own accommodations were Spartan, the bugs enormous, the heat unrelenting, and the work dirty yet satisfying. I was happily dreaming of taking an hour-and-a-half-long shower as we drove back from El

Paso to Colorado when Fred's words hit me like a dust storm, "Sometime I'd like to go down to Juarez for a year. What do you think?"

I thought, *no way*. This was a crazy idea. I loved my life and didn't want to give up everything to go to Mexico. But what I said was, "We can think about it," hoping this subject would never come up again.

For the next six years, we made our one-week journey to Mexico, and Fred made his seventy-two monthly pleas for the year's sojourn. In April 2006, Fred had a mild heart attack, which intensified his determination to fulfill his dream. "Di, this is my wake-up call. I want to commit to a year in Mexico while I'm still young and healthy enough."

I responded cheerfully, "Okay. You supported me with my dream to start my own business. I guess it's time I support you in your dream." Inside, I was screaming, *No!* I didn't understand, even in my enlightened state, why I had to give up everything in order to give back. This had to be another scary lesson. I was to leave my safe life and leap into another world, using my trust and love of Fred as my parachute.

I couldn't conceive of a year away from my kids, grandkids, and friends. I couldn't fathom not getting to experience the daily happenings of our grandchildren. Our slated departure date would coincide with Rese's daughter Nora's first birthday. I'd miss a whole year of her life and was deathly afraid she wouldn't know me when we returned.

I didn't want to leave my king-sized bed, my fully equipped kitchen complete with oven, our wonderful shower with its multifunctional showerhead, our walk-in closet, our beautiful flower garden and green grass. I loved Colorado with its temperate climate, scarcity of bugs, and beautiful mountains. I knew I was going to be living in a small room crawling with cockroaches and other dreaded insects. For a year my life would be covered by a layer of dust and baked in an oven of oppressive heat. The lack of amenities seemed eerily similar to my stay at New Vrindaban when I visited Lee and Patrick after my nervous breakdown.

Perhaps the worst consequence of going to Mexico was selling my business. Through the years my business had grown. I now had a basement full of sewing machines and a full-time staff. I loved them. I loved the work. I loved my customers. Every part of my being resisted selling, but I was determined not to sow the seeds of resentment. This was Fred's dream. He'd honored mine; it was time to honor his.

We began our yearlong preparations for our move to Mexico. Our plan was to take everything of ours out of the house and rent it for a year. This plan included storing, giving away, or selling the house's innards. Despite the fact Fred was still perfect for me, he'd exhibited some mildly irritating traits through the years. He was a packrat. I watched in amazement as his dream of Mexico trumped his "packratism" when he actually began to get rid of some cherished items. In clearing out his garage, he sold everything from duplicate tools to all his fishing gear. Even though I believe strongly a collection doesn't fit in the packrat category, I followed suit by cutting down my herd of elephants from seven hundred to a more manageable five hundred.

By Christmas we had a little more space in our house to accommodate the multitude of people who attended our combination birthday celebration for Fred and farewell party. At the party's end, I turned off the lights and trudged up the stairs exhausted, thinking Fred was right behind me. I realized he wasn't when I heard a crash punctuated by yelling.

I found Fred at the bottom of the stairs holding his right wrist, moaning. "I wish you hadn't turned out the light. I got disoriented without the furniture," he said through gritted teeth on our way to the emergency room.

His timing and our weather couldn't have been worse for the move. We were having a frigid winter with record snowfalls. On moving day, all my children, their spouses, and ten grandchildren, ranging from ten months to fifteen years, helped to strip our house bare and move everything but our king-sized mattress to a storage facility.

Fred supervised the move on a Sunday football game day, his arm dressed in an orange Denver Broncos cast looking like half a goal post. Everyone helped; in our family, there are only a few slackers. Five-year-old Jason, Gina's youngest, was "turbo kid," and even Jaycee, Mandy's three-year-old daughter, helped.

When I glimpsed Jaycee carrying a large pillow, I called after her, "Hey, Jaycee, what are you carrying?" She stopped, turned, rolled her eyes, looked at me like I was crazy, and said simply, "A pillow." I was very aware she hadn't mistaken the pillow for a mattress. I rationalized that perhaps the pillow I'd carried as a three-year-old had been a lot bigger.

It had taken almost a year to sell the business, rent out our house, sell our furniture, and tie up loose ends, but on February 1, 2007, we arrived in Juarez. Fred was in charge of the program and groups totaling about three hundred fifty people. He managed thirty-one volunteer groups who used cinder blocks, mortar, plywood, and nails to build thirty-one homes. I used donated sewing machines, thread, and material to teach seventy-five women to sew while they taught me about simplicity, courage, and good humor.

The first week, a Mexican woman whose house we were to rebuild graciously invited me into her home. She was proud of her 8x8 one-room space. The walls were made out of cardboard and crates, and the floor was dirt. The only furniture was a double bed in which she and her four kids slept. The small amount of food and supplies were in sacks hanging on pegs from the wall.

I walked out of the house and began to cry. "We Americans are so fortunate and spoiled," I told Fred that evening as we gratefully perused our 10x10 casita complete with a lumpy double bed, a 13-inch television, a closet made out of a bunk bed standing on its end, and many bugs.

The first month in Mexico, our days were so busy I fell into bed each night exhausted. I didn't have the time or the luxury to be homesick. Who was I kidding? It was hard to connect with people when I didn't speak the language, and I missed my family and friends terribly. Even though we'd made some short trips back to Denver, I wished for my family and friends to experience Mexico with me.

This wish that I sent out into the universe must have landed gently on more than a few shoulders and been whispered into many ears, because in March the English-speaking visitors started arriving. My sister Jean, Fred's daughter Wendy, and a host of relatives and friends made the trek. In June, my three daughters with their five children drove a van to Juarez. They stayed for four glorious days. All our visitors were a great help in easing my homesickness. They also helped with our various tasks, including house construction, sewing classes, and lunch duty.

In addition to teaching sewing at four community centers and occasionally helping with the home building, I also helped serve lunch every day to the neighborhood children. They got the leftover food served to the workers at the *maquilas* (factories), which are so prevalent in Juarez.

All our cooking was done in the main cafeteria. We had cooks when the groups were there, and I cooked for us, Fred, and two young men, Rush and Matao, who composed our family in Juarez. The cafeteria had everything I needed to cook, but it lacked a working oven.

In the eighth month of our stay, we moved into a small adobe house we'd fixed up. I was determined to add some color to my grey surroundings, so I painted the outside shutters, the bars on the windows, and the kitchen in my favorite color—turquoise. I painted the other three rooms in the colors that were available: green, purple, and orange. I was excited to have our own miniscule space complete with a small, eighteen-inch gas stove with an oven large enough to hold a tiny turkey. I was so ecstatic about the oven I started baking cookies. I became obsessed with cookie baking, and I simply couldn't stop. The thousands of cookies I made were eaten by Fred, me, and any and all visitors. I put a dozen cookies in bags for each of the seventy-five women in my sewing classes.

The month of January found us hopping from one party to the next, for everyone wanted to say good-bye. In the end, I didn't regret sharing Fred's dream. It had been a wonderful dream filled with color, lifelong friendships, laughter, light, Spanish, and cookies.

We returned stateside in February 2008, understanding we wanted to live more simply, not needing material goods to be happy. We moved back into our Arvada home. We brought home wonderful Mexican memories, some symbolized by decorations and ornaments for our walls. For a month, the only furnishing in our house was a queen-sized mattress, downsized from a king, on the floor in the basement. The transition from the poverty of Mexico to the abundance of our American life began there.

We immediately started on house projects. Fred and his brother tore out the carpet and put in a beautiful hardwood floor. I began to unpack all the decorative memorabilia from our past and hung it lovingly on the large, vaulted living room wall, adding our Juarez treasures.

I stepped back to admire my handiwork. My eyes traveled through time as each item on the wall evoked a feeling or a memory. This wall told the stories of my intense love of family and friends. As I gazed at the wall, I noticed about half my memories expressed themselves in turquoise. I was driven toward this color; in fact, I'd just purchased a white PT Cruiser and had specially ordered turquoise decals for it.

"Fred," I said, "this house looks pretty drab. Are you up for another project?"

"What color?" Fred responded.

"Have you noticed I'm partial to turquoise?"

Fred's eyes traveled to my turquoise blouse, up to my turquoise necklace and earrings, and glanced at the turquoise bracelets on my wrist as my finger pointed to the wall with turquoise memorabilia.

"No, I really haven't," he said with his tongue in his cheek and his dimples putting on a show.

"Well, I am, because the color makes me happy. Our project now is to paint the kitchen turquoise." And we did.

In the year 2010, we had a "cousin party." The party was in honor of two of Patrick's sons, Acarya and Ananda, who were visiting Denver. They especially wanted to see their first cousins; aunts, uncles, and second cousins were included, of course.

Our house was packed. The forty-person party consisted of all family members descended from Mom and Dad. The house filled with boisterous laughter and noise. I heard Mom's laugh everywhere, a contagious cacophony of joy radiating from the throats my children and grandchildren. The babies, in various stages of development, crawled, walked, and ran through the house. I could picture the *good* part of Dad, sitting under God's umbrella, looking down approvingly on his big family saying, "There's nothing more important than family. Families stick together."

My eyes traveled to the memory wall and down to the crowded couch where six or eight cousins were crunched together, some pushing and shoving, vying for position. My eyes moved to the right where JJ was lounging, fully extended, in the recliner. His eyes had a far-off look. He seemed to be looking through the festivities to another time. He wore his signature JJ smirk, radiating peace and contentment. I sat down in a chair next to my oldest child and said, "Hey, what are you thinking about?"

He turned his face toward me and said, "I was thinking how close you are to your brothers and sister. Then I was noticing the fact that this group"—his long arms swept the room—"seems so comfortable with each other. We're all close. We all truly like each other." He then looked at me with his deep brown eyes filled with soft intensity and said, "And Mom, then I was thinking…can you believe from so much tragedy came so much love?"

Final Notes

"Your story is amazing. Have you ever thought about writing a book?"

This comment, a familiar one from my various speaking engagements, came to me from a student in one of Kathy Bird's two-day trauma workshops. It was the middle of April 2009, and I had just finished an hour-long presentation about my past to a class of counselors and other professionals who were there to learn about trauma. I'd been a speaker in Kathy's classes once or twice a year since 2000, taking a couple years off for knee replacements and to live in Mexico.

Previously, I'd brushed this type of comment aside, but this time I paused to seriously consider the question. My response to the class was, "I've thought about it, but having tried it once before, you have to feel everything again in order to write it, and I'm not sure I'm willing to go through that kind of pain again."

Kathy adjourned the class for lunch, and there we were, the two of us. "You know, I think," Kathy said slowly, giving me a funny feeling life as I knew it was about to change, "if you wanted to, you could write that book. I don't believe you'd have to relive the pain to do it. You've done so much work on yourself, you're so spiritually sound, and your life is good today. I think the process of writing your story could be very healing."

This comment made sense to me. "Yes," I said slowly, "Maybe I could." I was thinking out loud, pondering the idea from a different perspective. "Maybe I don't need to be afraid of it. When I was considering it before with Oprah, I was in a very different place. I was still raising kids, married to Joe, and dealing with trauma. I'm on the other side now. I've come full circle. My story is complete."

With that thought, a surge of hope filled my body. *Yes, I think I could do this.* There was just one problem; I'd have to find a writer. I had strengths such as cooking, sewing, and mothering, but I knew writing wasn't one of them.

Before I knew it, out popped a bold question. "Kathy, do you want to write it with me?"

What I meant, which I didn't tell Kathy, was that I wanted her to write it. I knew she'd written a program about domestic violence. I had never read it, so I didn't know what kind of a writer she was, but I did know her and trusted her completely. I felt sure she'd tackle this project with compassion, understanding, and sensitivity.

The question seemed to startle Kathy. After a long pause, she said, "Okay." After another hesitation, she said, "We can certainly talk about it."

In an attempt to move the project along, I took the next step. "Let's get our husbands together and see if they'll support us." I knew without their support, there wouldn't be a book.

A week later, the four of us met at a restaurant. The husbands, it turned out, had much in common; they both loved good wine, fishing, sports, and were willing to support the project. They both agreed, however, that they didn't want to read it, Fred because it would cause too much anger, and Kathy's husband because of a traumatic history of his own.

At that meeting, Kathy asked me the first of many of thousands of questions to come. "Why do you want to write the book?"

That was one of her easier questions. I answered immediately, "I think telling my story has helped people." I used the example of speaking to the high school class where, because of my talk, a young man may have decided not to commit suicide. "By talking to counselors in your classes, I may have reached even more victims." Kathy nodded her agreement. "A book has the potential to reach the broadest audience of all."

"What do you think it would do for you personally?"

"For me?" The question snapped me back into my body. Even after all this time, I still had the tendency to think of myself last. To my surprise, the answer came easily. "Why, it would validate my life! It would give purpose to my pain. What's the point of pain if you don't learn from it and if you can't share what you've learned to help others?"

"It sounds like you're ready to write your book!" Kathy stated with admiration.

"I know I'm ready to try," I stated emphatically.

"Then, I'm ready to help," Kathy replied. Meanwhile the men were immersed in man-talk and had no clue a deal had been made.

Kathy and I met in August to discuss the project. I convinced her she was the perfect person to write the book because she had a full understanding of the subject matter and she knew me very well. I showed her my journal from our year in Mexico to stress the fact I shouldn't be the writer. That issue out of the way, we discussed my belief system. Kathy asked me what positive ideas had helped me through life. My answer embodied three major themes:

I believe we all have the power to choose our life. We have the power to control our destiny, rather than letting our circumstances control us. As adults, we have the choice to never think of ourselves as victims.

I came into this life to grow spiritually and to learn lessons. If one looks at life with the belief that everything happens for a positive reason, even if the reason is not apparent right away, then there is always a flicker of light at the end of the tunnel. Light leads to hope for tomorrow.

Dad thought death was better than shame. I believe secrets and shame fester into sickness. Talking and sharing bring health. The solution to shame is not death; it is sharing and living.

Neither Kathy nor I liked the first versions of the book. But I knew this project, like all of life, was a process. As the months passed, both Kathy's writing and my memory improved. Kathy's questions awakened sleeping memories, both good and bad. Even though I'd told my story hundreds of times, the written word seemed to bypass my brain and enter my soul. The process was impactful, healing, emotional, enlightening, and totally worth the time and effort.

Kathy was correct; I was healthy enough to tackle this project. The writing of the book certainly brought up some intense feelings, but I never felt I was reliving the debilitating shame, pain, or anger that has haunted my past. During the trauma-intensive Part I, we took many breaks. Finally, after many months of hard work, Kathy excitedly declared Part I finished.

I replied, "Well, my grandparents are pretty important, and there was that Christmas…"

She stared at me in disbelief. "In…Part…I?" Kathy enunciated each word.

I nodded.

"Diann," she said, squeezing her words out slowly. "If you want to ADD any more to Part I, I may have to do you bodily harm."

Reiterating one of the book's major themes, I answered, "Well, you can try, but I think I can take you, and I'll never be a victim again."

We laughed uncontrollably. After Kathy caught her breath, she conceded my point. She continued to ask questions, which continued to jog my memory banks for the next two years. Kathy, with little resistance, continued to include my additional stories where they fit. The book was finished, or so she thought, in December 2011. She, however, had a few more questions. Since my answers were often attached to long-forgotten memories, as late as February 2012, she added stories to all parts, including Part I. *I'm sorry, but I just can't think of everything chronologically. Kathy, it's really pretty simple: If you truly wish to stop the endless parade of stories, stop asking the questions!*

It's my fervent wish that my story will give help and hope to others in the same way so many helped me. It became abundantly clear, through this process, the book is a thank-you gift to all those who have helped me. It is especially a gift to all my children who have, from the very beginning, given me a reason to live.

I thank the universe and you, Mom, for allowing me to mother Vincent and Teresa. Being a good mommy to my babies gave me the light of purpose and self-worth, which provided hope through the dark experiences of childhood. Thank you, little Alan, the child-angel of our family, for saving our lives.

Thanks to all my siblings. You have been instrumental in my healing. Every one of you is handling our shared history to the best of your ability. We each have our own healing process. Thank you for supporting mine. A special thanks to Al for having the courage and fortitude to become and remain sober. You're an integral part of our close-knit family.

Thank you, Michelle Therese, for being my precious firstborn. I hope this book finds you and reassures you that you were given to your adoptive family with love. I hope to meet you someday.

Thank you, Cindy, for being a wonderful foster daughter. You let me give back and at the same time eased the pain of giving Michele Therese away. Thanks for being a wonderful big sister to my kids.

And finally, thank you, JJ, Rese, Gina, and Mandy for your love and acceptance. My love for you gave me a reason for living through the hard times. Being your mom gave me the purpose I needed to persevere. You provided me with hope as well as the impetus and desire to change the destructive patterns of my childhood. You continue to remind me daily how blessed I am to have you in my life.

I'm very close to and in constant contact with all of my children. I talk with JJ and Gina weekly. With Rese and Mandy, it's almost daily. Through the years, I've told them the basics of my tale, but they deserve much more. I was determined to tell my story openly and honestly in order to give them a truer and fuller picture of me. My hope is the book will, in turn, help validate their lives. After my children read the book, I phoned them to ask for their opinions about how it affected them personally.

I reached Mandy after work. She is a beloved high school teacher. Using tools learned from experience, she teaches classes in life skills. She is an involved single mother of two daughters.

My youngest is open-minded, thoughtful, and spiritual. It was evident in her response to my question that she'd read my story through that lens. She shared her thoughts easily and openly. "I didn't want to put the book down, but it was so emotional, I had to take little breaks in order to cry. You know me, Mom; I'm not a crier, but the book really affected me."

I taught my kids a lot of good things, but unfortunately, I was also a great example of how to repress feelings. I'd modeled "don't cry" most of my life. She explained that although she cried throughout the book, the deaths of Patrick and Stan were especially hard.

"I got so many insights into your life, Mom. It also gave me insights into my own childhood. The book explained a lot of things about you I didn't even know I needed to understand."

"Like what?" I asked, knowing I'd attempted to be very open with all my children as they were growing up. Mandy, being the youngest, probably received the healthiest mom simply because I was further along in my healing process.

"Like, I don't remember a day in my childhood you didn't snuggle with me. I took your affection for granted. Now I understand why snuggling was so important.

"The book helped me remember parts of my teenage years I'd forgotten. Seeing myself through your eyes has helped me be a better mother and teacher." Mandy told me my story is already working its miracles. She had given the manuscript to one of her students who had confided she was in therapy to deal with the trauma of incest. She reported to Mandy the book really helped her.

Next, I tried Gina. She was heading to the gym for a workout and had only a few minutes to talk. She is my independent, action-oriented daughter. Gina expresses her love through physical affection and by generously giving her time and effort to our family and others. She is more guarded when it comes to expressing her feelings. "The book messed up my emotions for six months. I had to cleanse my body in order to function. I didn't realize how much it would affect me. It was real emotional." Gina stopped, looking for words to describe her feelings.

I filled in with my best guess. "Our experiences were similar. Was it like looking in a mirror?"

"Yes! It was hard, at first, to look at myself, but now I'm fine. I'm really glad I read the book. It's actually helping me to understand my daughter better. Gotta go, I'm at the gym," she said. I detected some relief in her voice. "Love you. Bye."

Gina is married and has three children and two grandchildren. She and her husband own a successful business, and she is also a real estate agent.

I reached Rese next. Rese is an extremely busy married lady with three children. She is very involved in her children's lives and activities as well as being a real estate broker and a teacher's assistant at an elementary school. "Mom, let me call you back. Your question is really important. Let me gather my thoughts." That's my Rese: loving, thoughtful, and considerate.

About thirty minutes later she called. "Mom, things are still too busy for me to concentrate right now. Would it be okay if I take some time to think about your question and write my thoughts down?"

"Absolutely," I said, having some understanding of family demands.

Her touching words about the book made me cry. This is what she wrote:

There were parts that were very painful to read. But I know that pain has made you who you are today. Reading the book helped me experience your journey and in many ways get to know you better. I thank God every day that you are my mother. I've shared your story with many troubled souls over the years because you are a true inspiration. Everyone you have touched is a better person for having known you. I know my family and I are. I've always wanted to share my mom with those who are not so fortunate. Now I can. Thank you, Mom and Kathy, for writing this book.

I talked to JJ briefly. He told me he needed to deal with an issue with his son and he'd get back to me. He wished to write his thoughts down. Since he's a wonderful writer, I was delighted.

JJ is self-employed doing what he needs to do in order "to work to live," but his passions are his three teenaged children and his music. He is a nurturing father and a talented and versatile musician in a local band called Ironwood Rain.

A few days after my request, I received his letter. My tears flowed freely as his words spoke to my heart and soul. I knew then that no matter what happened with the book, the sharing of my turquoise life had been successful. My son's eloquent and beautiful letter is a testament to the healing power of love and hope:

Thank you, Mom, for so bravely facing your personal story in a way that can allow your own healing and that of others. As a child, I was only vaguely aware of many of the things that were going on in the big, adult world. I was protected and safe. It is interesting to see with grown eyes many of the dynamics that I never truly understood before. It makes me even more grateful for being born into the wonderful family we share. I strive to live up to the standards of love and acceptance that you have taught, and I pray that others may learn the same lessons without having to suffer such personal tragedies. Through your life, you have inspired dozens (maybe hundreds) of girls to learn from your strength and perseverance. This book can take that to the next level and perhaps inspire thousands. I will stand tall with you forever.

Acknowledgements

Diann and Kathy are grateful to:
Kathy Nelson, our first editor, for being interested in us as people and having the courage to take on a neophyte author. Katriena Knights, our second editor, for guiding us through the ins and outs of the book world and for helping us tighten up the story by getting rid of non-essential scenes, extraneous words, and overuse of the word "that" while remaining understanding and patient throughout the process. Artist extraordinaire, Darlene Maestas, for capturing the essence of *A Turquoise Life* on canvas. Marilyn Van Derber, for continuing to shine a beacon of hope for all sexual abuse survivors and for the willingness to read and comment on *A Turquoise Life*. Feather Berkower, Bob Cooper, and Joan Gabrielson for their dedication and passion in working for safety and health of children.

Kathy would like to thank:
Diann Kissell, one of the most courageous and wise people I know for trusting me to write her miraculous story and for making my life richer through friendship. What a wonderful journey! My husband Steve for his love and support, for reading the manuscript (even though he vowed not to), and for making astute and logical suggestions. Caroline Biagi for her excellent editing help, unflinching honesty both positive and negative, and more than an occasional meal. My brother, Brad Bird, for lending his *incredible* story-telling expertise to the project in its infancy. My sister, Leslie Ziemkowski, for her support and encouragement. My cheerleader sister-in-law, Jerri Cash, for reading, keeping, and loving, every single version of this book, even the roughest of drafts. My son, Chris Lowery, who not only read the book, but used his talents to design the front and back cover. My college buddies, Cindy Manley and Cynthia Rogers, who embody unconditional love and have been supportive through the entire process. My therapist friends, LaVada Glass-Judd and Doris Goodteacher,

for their insight and wisdom. Clare Alsko, Lynne Ervin, Becky Richmond, and Dianne Sievers, who have been invaluable in providing their time, resources, encouragement, and constructive criticism to the project. The many supportive friends and relatives whose names are too numerous to mention—a heart-felt thanks.

Diann would like to thank:
Kathy Bird, for agreeing to take on this project with me in the first place, for her patience with my cobwebbed memory, her wonderful humor, and the tremendous friendship that has been forged in the five years of building this book. To Fred, my prince charming and best friend for being supportive all through the process. My children JJ, Rese, Gina, and Mandy for their unconditional love and support. Jean for reading the book every step of the way and lending her editing expertise, even though it opened up painful memories for her. All my siblings for their unconditional love through all the years—I couldn't have survived without them. I have been blessed with innumerable friends throughout my life starting from kindergarten to the present. They have all been instrumental in helping me survive this crazy life. Some have been with me for many years—Vicki, Mona, Carolina, Oksana, Kathy H., Darlene, Annette, and Ermalinda. The rest—you know who you are—continue to remain in my heart, and I thank you.

The Diann/Kathy connection: Upon giving one of many hour-long presentations of her story to a class of counselors in Kathy's trauma workshop, Diann was again asked by one of the students if she had thought about writing a book. After adjourning the class for lunch, Kathy spoke to Diann in private, encouraging her to write her story if she wished to do so. She explained to Diann that, because of her recovery and the stability of her present life, writing her memoir might be a healing process for her as well as a way to help other victims. Diann liked the idea but knew writing wasn't her forte. She eventually asked Kathy if she would write her story. The minute Kathy accepted the project, a team was forged and the beginning of a book was born. The process of writing *A Turquoise Life* has met and exceeded both Diann's and Kathy's expectations by being healing, rewarding, enlightening, and empowering. They fervently wish the book will bring hope to many survivors of abuse and insight to those who wish to understand and support them.

Kathy Bird, M.A., L.P.C., CAC III has more than thirty years of experience as a psychotherapist specializing in all types of trauma including PTSD, domestic violence, childhood abuse, and dissociative disorders. She has a private practice in Lakewood, Colorado. For more than a decade, she taught workshops on trauma and domestic violence to counselors and other professionals. She is also the author of a nationally distributed domestic violence program. She loves to write, read, ski, hike, and spend time with family, Unlike Diann, cooking and sewing are not her forte. She lives in the foothills west of Denver with her husband Steve.

CPSIA information can be obtained at www.ICGtesting.com
Printed in the USA
LVOW07s0730080714

393254LV00001B/6/P